P9-DXN-458

THE TOTAL BOOK OF

HOUSE
PLANTS

Additional illustrations by

Dorothea Barlowe
Susan Korner
Enid Kotschnig
Manabu Saito
Elmer Smith
Arthur Singer

THE TOTAL BOOK OF
HOUSE
PLANTS

by RUSSELL C. MOTT

Illustrations by
ALAN SINGER

GREENWICH HOUSE
DISTRIBUTED BY CROWN PUBLISHERS, INC.
NEW YORK

This 1983 edition is published by Greenwich
House, a division of Arlington House, Inc.,
distributed by Crown Publishers, Inc., by
arrangement with Vineyard Books, Inc.

Manufactured in Hong Kong

**Library of Congress Cataloging in Publication
Data**
Mott, Russell C.
  The total book of house plants.
  Includes index.
  1. House plants.   2. Indoor gardening.
I. Title.
SB419.M8   1983   635.9'65   83-8954

ISBN: 0-517-416719

h g f e d c b a

CONTENTS

Foreword

Since ancient times, house plants have brightened the homes of people throughout the world. Today, as the outdoor world of trees and shrubs and vines continues to shrink, erased by highways and parking lots and shopping centers, they are more than ever essential to the well-being and inner tranquillity of all plant lovers.

In recent decades ecologists and nurserymen, growers and biologists have worked alongside one another to augment our knowledge of cultivating and breeding indoor plants and foliage. As a result, infinite new varieties and sophisticated new techniques of culture have come into being.

It is the purpose of this volume to set forth this diversified information simply and succinctly. The range of house plants covered is worldwide, extending from orchids to cacti, from begonias to African violets. In each case all relevant information is included in the simplest form possible—mixing soils, how and when to plant, use of fertilizers, repotting and starting new plants. For closely related plants with similar culture needs, such as the many varieties of begonias or geraniums, culture requirements are given in a general article within the relevant section; for all other plants with individual culture needs, the instructions accompany the article on each species of plant. In the case of the palm family, culture requirements for all the species cited are presented in a full-page chart.

Much attention is given to dish gardens and terrariums, tropical bonsai and hanging baskets, year-round care of patio plants and home culture and forcing of flowering bulbs. Included also are formulas for soilless potting mixes and new slow-release fertilizers, along with precise instructions as to light requirements, watering and temperature needs. The botanical name, family name, common name and original habitat of each ornamental plant add to the reader's knowledge of this fascinating and rewarding hobby or avocation.

What makes this book unique in its field, beyond any other factor, is the care and time and patience that have been spent on the illustrations. Seven artists were involved, and I am grateful beyond measure to Alan Singer, who illustrated the major portion of this book. My thanks go as well to Alan's father, Arthur Singer, who illustrated the jacket, to Manabu Saito, who illustrated the cacti section, and to Elmer Smith, who illustrated the orchid section. Credit for special renderings and drawings go to Dorothea Barlowe, Enid Kotschnig and Susan Korner.

Others to whom I am grateful for their help in reading the manuscript or making special contributions to the text include Richard Peterson, editor of the American Orchid Society Bulletin, and Gordon G. Dillon, executive secretary of the American Orchid Society Inc., Botanical Museum, Harvard University, Cambridge, Massachusetts; Dr. H. E. Moore, Jr., and Dr. Wm. J. Dress of the L. H. Bailey Hortorium, Dr. Kenneth Horst, associate professor, Plant Pathology Extension, and Dr. Raymond Fox, Department of Floriculture, all of Cornell University, Ithaca, New York.

Lastly, I am indebted to my good friend on the staff of Vineyard Books, Lucille E. Ogle, whose years of experience in the publishing field gave me guidance and encouragement in putting it all together.

R. C. M.
Ithaca, New York

This book is dedicated to
my wife BETTY,
who shares my love
for all growing things.

8

*Chrysanthemum blossoms
vary in
form and color*

HOLIDAY PLANTS

CHRYSANTHEMUM (*Chrysanthemum morifolium*) from China and *C. indicum* from China and Japan are the parents of most of the plants known to American growers as mums and in Europe and Australia as chrysanths. They are grown as pot plants and used as cut flowers for table arrangements, bridal bouquets and for spectacular flower displays both indoors and out. Flowering can be timed by regulating the day length, making blooms possible every month.

Colors offered are white, bronze, yellow, red, maroon and lavender pink, with pastel shades of each.

Flower form is varied. There are pompons with globe-shaped, compact flowers, some with flat, fluted or quilled ray florets. Disbudded pompons measure up to five inches in diameter. The smallest button pompons in colors mainly white and yellow are less than 1½ inches across.

Single and daisy types come in all sizes and forms.

Cushion types have tiered ray florets. Their dwarf growing habit makes them fine for potting.

Anemone-flowered plants have one or more layers of ray florets and a large raised center disk.

Spider chrysanthemums have curling tubular ray florets with ends shaped like a fishhook.

Fancy are Japanese types, which are rather shaggy in appearance. There are also feathery flowers that are carnationlike with cupped or twisted ray florets.

Hardy varieties sold as pot plants can be set outdoors to give flowers again in the autumn. It is well known that not all varieties sold are hardy. Only a few varieties cultured as florists' chrysanthemums are hardy to northern latitudes (check with your florist). When flowers have faded, cut the foliage back to about four inches and, as soon as the freezing weather is gone, plant outdoors.

Plant in a sunny location with a well-drained, well-prepared bed of garden soil. Addition of a complete garden fertilizer like a 5-10-5 is desirable. In hot climates protection from afternoon sun should be considered. Well-rooted cuttings can be planted directly in the garden bed. Vigorous single-stem sections are made when dividing a clump. Use the outside of the clump, discarding the woody centers. A second and third application of fertilizer during the growing season is beneficial. However, the last application applied two to three weeks before blooming, using a low-nitrogen type, will produce better quality flowers.

Pinch top growth when stems are five to six inches high to promote lateral growth. Select from one to four for continued growth. Continue pinching all shoots reaching five to six inches. In areas of early frost pinching should cease by mid-July.

If large blooms are desired, begin disbudding when buds are large enough to handle. Remove all flower buds except one or two per flower cluster; allow these to develop.

Plants not hardy enough to live over winter can be dug up, potted and moved indoors for late fall flowering. Grow as cool as possible. Give full exposure to sun and keep potting mix moist. Cuttings are made from suckers which sprout from the base of the plant, are rooted in peat, sand or vermiculite. Pot them up, moving to larger pots as needed. The short days of winter will naturally initiate buds, and flowering may take place February or March. Grow in a room about 60° F. Give full sun days but long nights of darkness. Do not expose the plants to any light during the night if you want flowers.

Home care for lasting quality of a potted chrysanthemum is the same as for most florist flowering plants. Provide bright light but not direct sun. Keep the temperature at night at least 10 degrees lower than in the daytime. Water daily, if needed, to keep pot moist.

Lilium longiflorum

EASTER LILY or **NOVEMBER LILY** (*Lilium longiflorum*) This beautiful lily from Japan is a main crop for flower growers all over the warm temperate world, producing its large white flowers in spring. It is often bought just as its first flower is about to open. Other buds will then open in the home. The yellow floral parts, the male anthers, may be removed as each bud opens to prevent pollen staining the white petals.

Before 1940 most of the bulbs were grown for forcing in Bermuda and Japan. Through breeding and selection, researchers in the United States developed varieties which grew successfully in Southern states and in the Northwest. Bulbs treated for forcing are shipped to greenhouse growers by the thousands for Easter sales each year.

After flowering, the plant, which grows from a lily bulb, may be moved to a sunny garden. The survival of forced Easter-lily bulbs in a garden depends on where the bulbs were grown for forcing. Those grown in northern regions, for example, would probably survive in temperate areas, while those from southern regions may survive only in a warmer climate.

Plant outdoors when danger of freezing is past. Carefully remove bulb with soil mass and roots intact. Dig hole large enough so that the bulb will set eight to nine inches below the ground. A couple of handfuls of coarse sand or gravel at the bottom will facilitate good drainage. A tablespoonful of garden fertilizer mixed with the backfill will furnish food for continued growth. Sometimes a forced lily will bloom again in late summer. Normal blooming time is summer, but forced bulbs may need another year to build up strength for flowering. It is inadvisable to plant forced Easter-lily bulbs in the same area with garden lilies because of a chance of virus transmission.

In the home provide bright light, out of direct sun. Keep low temperature at night, check water need daily. If plant is foil-wrapped, punch holes in the foil bottom so excess water drains away.

CYCLAMEN *(Cyclamen persicum)* is a very popular winter pot plant, particularly in Europe, Australia and the United States. Most modern cultivars are sold under the name *Cyclamen persicum grandiflorum*. The typical shuttlecock-shaped flowers come in shades of pink, red, lilac, orchid-purple and white. The leaves of some cultivars are boldly patterned with silver. In table arrangements the flowers are as attractive as sweet peas. Later the same plants are sold as potted plants.

Blooming plants are available from autumn until spring, usually offered with several flowers and buds in all stages of development. The cyclamen is difficult to grow as a house plant because of its low temperature requirement.

This plant must have a cool place to survive. High day temperatures cause flower buds to wither and leaves to yellow.

Check the plant for water daily. If plant dries out, submerge the pot in water for 15 minutes.

Cyclamen persicum

HYDRANGEA *(Hydrangea macrophylla)* is a native of Japan, where it grows as a woody shrub about 12 feet tall. The large flower head is composed of a number of florets that are produced in late spring and early summer. The showy parts are the large sterile florets while the fertile ones are small and inconspicuous. The fertile complete flowers are hidden in the inflorescence. The color range is white, pink, red, lavender, blue and purple.

It is a plant sold in the Northern Hemisphere for Easter and other spring holidays. The flowers will last for at least six weeks.

Care in the home requires much water and as low a temperature as possible. Give bright light and no more than four hours of direct sun.

New plants may be started from cuttings in late summer.

In potting, add lime to the compost for pink varieties only; for the blue flowers the compost must be completely lime free. Use mix formula A.

Hydrangea macrophylla

Primula malacoides

Calceolaria herbeohybrida

FAIRY or **BABY PRIMROSE** (*Primula malacoides*) is a perennial species, but is usually grown as an annual. Flowering plants are usually found in the market early in the year and are available throughout spring. The dainty flowers range from pinks and reds to purple and white and many single and double cultivars have been raised. Since it is produced in a greenhouse, cool home temperatures are required. Keep moist in a bright window with indirect sun.

The variety Rinepearl White is grown commercially and comes in mixed colors of white, rose and carmine.

ENGLISH PRIMROSE (*Primula polyantha*), polyanthus primrose, is in flower markets from winter to spring. Usually potted in five-inch pots with fresh green leaves bearing flowers one to two inches in diameter, it comes in mixed shades of orange, red, yellow and mahogany.

This hardy species may be planted outdoors in a shady spot when frosty weather is gone. An excellent plant to combine with spring-flowering bulbs. A cool, moist climate suits them best, so this one is for northern gardeners to enjoy. Keep moist.

CALCEOLARIA (*Calceolaria herbeohybrida*) is known as "pocketbook plant." It is an old-time florist favorite and one of the most showy and interesting of all potted flowering plants. Calceolarias have coarsely toothed, soft, hairy leaves measuring to six inches long. The flowers are composed of an upper and lower lip; the lower lip is very large and inflated, more or less slipperlike. Some varieties produce flowers that are two inches in diameter and borne close to the foliage. Grown as an Easter plant, it comes in red, pink, maroon and yellow flower colors with orange, red and purple dots.

It is not suitable for areas where minimum temperatures habitually exceed 60°F.

Take care of the plant in the home as you would the primrose. Lots of water, no direct sun and as cool temperatures as possible to help it last. As a biennial, it has finished its flowering when the blooms have faded.

Senecio cruentus

CINERARIA *(Senecio cruentus* syn. *Cineraria cruenta)* is another pot plant which has low temperature culture requirements. It is a biennial and so is discarded when the flowers have faded, and new plants must be bought or grown. An inexpensive flowering pot plant, it is found in shops from late winter to spring. Numerous varieties are grown, with the colors of the daisylike flowers ranging from red and pink through mauves and purples to blue and white. Several bicolored forms are also grown.

One of the most widely grown varieties is Festival. Its compact, well-rounded growth habit combines with larger flower heads of medium-size flowers.

To keep it healthy in the home, grow it as cool as possible. It should not dry out and should be shaded from direct sunlight.

Cinerarias are excellent as container plants for patio decoration. Sow the seed in late fall for plants to set out in March. Seedlings potted in three- to four-inch pots using mix A should be shifted gradually to avoid becoming pot-bound until they reach desired container size. Feeding every two weeks with a water-soluble fertilizer will produce vigorous flowering plants. Six- or eight-inch size pot specimens are effective when combined with begonias and other foliage plants on a terrace.

A related vine for outdoor culture in mild regions is *Senecio confusus,* or Mexican flame vine. A twining vine, needing the support of a trellis, it reaches 10 to 12 feet. It will die back to ground if subjected to a mild frost but will grow again from roots. The daisylike flowers are produced in large clusters of a startling orange-red color with golden centers. It will flower all winter where the weather is mild.

It can be grown also in a hanging basket and is effective when cascading over a wall.

Easily propagated from cuttings, this flame vine is subject to red spiders and aphids, unfortunately.

*Euphorbia
pulcherrima*

POINSETTIA (*Euphorbia pulcherrima*). Tropical Mexico and Central America are its native habitats. It is the most popular and showy flowering plant of subtropical climates and temperate interiors. Hybridizers have developed beautiful Christmas colors of red, white, pink and even pale yellow floral leaves or bracts. The true yellow and green flowers are inconspicuous at the center of the bracts.

Display in full sun, if possible. Leaves will sometimes drop because of poor light. Temperature can be warm.

Too low humidity can cause leaf drop. Keep moist.

Fresh plants from the florist are a joy to see each Christmas. When properly cared for, they will last for several months. When the colorful bracts have faded, the plant should be discarded in favor of other seasonal flowering plants.

THE LEGEND OF THE POINSETTIA:
On a Christmas Eve long ago Pepita was sad. This little Mexican girl wanted more than anything to give a fine present to the Christ child at the church service that evening. But she was very poor and had no gift. As she walked sorrowfully to church with her cousin, Pedro, he tried to console her. "Pepita," he said, "I am certain that even the most humble gift, given in love, will be acceptable in His eyes." So Pepita gathered a bouquet of common weeds from the roadside and entered the church. As she approached the altar, her spirits lifted. She forgot the humbleness of her gift as she placed it tenderly at the feet of the Christ child . . . and there was a miracle! Pepita's insignificant weeds burst into brilliant bloom. They were called **Flores de Noche Buena**—*Flowers of the Holy Night. We call them poinsettias.*

Courtesy, Paul Ecke, Encinitas, California.

CHRISTMAS PEPPER or ORNAMENTAL CHILLI (*Capsicum annuum conoides*). This is an attractive plant originating from Central and South America. It has cone-shaped berries which are in fact miniature peppers. The edible, upright cone-shaped fruits are pungent to taste and display red, purple and cream colors. Although a perennial, it is grown as an annual.

Place in full sunshine, if possible. Yellowing or dropping of leaves is caused by low light. This ornamental pepper requires cooler than normal room temperature for lasting quality. Keep soil moist. A dry soil will cause leaves to turn yellow and drop. Water daily, if needed.

The Christmas Pepper is an annual and should be discarded after its beauty is past.

If you wish to grow your own, sow the seed in May or June. Treat the same as Jerusalem cherry seedlings. Plunge the pots in the soil out of doors. A pinch is necessary to shape the plant. A final shift to desired pot size is made in September when the plants are moved inside.

JERUSALEM CHERRY (*Solanum pseudo-capsicum*). The Christmas or Cleveland cherry is a Christmas potted plant with shiny green leaves and large orange-scarlet cherrylike fruit. A yellow fruited strain is also grown.

Cherry plants need full sun and a cool room at night. As for all fruit-bearing plants, potting mix should be moist, otherwise leaves and fruit drop.

Plants may be kept after fruit has dropped. For best flowering and fruit set plant outdoors in summer. Some leaf drop occurs due to root disturbance when lifted in fall.

To grow your own, sow seeds early in February. Fluorescent light for a 14-hour day and 50° temperature are desirable. Pot seedlings in peat pots, then four-inch pots, before moving outdoors for summer. Pinch back now and then to encourage bushiness. Do not pinch after July 1. In September lift pots and make final shift to a five- or six-inch pot; move indoors. Fruit will turn bright orange-red for Christmas.

REMARKS: The berries contain toxic substances and should never be eaten.

Capsicum annuum conoides

Solanum pseudo-capsicum

AZALEA. *Rhododendron indicum* and *R. obtusum amoenum* are the two main parents of the hybrid varieties grown as florists' pot plants today. They are the most showy of the spring-flowering pot plants and are available in a wide range of colors from white and yellow to red and violet with both single and double flowers.

A class known as *Kurume* is probably the hardiest for outdoor planting of any of the forcing types. Your florist can tell you the variety name. The plants will winter outdoors in the more temperate regions.

When frosty nights are gone, the *Kurumes* can be planted out. Azaleas planted outdoors grow best in a sunny location or with partial shade and protection from the wind. In dense shade they become spindly and bloom sparsely. A likely location is under oak trees or pines, which have deeply penetrating roots. Shallow tree-root locations such as those under elms or maples are to be avoided.

Azaleas do best planted in straight coarse peat moss as it comes from the bale. Lumpy peat assures good aeration and drainage.

Dig hole larger than the ball of roots. Discard the existing soil and backfill with peat. A layer of sand or gravel in the bottom will afford good drainage. Set the plant only to the depth it was in the pot.

After planting, water heavily and never let dry out thereafter. When plants are set, apply a mulch about two inches deep, using peat moss, pine needles or leaf mold to conserve moisture. Much attention must be given to watering the first year.

If chlorotic foliage appears—*i.e.,* yellow leaves—it may be caused by a lack of iron. Apply iron sulfate or chelated iron according to directions on the package.

All azalea varieties sold by florists are handled alike in the home. Keep the plant in a cool spot while in flower, especially at night. A warm, dry atmosphere will make it bloom quickly; hence the blossoms will last only a short time. Keep the plant in a cool, sunny location and remove the faded flowers as soon as they wilt. Daily watering is necessary.

Unless you live in a mild climate, it is too much trouble to keep it for another year.

Rhododendron hybrids

Kalanchoe blossfeldiana

KALANCHOE (*Kalanchoe blossfeldiana*), an attractive long-lasting plant with showy red flowers, is available for Christmas and for Valentine's Day. 'Tetra Vulcan' is a variety grown most commonly today. It is a natural dwarf and bushy type with large red flower heads.

The average height of most varieties is eight to 12 inches. The plants, popular for their compactness, bear masses of four-petaled flowers ¼ to ½ inch in diameter. Flower colors come in shades of red; one variety is yellow. Named varieties grown are 'Scarlet Gnome,' 'Tom Thumb' and 'Brilliant Star.' 'Yellow Tom Thumb' is a variant of red 'Tom Thumb.' 'Jingle Bells' is a trailing type that is appropriate for hanging baskets. It has large, bell-shaped flowers. Taller-growing varieties known as Swiss Strain are also available to the trade.

To start new plants, make terminal cuttings in the fall or sow seed in the spring.

The plant's low-temperature require-ments for successful flowering limit its use as a flowering house plant. Instead, it may be grown as a foliage plant at room temperature, giving it culture as for any succulent plant.

The plant's water requirements are on the dry side.

A schedule for flowering at different times of the year as used by some commercial flower growers follows:

Temperature of 60° specified.

Shading plants by black-cloth treatment, giving total darkness from 5:00 P.M. to 8:00 A.M.

Seed started from January to July.

Shade applied July 20 to September 20 will produce flowering plants in mid-October.

Shade applied August 15 to October 1 will flower plants by early December.

Shade applied September 1 to October 15 will give flowering plants for Christmas.

Flowering will occur without black-cloth treatment if grown at 50°.

FLOWERING HOUSE PLANTS

Amaryllis (*Hippeastrum* hybrids)

A native to the Peruvian Andes. Bulbs are available at garden stores and florist shops. Hybrid strains have a color mixture ranging from pure white to rose, red, carmine, crimson and candy-striped flowers. "Prepared" bulbs are imported into many areas from Holland and will flower in the Northern Hemisphere for Christmas. Allow about eight weeks to flowering.

Seed pods develop rapidly after pollination. They are mature within four or five weeks. Pods should be picked as soon as they turn yellow and begin to split open. Remove the seed from the pod, allow it to dry for a few days and then plant. Use mix formula D in a flat or shallow container that has good drainage. Provide shade for germination, then increase light to full sunlight for development of seedling bulbs. Transplant to individual pots as soon as seedlings are large enough to handle.

LIGHT: Indirect sun is needed when the bulb starts to flower. Partial shade helps to bring out brilliant color of flowers.

TEMPERATURE: A warm temperature is needed for forcing into flower; cool conditions make flowers last longer.

MOISTURE: Water well after potting, then water on the dry side until root growth is started. Then keep moist while in leaf.

PROPAGATION: Propagate from seed (three years to flowering) or offset bulbs at potting time (two years to flowering).

POTTING: Use a well drained potting mix B, potting the bulb into a five- to seven-inch pot. Allow one inch of mix around the bulb. The bulb is potted to leave the upper third exposed above the mix level.

FERTILIZER: Apply water-soluble fertilizer once a month during growth season.

INSECTS: Amaryllis is subject to spider mites and mealy bugs.

REMARKS: After bulb has flowered, place outdoors in a semishady location for summer growth. In fall, when leaves dry down, store in a cool, dry location until signs of growth appear in late fall or winter.

Hippeastrum vittatum

Kafir Lily *(Clivia miniata)*

A native to South Africa and a member of the amaryllis family. Three species are available: *C. miniata,* salmon red funnel-shaped flowers; *C. cyrtanthiflora,* tubular flowers, orange, red and green; *C. nobilis,* tubular flowers, brilliant orange-red with green tips. In addition, several hybrids have been raised. Flowering period is late winter and early spring. Flowers are followed by ornamental red berries.

Flowering-size plants usually grow best in eight- to ten-inch pots and do best when left undisturbed. When masses of the tuberous thick roots seem to be replacing the potting mix, it is time to repot.

When repotting is needed, the best time to do so is after flowering in the spring; divide the plant, if necessary. Do not cut into more than two sections. The larger the section, the more leaf surface, the better the chance of flowering.

The Kafir lily is a large plant that usually occupies much space; some plants attain 18 to 24 inches in height and are as broad. It is hardly an apartment dweller, but it is an excellent plant to use on the outdoor patio in summer for decoration.

Belgian and Zimmerman hybrids, grown in the United States, offer outstanding foliage and flower characteristics. Plants grown outdoors are planted in borders with plants such as ferns, azaleas and other shade types. Plant in rich soil with top of tuber above soil line. Leave undisturbed for several years to obtain the best bloom.

LIGHT: When grown outdoors they need high light and protection from sun; bright indirect light indoors.

TEMPERATURE: Winter temperature cool, spring warm.

MOISTURE: Keep moist in growing period, water sparsely in winter.

PROPAGATION: By seed or by division.

POTTING: When extremely pot-bound, repot (probably every three or four years). Use mix A.

FERTILIZER: Apply water-soluble fertilizer once a month during growing period.

INSECTS: Mealy bugs.

Clivia miniata

Allamanda

(A. cathartica hendersonii)

Also known as Golden Trumpet, a vinelike shrub, eight to ten feet high, it comes from Brazil. Can be grown as a potted house plant. It produces golden-yellow funnel-shaped flowers. Prospers if grown in a conservatory, greenhouse or on an enclosed sun porch. *A. neriifolia* is more shrublike, having golden-yellow flowers striped inside with reddish-brown.

The plant's small, oleanderlike leaves are arranged in whorls around the stems. This species flowers in late winter and early spring. It is propagated by cuttings and also seeds when produced.

Another variety is *A. williamsi*, which produces smaller blooms in less profusion than *A. cathartica hendersonii*. It is propagated by air layering and also by cuttings.

LIGHT: Very high. Full sunlight is required for best growth and flowering.

TEMPERATURE: Provide warm temperature for growing, cool in winter.

MOISTURE: Keep moist in growing period, dry in winter.

PROPAGATION: Stem cuttings from mature growth in spring; air layering.

POTTING: Mix B.

FERTILIZER: Should be fertilized monthly in spring and summer.

INSECTS: Subject to aphids, red spider mites.

PRUNING: When plants cease flowering in winter, prune back and give less water.

Allamanda cathartica hendersonii

Star Jasmine
(Trachelospermum jasminoides)

Also called Confederate or Chinese star jasmine, it is a twining, vinelike shrub from southern China. It is not a true jasmine, belonging to the dogbane or *Apocynaceae* family. With support it will twine to 20 feet. Without support and with pinching back it makes a spreading shrub or ground cover. The new foliage is glossy green, becoming lustrous dark green as it matures. Leaves measure to three inches long. Flowers are white, star-shaped, one inch across, borne in clusters and fragrantly sweet. Heaviest bloom occurs in late spring to early summer. A popular plant for greenhouses.

It may be trained in any shape or direction desired. Train on columns, walls or balconies by providing a cord tied for direction. For training start with a staked plant or one that has not been tip-pinched to make it bushy. Choose a spot where its fragrance can be enjoyed or where night lighting can pick up its white blossoms.

Train as indoor potted plants by occasionally tip-pinching wiry vine type of growth. Young plants are slow to start and are grown warm until plant matures.

LIGHT: Very high. They do best in direct sunlight in winter and filtered sunlight in summer.

TEMPERATURE: Warm temperatures are needed for seedlings, cool for mature plants.

MOISTURE: Keep moist in summer, dry in winter.

PROPAGATION: Use stem cuttings of half-ripened wood in spring with a hormone rooting aid. Use any rooting medium.

POTTING: Mix B.

FERTILIZER: Fertilize with water-soluble solution monthly in spring and summer. No fertilizer in winter. When blooms fade, withhold water to cause more flowering.

INSECTS: Red spider mites, mealy bugs and scale insects.

REMARKS: Place in cool room for rest period in winter.

Trachelospermum jasminoides

Bougainvillea glabra

Bougainvillea *(B. glabra)*

Is native to South America and a member of the four-o'clock family or *Nyctaginaceae*. They are named after the French navigator Louis A. de Bougainville (1729–1811), who discovered the plants in Rio de Janeiro.

The floral bracts that surround the small inconspicuous flowers are the showy parts. *B. spectabilis*, a species grown in frost-free areas, is less desirable for container culture because of its tall growing habit and thorny stems. Many intermediate botanical varieties and forms have been developed by hybridizers. Bougainvilleas can be grown as potted specimens trimmed for bushy forms, as tree forms and hanging baskets.

Some desirable varieties for container plants grown in many tropical areas are:
B. 'Afterglow'; orange, turning pink, a sport of *B.* 'Crimson Lake'
B. 'Alba'; common white with greenish cast
B. 'Barbara Karst'; bright deep orange, long-blooming season, vigorous
B. 'Bois de Rose'; very good pink, long-blooming season
B. 'Crimson Jewel'; glowing red, adapted to basket culture
B. 'Hugh Evans'; vigorous, good foliage, no fixed season of bloom
B. 'Lady Mary Baring'; golden yellow, bushy
B. 'Mahara'; dark red, double flowers, dwarf, long-lasting bracts
B. 'Manilla Red'; large clusters of double red flowers. Train to trellis
B. 'Scarlet O'Hara'; fast-growing climber, large deep purple bracts, winter bloomer

LIGHT: Very high. Needs bright sunlight.

TEMPERATURE: Warm temperature is necessary.

MOISTURE: Keep moist, although less water required after pruning.

PROPAGATION: Use stem cuttings of pencil thickness, six to eight inches long. Best time is in spring after flowering. Root in sand and peat. Rooting hormone is helpful. Keep moist. Two to three months for roots to develop.

POTTING: Pot in any basic mixture. Grow flowering-size plants in gallon-size containers. Roots do not mesh to form ball, so disturb as little as possible.

FERTILIZER: Apply complete fertilizer solution once a month for young plants. Feed established flowering plants only late spring and summer.

INSECTS: Mealy bugs, aphids, red spider mites.

Passionflower
(Passiflora X alato-caerulea)

Most species came from South America. Natural, fast-growing climbing vines produce edible fruits used in the tropics for flavoring sherbets, juices and jams; some varieties are eaten with sugar directly from the pod with a spoon.

It is best grown by training on a trellis or other supports, or about the casement of a picture window. The flowers open and last for one day only. Florists cement the sepals and petals with a few drops of candle wax to make them last for several days. They can be floated in a bowl of water or can be worn as a corsage.

Other species for home culture are: *P. caerulea* (parent of *X alato-caerulea*), having three- to four-inch pink and blue flowers and gray-green foliage.
P. coriacea, with small green, yellow and purplish flowers and leathery green leaves, curiously formed, appearing to be attached crosswise, with two lateral points.
P. trifasciata, small greenish flowers and leaves with gray and purple coloring along the three veins of the leaf.

LIGHT: High, full sun in winter; responds to fluorescent-light growing.

TEMPERATURE: warm.

MOISTURE: Needs moisture year round.

PROPAGATION: Seeds or terminal cuttings of half-ripened wood, with several nodes to a cutting. Rooting hormone beneficial.

POTTING: Any basic well-drained mix is suitable for potting. Mix B.

FERTILIZER: Feed once a month with water-soluble fertilizer. Omit in winter months after cutting plants back.

INSECTS: Red spider mites and mealy bugs.

REMARKS: Outdoor summer growth on patio gives vigorous healthy plants as well as profuse flowering.

Passiflora X alato-caerulea

Glory Bower or Bleeding Heart Vine
(Clerodendrum thomsoniae)

A vinelike plant named for the wife of W.C. Thomson, a missionary at Old Calabar on the west coast of tropical Africa who in 1861 sent specimens of this plant to Edinburgh, Scotland. May be grown as a vine, a trellis plant or a hanging basket. European growers have produced clerodendrum as a pot plant for many years. Recent research at Cornell University has adapted this plant for crop production in the United States. The colorful white bracts and red flowers provide an unusual and attractive plant for home and office.

LIGHT: Normal short days and high light intensity of full sunlight or fluorescent light promote flowering.

TEMPERATURE: Grow at 70° nights. Lower temperatures inhibit growth. Higher temperatures enhance growth but inhibit flowering.

MOISTURE: Keep moist.

PROPAGATION: Propagate by means of two-node stem cuttings. Keep moist (polyethylene bag). Summer-propagated plants flower in about 12 weeks after cuttings are started. Use any rooting medium.

POTTING: Use potting mix formula B. Plant one to three rooted cuttings per pot, depending on the size of specimen desired, and use a four- to five-inch pot.

FERTILIZER: Water-soluble fertilizer is needed once a month or use slow-release type according to direction.

INSECTS: Susceptible to red spider mites, mealy bugs, aphids and white flies.

PRUNING: If more than one cutting is used in a pot, pinching is not necessary. If a single cutting is used, the new shoots should be pinched when they are one to two inches long. Remove only the top (soft pinch).

REMARKS: High temperature and low light intensity can cause a serious problem with bud and flower drop. High light intensity or low temperature (below 60°) prevents bud drop. Susceptible to leaf spot diseases. Remove infected foliage; avoid splashing water.

Clerodendrum thomsoniae

Glory or Climbing Lily
(*Gloriosa rothschildiana*)

A native to tropical Africa. Walter Rothschild cultivated this lily in England with tubers imported from Uganda, Africa. The generic name *Gloriosa* comes from the Latin *gloriosus*, full of glory. The only climbing bulb, *G. rothschildiana* grows as a vine, reaching six to ten feet with its red and yellow flowers. *G. superba* grows as tall but with smaller flowers that have narrow but crisped green petals turning to yellow and finally orange-red as they mature. *G. superba lutea* is a variety having all-yellow flowers.

Its climbing habit with tendril-like prolongations of leaves needs a trellis or stake for support. The blooming season is summer to late autumn. Tubers normally are started in spring after a dormancy period. In warm, frost-free areas, they can be planted outdoors or in large containers for patio growing. A light shade from direct sun is beneficial.

LIGHT: High.

TEMPERATURE: Grow at cool temperature not to exceed 65°.

MOISTURE: Moist soil is needed.

PROPAGATION: Propagate either by seed or division of tubers when dormant. Its tubers, similar to those of dahlias, are easily separated when dormant. Select larger-sized new tubers with healthy growing tips for starting new plants. Make division when new growth appears.

POTTING: Use mix A or B. Set tubers horizontally four inches deep.

FERTILIZER: Apply water-soluble fertilizer every two weeks until flowers fade.

INSECTS: Red spider mites.

REMARKS: Gloriosa tubers can be started at any time of the year after a couple of months of rest. Two blooming periods a year may be had since the growth cycle is completed within six months. In warm countries, leave in the ground the year round. In colder regions, dig in the autumn before frost. Carefully clean soil from tubers and store in peat moss at 50°–60°.

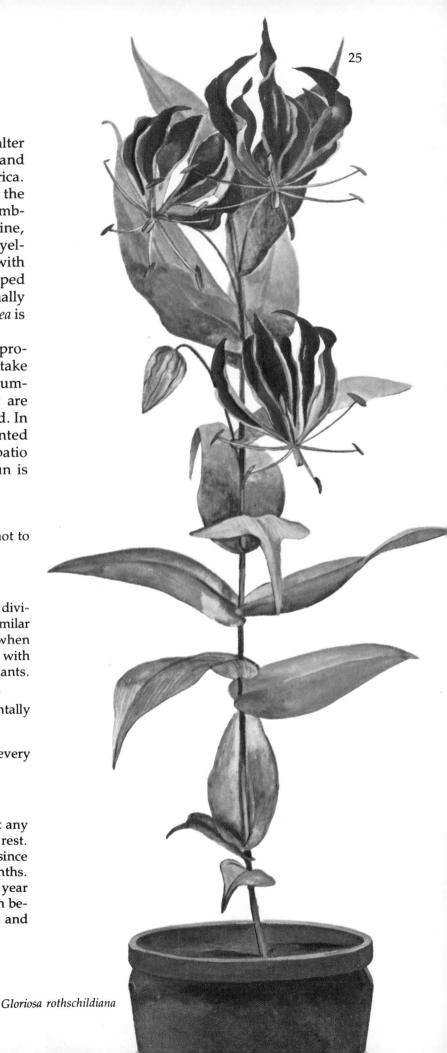

Gloriosa rothschildiana

Natal Plum *(Carissa macrocarpa)*

C. macrocarpa, a plant species from South Africa, is a shrub with thornlike spines used as a hedge in the south. It is often planted by the seashore because it is unaffected by salt spray and wind.

The varieties *C. macrocarpa* 'Boxwood Beauty,' with glossy dark-green leaves, and *C. macrocarpa nana*, with similar but smaller leaves, are dwarf clones; they make attractive ground-cover plants in the south and desirable potted plants for home culture indoors. Other varieties are *C. macrocarpa* 'Green Carpet,' a dense spreading growth resembling a carpet of green. Also *C. macrocarpa* 'Tomlinson' with dwarf compact growth to 2½ feet high, extending horizontally to three feet. Without thorns, its slow growth makes it a nice tub plant for summer patios. These varieties, available in the United States, do well in terrariums because of their dwarf growth habit.

The fragrant white flowers occur irregularly throughout the year. Fruiting and flowering often occur at the same time. The fruits are eaten as plums and also used for jelly and preserves.

LIGHT: High light; will stand full sun.

TEMPERATURE: Cool nights and warm days.

MOISTURE: Needs moist soil condition.

PROPAGATION: May be propagated at any time from stem cuttings; rooting hormone beneficial.

POTTING: Use mix B in three-quarter-size pots or containers.

FERTILIZER: Fertilize with water-soluble solution monthly.

INSECTS: Mealy bugs.

PRUNING: Prune to shape and keep low or for bonsai effect.

Carissa macrocarpa 'Boxwood Beauty'

Gardenia jasminoides

Gardenia *(Gardenia jasminoides.)*

The gardenias of today which grow in tropical gardens or as potted plants are forms or grafted varieties of *G. jasminoides*; some may be *G. jasminoides veitchii*. Florists grow them as pot plants for spring sales and harvest the cut flowers for corsages. Popularity of this flowering plant is attributed to its large fragrant white flowers. Its dark glossy green foliage makes it attractive as a house plant.

However, when its complexity of culture is understood, it becomes a challenge to grow, and one may decide that it is not a good house plant for today's environment.

It should be understood that the flowering period is largely determined by night temperatures between 62° and 65°. Above 65° will increase vegetation growth but decrease growth of flower buds and increase bud drop.

LIGHT: Gardenias need at least four hours of full sunlight daily.

TEMPERATURE: Night temperature must be a cool 62° to 65°.

MOISTURE: Soil must be moist at all times. Drying causes chlorosis and bud drop.

PROPAGATION: Propagate any time from terminal cuttings. Insert the potted cutting in a plastic bag. Rooting hormone is beneficial.

POTTING: Use mix A without limestone; the gardenia requires pH 4.5–5.5. Add acid fertilizer to mix.

INSECTS: Susceptible to mealy bugs, red spider mites, scale insects and root nematodes.

FERTILIZER: Apply water-soluble type once a month at recommended strength. Iron chlorosis, evidenced by yellow-green leaves toward top of plant, can be corrected by one or two applications of a chelated iron solution.

REMARKS: Culture in the home is further complicated by the plant's susceptibility to disease. Leaf troubles such as tip burn (black tips) are caused by lack of moisture. Leaf spots are caused by fungi; brown leaf margins are caused by nutritional deficiencies; sooty mold is another problem. These are described in the chapter on diseases, pages 202 and 203.

All of these and more may contribute to failure with gardenia culture in the home.

28

Spathiphyllum
'Mauna Loa'

Strelitzia
reginae

Anthurium
scherzerianum

Bird-of-Paradise Flower
(Strelitzia reginae)

Dedicated to Queen Charlotte Sophia, of the house of Mecklenburg-Strelitz, wife of George III. A slow-growing plant from Transkei, South Africa, it belongs to the banana family. Potted specimens grow to five feet. The exotic flowers resemble a tropical bird with vivid colors of red, orange and blue. Flowering period occurs usually in early summer and lasts until late autumn. Individual flowers last a few weeks in bloom.

LIGHT: It needs very high light, with full sun in winter and light shade if outdoors.

TEMPERATURE: Warm temperatures suit it well.

MOISTURE: Dry soil conditions.

PROPAGATION: When propagating from seed, allow six to eight years to flowering. If by division of clumps, three to four years to flowering.

POTTING: Use mix A. Grow in large containers and repot only when necessary. Large undisturbed clumps bloom the best.

FERTILIZER: Apply water-soluble fertilizer monthly or top-dress with slow-release fertilizer as recommended on container.

INSECTS: Susceptible to mealy bugs.

REMARKS: Sink pot in ground or set on patio during summer.

Flamingo Flower
(Anthurium scherzerianum)

One of the world's loveliest, most exotic flowers.

  A. andraeanum has a variety of colors, larger leaves and flowers and an upright habit of growth. It is a popular cut-flower crop for Christmas in Hawaii. It does best under greenhouse culture, where atmospheric humidity and watering can be better controlled and maintained. *A. scherzerianum* is better suited for house culture because of its habit of low growth. Flowering is continuous under good culture, and the brilliant scarlet flower bracts last a month or more. Flowers are excellent when they are cut for floral arrangements.

LIGHT: Medium light is best.

TEMPERATURE: Warm.

MOISTURE: Soil should be moist.

PROPAGATION: By seed or by separation of root-bearing side shoots from the main stems.

POTTING: Orchid mix D should be used. Or use equal parts of sphagnum moss and fine fir bark or shredded tree fern fiber.

FERTILIZER: Apply water-soluble solution once a month to *A. scherzerianum* and every two weeks to *A. andraeanum*.

INSECTS: Aphids, mealy bugs.

REMARKS: Keep upright growing stems covered with sphagnum moss and keep moist.

White Flag
(Spathiphyllum 'Mauna Loa')

Species of *Spathiphyllum* are found growing from Mexico to Peru and Brazil. For the most part they grow in foothills of mountains, in moist shady places along edges of rivers and streams. *S. clevelandii*, more typically a species, is less robust than *S.* 'Mauna Loa,' which has smaller flowers and leaves. Both types seem tolerant of artificial light and low atmospheric humidity as long as the root ball is constantly moist. Flowering occurs infrequently throughout the year.

LIGHT: Medium light is required; filtered sunlight in winter.

TEMPERATURE: Warm.

MOISTURE: Moist soil conditions are required at all times.

PROPAGATION: By division. It does best when undisturbed. Divide to larger clumps.

POTTING: Use mix A. Shift to larger pots not more than once a year.

FERTILIZER: Feed once a month with water-soluble fertilizer.

INSECTS: Mealy bugs, red spider mites.

REMARKS: Flowers are long-lasting when cut and placed in water.

Acalypha hispida

Justicia brandegeana

Chenille Plant *(Acalypha hispida)*

A native shrub from the East Indies, cultivated as hedges and bedding plants. It is an interesting flowering-foliage plant for the greenhouse and house culture. Its fuzzy minute red flower bracts are long pendant spikes and are often called 'Red-Hot Cat Tail.' Another species, *A. wilkesiana*, possesses striking foliage of red copper and pink color tones. The flowers of this species are less conspicuous.

LIGHT: High. Bright sun is needed in winter.

TEMPERATURE: Warm daytime and cool night temperatures are necessary.

MOISTURE: Soil should be kept moist.

PROPAGATION: Terminal cuttings of summer growth or shoots from cut-back plants in spring.

POTTING: Use mix A. Move to larger pot when root-bound.

FERTILIZER: Apply water-soluble solution once a month.

INSECTS: Red spider mites, mealy bugs and white flies attack it.

REMARKS: Prune severely to rejuvenate old plants in spring. Start new plants for replacement of old from cuttings.

Shrimp Plant

(Justicia brandegeana; Beloperone guttata)

Found growing in Mexico, with its white flowers beneath showy overlapping reddish-brown bracts, it is so named because of its resemblance to that tasty morsel from the sea. A cultivar with yellow bracts instead of copper is *J. brandegeana* 'Yellow Queen.' Flowering seems continuous since the bracts remain attached to the plant after the flowers fade.

LIGHT: It needs good high light.

TEMPERATURE: Warm day and cool night temperatures.

MOISTURE: A moist soil is required.

PROPAGATION: Terminal cuttings.

POTTING: Use mix A.

FERTILIZER: Use water-soluble solution monthly.

INSECTS: This species is very susceptible to red spider mites, mealy bugs and white flies.

PRUNING: Prune old plants to eliminate straggly growth and maintain bushy character by pinching out tip growth.

Fuchsia *(Fuchsia hybrida)*

A group name for hundreds of cultivated hybrid fuchsias. Each year new varieties too numerous to mention are added to the list. Single- and double-flowered varieties suitable for hanging baskets, pot culture, espalier training, pyramids and standards or tree forms are available.

Additional information regarding fuchsia varieties may be obtained from nursery catalogs. The American Fuchsia Society has its headquarters at 738 22nd Ave., San Francisco, California 94121.

LIGHT: High. Direct sun in winter, light shade in summer.

TEMPERATURE: Cool, especially at night.

MOISTURE: Moist at all times. Daily watering sometimes necessary for hanging baskets.

PROPAGATION: Terminal cuttings of soft wood two to three inches long, in medium of half coarse sand and half vermiculite.

POTTING: Mix A or B is required when potting; good drainage is essential. Repot once a year to larger pot.

FERTILIZER: Fuchsias are heavy feeders, so apply water-soluble solution every two weeks in summer, once a month in winter.

INSECTS: They are susceptible to aphids, mealy bugs, scale insects and white flies.

PRUNING: Pinch tips out occasionally to make bushy growth. Prune back late fall or spring to promote new growth for flowering. Cut off fruits to get more flowers.

REMARKS: Fuchsia flowers best in long warm days following a cool growing period. Put plants outside as soon as danger of frost has passed. Bud drop caused by high temperature and poor light.

F. 'Rose of Castile'

F. 'Display'

F. 'Thalia'

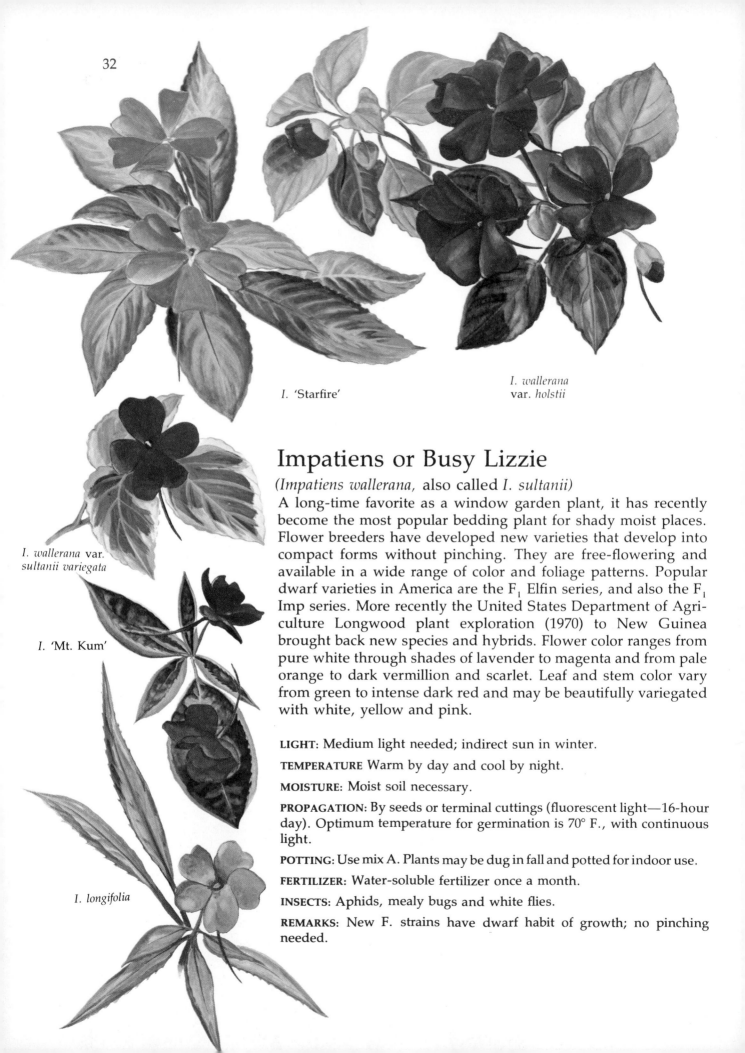

I. 'Starfire'

I. wallerana
var. *holstii*

I. wallerana var.
sultanii variegata

I. 'Mt. Kum'

I. longifolia

Impatiens or Busy Lizzie

(Impatiens wallerana, also called *I. sultanii)*

A long-time favorite as a window garden plant, it has recently become the most popular bedding plant for shady moist places. Flower breeders have developed new varieties that develop into compact forms without pinching. They are free-flowering and available in a wide range of color and foliage patterns. Popular dwarf varieties in America are the F_1 Elfin series, and also the F_1 Imp series. More recently the United States Department of Agriculture Longwood plant exploration (1970) to New Guinea brought back new species and hybrids. Flower color ranges from pure white through shades of lavender to magenta and from pale orange to dark vermillion and scarlet. Leaf and stem color vary from green to intense dark red and may be beautifully variegated with white, yellow and pink.

LIGHT: Medium light needed; indirect sun in winter.

TEMPERATURE Warm by day and cool by night.

MOISTURE: Moist soil necessary.

PROPAGATION: By seeds or terminal cuttings (fluorescent light—16-hour day). Optimum temperature for germination is 70° F., with continuous light.

POTTING: Use mix A. Plants may be dug in fall and potted for indoor use.

FERTILIZER: Water-soluble fertilizer once a month.

INSECTS: Aphids, mealy bugs and white flies.

REMARKS: New F. strains have dwarf habit of growth; no pinching needed.

Oxalis species

O. martiana
aureo-reticulata

O. ortgiesii

O. hedysaroides

Wood Sorrel (Oxalis species)

A large genus of about 400 species found growing throughout the tropics, belonging to the Wood Sorrel family or *Oxalidaceae*. The leaves of the plants resemble clover, having three leaflets. The roots are semibulbous like tubers. Several species are troublesome weeds in gardens and greenhouses, especially in warm climates. Others are grown in hanging baskets or on the windowsill. *O. martiana aureo-reticulata*, known as Sour Clover, produces large leaves and carmine-rose flowers with red lines radiating from a white throat. *O. ortgiesii*, named Tree Oxalis because of its taller growth habit, has large leaves, fish-tailed at the ends, and small yellow flowers borne five to ten in a cluster at the tops of small stems. *O. hedysaroides*, called Firefern, is well named for its fernlike foliage of a glowing satiny-red. Its bright yellow flowers are in sharp contrast to the showy leaves.

LIGHT: High light and full sun required. Flowers open on sunny days, go to "sleep" at night and in dull weather.

TEMPERATURE: Warm day and cool night temperatures suit this plant.

MOISTURE: Soil must be moist for growth. After foliage withers, keep dry until fall.

PROPAGATION: From seeds, divisions or bulblets separated at repotting.

POTTING: Use mix A and repot once a year when growth starts. Pot three to four bulbs in five-inch pan.

FERTILIZER: Feed once a month during the summer with water-soluble fertilizer.

INSECTS: Subject to mealy bugs, red spider mites and white flies.

BEGONIAS

Grown as potted flowering plants, as foliage plants, bedding plants and as hanging baskets. The many species and varieties fall into three groups: fibrous-rooted, tuberous-rooted and rhizomatous.

The fibrous-rooted types, which have a central stalk, are extremely variable in foliage and flowers and include many free-flowering forms.

Tuberous-rooted kinds are mainly summer-flowering, with large camellia-type single and double flowers.

The rhizomatous types are distinguished by creeping rhizomes and large and small, beautifully colored leaves.

RIEGER ELATIOR BEGONIAS of the florist industry are a 1971 introduction to the United States and Canada from Europe. They were brought in by J. C. Mikkelson of Mikkelson's, Inc., the exclusive licensing agency for the Rieger Company of Nürtingen, West Germany.

Many begonias are offered in florist shops and garden stores along with poinsettias, azaleas and chrysanthemums. Their long-lasting spectacular blooms make them highly desirable for home embellishment.

For home culture the requirements are not difficult. High light exclusive of direct sunlight is of first importance. The potting mix must be kept moist. Drying out weakens the plant, making it susceptible to disease. Similarly, good aeration is important. A sun porch or outdoor patio is an excellent location for summer culture. Most varieties will flower continuously with proper care.

Fertilize only at half strength once a month. Too much fertilizer will slow down flower production.

There are two basic types:

'Schwabenland Red' is the predominant variety, with medium-red flowers and a distinct yellow eye. Other varieties have flower-color shades of pink, rose and orange.

Most of the Schwabenland varieties will flower the year round. In Europe, they are used extensively as attractive flowering house plants.

Aphrodite types are useful as hanging baskets because of their habit of growth. A new Aphrodite variety introduced in 1972, 'Amoena,' has a two-tone color effect of pink and yellow double flowers. Other varieties include Aphrodite 'Cherry Red,' 'Red,' 'Rose,' and 'Pink.'

*Rieger elatior begonia
(Begonia X hiemalis)*

BEGONIA SEMPERFLORENS is the fibrous-rooted or wax-leaf type, and hybrids of it are the most widely cultivated of the begonia family. It is offered in the spring by nurseries and garden stores for use as a bedding plant in gardens and in containers. Flowering occurs, regardless of the length of day, thus making it adaptable as a house plant for the sunny window sill.

For many years wax-leaved varieties have been grown as pot plants and only occasionally used for bedding plants. Today, as a result of breeding new varieties both in the United States and Europe, there are many excellent F_1 hybrids. Most garden stores offer them in "packs," as they do for petunias and marigolds.

Two groups of plants are available: dwarf, which averages three to five inches tall when grown in pots, and an intermediate group that grows about four to eight inches high in pots. Each of these groups is further divided into green-leaved plants and bronze-leaved plants. Growing the bronze-leaved plants in full sunlight intensifies the bronze foliar color in some varieties.

A few of the dwarf-class varieties, identified as F_1 hybrids, created by plant breeders are: B. 'Scarlotta,' bright scarlet; B. 'Gin,' bright rose; B. 'Vodka,' bright scarlet; B. 'Viva,' pure white.

Another series of the variety 'Cinderella' is about ten inches tall. It produces about 50 percent extra-large flowers having a bright golden pincushionlike center. The leaves are larger than the regular fibrous type. Colors available are rose, white and a mixture. A fibrous-rooted double-flowering strain is also available. It produces about 50 percent doubles. Australian nurseries offer several varieties of *Begonia semperflorens*, including "Thousand Wonders."

Plants are started from seed, which is very fine and must be sown thinly on a *moist* surface. The seed container is covered with a piece of glass to reduce the need for frequent watering. A light sandy medium with sifted sphagnum moss will help maintain moisture. Seed usually germinates in about two weeks when given 70°. After germination, water the seedlings with a water-soluble fertilizer solution at half strength. When large enough to handle, transplant seedlings to 2½-inch pots.

Terminal cuttings made in the fall will grow into fresh plants for winter.

This group is also suitable for pot-plant culture. It has larger flowers than the regular fibrous group. The flowers are extra large and showy, with large bright golden-yellow centers. Plants are available in white, rose and a mixture of flower colors.

Begonia semperflorens

36

Begonia tuberhybrida pendula flore pleno

TUBEROUS BEGONIA *(Begonia tuberhybrida)*, sometimes called Camellia-flowered begonia, is a hybrid group derived from several South American species of begonias. The group is mainly summer- and fall-flowering. Plants are used in outdoor beds and containers. If they are grown for more than eight to ten weeks in the dry atmosphere of the home, they become weak and spindly.

Their flowers are remarkable for size, beauty and diversity of color, form and texture. Flowers are mostly double with plain, ruffled and frilled edges.

CULTURE OF TUBEROUS BEGONIAS
Starting dormant tubers
Tubers are started in the spring or whenever the pink vegetative buds start to show. Place them in pots or flats for starting. Use a medium of one third peat moss and two thirds sand or perlite. Peat moss alone holds 90 percent of its weight in water when saturated, thus is not recommended without amendment because it tends to pack and become soggy, excluding air. A coarse hardwood leaf mold or hardwood bark soil amendment may be used as a substitute.

Space tubers to allow for heavy root development. Bury by covering with half an inch of the medium. Water the container of tubers carefully to distribute moisture evenly, avoiding soggy wetness. Place container at a warm temperature of 65° to 75° in high light, but shield from direct sun.

Transplant to pots or outdoor prepared beds when the first two leaves have reached full development. Danger of frost must be past before planting outdoors. Rooting is usually heavy at the two-leaf stage, and the tuber will adjust to transplanting. Begonias are shallow rooting, requiring shallow containers such as an azalea pot rather than a standard-size pot. Choose a pot size that allows two inches between the tuber requiring a six-inch pot and larger tubers requiring an eight- or nine-inch pot. Use potting mix B. Fill pot two thirds full and position tuber; finish filling around root mass with mix. Firm medium and finish by covering root mass lightly with one-quarter inch of potting medium. Water carefully until water seeps from drainage hole in bottom of pot. When danger of frost is past, set pots outdoors on patio or other area where high light prevails but not in direct sun or dense shade.

For transplanting in outdoor beds, the prime considerations are: *perfect drainage* and location of planting area in relation to *sun*. Prepare planting bed to consist of one third peat moss or leaf mold or bark soil amendment, one third coarse sand and one third sandy loam. Well-rotted cow or steer manure can be added but must be mixed well. The bed should be spaded and worked with components a month in advance of planting. Addition of a garden fertilizer during bed preparation is recommended. Dig holes large enough to receive the mass of roots without crowding, replacing soil to barely cover top of tubers. Firm in place and add water carefully. Soil should not be in contact with stem of plant.

Suggested planting areas are north sides of buildings, under trees of light shade or lath houses. The correct degree of light and shade will produce strong compact plants and profuse blooms. They will not perform satisfactorily in complete shade or in a bright sunny spot. If too shaded—no blooms. If excess sun—stunting and burn.

Digging tubers and dormant storage
Potted begonias can be forced into dormancy at any time by gradually withholding water. Growing should be encouraged through November, if possible, to increase size of tubers and storage of food for the next year. Bedded begonias growing in colder regions, where chance of early frost may injure plants, can be lifted with a large amount of soil and set in a frostless basement or garage, where they will gradually mature and dry down. A first light frost will not harm the tubers.

When bedded plants or pot begonias drop their foliage the stem will dry and break free from the tuber. Wash all soil from tubers and dry in sunshine for a few days until tuber is hard and dry. Be sure to remove all traces of stem tissue from tuber to prevent decay and infestation. Store in open trays or boxes in a cool, dry place until the pink vegetative buds appear. These are usually visible in spring. Then start over again as outlined for starting dormant tubers.

Tuberous begonias are also started from seed.

Begonia tuberhybrida pendula flore pleno is the Basket begonia. It is a very popular plant, taking the lead for summer-flowering baskets on the patio or the porch. Its pendant habit comes from the species *B. boliviensis* and its varieties come with red, rose, salmon, yellow and white flowers. Basket begonia tubers, which do not sprout more than two branches at the beginning of the season, should have the tips pinched off when the first flower bud appears. This will make a fuller basket.

All tuberous begonias need semishade, cool temperature and moisture. An application of water-soluble fertilizer once a month encourages luxuriant growth and flowering.

Begonia tuberhybrida

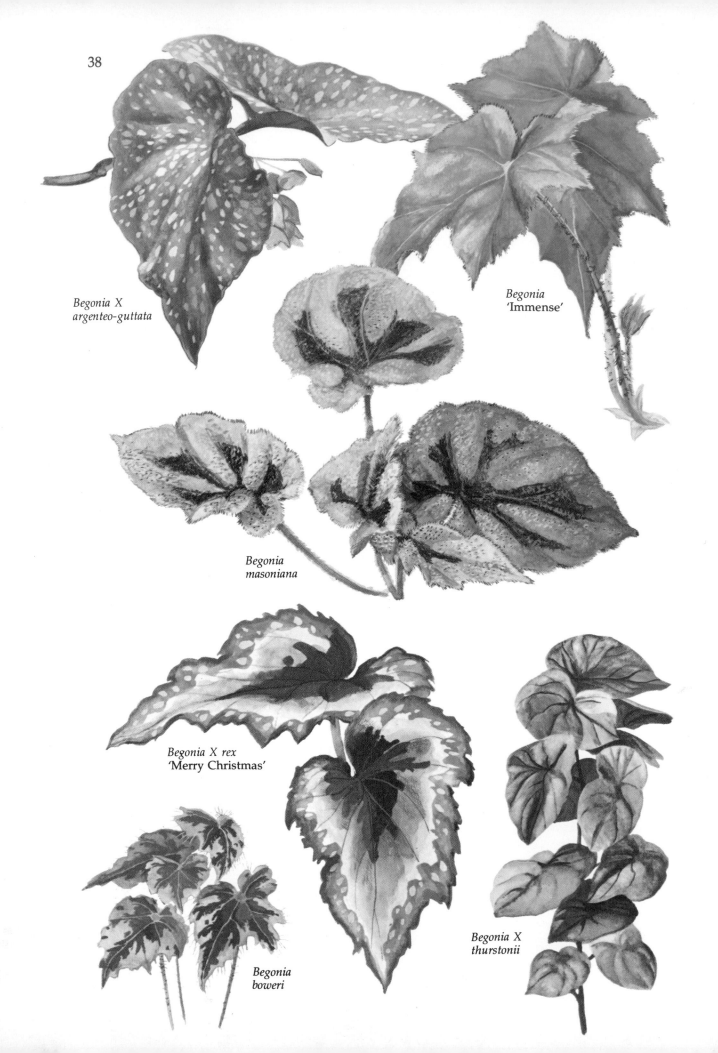

38

*Begonia X
argenteo-guttata*

*Begonia
'Immense'*

*Begonia
masoniana*

Begonia X rex
'Merry Christmas'

*Begonia
boweri*

*Begonia X
thurstonii*

BEGONIA X REX is of the rhizomatous group, is the foliage plant of the family and has many hybrids with brightly colored tapestrylike leaves. Some are upright, but most are creeping. *B. X rex* 'Merry Christmas,' as illustrated, is one of the many varieties. Dwarf types of rex are among the miniatures of the begonia family. Most of them are excellent for small pots and terrariums. Rex begonias need shade from direct sun from late winter to late fall. Supplemental fluorescent lighting is beneficial in the winter from early in the morning until late at night. Repotting of rex begonias is necessary when the rhizome outgrows the pot. Use a shallow or azalea-type pot because of the plant's shallow root system. Mix A for potting or a mixture composed of 50 percent peat for moisture-holding capacity. Like other members of the family, rex varieties like a moist mixture. Avoid a potting mixture that remains soggy wet, which may cause the rhizome to rot. Fertilize rex plants once a month, except in winter. Winter is a period of semirest for some varieties, and at that time some leaf drop may occur.

Propagation

Propagation of rex is accomplished in a number of ways. Division of the rhizome can be done at repotting time. Cut the rhizome into pieces one to two inches long and press into the potting mix longitudinally to a depth of one half the diameter of the rhizome. Keep moist and warm until shoot growth appears.

Another method is by leaf and petiole cutting; the new plant sprouts from the base of the stem. Still another is to cut the leaf into pie-shaped wedges, each having one main vein; insert the leaf base a half inch into the potting medium; position at a 45° angle. Another method is to slit the main vein of the leaf at numerous places on the back side. The slit leaf is then laid on the moist rooting media and fastened with a hairpin.

BEGONIA MASONIANA, the Iron Cross Begonia, is considered one of the most beautiful begonias in cultivation. This species was introduced from the gardens of Singapore and is thought by some to be a rex, although it is truly a rhizomatous type. Start new plants by division of the rhizomes and by leaf and petiole cutting.

BEGONIA X ARGENTEO-GUTTATA, called Trout Begonia and often referred to as Angel Wing Begonia, has leaves arranged at an angle resembling angel wings. It is a cane-stem type and becomes bushy when soft-pinched. Propagate by terminal cutting or by sectional cuttings.

BEGONIA BOWERI, is a rhizomatous type native to southern Mexico. Its popular name, Eyelash begonia, comes from the erect white hairs evenly spaced along the margins of the vivid green leaves. The margins of the leaves are spotted with black and purple patches. The flowers appear during the winter and spring months and are of a characteristic pink color. It is in the dwarf section of begonias, useful for dish gardens and terrariums. New plants can be started in the spring by division of the rhizomes. Cut off the old leaves and let the new ones develop.

BEGONIA 'IMMENSE' is a seedling offspring of *B. x ricinifolia* and is a robust plant with large, starlike, light-green waxy leaves. The upper surface of the leaf is covered with very short bristlelike hairs; the margins of the leaves and the leaf petioles are covered with short red hairs. The flowers are pink, and new plants are started by division, as are *B. rex* and other rhizomatous types.

BEGONIA X THURSTONII is a fibrous-rooted type, a hybrid between *B. metallica* and *B. sanguinea*. Pinching out the terminal growth makes it a desirable, bushy house plant. Red-colored petioles are covered with white hairs. Its leaves have a glossy bronze-green color on the top surface, with the red color of the stems on the under surface. Its flowers are light red. Start new plants by stem cuttings and by division of the larger plant at repotting time in the spring.

GERANIUMS

A native plant species, **Pelargonium hortorum,** *from South Africa. The geranium has been popular for over a century and ranks worldwide as the most important and useful plant today. As a sun-loving plant it is excellent for the greenhouse, yet it grows in the home with full sun exposure or under fluorescent lights for a 16-hour day. A popular pot plant, it is sold by florists and garden stores for Easter and Mother's Day. It is used in porch boxes, in containers for patios and in cemetery urns. In the United States, Canada, Alaska and in northern Europe it is planted in gardens as a bedding plant. It is ever-blooming throughout the entire season. It is seldom found in southern climates where temperatures exceed 85°, yet it will tolerate temperatures as low as 28°.*

Varieties of P. hortorum *are used by growers as the main crops for indoor-outdoor plants. The matter of varieties changes considerably with demands of the consumers and markets in different parts of the world. Red, pink and white with shades of dark and light colors are offered. Hundreds of cultivars have been created and it is best to consult the catalogs of local nurserymen before buying.*

Some varieties available in America are:

Red—'Red Perfection,' dark red
  'Irene,' an excellent bright scarlet-red
  'Sincerity,' a dark orange-red
  'Cardinal,' a robust dark red
  'Imp. Ricard,' a dependable large-flowered brick-red

Pink—'Skylark,' a large medium-pink
  'Genie,' a free-flowering rose-pink
  'Enchantress Fiat,' an excellent light salmon-pink
  'Penny,' a semidouble neon-pink
  'Salmon Irene,' an excellent medium salmon

White—'Snow Mass,' one of the better whites
  'Modesty,' a white 'Irene'

A few noteworthy cultivars grown in Great Britain are:

Crimson—'Distinction,' rounded leaf marked with a dark brown zone close to margin of the leaf

Coral—'Fiat,' a semidouble flower

Pink—'Gazelle,' salmon pink flower, a dark purple zone near the center of the leaf

Culture of geraniums

TEMPERATURE: For the production of geraniums in greenhouses a temperature of 60°–65° Fahrenheit is recommended. In the home, maintain a warm temperature during the day but keep plants cool at night.

MOISTURE: Geraniums are kept moist but not excessively wet, which is contrary to an early concept of growing on the dry side. Withholding water may cause yellowing and dropping of the leaves. Pots or planters must have drain holes to allow excess water to flow out.

PROPAGATION: Use terminal cuttings 2½ to four inches long and leave as many leaves attached as possible. A good medium for rooting is a coarse sand or a peat and perlite combination. Water the pots or flats of cuttings on the dry side for the first two weeks to encourage callus formation. Thereafter, more moisture added to the medium will encourage rooting. Enclosure within a polyethylene bag is beneficial to prevent cuttings from wilting. The use of a rooting hormone will hasten rooting, though it is not essential.

SEED (new strains): A major development in geranium culture is growing from seed. Carefree is a well-known strain that comes in red, scarlet, white and shades of pink. An American strain, Nittany Lion, and the Moreton hybrids show colors similar to the Carefree series. Commercial growers grow a four-inch potted flowering plant in 120 days from seed.

POTTING: Mix A or well-aerated soilless mix is used for potting cuttings and growing. The well-rooted cutting may be potted directly into a four-inch pot.

FERTILIZER: Application to growing geranium plants once every two weeks in summer and once a month in winter will produce a healthy plant and encourage subsequent flowering. Use of a complete water-soluble fertilizer solution is recommended. A slow-release type incorpo-rated into potting mixture or top-dressings may also be used.

INSECTS AND DISEASE: These often cause problems with geraniums. White flies, mealy bugs and aphids are the troublesome insects. Geraniums are very susceptible to bacterial stem and leaf rots. Fungous infection by pythium produces blackened stems near base of young plants. It can be avoided by using sterilized mixes and by not overwatering. Sanitation is the best method of control. For home gardeners, it is better to discard old diseased plants and grow new plants.

IVY-LEAVED GERANIUMS A recent craze for hanging-basket plants has brought new interest in the vining ivy-leaved geranium for home culture and greenhouse. Known botanically as *Pelargonium peltatum*, a species with many varieties; differs from *P. hortorum* in its trailing, drooping or somewhat climbing habit. Its leaves and stems are somewhat succulent and smooth. An old favorite, Sunset Ivy geranium, *P.* 'L'Elegante,' has green-and-white variegated leaves which take on pink color when grown dry.

Pelargonium 'L'Elegante'

P. X hortorum
'Mrs. Henry Cox'

P. X hortorum
'Maréchal MacMahon'

P. X hortorum
'Distinction'

P. X hortorum
'Cherry Sundae'

Some other outstanding varieties are:
P. 'Charles Turner,' a profusely blooming large flower of deep pink.
P. 'Barbary Coast,' with extra-large lavender flowers, a new variety.
P. 'Intensity,' with bright orange-scarlet flowers.
P. 'Mexican Beauty,' a long trailing variety with large dark-red flowers.
P. 'Queen of Hearts,' sturdy arching stems bearing double white flowers, each petal having a red spot.

SCENTED-LEAF GERANIUMS Some of the scented-leaved types of pelargoniums were among the first discovered in cultivation centuries ago and are still grown today. A light pressure on the leaf between the thumb and forefinger releases the plant's fragrance.
Some of these are:
P. graveolens, with rose-scented leaves, used in cookery and perfume.
P. crispum, mildly scented, used in finger bowls or hung in closets.
P. X fragrans, the "nutmeg geranium."
P. tomentosum, the "peppermint geranium," strongly scented, of sprawling habit.

Other more recent introductions are P. X 'Clorinda,' eucalyptus-scented with oak-shaped leaves, and P. 'Old Spice,' with strong apple and nutmeg fragrance.

FANCY-LEAVED GERANIUMS: These include geraniums with green and white foliage, also some with bronze and gold and others with multicolors.
P. X hortorum 'Flowers of Spring' has glistening bright-green leaves with wide cream-colored border and red blooms.
P. X hortorum 'Lady Esther,' with double red flowers and mottled foliage. Varieties have bronze and gold foliage; for instance, P. X hortorum 'Alpha,' a small bushy habit of growth, bearing single scarlet flowers in profusion.
P. X hortorum 'Contrast' has leaves bordered bright yellow, splashed scarlet and brown; scarlet flowers.
P. X hortorum 'Filigree' produces lobed, sil-

very green leaves bearing a wide cream border and zoned with pink and brown; deep salmon flowers.

P. X hortorum 'Golden Oriole' bears small shiny yellow-green leaves with rust-red zones; salmon flowers.

P. X hortorum 'Happy Thought,' an old English variety, bright-green leaves with a large cream-yellow butterfly marking, bearing single flowers of red and scarlet.

P. X hortorum 'Skies of Italy,' a dwarf with maplelike leaves, green and creamy margins, brown zones tinted with orange, red and crimson; single scarlet flowers.

DWARF AND CACTUS-FLOWERED GERANIUMS Dwarf varieties grow nine to ten inches tall in pots and are available in a variety of colors. Some have double blooms and some single.

P. X hortorum 'Robin Hood' is a semidwarf compact with zoned foliage and produces a profusion of cherry-red double flowers.

P. X hortorum 'Gina,' a heavy bloomer with double white flowers.

P. X hortorum 'Cherry Time' has double orange-red flowers borne above a dense growth of yellow-green leaves with faint bronze zonings. The cactus-flowered types, often called poinsettia geraniums, have narrow flat petals, sometimes twisted or rolled in an interesting variation of flower form.

This series includes:

P. X hortorum 'Poinsettia,' with dense double globular flowers and narrow rolled and twisted petals of bright scarlet.

P. X hortorum 'Noel,' with double white flowers, rolled and twisted.

P. X hortorum 'Southern Cross,' with double coral-red flowers, characteristic of the poinsettia geranium.

Other dwarf varieties offered have intriguing names such as 'Fairy Tales,' a tricolor variety; 'Doc,' a red; 'Dopey,' pink and white; 'Sneezy,' red and white; 'Grumpy,' dark red. There also are the light salmon 'Tweedledee' and the dark salmon 'Tweedledum.'

P. X hortorum
'Pompeii'

P. X hortorum
'Pink Poinsettia'

P. 'Prince
of Orange'

P. graveolens
'Lady Plymouth'

AFRICAN VIOLETS AND RELATIVES

African Violet
(Saintpaulia ionantha)

The African violet has been a popular and easy-to-grow house plant since its introduction into cultivation. It is a member of a large, interesting and diversified family; botanically *Gesneriaceae,* referred to by the gardeners who grow any of the related genera as Gesneriads. Saintpaulia cultivars numbering several hundreds have originated from crossing the many different wild forms native to tropical East Africa. In recent years related genera developed in America have become as popular as the violet, and genera such as gloxinia, *Columnea Episcia* and others are cultivated by specialists and offered to the trade.

Gesneriads are recognized by their wheel-shaped, tubular or bell-shaped flowers, some of which are brightly colored, some speckled and others even bicolored. Leaf surfaces are often velvety or hairy and some are thick and succulent. Their habitat is greatly varied, from tree-dwelling epiphytic kinds to those that thrive alongside tropical waterfalls and mountainous streams. One is reported to withstand frost.

LIGHT: A main requirement. A light intensity of about one-tenth of summer sun or an intensity equal to that of direct winter sun is best for flowering in the home. Young plants will grow at less than that but need more light for flowering. Plants growing on windowsills must be protected from direct sun. A combination of cool white and warm white fluorescent lights located six to eight inches above the plants, giving illumination for 16 hours a day, is recommended

'Paul Bunyan'　　　'Wintergreen'　　　'Blue Nocturne'

'Blue Canoe'　　　'Firebird'　　　'Blue Warrior'

for growing without daylight. Plant-growing lights may also be used.

TEMPERATURE: Warm. 60° to 75° is required for growth. Lower than 60° causes the foliage to become pale green and curl at the margins. Cold drafts or contact with a cold windowpane causes yellow blotches to appear on the leaves.

WATER: As important as light. Overwatering can be fatal to African violets. The potting mix should be kept just moist at all times. Water can be applied on the surface or as capillary water from below. If watered from below, set pot in a pan of water but remove as soon as moisture appears at mix surface. Tepid water (65° to 70°) is best, because colder water causes permanent discoloration and spotting on contact with foliage.

PROPAGATION:

Step 1. Select a large, healthy leaf and cut from plant with a one-inch-long petiole attached. Use a razor blade or sharp knife.

Step 2. For rooting use a 2½-inch-size plastic pot filled with a medium consisting of one half peat moss and one half sand or perlite. Another medium that is just as good is vermiculite. Moisten medium and press firm. Using a dowel, dibber or pencil, make a hole in the center to receive the petiole. Insert petiole to leaf blade. Place pot in polyethylene (polythene) bag. Remove the polyethylene bag as soon as shoot growth appears.

Forsythe pot method is a convenient way to root several cuttings. Place a smaller pot (2¼") with a corked drainage hole inside a large pan of clay or plastic that is filled with a propagation medium. Fill the small pot with water. The water will seep through, keeping the propagation material continually moist.

Step 3. When the cutting has rooted, a cluster of plants will form at the base of stem. When large enough to handle, remove and pot into a small pot, using mix A for growing on.

Step 4. When plants are four or five months old, divide the crown into single plants. A later shift will bring the plants to a finishing four-inch pot.

'Norlina'

'Lili Belle'

'Fury'

'Wild White'

'Blue Boy-in-the-Snow'

'Plum Tipped'

Saintpaulia ionantha 'Hot Drops'

POTTING: Mixture A is recommended because of its high moisture capacity. Mixtures containing leaf mold and soil must be steam-sterilized at 160° for 30 minutes before use.

FERTILIZER: Fertilize African violets only when they are established in the pot. They are not heavy feeders. Use a water-soluble fertilizer once a month according to the manufacturer's directions.

INSECTS: Mainly mealy bugs and aphids.

DISEASE: Several diseases occur, such as mildew, crown and root rot. Most diseases can be avoided by using care in watering. A well-drained aerated potting mix will prevent excess water from standing about the crown of the plant. Using a sterilized potting mix also helps to prevent disease problems. Spraying plants with a sink spray, using tepid water, cleans and refreshes.

BREEDING: Breeding violets for new forms and color is a challenge and can develop into an exciting new hobby. It has been learned that the progeny of a single cross often show several characteristics that were not apparent in either parent plant. Sometimes several generations are required to find the answer.

Since the period of time from sown seed to a flowering plant is about the same as that from cutting to mature plant, no time is lost. A cutting produces only one plant, whereas seeds from a single pod produce many.

For breeding, choose a well-developed, not faded, flower for both parents. Remove the flower from the plant chosen as a male parent and with a razor blade open or slit the anthers, thus releasing the yellow pollen grains. The anthers are then carefully rubbed over the stigma of a flower on the plant selected as the seed-bearing or female plant until it is covered with pollen. A sticky substance on the stigma holds the pollen grains until the flower is fertilized. If the "cross" takes, although not every one will, a tiny seed pod will begin to form about two weeks after pollination. Six to nine months are required for the seed pod to mature fully. After the pod has developed fully, the seed either can be stored (60° to 65°) in a dry place or sown immediately. Mature seed pods are ready for harvest when they shrivel, dry and turn brown on the plant.

Sowing seeds requires special care, as the seeds are fine as dust. A clean sterilized plastic or clay pot covered with a glass plate or polyethylene bag is satisfactory for germinating seed. Use the seed-sowing mix D as suggested in the chapter on soilless potting mixes. Seeds are sprinkled very thinly over the surface of mix and placed in a tray of water for subirrigation.

Fluorescent lighting or curtain-shaded sunlight will fulfill the light requirement. Seedlings will appear in about three weeks. When the seedlings are a half inch or so high they should be transplanted singly to individual pots of two-inch size.

MINIATURE AFRICAN VIOLETS. Breeders and hybridizers have developed miniature or dwarf cultivars and semidwarf varieties as well as some trailing types. A variety of flower colors are offered and a variation of leaves. Growers have learned that the miniature violets respond to higher light intensity than regulars and also use more fertilizer. The development of suckers is prolific, and it is desirable to thin these out regularly every two or three weeks. Tweezers are handy tools for this operation.

Cultural requirements such as temperature, moisture, potting materials and insect control are the same as for large violets. When to repot is a question. A 2½-inch pot is generally used. A shift to a large pot is considered when the diameter of the plant becomes two-thirds larger than the pot.

To facilitate watering these small pots, it is suggested that pots be plunged into trays of moist sand, providing the plants with a constant supply of moisture through the sub-irrigation method.

The Magic Flower
(*Achimenes*—Species and hybrids)

A very popular, flowering-sized house plant growing naturally in the Caribbean, Mexico and Central America. *Achimenes,* which is summer-flowering, makes wonderful hanging baskets as well as potted specimens. Flowers vary in size from one-half to three inches across and usually cover the plant with cascades of blooms. The flowers are very colorful in pastel shades of orange, red, lavender and some white.

For hanging baskets there are *A.* 'Wetterlow's Triumph,' bright pink; *A.* 'Margarita,' pure white; *A. puchella*, orange-red; and many others. There are varieties with dwarf tendencies that are good as table plants—for example, *A.* 'Adele Delhaute,' large,

A. 'Paul Arnold'

A. 'Ambroise Verscheffelt'

purple-violet; *A.* 'Charm,' pink; *A.* 'Little Beauty,' large pink flowers. There are tall, upright varieties, some of which require staking, and many others that are bushy types.

LIGHT: High; partial shade outdoors in summer.

TEMPERATURE: Warm. Storage in winter at 55°.

MOISTURE: Moist. Drying causes dormancy. Use warm water to prevent leaf spotting.

PROPAGATION: Scaly rhizomes, cuttings, seed. Start seed in late winter.

POTTING: Formula B. Plant rhizomes five to six in a four- or five-inch shallow pot. Set one-half to one inch apart and cover one inch deep.

FERTILIZER: Apply water-soluble fertilizer once every two weeks when growing in soilless mix.

INSECTS: Mealy bugs, spider mites.

PRUNING: On taller varieties pinch out tips when three to four inches tall.

REMARKS: *Achimenes* go dormant for the winter. Gradually stop watering in late fall. Cut off wilted foliage to ground. Store in pots at 55°. Repot in spring when new shoots appear.

Aeschynanthus pulcher

Lipstick Plant
or Royal Red Bugler
(*Aeschynanthus pulcher*)

A climbing epiphytic plant producing roots at the nodes, clinging to trunks and branches of trees in the jungles of Java. Produces brilliant-scarlet tubular flowers in clusters at the tips of the branches in the spring. The trailing habit of growth makes it a good basket plant.

Other varieties worthy of growing are *A. x splendidus*, *A.* 'Black Pagoda' and *A. pullobia*.

LIGHT: High, but no direct sun in the summer.

TEMPERATURE: Warm.

MOISTURE: Dry; moist atmosphere in summer.

PROPAGATION: Stem or terminal cuttings, division.

POTTING: Mix B or a well-drained and aerated mix as for other epiphytes.

INSECTS: Mealy bugs, red spider mites, white flies.

PRUNING: Thinning out of old flowered branches encourages new growth.

Gloxinia (*Sinningia speciosa*)

The florist gloxinia and species; easy to grow under home conditions; native to Brazil. Woody tuberous-rooted; most species are rosette-type plants ranging in size from two inches to two feet across. Flowers are small to large, slipper-shaped and bell types in many color patterns as well as various pastel shades. Tubers are purchased from garden stores in early spring for summer bloom. *S. barbata*, *S. eumorpha* and *S. regina* are species types worthy of growing for the plant collector. The miniature species *S. concinna* and *S. pusilla* (the world's smallest gloxinia) have been hybridized to produce many interesting varieties. All are identified by trumpet- or slipper-shaped flowers. Plants measure from two to three inches across to not more than one to three inches high. They are ever-blooming and grow well in terrariums. Some better known are *S.* 'Bright Eyes,' *S.* 'Cindy,' *S.* 'Doll Baby,' *S.* 'Freckles' and *S.* 'White Sprite.'

Sinningia speciosa

Columnea rubra 'Morton'

Columnea gloriosa

Columnea crassifolia

LIGHT: Medium to high; no direct sun.

TEMPERATURE: Warm, with ventilation.

MOISTURE: Moist (high humidity of terrarium).

PROPAGATION: Seeds, division of tubers, leaf cuttings.

POTTING: Mix B. Plant miniatures in 1¼- to three-inch pots. Florist type in five- to six-inch size.

INSECTS: White flies, mealy bugs, aphids.

REMARKS: Rest periods, few days to several weeks, but 14 to 16 hours of fluorescent light prolongs flowering.

Goldfish Plant *(Columnea)*

Fibrous-rooted gesneriads with showy scarlet, orange or yellow flowers from the rain forests of Central and South America. Many are wild species, but hybrids have been created that are tolerant of the adverse conditions of the home. Two types: slender stem vines for hanging baskets and those with stiff upright growth for pot culture. Some of the better basket types, raised chiefly in America, are hybrids of *C. gloriosa:* *C.* 'Cascadilla,' *C.* 'Yellow Gold' and *C.* 'Early Bird.' Upright types include *C.* 'Cornellian,' *C.* 'Cayugan' and *C.* 'Yellow Dragon.' These plants are more tolerant of home culture. Most are seasonal in blooming habits, but through selection of hybrids or species, plants can be in bloom all year.

LIGHT: Bright; indirect sun.

TEMPERATURE: Warm, with exceptions: *C.* 'Stravanger,' *C. hirta* and *C. microphylla,* which require 50° to 59° for bud formation.

MOISTURE: Dry, with atmospheric moisture if possible.

PROPAGATION: Seeds, stem and terminal cuttings, division.

POTTING: Mix B, loose epiphytic type.

INSECTS: Mealy bugs.

REMARKS: Cut off old flower stems to stimulate formation of new shoots.

50

Kohleria amabilis

Temple Bells
(Smithiantha zebrina syn. *Naegelia zebrina)*

A native to the mountains of Mexico. Another species, *S. cinnabarina*, has heavily spotted contrasting red and yellow flowers with dark-green heart-shaped leaves. Also available are crosses between *Smithiantha* and *Achimenes* resulting in a hybrid labeled *X Eucodonopsis*. Crosses between *S. fulgida*, *S. cinnabarina*, and *S. zebrina* have produced cultivars noted for their unusual large flowers and colors ranging from pale peach to deep red. *Smithiantha* flowering period is from late summer to winter.

LIGHT: Indirect sunlight. Fluorescent lighting for 12 to 14 hours a day.

TEMPERATURE: Warm.

MOISTURE: Moist; high humidity if possible.

PROPAGATION: Division of scaly rhizome. Leaf-petiole cutting.

Kohleria *(Kohleria amabilis)*

A native to the mountains of tropical America. A plant easy to grow in the home or greenhouse. Tubular flowers appearing along the stem are showy, speckled with deeper contrasting color. Can be grown as trailing or upright with support. *K. amabilis* has pink flowers with reddish-purple dots, black veins and is dwarf in habit of growth. Hybrids of *amabilis* include *K.* 'Rongo,' which is almost ever-blooming. *K.*

LIGHT: High; no direct sun. Flowering under long-day conditions: 16 hours under artificial light.

TEMPERATURE: Warm.

MOISTURE: Moist.

PROPAGATION: Terminal cuttings, division of scaly rhizomes.

POTTING: Mix B.

INSECTS: Mealy bugs, white flies.

REMARKS: Cut back after flowering. Sprouts will grow from scaly rhizomes without rest period.

Smithiantha zebrina

Rechsteineria cardinalis

POTTING: Repotting and dividing, put one rhizome to a four- to five-inch pot. Mix A.

FERTILIZER: Apply water-soluble type once a month during spring and summer when plants are in active growth.

INSECTS: Mealy bugs, white flies.

REMARKS: After flowering, gradually withhold water to give semirest period until new growth commences.

Cardinal Flower

(*Rechsteineria cardinalis*)

It is closely related to the gloxinias in the family *Gesneriaceae.* The native habitat of the genus ranges from Brazil to Central America and into Mexico. Flowers are less showy than gloxinia, being rather slender, tubular, of red and orange colors, one to 2½ inches long. Low-growing species like *R. cardinalis, R. macropoda* and *R. leucotricha* are the best species for indoor culture. *R. macropoda* differs from *R. cardinalis* in that it has large, less velvety leaves and orange-red flowers, but it lacks the hood characteristic of *R. cardinalis. R. leucotricha* resembles *R. cardinalis* except that sometimes it produces long center stems with leaves and flowers at the end. Its leaves are unusual, being covered with dense silvery wool which also covers stems and flowers.

The color of the flowers is bright salmon-red. Flowering of *R. cardinalis* takes place from late fall to Christmas, making it a good gift plant.

LIGHT: High; indirect sunlight or 14 to 16 hours of fluorescent lighting.

TEMPERATURE: Warm.

MOISTURE: Dry, but followed by a thorough soaking.

PROPAGATION: Leaf-petiole cuttings at any time. Seeds.

POTTING: Mix B. Repot when new shoots start to grow.

FERTILIZER: Apply water-soluble fertilizer during summer and fall once a month.

INSECTS: Mealy bugs and white flies.

PRUNING: Cut off old stems after flowers have faded. New shoots will grow after a short rest period.

REMARKS: Tubers grow larger each year and need repotting when new shoots develop.

E. 'Bronze Queen'

E. 'Acajou'

E. 'Ember Lace'

Flame Violet

(Episcia cupreata var. cupreata)

Grows wild in Colombia and Venezuela. Foliage patterns are variable due to variants and mutants. Veins of leaves are often pale green or silvery, but all flower colors of *E. cupreata* are orange-scarlet. A species, *E. dianthiflora*, has small velvety green leaves and large heavily fringed white flowers.

Most episcias have trailing habit, but some grow erect, such as: *E. punctata* with magenta-spotted flowers; *E. melittifolia* has purple-pink flowers; *E. decurrens* has white flowers. *E.* 'Cygnet,' introduced by Cornell University, is a cross between *E. dianthiflora* and *E. punctata*.

Many excellent commercial cultivars are available. Those with orange and red flowers seem to be the best-flowering. Among the many are *E.* 'Acajou,' *E.* 'Chocolate Sol-dier,' *E.* 'Cameo,' *E.* 'Filigree,' *E.* 'Jean Bee,' *E.* 'Moss Agate.' *E.* 'Ember Lace' has pink flowers and variegated foliage. *E.* 'Tropical Topaz' has bright green leaves and yellow flowers.

LIGHT: High; give more intensity than for African violets.

TEMPERATURE: Warm. Below 55° injures foliage as if frozen.

MOISTURE: Moist. Never let stand in a saucer of water.

PROPAGATION: Stem cuttings, runners.

POTTING: Mix B. Best grown in hanging baskets or raised pots.

INSECTS: Mealy bugs, white flies.

REMARKS: Removal of stolons or runners encourages flowering.

Cape Primrose

(Streptocarpus X hybridus)

From moist wooded mountain gorges of tropical Africa. The genus comprises numerous species with variable growth habits. The many colors and hybrids of *Streptocarpus* have made it a favorite among plant people. It is used not only as a potted plant, but its cut flowers are used in making flower arrangements and are made up as corsages.

Streptocarpus is not hardy like true primroses and is usually grown indoors or in greenhouses. In temperate regions they are sometimes set in an outdoor flower border in a shady spot and grown like annual bedding plants.

The common hybrid varieties are easily raised from seed. Seed sown in early spring will flower by early winter. Successive sowings will give a succession of blooms throughout the year. Seed is very fine and is counted at an estimated 1,500,000 to the ounce. Refer to the section on page 197, Starting Plants from Seed, for instructions about sowing fine seed. Those best suited for home culture are hybrids from parentage with *S. rexii*. Flowers are large, nodding trumpet-shaped of purple, light to dark blue, deep crimson to white. *S.* 'Constant Nymph' with blue flowers and *S.* 'Massen's White' with pure white flowers are extremely floriferous. *S. saxorum*, a branching stem type, has fleshy medium-green leaves with nodding light lavender-blue flowers; it blooms for six months at a time.

LIGHT: High, exclusive of direct sun. Fluorescent lights are beneficial.

TEMPERATURE: Warm.

MOISTURE: Moist; never let dry.

PROPAGATION: Seed, division of crown, leaf cuttings by nicking the midrib in one or two places and setting the leaf on moist medium, or cutting in three-inch sections. (*S. saxorum:* seed and stem cuttings.)

POTTING: Use mix B.

FERTILIZER: Feed water-soluble, type once a month at half strength. Responds to foliar application at the above rate.

INSECTS: White flies, mealy bugs, aphids.

REMARKS: An "easy-to-grow" house plant.

S. 'Constant Nymph'

P. 'Red Emerald'

FOLIAGE PLANTS

Philodendrons are the favorites of all foliage plants. Their popularity exists because of their tolerance to indoor growing conditions of low light, dryness and warm temperature. Their tough, leathery, glossy green leaves exhibit a most attractive live appearance. A variety of species and hybrids offers many different kinds of leaf shapes and sizes.

The decorator is offered two types to choose from: vining and self-heading.

Vining types such as P. 'Florida,' P. hastatum and P. 'Red Emerald' really do not climb but when given support will conform to it. The support can be anything decorative that is water absorbent. Sections of tree fern are excellent as supports; wire and sphagnum-moss totem poles or slabs of redwood bark that will furnish the plant's stem with moisture also help the plant to grow better.

Philodendron 'Red Emerald'

Another fine hybrid of the philodendron group. Its climbing habit of growth requires support in the way of a trellis. Its leaves are large. The stem and leaf petioles are red, with light-green, arrow-shaped leaves.

LIGHT: Medium.

TEMPERATURE: Warm.

MOISTURE: Moist.

PROPAGATION: Stem cuttings, air layering.

POTTING: Mix B. Repot at least once a year.

FERTILIZER: Apply water-soluble type once every two to three months.

INSECTS: Mealy bugs, red spider mites.

PRUNING: Air-layer top to start new plants. Cut back to ground if losing lower leaves.

P. scandens
subsp. *oxycardium*

Heart-Leaved Philodendron

(Philodendron scandens subsp. *oxycardium)*

The most common and popular of all the philodendrons. It is used in combination with other plants for dish gardens, as a ground cover for large planters, trained upright on totems and in hanging baskets.

LIGHT: Low to medium.

TEMPERATURE: Warm, but will survive short cool spells.

MOISTURE: Moist.

PROPAGATION: Terminal cuttings, leaf-petiole cuttings.

POTTING: Mix B. Repot when plants are root-bound or appear too large for the container.

FERTILIZER: Feed water-soluble type once a month.

INSECTS: Red spider mites, mealy bugs.

Panda Plant

(Philodendron bipennifolium)

Often referred to as "Fiddle-leaf philodendron." A climbing type with large rich green leaves, it is a long-time favorite as a house plant. Climbing types in the home do not really attach to support but must be tied to it.

A water-holding column of sphagnum moss packed in wire or plastic mesh, tree-fern stem totem or slabs of redwood bark that hold moisture make the plants grow better.

LIGHT: Medium to high. High light exclusive of direct sun is best.

TEMPERATURE: Warm.

MOISTURE: Moist.

PROPAGATION: Air layering of leafy tops; sectional cuttings.

POTTING: Mix B.

FERTILIZER: Feed water-soluble type once a month; controlled-release type twice a year.

INSECTS: Mealy bugs.

PRUNING: It is natural for most philodendrons to drop older leaves occasionally in the home. Air-layer tops or cut back to short stub to grow again.

REMARKS: Wash foliage once a month.

P. bipennifolium

P. selloum

Philodendron
(Philodendron selloum)

Sometimes called "Saddle-leaved philo-dendron," it is a member of the large aroid family *Araceae*. Philodendrons, favorite indoor ornamentals, are available in many different sizes and leaf shapes. Some are climbers and some are erect and self-supporting. An exceptional cultural note: Some varieties of *P. selloum* are susceptible to a bacterial leaf-spot disease brought on by moist potting soil and high atmospheric moisture. Therefore, it should be cultured on the extreme dry side. *P. selloum*, a self-heading type, is much used as an interior-decoration plant. Another self-supporting type is *P. wendlandii* and its hybrids. It grows a rosette of thick, waxy green, broad leaves with a thickened midrib and a short bulblike petiole. It looks much like a bizarre bird nest.

LIGHT: Medium to high. Grows best in high light, but not direct sun.

TEMPERATURE: Warm.

MOISTURE: Dry. Plants can become conditioned to less frequent watering where light intensity is low.

PROPAGATION: Air layering of tops of old plants and sectional cuttings.

POTTING: Mix B. Repot only when root-bound.

FERTILIZER: Feed water-soluble type once a month or apply controlled-release type every four months.

INSECTS: Red spider mites, mealy bugs.

REMARKS: Dust or wash foliage once a month to restore luster of leaves.

Elephant's Ear
(Philodendron hastatum syn. *P. domesticum)*

A species climber from Brazil, a long-time favorite as a house plant. Its popularity has given way to many fine hybrids. It is a lush grower with fleshy, green, arrow-shaped leaves. As an adult form, the leaf shape changes to more broadly arrow-shaped with more wavy appearance. It has an outstanding inflorescence, consisting of a pale-green spathe suffused with red inside. Flowering occurs on mature plants. This is usually not experienced indoors, because they are seldom allowed to grow over four feet tall.

P. hastatum variegatum is a striking mutant of *P. hastatum.* Its fleshy, light- to dark-green leaves are irregularly variegated and splashed with nile green, yellow and creamy white.

This is one of the many desirable characteristics of the philodendron group. A variety of sizes, shapes and textures offers the decorator much style to choose from.

Culture as for Heart-Leaved Philodendron.

Self-heading varieties such as *P. selloum, P. wendlandii, P. squamiferum* and hybrids of these make short, broad sets of leaves that radiate from a central crown.

An exciting experience takes place when a philodendron flowers. Older plants will reach an adult stage when grown on tall totems—provided that heat, light and moisture are at optimum levels. The flowers look somewhat like calla lilies, with a boat-shaped bract surrounding a club-shaped, spikelike structure. The bracts are sometimes colored greenish white or reddish.

In spite of the very best growing conditions, philodendrons naturally drop lower leaves in time, exposing the bare stem. To remedy this, one can either air-layer, rooting the stem and cutting it off to pot up, or cut plant back to a stub and start over again. Best advice is to toss the plant out and buy a fresh new one to take its place.

When aerial roots form, train them to travel down the totem and into the potting mix. They function by taking up water and nutrients to supply the tops.

P. hastatum

Caladium hortulanum

Fancy-Leaved Caladium
(Caladium hybrids*)*

Members of the popular ornamental family *Araceae,* they are native to the hot humid Amazon basin of Brazil.

Tubers are raised commercially for forcing as potted foliage plants and for bedding out of doors in warm climates. Tubers are available in grades, expressed in inches of diameter. A "No. 3 size," measuring three quarters to one inch, is the smallest; a "Mammoth" measures 3½ inches or more. Some specialists store tubers under controlled conditions, making them available at any time of the year.

The tubers may be started directly in flowering-size pots at home by following the simple rules of culture.

In America several hundred cultivars have been produced by plantsmen with leaves in shades of red, green and white, often overlain with red or white markings. The most popular grown is 'Candidum'— white with green veins.

A few of many fine varieties are:
'Carolyn Whorton': Fine for pots. Rose, darker veins, green hue.
'Edna': Excellent pot plant. Large glossy leaves. Brilliant red.
'Frieda Hemple': Dwarf, all-purpose red.
'Mrs. Arno Nehrling': Bronze turning white, pink hue, red mid-ribs.
'Fanny Munson': Excellent, brilliant pink with deeper veins.

A variety of caladium leaves, showing different colors and patterns

'Lord Derby': Transparent rose with dark ribs. Bushy.

A distinct class differing from the regular fancy-leaved varieties in leaf appearance is that of the lance-leaf or strap-leaf varieties. Leaves are narrower and the plants grow shorter. They are better adapted for outside beds or in pots for patio growing.

LIGHT: Medium. Avoid direct sun. Leaf burn will occur if exposed to direct sun.

TEMPERATURE: Warm. Temperatures below 70° should be avoided.

MOISTURE: Moist at all times. Excessive moisture and poor drainage may induce root rot. Leaf burn will result from direct sun.

PROPAGATION: Division of tubers at potting time.

POTTING: 100 percent sphagnum peat moss for starting and growing on. Plant in pots or flats (boxes), covering about one inch deep. One tuber will need a four- to five-inch pot.

FERTILIZER: Water-soluble feeding once a month will increase tuber size for next year.

INSECTS: Slugs, in outdoor beds.

REMARKS: When leaves begin to wither, water less frequently until tuber is dormant. Store in pots at 65° to 70° in a heated, well-ventilated area for about four months. Remove from pot, clean off medium and start in spring. Bottom heat of 80°-85° will hasten development of shoot growth.

P. griseo-argentea

P. argyreia

Peperomia

A genus of succulent and semisucculent plants from the subtropics, and mainly of South America. A popular plant because it is one of the exceptions to the rule—"always moist." Its compact, dwarflike growth makes it useful for dish gardens and as a foliage pot plant for the coffee table or windowsill. Foliage plant specialists are constantly selecting new and better peperomia varieties.

Ivy peperomia in America is *Peperomia griseo-argentea*. In Brazil it was known as *P hederaefolia* and has been introduced in Europe under the same name. A plant of bushy habit with shieldlike, quilted leaves, blotched with glossy silver; the veins of the leaf are purplish olive. A cultivar found in California is *P. griseo-argentea* 'Blackie' with metallic olive-green to blackish, coppery leaves.

Peperomia scandens variegata a semierect, creeping plant suitable for table display. It is fast-growing, filling a four-inch pot in four months from a rooted cutting under fluorescent lighting. An all-green leaf form is *P. scandens*, which resembles a miniature philodendron with its heart-shaped leaves.

P. argyreia, watermelon peperomia, from Brazil, with long, upright flower spikes is very attractive and tolerant of dryness.

P. caperata 'Emerald Ripple,' a natural cultivar from Brazil, is very popular with its heart-shaped, rippled leaves and upright flower stalks of tiny, greenish-white flowers.

P. obtusifolia variegata, a variegated-leaf type similar in growth and description to *P. obtusifolia*, is now identified by taxonomists as *P. floridana*; *P. obtusifolia variegata* is general terminology referring to variegated-leaf

P. scandens variegata

P. caperata
'Emerald Ripple'

P. obtusifolia
variegata

forms with similar characteristics. Among the cultivars listed are *P. obtusifolia alba*; *P. albo-marginata*; *P.* 'Gold Tip,' an American introduction; also *P. lougenii*, a miniature version and another miniature, *P. minima*.

P. floridana (*P. obtusifolia*) today is still a popular dish-garden plant propagated by the thousands in Florida nurseries.

P. rotundifolia, formerly called *P. nummularifolia*, was introduced from Puerto Rico and Jamaica. It is a common ground-cover plant found in the Luquillo rain forest of Puerto Rico. It is a ground-cover creeper with threadlike green stems rooting at each node with tiny, succulent, round, thick leaves measuring only one-third of an inch. It is an excellent plant for terrarium landscapes and for miniature gardens of all kinds.

P. metallica is an attractive, erect, bushy type, low-growing with red stems bearing narrow, waxy leaves of a metallic luster. The underside of the leaf is silvery.

LIGHT: Medium; indirect sun in winter.

TEMPERATURE: Warm.

MOISTURE: Dry. Allow mix to become moderately dry before watering.

PROPAGATION: Terminal cuttings from branching types. Leaf-petiole cuttings for stemless varieties. Rooting medium of coarse sand to provide good drainage. Division of crown of older plants.

POTTING: Mix B for good aeration and drainage.

FERTILIZER: Feed large established plants once every three months with water-soluble fertilizer.

INSECTS: Mealy bugs.

PRUNING: Pinch out tips of stem varieties to encourage branching for compact growth.

P. rotundifolia

Helxine soleirolii

*Pilea
cadierei*

*Pilea
involucrata*

Mind Your Own Business or Baby's Tears *(Helxine soleirolii)*

A plant native to Corsica and Sardinia belonging to the nettle family. A very popular plant for home culture because of its matlike creeping habit.

LIGHT: High. Medium light causes elongation of stems, giving a trailing habit of growth.

TEMPERATURE: Warm. Cool nights beneficial.

MOISTURE: Moist at all times. Leaves readily injured if allowed to dry.

PROPAGATION: Division of clump. A small piece spreads rapidly.

POTTING: Mix A.

FERTILIZER: Apply water-soluble type at half strength every two weeks.

INSECTS: White flies, mealy bugs, slugs.

Aluminum Plant

(Pilea cadierei)

Pilea is another genus of the nettle family with several species in cultivation; used as table plants in the home and office or combined with other plants in dish gardens. The outstanding leaf characteristic is its pretty silver patterning. The average height is around 12 inches.

   P. 'Moon Valley,' probably a natural hybrid from the wild, is popular; has a rough textured leaf surface. The center portion of the leaf is blotched brownish with the margin diffused with tawny gold.

   Other species available are *P. involucrata* or 'Panamiga,' the friendship plant, and *P. microphylla*, the artillery plant.

LIGHT: High. Fluorescent light for 16-hour day.

TEMPERATURE: Warm.

MOISTURE: Dry but not completely.

PROPAGATION: Stem cuttings and division.

POTTING: Mix B.

FERTILIZER: Feed with water-soluble type at half strength once a month.

INSECTS: Mealy bugs, aphids and white flies.

PRUNING: Soft-pinch to maintain bushiness.

Piggyback Plant
(*Tolmiea menziesii*)

A hardy outdoor plant native to the West Coast of the United States, where marine influences bring about mild winter weather. For the home or office it makes an excellent table plant, surviving under the most adverse conditions. However, it requires a cooler temperature than most living environments to do really well.

LIGHT: High. Light shade from direct sun in summer.

TEMPERATURE: Cool. A windowsill or cool entrance hall is best.

MOISTURE: Moist at all times.

PROPAGATION: Leaf and petiole cuttings, using leaves on which a plantlet has formed. Insert so base of leaf rests on medium.

POTTING: Mix A.

FERTILIZER: Feed water-soluble type monthly during summer to established plants.

INSECTS: Mealy bugs and white flies.

Tolmiea menziesii

Sensitive Plant (*Mimosa pudica*)

A member of the pea family, *Leguminosae*, this plant comes from continental tropical America. A fascinating plant attraction for children and adults. The leaves and branches droop and fold up quickly when touched or otherwise disturbed. Following collapse, recovery to fully expanded leaves occurs in from several minutes to a half hour, depending on temperature.

LIGHT: High. Sunny window sill for best results.

TEMPERATURE: Warm.

MOISTURE: Moist. Dryness causes leaf drop.

PROPAGATION: Seeds sown annually.

POTTING: Mix B. Transplant seedlings to a four-inch pot.

FERTILIZER: Feed water-soluble type every three weeks when plant appears pot-bound.

INSECTS: Mealy bugs and red spider mites.

REMARKS: Sow seeds in early spring. Save seeds produced by the plant.

Mimosa pudica

Rhoeo spathacea

Classic Myrtle
(*Myrtus communis microphylla*)

A compact bushy plant with dark-green foliage grown by European plantsmen for wedding embellishment. It is sheared into globe shapes on short or tall treelike stems. Also used in dish gardens and as potted foliage plant specimens. Fragrant, tiny white flowers and aromatic foliage.

LIGHT: High.

TEMPERATURE: Cool to warm.

MOISTURE: Moist soil conditions are needed.

PROPAGATION: By terminal cuttings at any time.

POTTING: Use Mix A, repot in spring. Use three-quarter-size containers or shallow pots for appearance.

FERTILIZER: Apply water-soluble fertilizer solution spring, summer and fall.

INSECTS: Susceptible to red spider mites, mealy bugs and scale insects.

PRUNING: Shear in early spring to maintain shape. Occasionally remove sprouting lower branches on stem.

REMARKS: Susceptible to *Botrytis* (gray mold). Needs good aeration.

Moses-in-the-Cradle
(*Rhoeo spathacea*)

A single-species plant of the spiderwort family *Commelinaceae*, found growing in Mexico and the West Indies. So named because of the appearance of small, white flowers in a boat-shaped bract at the base of the overlapping leaves, resembling a baby in a cradle. Equally attractive is *R. spathacea variegata,* a variegated form which has leaves longitudinally striped with yellow. Use as a single table plant or in a hanging container.

LIGHT: Medium to high. Direct sun will intensify purple coloration of under-leaves. Filtered sunlight in summer.

TEMPERATURE: Warm. Sensitive to cold and drafts. Lower night temperatures beneficial.

MOISTURE: Dry.

PROPAGATION: Division of clump. Oldest stalks discarded in favor of new shoots. Also by seeds.

POTTING: Mix B. Repot once a year.

FERTILIZER: Feed established plants once a month with water-soluble type.

INSECTS: Mealy bugs.

Myrtus communis microphylla

Maranta leuconeura kerchoveana

Maranta leuconeura massangeana

Prayer Plant
(Maranta leuconeura kerchoveana)

Of the arrowroot family *Marantaceae*, native to tropical America. A table plant often used in combination with other foliage for planters. Also useful in terrariums. The name "prayer plant" comes from the movement of the plant's leaves in darkness to a vertical position that makes them resemble hands in prayer. During the day they assume the normal horizontal position. This reaction to darkness can be created artificially by turning a table light off and on at intervals.

Another attractive variety, *M. leuconeura massangeana*, has leaves of satiny bluish green with fishbone pattern of pink veins radiating off the center rib of the leaf to the margin.

Calathea makoyana, the "peacock plant," a related genus to *Maranta*, requires similar culture and is interestingly different enough to be in demand. Its oval leaves are surfaced with a feathery design of opaque olive-green lines and ovals in a translucent field of pale green-yellow with purplish coloration beneath. "As beautiful as a peacock's feathers" rightly describes its markings and colora-tion. Its cultural requirements are warm temperature, a moist atmosphere (like ferns), medium light intensity and a moist potting mix.

Other Marantas are *M. leuconeura erythro-neura*, similar to *massangeana* except with bright red veins instead of silver, and *M.* 'Bi-color,' with leaves of gray feathered design, fading to grayish green at edge, purple beneath. *M. repens* is a low plant similar to *M. leuconeua kerchoveana* with smaller leaves.

LIGHT: Medium. High in winter, exclusive of direct sun.

TEMPERATURE: Warm.

MOISTURE: Moist.

PROPAGATION: Division of clump in spring. Terminal cuttings of new shoot growth.

POTTING: Mix B when new growth appears in spring, after a semirest period.

FERTILIZER: Once a month with water-soluble type from spring to fall, after root system is established.

INSECTS: Red spider mites, mealy bugs.

REMARKS: *M. leuconeura kerchoveana* does best after a semirest period in winter. Water less frequently so that leaves turn yellow. Do not dry out completely.

Umbrella Plant
(Cyperus alternifolius)

A bog plant of the sedge family *Cyperaceae*; from Africa, but grows also in West Indies and South America. These rush or grasslike plants differ from true grasses because of their three-angled solid stem and differing floral structure. It grows planted in aquariums, yet will survive as a pot plant when kept constantly moist. Valued for its striking form and interesting Oriental silhouette pattern, it makes an attractive addition to the water-lily pool in summer. When given ample pot room it will grow three to four feet in height.

C. *alternifolius gracilis* is similar, but with very slender stalks and leaves; grows about 18 inches tall. C. *alternifolius nanus* is a dwarf form.

C. *papyrus* is the papyrus plant used by Egyptians for paper-making since 2750 B.C. Its tall growing habit prohibits its use in most homes, but it is attractive in indoor shopping precincts or malls.

LIGHT: High; full sun in winter.

TEMPERATURE: Cool to warm.

MOISTURE: Moist. Drying out will cause the tips of leaves to turn brown.

PROPAGATION: Division of the roots, leaf-petiole cuttings, seeds.

POTTING: Mix A. Divide and repot the vigorous sections when clump becomes too large. Use the smaller outside divisions and discard the overgrown centers. If plants have been outside for summer, repot in the fall before moving in for the winter.

FERTILIZER: Feed water-soluble type at half strength every two weeks in summer or use slow-release type as manufacturer directs.

INSECTS: Red spider mites, mealy bugs.

PRUNING: Cut off dead or broken stalks from the base of plant to make room for the new shoots to develop.

REMARKS: The papyrus plant as well as C. *alternifolius* are much used by flowing arrangers; also for bottle and water gardens.

Cyperus alternifolius

Aglaonema commutatum 'White Rajah'

Aglaonema modestum

Chinese Evergreen
(*Aglaonema modestum*)

From China and the Philippines, it is a member of the aroid family *Araceae*. Several fine varieties comprise the group, all of which make excellent house plants. Their adaptability to survive low light intensity in the home and their ability to grow in water without soil make them useful for many arrangements. Used in floral decoration, for offices and foyers, for water gardens, even for planters and containers in shopping malls or precincts. Generally classified as a table plant.

A. crispum, formerly known as *A. roebelinii*, is a large-leaved robust species with gray blotches on either side of a darker green midrib. Useful in larger planters, it grows to a height of three feet.

A. commutatum is a slow-growing small-leaved species, its leaves lightly marked with gray. Much in demand for dish gardens and terrariums.

A. commutatum 'White Rajah' is a very attractive cultivar; its narrower leaves, heavily marked with white, resemble a *dieffenbachia*.

A. commutatum 'The Queen' is a cultivar selected from hundreds of seedlings possessing narrow pointed leaves. The stems are green, with leaf petioles flecked with cream color. It is a choice specimen.

A. commutatum 'The King' is similar to 'The Queen' but with cream-colored stems and leaf petioles flecked with green.

LIGHT: Low; excellent for dark corners. North window light.

TEMPERATURE: Warm.

MOISTURE: Moist at all times.

PROPAGATION: Seeds, cane layering, terminal cuttings, division of crown, air layering.

POTTING: Mix B. Repot once a year and only when pot-bound.

FERTILIZER: Apply fertilizer once a month to established plants.

INSECTS: Mealy bugs.

Podocarpus macrophyllus maki

Southern Yew
(Podocarpus macrophyllus maki)

It is also called Chinese podocarpus, Japanese yew or Buddhist pine; family *Podocarpaceae*. It is cultivated as an evergreen shrub for hedges in warmer climates and is used extensively as a container plant indoors in colder areas. Its apparent ability to withstand cool drafts makes it useful for embellishment of entrances to hotels, shopping malls and even the hallway of the home. It is usually grown to six feet as a floor plant; it can be pruned and sheared to maintain a desired height and shape. Seedling plants are used in dish gardens and even in terrariums. *P. gracillior*, whose habit is more pendulous, will vary with culture. Seedlings are more upright in growth pattern.

LIGHT: High; some direct sunlight.

TEMPERATURE: Cool to warm. Maintains best at cooler temperatures.

MOISTURE: Moist. May be adjusted to dry situation at cooler temperatures.

PROPAGATION: Terminal cuttings. Chemical hormone rooting aid beneficial.

POTTING: Mix A. Repot only when root-bound; once every two years probably sufficient.

FERTILIZER: Apply water-soluble type once every two months from spring to autumn; controlled-release type once every four months.

INSECTS: Mealy bugs, scale insects.

PRUNING: Prune and shear in spring of year, if desired.

Variegated Mock Orange

(Pittosporum tobira variegata)

Evergreen shrub from Japan; family *Pittos-poraceae*, grown as favored ornamentals and useful as container plants and in planters. Like *Podocarpus*, these plants will withstand dry, cool and drafty conditions.

P. tobira with all-green leaves grows to be a little larger and more robust than the *variegata* form. Clusters of creamy-white flowers are not uncommon on the plants, appearing in spring with the fragrance of orange blossoms.

Both sorts are adaptable to full sun and useful for outdoor summer growing on the patio or penthouse terrace. Display as floor plants.

LIGHT: High; some direct sunlight.

TEMPERATURE: Cool to warm. Can tolerate slight frost.

MOISTURE: Moist to dry. Will acclimate to dry condition.

PROPAGATION: Terminal cuttings with chemical rooting aid.

POTTING: Mix A. Repot only when root-bound.

FERTILIZER: Apply water-soluble type once every two months from spring to autumn. Controlled-release type every four to five months.

INSECTS: Mealy bugs, aphids, scale insects.

PRUNING: Usually not necessary. Plant can be trimmed to maintain height of five to six feet.

Pittosporum tobira variegata

Cordyline terminalis

Ti Plant *(Cordyline terminalis)*

An economic type of plant in its native habitat of Polynesia, where it is used for roof thatching and hula skirts. Another plant of the agave family *Agavaceae*. Many commercial forms are available, with variegated foliage ranging from mahogany red to pink and coppery tones. *C. terminalis* 'Firebrand' is an excellent red-leaved type. *C. terminalis* var. 'Ti' from Hawaii, used for growing grass skirts, is much merchandised as "Ti logs" from stem-sprouting new plants.

Artificial lighting of high intensity will provide necessary illumination for fairly successful indoor culture.

LIGHT: Very high.

TEMPERATURE: Warm.

MOISTURE: Moist. *Never let dry.*

PROPAGATION: Terminal cuttings, cane cuttings, seed. Layer "logs" or canes to half an inch deep in peat and sand or sphagnum moss. When shoots develop three to four leaves, cut off, root and pot.

POTTING: Mix B. Repot only when pot-bound.

FERTILIZER: Feed once every three to four months when plants are established.

INSECTS: Red spider mites.

Aphelandra squarrosa dania

Zebra Plant

(Aphelandra squarrosa dania)

The original species of this very attractive best seller of novelty plants comes from Brazil. The family is *Acanthaceae*. It thrives on moisture and medium light. The zebra plant has proven to be an excellent house plant when its culture is understood. Just don't let it dry out! The hybrid *dania* is a stocky, compact form with very showy white-veined, glossy deep-green leaves. It was selected from a cross between *A. squarrosa leopoldii* and *A. squarrosa louisae*.

LIGHT: Medium to indirect bright light.

TEMPERATURE: Warm.

MOISTURE: Moist at all times.

PROPAGATION: Grows from single-eye cuttings —that is, a leaf and bud with half a stem section attached. Keep moist in propagation medium.

POTTING: Mix A.

FERTILIZER: Feed once a month with water-soluble fertilizer when in good growth.

INSECTS: Mealy bugs.

PRUNING: Pinching will encourage flower buds to develop.

Aspidistra elatior variegata

Cast-Iron Plant

(Aspidistra elatior variegata)

A member of the lily family, *Liliaceae,* native to China. So called because of its ability to withstand neglect, low light and dryness. It is another plant species ranking with *Sansevieria* for toughness. It was used for many years as decoration in barbershops, in the old saloons and in restaurants. Probably it is less used today because of its slow habit of growth when compared with philodendron and other ornamentals.

A. *elatior,* the all-green leaf, is not as attractive as *variegata,* but its dark-green broad leaves are excellent for contrast in combination with other ornamentals.

LIGHT: Low.

TEMPERATURE: Cool to warm.

MOISTURE: Moist. Will condition to dry category.

PROPAGATION: Division of the clump.

POTTING: Mix A. Repot only when pot-bound; probably every two to three years.

FERTILIZER: Water-soluble type every two months or controlled-release type every three to four months.

INSECTS: Mealy bugs, scale insects.

REMARKS: Occasional washing of the broad leaves enhances the beauty of the dark-green or variegated leaf.

Variegated Screw-Pine
(Pandanus veitchii)

A genus of the *Pandanaceae* or screw-pine family. So called because of the twisted arrangement of the densely borne narrow leaves, which resemble those of a pineapple but are glossy and white-edged. The fruit of mature plants is cone-shaped but rarely borne on pot-grown plants. It is native to the Pacific islands. Plants are often considered undesirable as house plants because of the spines on the leaf edges. Growing to a height of three to four feet, it is used as a floor plant.

When growing on the beaches of the South Pacific the plants produce stout stilt (aerial) roots that serve to anchor the plants against the force of the winds.

LIGHT: Medium to high. Direct sun in winter is beneficial.

TEMPERATURE: Warm.

MOISTURE: Dry. Drench with water and let dry completely before wetting again.

PROPAGATION: Suckers which grow from the base of the plant.

POTTING: Mix B. Repot when crowded in pot every two or three years.

FERTILIZER: Apply water-soluble type to established plants every two months except in winter. Use controlled-release type twice a year—early spring and late summer.

INSECTS: Mealy bugs.

REMARKS: Stilt roots developing on larger plants may be directed back into the pot.

Pandanus veitchii

Fatshedera lizei

Tree Ivy *(Fatshedera lizei)*

An excellent house plant because it is tolerant of almost any environment, withstanding even temperatures to 35° without injury.

An unusual bigeneric cross first noticed in a nursery in France half a century ago between Irish ivy *Hedera helix hibernica* and Moser's Japanese fatsia *Fatsia japonica moserii*, it climbs like an ivy yet grows as a shrub by pruning.

Fatshedera lizei variegata is offered by some nurseries as possessing white-bordered leaves.

Fatsia japonica, Japanese aralia, the related species of *F. japonica moserii*, is a bold, attractive plant with a tropical appearance. Its large, glossy, dark-green leaves measure up to 18 inches across. Deeply lobed and fan-shaped, they are borne on long stalks or petioles. The plant, not of branching habit, will grow up to eight feet tall. Its culture is simple. It requires a moist potting condition, responds to monthly applications of water-soluble fertilizer and tolerates a cool to warm temperature and a medium to high light intensity.

Older plants will flower with good culture, but it is advisable to remove flowers to promote normal leaf growth.

Its habit of growing suckers at the base offers opportunity to start new plants. It is also propagated from seed.

F. japonica moserii is a much slower, more compact cultivar.

LIGHT: High. Takes direct sun in winter.

TEMPERATURE: Cool to warm.

MOISTURE: Moist.

PROPAGATION: Terminal cuttings, sectional cuttings. Chemical rooting aid beneficial.

POTTING: Mix A.

FERTILIZER: Feed water-soluble fertilizer once a month.

INSECTS: Aphids, scale insects, mealy bugs.

PRUNING: Tall plants tend to become leafless on lower stems. Can be trimmed back to start again. Pinch tip growth to control height.

REMARKS: Needs support. A good indoor-outdoor plant for summer patio growing.

Dizygotheca elegantissima

False or Spider Aralia

(Dizygotheca elegantissima)

Native to the Pacific islands, an attractive plant, three to eight feet tall. It is used in large planters or as a house plant in its juvenile stage when its lacy leaves are divided, fanlike, into narrow leaflets about three-eighths of an inch wide and four to nine inches long, with notched edges. The top surface of the leaf is dark, shiny green and reddish-brown beneath. Mature plants are useful in shopping enclosures because they have much larger leaves—to 12 inches in length and three inches in width.

It combines well with broad-leaf foliage plants. It is most attractive as a specimen with three plants potted together. It suggests a decorative Oriental motif.

LIGHT: High; indirect sunlight.

TEMPERATURE: Warm.

MOISTURE: Moist. Water-logged or dry soil will cause leaf drop.

PROPAGATION: Terminal and sectional stem cuttings. Chemical rooting aid beneficial. Air layering of large specimens.

POTTING: Mix B. Shift to larger pot once a year in spring. Provide large container with drainage.

FERTILIZER: Water-soluble type once a month, every two months in winter.

INSECTS: Red spider mites, mealy bugs and scale insects. Weekly spraying of foliage with tap water controls insects and cleans foliage.

PRUNING: Pinch out tips or prune to maintain shape.

Monstera deliciosa

Hurricane *(Monstera deliciosa)*

One of many climbing plants of the *Araceae* family, originates in Mexico and Central America. It is widely used as an indoor decorating plant, but many home gardeners and florists in America misname it as "split-leaf philodendron."

Monstera is distinctly different from philodendron in appearance, particularly its leaf. During the young stage, this plant develops leaves that are solid or have slight indentations. When mature, the indentations deepen and holes appear in the leaves, as in a slice of Swiss cheese.

How can one tell the difference? *Monstera* has an easily identifiable plant structure called "geniculum" at the junction of the leaf stem and the leaf blade. The geniculum is described as bent like a knee. Such a struc-ture is never present in philodendron, which has smooth and straight petioles or leaf stems.

LIGHT: High to medium. Low light is the main cause of the topmost leaves reverting to the juvenile form.

TEMPERATURE: Warm.

MOISTURE: Moist; may be conditioned to dry category.

PROPAGATION: Leaf-bud cuttings, cane layering, air layering, seeds.

POTTING: Mix B. Use two or three stems in a pot for nice specimens.

FERTILIZER: Feed water-soluble type once a month or slow-release type every four months.

INSECTS: Mealy bugs.

PRUNING: A climbing plant; should be pruned from time to time to limit growth and maintain desired height and shape.

Java Fig *(Ficus benjamina)*

An excellent indoor plant for home or office from India, Malaysia and the Philippines. A member of the fig family *Moraceae*.

Ficus microcarpa (retusa nitida), or Laurel fig, is the more common species in cultivation but not as graceful as *F. benjamina exotica*. Its growth habit is upright branching that will eventually form a crown, becoming semiweeping in habit.

Plants react to pruning in spring by sprouting new growth. They may be trained as "espaliers" or "standards."

In contrast to either species here described is *F. pumila*, creeping fig. Having a most unfiglike habit of growth, this creeping, climbing plant fastens itself to wood, masonry and even metal. It is most useful in its juvenile stages. The delicate tracery of branches bearing tiny heart-shaped leaves, up to half an inch across, will soon cover an inside masonry wall or brick chimney, if desired. In milder climates it is used on the outside for the same landscape value. It is an excellent ground cover for the top of tree-sized containers or for planting pockets. It makes a good hanging basket and helps, in the form of small, rooted cuttings, to landscape terrariums.

If allowed to grow to adult stage, its neat little leaves develop into large leathery oblong leaves, two to four inches long, bearing large oblong fruits on its stubby branches.

LIGHT: Medium. Semishaded location outdoors in summer.

TEMPERATURE: Warm.

MOISTURE: Moist. Drying out causes leaves to turn yellow and drop.

PROPAGATION: Terminal cuttings; rooting hormones beneficial. Air layering.

POTTING: Mix A.

FERTILIZER: Feed every three months with water-soluble type for established plants.

INSECTS: Usually insect-free. Possibly mealy bugs.

PRUNING: Prune occasionally to maintain shape and create bushy form.

Ficus benjamina

Rubber Plant
(Ficus elastica decora)

A member of the fig family *Moraceae* (not a relative of the commercial rubber-producing plant *Hevea brasiliensis*). The less frequently seen true species, *F. elastica*, is a forest tree in Malaysia and India. *F. elastica decora* is a seedling sport and a great improvement over the old-fashioned rubber plant of Grandmother's day. The dark-green, leathery leaves grow in a wide spiral formation from the main trunk. Each leaf is attached by a small petiole or stalk about two inches long. The leaves measure nine to 12 inches in length and five to seven inches wide. While growing, a new leaf is enveloped in a bright red sheath. Later, as the leaf expands, the sheath turns brown and drops off.

F. elastica doescheri is the only large-leaved variegated ficus. Its looks are similar to *F. decora,* but the leaves are narrower and longer. The young leaves are attractive, having broad, irregular cream-colored markings near the edges that narrow as the leaf matures. The center of the leaf is two shades of green in irregular patches. The midrib of the leaf is pink. Although a truly handsome and decorative plant, it is, however, more delicate than *F. decora* in that it requires a warm temperature and must never become dry.

LIGHT: High for best growth. Will condition to medium.

TEMPERATURE: Warm.

MOISTURE: Moist. Drying of root ball causes lower leaves to drop.

PROPAGATION: Air-layering method. Rooting in several weeks. Cut off just below roots and pot, sphagnum and all. See instructions on air layering in the chapter on starting plants, page 196.

POTTING: Mix A. Repot only when pot-bound. Avoid severe root pruning.

FERTILIZER: Feed monthly.

INSECTS: Mealy bugs.

PRUNING: Soft pinch of terminal growth will limit top growth and encourage side branching.

REMARKS: Sponge with water and detergent once a month to remove dust.

Fiddle-Leaf Fig *(Ficus lyrata)*

Another plant of the fig family from tropical Africa. Its large, bold, thick, violin-shaped leaves measure to 15 inches long and ten inches wide, with prominent veins and a glossy surface. Its large-sized leaves and shrubby habit of growth make it desirable as an accent plant in planters. To promote branching and to restrain top growth, pinch young top growth. An excellent large specimen plant when two or three stalks are planted together. When cultural conditions are right, plants will grow upright. Sometimes stakes and tying are needed to keep them vertical.

Another species not mentioned elsewhere is worth some space here. It is called the mistletoe fig, *Ficus diversifolia*, which is a slow-growing, small, shrublike plant making a good house plant. Also a fine subject for training as an indoor tropical bonsai. Its leaf shape is interestingly variable; some are round, some are pointed. A gray overcast webbing effect gives the appearance of dust accumulation on the leaves, but it is normal. Fruits are produced on small plants. They are borne on short stems at the axil of leaf petiole and stem. The early stage is green, turning dull yellow or reddish at maturity.

LIGHT: Medium. A light shade from sun, if used on patio in summer.

TEMPERATURE: Warm

MOISTURE: Moist.

PROPAGATION; Air layering. Difficult from terminal cuttings. Refer to the chapter on starting new plants, page 196.

POTTING: Mix A. Shift to larger pots when rooting indicates; necessary to support large top growth.

FERTILIZER: Apply water-soluble type once every three to four months.

INSECTS: Mealy bugs. Otherwise insect-free.

PRUNING: To encourage branching, make soft pinch when plants are young.

REMARKS: Sponge leaves occasionally with mild soapy water to remove dust and help prevent insect infestations.

Ficus elastica decora

Ficus lyrata

Dieffenbachia picta superba

Dieffenbachia amoena

Dumb Cane
(*Dieffenbachia amoena*)

There are various species and varieties, known as mutants of *dieffenbachia,* belonging to the *Araceae* or arum family and native to South America. Growers have selected desirable varieties for indoor culture.

Many other kinds are available for indoor culture from the species known as either *D. maculata* or *D. picta. D. m. exotica* is more compact than *D. amoena*, with smaller leaves. Edges of leaves are dark green with much creamy variegation; midrib of leaf is creamy white.

Another *D. maculata*, 'Rudolph Roehrs,' is a large-leaved, tall grower with leaves of pale chartreuse blotched with ivory and edged with green.

D. maculata superba has a stout trunk with large, thick leaves growing close to the stalk measuring three times as long as they are broad. Leaves heavily blotched with cream.

It is an ideal plant for the patio in summer. Protection from sun and wind must be provided with roof and lattice work.

LIGHT: Medium.

TEMPERATURE: Warm.

MOISTURE: Dry, but not extremely so. Water as soon as surface looks dry.

PROPAGATION: Air layering, cane cuttings, terminal cuttings. Use sphagnum moss as medium.

POTTING: Mix B. Will grow very well in pure sphagnum moss. Some varieties produce offsets and may be separated at repotting time. Repot when root mass tends to push plant upward from the pot.

FERTILIZER: Feed every three to four months. Plants cultured in sphagnum moss will need a water-soluble fertilizer solution once a month.

INSECTS: Red spider mites, mealy bugs.

PRUNING: Overgrown leggy plants, cut back almost to the base, will sprout and grow into a bushy plant.

REMARKS: The common name Dumb Cane refers to the fact that if parts of the plant are eaten, the acrid sap will injure the delicate tissues of the mouth and throat and cause painful swelling.

Striped Dracaena
(Dracaena deremensis warneckei)

A member of the agave family, *Agavaceae,* and native to tropical Africa. Grown in tropical regions for use in the horticulture trade.

A slow-growing plant with palmlike leaves, adaptable to areas of low light intensity. Used as a small pot plant for the end table or larger plants in tubs used as floor specimens. Also used as an accent plant for planters in combination with other plants.

LIGHT: Medium.

TEMPERATURE: Warm.

MOISTURE: Moist.

PROPAGATION: Cane, air layering.

POTTING: Mix A. Repot only when root-bound and plant has become too large for pot.

FERTILIZER: Apply water-soluble type once every three to four months to established, well-rooted plants.

INSECTS: Mealy bugs and red spider mites.

PRUNING: Tall leafless stalks can be cut back after air layering, and new shoots will develop.

Dracaena deremensis warneckei

Malaysian Dracaena
(Pleomele reflexa)

A fine indoor plant recently attaining popularity, belongs to the agave family, comes from Madagascar (Malagasy Republic). Its rosettes of dark-green leaves arranged along the main stem make it an excellent decorator plant. *Dracaena thalioides* is also an attractive indoor type.

LIGHT: Medium.

TEMPERATURE: Warm.

MOISTURE: Moist. *Never let it dry out.*

PROPAGATION: Air layering, terminal cuttings. Chemical rooting aid beneficial.

POTTING: Mix A.

FERTILIZER: Water-soluble feed once every three to four months.

INSECTS: Apparently free.

PRUNING: May be cut back to maintain size; trimmings rooted as cuttings.

Pleomele reflexa

Dracaena fragrans massangeana

Dracaena godseffiana

Corn Plant
(Dracaena fragrans massangeana)

An old-fashioned house plant from Upper Guinea and a member of the agave family, *Agavaceae*. An attractive decorator item can be created by rooting canes of large diameter and placing two or three in a container. A variation in height, with a rosette of leaves at the top, makes an interesting modern plant specimen. *D.f. massangeana* has green leaves with a gold center.

   D. deremensis 'Janet Craig' is offered as a green form.

LIGHT: Low to medium.

TEMPERATURE: Warm.

MOISTURE: Moist.

PROPAGATION: Cane cuttings or air layering. Woody cane rooted directly in pots.

POTTING: Mix A.

FERTILIZER: Feed water-soluble type every three to four months.

INSECTS: Spider mites, mealy bugs.

PRUNING: May be cut back if too tall; will sprout new shoots.

Gold-Dust Dracaena
(Dracaena godseffiana)

This is a small dracaena compared with the rest of the genus. Excellent for home culture in planters for table or desk. With its cream-spotted leaves, it combines well with English ivy, philodendron or other green vines. A member of the agave family, or *Agavaceae*, it comes from Upper Guinea.

LIGHT: Medium.

TEMPERATURE: Warm.

MOISTURE: Moist.

PROPAGATION: Stem cuttings. Chemical rooting aid beneficial.

POTTING: Mix A. Repot only when extensive root system develops.

FERTILIZER: Apply water-soluble type once every three months.

INSECTS: Usually free, but red spider mites can be a pest.

PRUNING: Not necessary to prune or cut back.

Madagascar Dragon Tree
(*Dracaena marginata*)

From Madagascar (Malagasy Republic), it is another plant of the agave family, *Agavaceae*. Older plants with branching habit are both exotic in appearance and decoratively useful. It is a slow grower, yet very durable when grown under good cultural conditions.

LIGHT: Medium bright light, exclusive of direct sun, is best.

TEMPERATURE: Warm.

MOISTURE: Moist. Must have good drainage.

PROPAGATION: Terminal stem cuttings best.

POTTING: Mix B.

FERTILIZER: Water-soluble feeding once in three to four months.

INSECTS: Red spider mites, mealy bugs.

PRUNING: May be pruned, if necessary. Will make new shoot growth when cut back.

REMARKS: Plant stems may be trained to shape by using stiff wire and tying, as in bonsai culture.

Dracaena marginata

Sander's Dracaena or Ribbon Plant
(*Dracaena sanderiana*)

Another small planter-type plant of the family *Agavaceae* from the Cameroons.

Plants offered today are mostly cultivated forms which have been selected for their more striking variegation and intense coloring of foliage. This plant's growth habit of producing stately upright stems or stalks makes it a good accent plant.

LIGHT: Medium.

TEMPERATURE: Warm.

MOISTURE: Moist (a characteristic of all species and varieties of this group).

PROPAGATION: Stem cuttings and cane cuttings.

POTTING: Mix A. Repot only when pot-bound.

FERTILIZER: Feed once in two to three months when roots are abundant.

INSECTS: Fairly clean of pests. Check for red spider mites occasionally.

PRUNING: Trim tall plants to limit upright growth.

Dracaena sanderiana

Umbrella Tree
(Schefflera actinophylla)

Commonly known as Australian umbrella tree, it is a member of the aralia family. It is a native plant of Queensland, Australia, and is widely cultivated as a large shrub or small landscape tree in Hawaii, southern Florida and California.

As an indoor plant, it can be trained to grow as a bonsai, a dwarf pot plant or a large tub specimen for shopping enclosures.

LIGHT: High, exclusive of sunlight for best maintenance. Will condition to survive with low light.

TEMPERATURE: Warm; will tolerate cool.

MOISTURE: Dry for slow normal growth. Moist with high light for rapid growth.

PROPAGATION: Seeds, air layering, and terminal cuttings.

POTTING: Mix B.

FERTILIZER: For fast growth, use moist category, high light, and fertilize once a month. For slow growth, use dry category, low light, and fertilize once in four months.

INSECTS: Make sure you are buying insect-free plants. Red spider mites and scale are often found on these plants.

PRUNING: Growing tips may be pruned back to encourage side growth.

Schefflera actinophylla

Araucaria heterophylla

Norfolk Island Pine
(Araucaria heterophylla)

An evergreen tree and a member of the *Araucaria* family from the Norfolk Islands in the South Pacific. It is an excellent plant for hotel foyers, shopping malls and interior home environments. They make excellent potted Christmas trees for the table or floor plants in the home and in public places.

Its selection as an indoor plant depends on its adaptability, but you must strive to provide the best environment.

LIGHT: High, exclusive of direct sun for best quality.

TEMPERATURE: Cool. Will tolerate warm. A subtropical plant, it will not take temperatures for long below 40° without showing damage.

MOISTURE: Moist. Ball of roots must not dry out at any time.

PROPAGATION: Seeds. Cuttings are made only by trained nurserymen.

POTTING: Plants received from growers can remain in the same pot for approximately a year. Mix B.

FERTILIZER: Water-soluble feeding every six weeks.

INSECTS: Scale sometimes found.

PRUNING: Removing the leader growth will maintain size, if necessary.

REMARKS: Sponging foliage at feeding time will improve plant's appearance. Use warm water with a few drops of dish-washing detergent.

Ivy *(Hedera helix)*

The ivy plant is an evergreen, clinging vine native to Europe and Asia. In ancient Greece it was called cissos *because, according to a mythological legend, it was named after the nymph Cissos, who, at a feast of the gods, danced with such joy and abandon before Dionysus that she fell dead from exhaustion at his feet. Dionysus was so moved by her performance and untimely death that he turned her body into the ivy, a plant which graciously and joyfully entwines and embraces everything near it. The ivy, dedicated to the wine god Dionysus, is hung even today in wreaths over the doors of taverns and wine shops.**

The English ivy *(H. helix)* is one of the most useful house plants.

LIGHT: High. Very high in winter with full sun. Shade in summer.

TEMPERATURE: Cool.

MOISTURE: Moist, with good drainage.

PROPAGATION: Terminal and sectional cuttings.

POTTING: Formula B.

FERTILIZER: Feed water-soluble type once a month.

INSECTS: Aphids, red spider mites, mealy bugs and scale.

PRUNING: Soft-pinch tips of branches to encourage branching.

REMARKS: An excellent ground cover in temperate climates.

Cape Ivy
(Senecio macroglossus variegatus)

Sometimes called the variegated wax vine, which describes its waxy, succulent leaves. This species comes from Cape Province, and it is of the family *Compositae*. It has proven to be a good house plant for dry interiors.

LIGHT: Medium.

TEMPERATURE: Warm.

MOISTURE: Dry.

PROPAGATION: Terminal cuttings.

POTTING: Mix A.

FERTILIZER: Once every two to three months.

INSECTS: Mealy bugs.

PRUNING: Prune off trailers to make plant compact.

Swedish Ivy
(Plectranthus australis)

Probably the fastest-growing of all house plants, it is ideal for hanging baskets. The species comes from Africa and Australia and botanically is of the mint family, *Labiatae*.

LIGHT: Medium to high.

TEMPERATURE: Warm, but growth is slower at cooler temperatures

MOISTURE: Moist.

PROPAGATION: Terminal and sectional stem cuttings. Will root in water.

POTTING: Mix A. Shift to a larger-sized pot when plant becomes root-bound.

FERTILIZER: Feed once in two to three months with water-soluble fertilizer.

INSECTS: Mealy bugs, white flies.

PRUNING: Pruning from time to time will keep plants bushy.

German Ivy *(Senecio mikanioides)*

A fast-growing, ivylike plant from South Africa, it belongs to one of the largest families of plants, *Compositae*. In contrast to German Ivy, other plants of the same genus exhibit thick succulent stems and leaves. *Senecio crassissimum* looks much more like a crassula than its counterpart, the German Ivy.

Cuttings from the plant may be started in water and placed in attractive bottlelike containers to grow as water plants.

LIGHT: Medium.

TEMPERATURE: Warm.

MOISTURE: Moist.

PROPAGATION: Terminal cuttings.

POTTING: Mix B.

FERTILIZER: Feed with water-soluble type once a month.

INSECTS: Mealy bug and red spider.

PRUNING: A soft pinching from time to time will encourage bushiness.

---

* Lehner, Ernst and Johanna, *Folklore and Symbolism of Flowers, Plants, and Trees,* published by Tudor Publishing Company, New York, N.Y., 1960. "Ivy," John Gerard's *The herball generall historie of plantes,* Adam Islip, London, 1633.

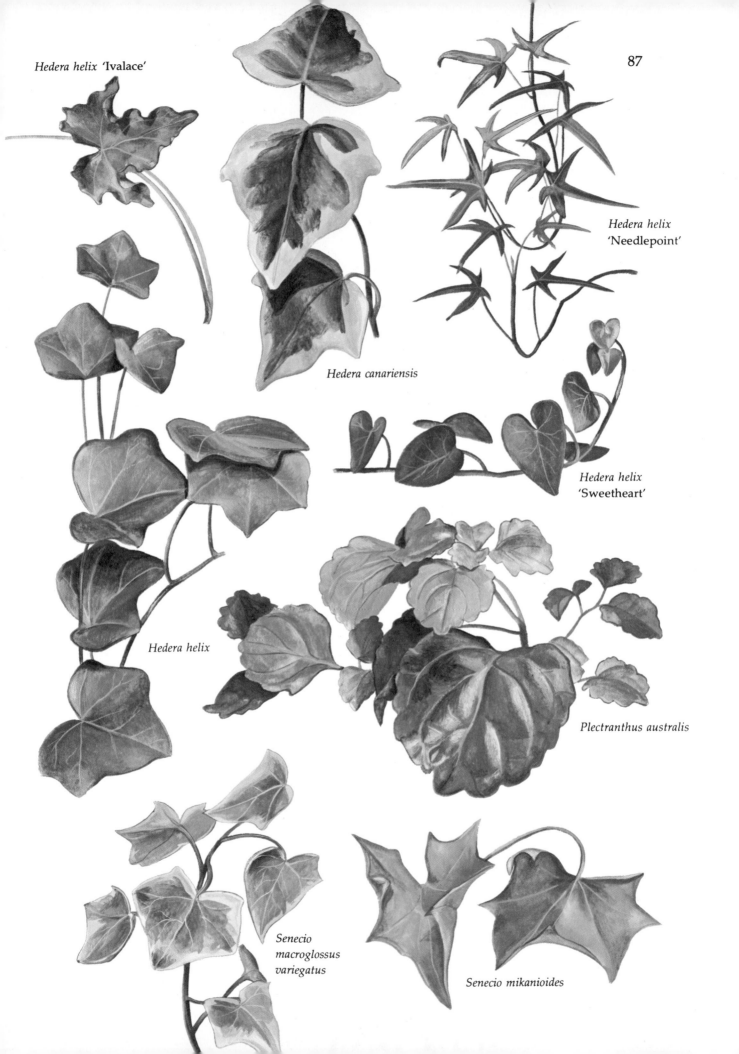

Hedera helix 'Ivalace'

Hedera helix 'Needlepoint'

Hedera canariensis

Hedera helix 'Sweetheart'

Hedera helix

Plectranthus australis

Senecio macroglossus variegatus

Senecio mikanioides

Chlorophytum comosum mandaianum

Spider Plant
(Chlorophytum comosum mandaianum)

A longtime favorite house plant because of its cascading stems producing small white flowers, followed by small plantlets. Its native habitat is South Africa, and it is a member of the lily family, *Liliaceae*. The popularity of spider plants today has increased with the use of hanging baskets, which create a natural environment for its habit of growth.

A cultivar relative, *C. comosum variegatum,* is a more vigorous plant with leaves measuring ten to 15 inches long and about one inch wide, with margins edged with white.

LIGHT: Medium to high.

TEMPERATURE: Warm.

MOISTURE: Moist.

PROPAGATION: Take plantlets forming roots and pot up.

POTTING: Mix A. Repot only when root-bound condition exists.

FERTILIZER: Feed water-soluble type once in three to four months to established plants.

INSECTS: Mealy bugs.

PRUNING: Older leaves tend to brown at tip end and become unsightly. May be removed at the base. New leaves will develop from the rosette-like growth of the crown.

Grape Ivy *(Cissus rhombifolia)*

A table plant sometimes grown in hanging baskets. It is native to northern South America and is of the grape or vine family *Vitaceae*; thus its name "Grape Ivy."

A very attractive plant for any indoor location. It is sometimes used as a ground cover for large floor planters. A sport, *C. rhombifolia mandaiana,* is more compact, with darker green leaves of a waxed appearance.

LIGHT: Medium.

Zebrina pendula

Tradescantia albiflora albovittata   *Gibasis geniculata*   *Tradescantia purpusii*

TEMPERATURE: Cool, but will grow at warm temperature with high light.

MOISTURE: Moist.

PROPAGATION: Terminal cuttings, slow to root. Hormone rooting aid beneficial.

POTTING: Mix A.

FERTILIZER: Feed established plants once a month.

INSECTS: Mealy bugs.

PRUNING: Long tendril-like stems can be cut back to make plant more bushy.

See illustration on page 166.

Wandering Jew
(Tradescantia albiflora albovittata)

A creeping type of plant used as a ground cover in warm countries and under benches in greenhouses. Probably best grown as a hanging-basket plant. A native of South America, it belongs to the family *Commelinaceae*. Its many related species differ in minor botanical characteristics. *Zebrina pendula*, also called Wandering Jew, is worthy of mention. Its leaves are of similar shape, deep green to purple, with two broad vertical bands of silver above and purple suffused beneath.

Both species will adapt to growing in water. They will last for several months by changing water once a month and adding a few drops of fertilizer solution.

LIGHT: Medium.

TEMPERATURE: Warm.

MOISTURE: Moist.

PROPAGATION: Terminal or sectional stem cuttings.

POTTING: Mix B.

FERTILIZER: Apply liquid-soluble fertilizer once a month.

INSECTS: Red spider mites.

PRUNING: Trim back to encourage bushiness.

Fittonia verschaffeltii argyroneura

Fittonia verschaffeltii

Mosaic Plant *(Fittonia verschaffeltii)*

A ground-cover type plant coming from South America, and a member of the *Acanthaceae* family. The plant's requirements for much moisture and humid atmosphere make *Fittonia* a desirable plant for terrarium planters. The variety *F. verschaffeltii argyroneura* is more commonly seen, with a lighter green leaf having white veins and midrib. *F. verschaffeltii* has a thicker leaf and is better adapted to growth as a table plant in open containers.

LIGHT: Low to medium.

TEMPERATURE: Warm.

MOISTURE: Moist.

PROPAGATION: Terminal cuttings mostly easily rooted in peat moss in closed containers of polyethylene (polythene) bags. Cuttings wilt quickly after being cut and exposed to air.

POTTING: Mix B or sphagnum moss with liquid fertilizer feeding.

FERTILIZER: Feed established plants once in three to four months with water-soluble fertilizer.

INSECTS: Relatively free. Mealy bugs and slugs, if grown as greenhouse ground cover.

PRUNING: Overgrown plants may be cut back to main creeping stems to sprout new growth.

REMARKS: Grow several plants on a vertical plaquelike support. Construct a simple frame of wood or three-inch-wide material and stuff with sphagnum moss. Seal moss into the frame with half-inch wire mesh. Plant cuttings directly into moss through the wire. Suspend in a polyethylene bag until established. Feed with half-strength water-soluble fertilizer every two weeks.

Coleus *(Coleus blumei)*

One of the most common and easily grown foliage types of plants, coleus belongs to the square-stemmed mint family, *Labiatae.* The original species comes from Java. Plantsmen have selected many cultivars that offer plants in groups with similar size and foliage characteristics.

In America three forms are grown. A "small-leaved class" is popular for house culture and is easily propagated by cuttings. The "rainbow class" offers plants of medium size, free-branching and bushy. This group is easily propagated from seed with selected color range, the most popular being shades of red. A third class, known as "Exhibition," is distinguished by extra large leaves, but is really not suited for home cul-ture. A new strain, "Carefree," grown from seed, comes almost 90 percent true to type. Its foliage is fringed and lobed like an oak leaf. The plants are grown basically for their foliage, which comes in shades of jade, gold, bronze, yellow, red and white.

LIGHT: High for indoor culture.

TEMPERATURE: Warm.

MOISTURE: Moist

PROPAGATION: Terminal cuttings; seed germinates in ten to 15 days at 65° with artificial light.

POTTING: Mix A.

FERTILIZER: Water-soluble feeding once a month.

INSECTS: Mealy bugs, red spider mites, white flies.

PRUNING: Soft-pinch from time to time to make compact growth and to prevent legginess.

Coleus blumei varieties

Hoya carnosa compacta

Hoya carnosa variegata

Wax Plant *(Hoya carnosa)*

Wax plants are native to an area extending from East Asia to Australia. A characteristic of milky sap places it in the milkweed family, *Asclepiadaceae*. Most of its species are climbing vines with leathery leaves bearing white to pink flowers.

They are most effectively displayed growing on supports of trellis, stiff wire loop or totems. The peduncles or stalks that bear the flower cluster should not be removed when picking the flowers, because more blooms will form here year after year.

H. carnosa variegata is an attractive type with blue-green leaves broadly edged with creamy white or, often, pink coloration. *H. carnosa compacta*, known as "Hindu Rope," with twisted leaves resembling braided rope, is a curiosity. *H. bella*, a dwarf with upright to drooping growth patterns, produces small waxy-white parachute clusters of white flowers with purple centers.

LIGHT: High.

TEMPERATURE: Cool to warm.

MOISTURE: Dry. More water given in summer.

PROPAGATION: Terminal and leaf-bud sectional cuttings. Rooting best in coarse peat and perlite medium, not too moist.

POTTING: Mix B.

FERTILIZER: Apply water-soluble solution once a month in summer only.

INSECTS: Mealy bugs.

Rosary Vine *(Ceropegia woodii)*

One of a hundred species cultivated as house plants. A plant belonging to the same family as *hoya*, of the milkweed family, *Asclepiadaceae*. It is often referred to as the "string of hearts" because of the trailing threadlike stems.

It is a small vine with leaves in pairs on short petioles rising from a tuberous base. Its leaves are heart-shaped, thick and succulent, about two-thirds of an inch long. The surface of the leaf is dark green, with whitish veins. The little tubers that form from the trailing stems are used to start new plants. Flowers are small, dull pink or purplish in color; not showy, but of very interesting structure. It grows best in pots. Thrives in low light intensity with atmospheric moisture.

Other species less interesting and better suited for a greenhouse but with intriguing flowers are: *C. debilis* from Nyasaland, a threadlike vine with cordlike roots and linear leaves. The flowers are greenish, marked with purple; *C. dichotoma*, an erect form that comes from the Canary Islands. It is a succulent with jointed forked green stems and scattered linear leaves. Its yellow flowers are interesting and attractive.

Rosary Vine can be displayed attractively with its drooping, trailing growth in small exotic containers on a shelf or as a hanging basket.

C. fusca from the Canary Islands also is an upright, succulent shrub similar to *C. dichotoma*. Its forked, cylindrical columns appearing restricted at joints are gray to purplish in color. The flowers are brown and yellow.

C. barkleyi from Cape Province is a slender vine with cormlike roots similar in growth habit to *C. woodii*. Succulent leaves with silver-white veins and flowers greenish veined with purple.

C. elegans is a trailing vinelike plant from India. Its leaves are oval-shaped, not succulent. Flowers are tubelike or expanded funnel shape. Color is whitish blotched with purple; top lobes are united in the center and edged with long, dark hairs.

LIGHT: Medium.

TEMPERATURE: Warm.

MOISTURE: Dry. Follow with a thorough drenching. In winter, water only occasionally to keep the leaves from shriveling.

PROPAGATION: Sectional stem cuttings with tuberlike roots attached. Pot them up for growing on in regular potting mix.

POTTING: Mix B. Use shallow pots of large proportion because of its surface rooting habit.

FERTILIZER: Water-soluble fertilizer solution applied once in three to four months. Do not feed in winter.

INSECTS: Apparently free.

PRUNING: Seldom needs pruning. Trimmings having tubers attached can be used to start new plants.

Ceropegia woodii

Syngonium podophyllum

Syngonium
(Syngonium podophyllum)

Native to the American tropics, of the family *Araceae*. They are climbing plants with arrow-shaped leaves. The juvenile or young plants are cultivated and grown in planters as small pot specimens for end tables, desks or bookshelves. When the plants become older, they enter an adult phase of growth and require support. The leaves then change from arrow-shaped to fan-shaped leaves about ten inches in size; they also lose their white leaf markings and become all green.

S. podophyllum 'Emerald Gem' is a more compact-growing cultivar, more of a creeper with all-green leaves. Other cultivars are offered by the trade.

S. podophyllum albolineatum 'Ruth Fraser' is a horticultural selection, available in America, and showing a distinct improvement in variegation.

S. podophyllum 'Imperial White' is more compact, with broad, glistening, arrowhead-shaped leaves in the juvenile stage. Margins of leaves have a greenish border and are greenish-white inside.

LIGHT: Medium.

TEMPERATURE: Warm.

MOISTURE: Moist.

PROPAGATION: Terminal cuttings, seed and division.

POTTING: Repot, using mix B, when plants become crowded. Divide at this time, if necessary.

FERTILIZER: Apply water-soluble fertilizer every three to four months.

INSECTS: Mealy bugs and red spider mites.

PRUNING: Pruning off climbing growth will retain juvenile form.

Devil's Ivy

(Epipremnum aureum–Pothos aureus)

A member of the *Araceae* family. Authorities on nomenclature differ in their opinions regarding the name of this genus. Sometimes listed as *Scindapsus aureus*, *Raphidophora aurea* and recently as *Epipremnum aureum*. The devil's ivy is one of the most popular of the climbing or vining foliage plants. In its native habitat, adult plants produce leaves about two feet in length, while leaves of the juvenile plants used for interiors are two to three inches in length. Offered by nurserymen are *E. aureum (P. aureus) wilcoxi*, which has leaves marked with yellow blotches or streaks of color. Another strain is *E. aureum (P. aureus)* 'Marble Queen' with foliage marked with white instead of yellow splashes. The plant is very versatile. It is a favorite as a small pot specimen for end table or desk, used as a filler plant in planters, as well as for small and large totem specimens from 12 to 48 inches tall.

LIGHT: Medium.

TEMPERATURE: Warm.

MOISTURE: Dry.

PROPAGATION: Leaf-bud cuttings, stem cuttings. Propagation medium is kept slightly dry at start to promote callus before rooting. When roots form, add more moisture.

POTTING: Mix B.

FERTILIZER: Feed established plants once every three to four months.

INSECTS: Red spider mites and mealy bugs.

PRUNING: Pinch tips or cut back to control growth when necessary.

REMARKS: Totems of sphagnum moss enclosed in wire or plastic mesh encourage climbers to develop roots.

Epipremnum aureum 'Marble Queen'

Epipremnum aureum

Gynura 'Purple Passion'

Purple Passion Plant

(*Gynura* 'Purple Passion')

A member of the large family *Compositae*, it is a cultivar of uncertain origin. It has recently become a popular plant because of its velvety purple leaves. The orange composite flowers contrast vividly with the purple color of the foliage.

Unfortunately the fragrance of the flowers is objectionable to most people, and they are usually trimmed out as soon as they open.

It may be used as a specimen pot plant for a table, desk or window sill.

LIGHT: High.

TEMPERATURE: Warm.

MOISTURE: Dry.

PROPAGATION: Terminal cuttings.

POTTING: Mix B.

FERTILIZER: Feed once a month; established plants only.

INSECTS: Red spider mites and white flies.

PRUNING: Pinch occasionally to encourage development of new growth that produces best purple coloration.

Kangaroo Vine

(*Cissus antarctica minima*)

Originating from New South Wales, Australia, hence its name, this plant is a member of the vine family, *Vitaceae*.

C. antarctica minima, a compact dwarf *Cissus*, has small leaves, is a slow grower with free-branching habit, making it very desirable as a house plant.

C. antarctica, a better-known species, is very similar, but with long shrublike growth of coarse, leathery leaves.

LIGHT: Medium to high.

TEMPERATURE: Cool to warm.

MOISTURE: Moist.

PROPAGATION: Terminal and sectional stem cuttings. Chemical rooting aid is beneficial.

POTTING: Mix B. Repot about once a year.

FERTILIZER: Apply water-soluble fertilizer once every two to three months.

Cissus antarctica minima

Saxifraga sarmentosa tricolor

Saxifraga sarmentosa

INSECTS: Relatively free. Occasionally mealy bugs.

PRUNING: *C. antarctica* needs occasional cutting back of long tendril-like stems.

Strawberry Geranium

(Saxifraga sarmentosa, S. tricolor)

A common name that to some is misleading yet descriptive. It belongs to neither the strawberry family nor the geranium family. Botanically it belongs to the Saxifrage family, *Saxifragaceae*. Its region of origin is East Asia. Its running, plant-producing strawberry habit and bicolor foliage have sustained its popularity through the years. The plant *S. sarmentosa*, with an upper-leaf surface of gray-green with white veins and under-leaf surface of reddish color, is more vigorous than *tricolor*. Both types are used as table plants, in planters and in small hanging containers.

The culture of *tricolor* requires attention because certain phases are critical to its behavior as a healthy plant. It must have a cool, humid atmosphere; a soil or potting mixture of low nutrition. It takes less water than its relative. Grow it on the dry side. A summary of culture follows.

In cool areas with milder winters *S. sarmentosa* is grown as an outdoor ground cover and is attractive in the rock garden.

LIGHT: Medium. *S. sarmentosa* will take full sun.

TEMPERATURE: Cool.

MOISTURE: Moist to dry. *S. sarmentosa* needs more moist conditions than *S. tricolor*.

PROPAGATION: Runners and division of the crown. To increase runner production, set plants in large tray or greenhouse flat to encourage more plantlets to form. When rooting, cut off and pot up.

POTTING: Mix B. Both varieties make attractive additions to old-fashioned strawberry pots.

FERTILIZER: Feed established plants only once in three to four months.

INSECTS: Mealy bugs.

PALMS

Palms, the aristocrats of the foliage plants, are only really successful in centrally heated homes where there is plenty of room. The variety of shapes, sizes and textures available makes palms very useful for decorating the interiors of homes, modern office buildings, shopping malls and outdoor patios in summer.

The price of a palm may seem high in comparison to the price of other plants, but when one knows its durability and longer life, it is a good investment.

PARLOR PALM (*Chamaedorea elegans*). A native of Mexico and of the family *Palmae*, it is grown commercially by the tens of thousands in warm climates. A small dwarf with thin, dark-green feathery leaves, this single-stem palm is used in every kind of container from terrariums to dish gardens to single specimens. Also used with three in a pot as a table or desk plant. A curiosity that is surprising to many is that this palm produces flowers when only one foot tall; since these resemble buds rather than flowers, they are sometimes mistaken for insects.

Flowers are borne in yellow clusters and often extend on stalks above the foliage.

Chamaedorea elegans

Chamaedorea elegans is a dioecious palm. Each sex is confined to separate plants and will not produce viable seeds unless both sexes are found in flower at the same time. Seeds are available, but one must be sure one is purchasing fresh seed.

It is reported that *Chamaedorea elegans* can be propagated by air layering. Sphagnum moss is wrapped about the stem near the top in the form of a ball and kept moist. After several months roots will develop, the top cut from the lower trunk and potted in soil. It is probable that this method could be duplicated for any of the *Chamaedorea* species which have the habit of sending out adventitious roots from the stem.

Many nurserymen and florists sell this palm under its erroneous name of *Neanthe bella* but its correct name is *Chamaedorea elegans*. The parlor palm's tolerance to desert-like conditions, to low light intensity and resistance to below average home temperatures make it the number one house plant.

COCONUT PALM (*Cocos nucifera*). Although its original habitat is not definitely known, it probably came from the Old World tropics. It is a useful tree whose main products are copra—a source of widely used oil—and desiccated coconut and fiber. Travelers in tropical and subtropical regions have long admired the scenery created by the graceful curving, erect trunks topped by majestic crowns of glossy, feathery fronds. Many trunks reach 100 feet, yet it is recommended here as a house plant in the seedling stage.

A sprouting coconut grown in a container with half its husk exposed becomes a home conversation piece. It grows slowly and will last for several years before it outgrows its welcome as a large tree. Only an expert can pick a coconut viable for germination, so it is best to purchase one already started. Its care is simple. Keep it moist. Add fertilizer once in two months and watch for the usual insects.

PIGMY DATE PALM (*Phoenix roebelenii*). Found growing in Laos on the Mekong River in the family *Palmae*. A very graceful palm as a miniature pot plant and as a floor specimen, having many small flat leaves or fronds arising from a central crown. It is a slow grower and found to be more attractive when two or three plants are put together in a container. Good drainage must be provided in its pot, and overpotting should be avoided.

The ultimate size of *P. roebelenii* as a well-grown plant comprises 30 to 40 leaves, making a diameter of four to six feet. The leaves are borne on a trunk approximately four inches in diameter. The attained height ranges from three to five feet. It is tolerant of low temperature, excessive sun, winds and cold. It has reportedly survived a temperature drop to 18° Fahrenheit.

BUTTERFLY PALM (*Chrysalidocarpus lutescens*). It is also known as Areca palm and it belongs to the family *Palmae*. Its native habitat is Madagascar (Malagasy Republic), yet it is found growing in many places in the tropics. Its very tropical appearance, with feathery foliage arching widely from tightly clustered leaf bases, makes it an excellent decorator plant for the home, office and industrial interiors. As a floor plant, the average size obtainable is four to eight feet. It is a clustered-stem type, making it a good specimen palm. The size of the container regulates its growth. Foliage color is normally green.

Chrysalidocarpus lutescens

Phoenix roebelenii

Chamaedorea siefrizii

Rhapis excelsa

Howea belmoreana

REED PALM (*Chamaedorea siefrizii*). Its native habitat is the Yucatan peninsula of Mexico. A tall, upright, clustered-stem palm with narrow bamboolike foliage, it is a favorite for indoor planting. Average size offered ranges from three to eight feet. It will withstand lower than normal temperatures, making it an ideal plant for tubs on patios in warmer climates.

The genus *Chamaedorea* has many other favored species. Those most desirable as house plants are listed in the table on Handling and Care of Potted Palms. Similar to *C. siefrizii* is *C. erumpens*, known as the bamboo palm. A cluster-type palm, it has bamboo-like stems with thin, feathery, dark-green, recurved leaves loosely distributed from top to bottom. The average size offered is from three to nine feet.

C. cataractarum is available in two- to three-feet sizes. It is a dwarf, compact, clustered-stem type. Its featherlike, dark-green leaves originate alternately from branching stems, prostrate and forked.

Protection of the plant from direct sun should be provided, and watering is a prime consideration.

Drying of the soil ball can cause injury to small feeding roots that are characteristic of palms. Only a few palms can withstand dry soil conditions.

A test to make sure sufficient water is added is to be sure the excess water emerges from the drainage hole at the bottom.

BELMORE SENTRY PALM (*Howea belmoreana*) of the family *Palmae* has been cultivated for many years for florists' use and decoration. Formerly known under the name of Kentia, it is native to Lord Howe's Island in the South Pacific Ocean, hence the name *Howea*. Today it is cultivated by the thousands in the state of California to be used as decorator palms in the indoor-landscape business. It has thick, leathery, dark-green leaves that arch from a center axis, then droop downward with leaflets becoming slender, to pointed tips. An excellent floor plant, usually available from three to six feet tall, potted in six- to eight-inch-size containers.

The only other species of *Howea* is *H. forsterana*, referred to as the Forster sentry palm. It also comes from Lord Howe's Island. It is faster-growing and of larger proportion than *H. belmoreana*. The leaflets are not arching but flat to the center axis. A hardier palm, it will resist cool temperature, lack of strong light and some neglect.

Its rating as a favorite house plant is second only to *C. elegans*, the parlor palm. Its tolerance to below-average house temperatures, low light intensity and ability to withstand dryness makes it useful for the office and other industrial embellishment. Its water requirements, as with most palms, are on the moist side. Use as a single-stem plant or pot two and three together to make spectacular floor specimens. For potting use formula A. New plants may be started from seed in warm-temperature chambers.

LADY PALM (*Rhapis excelsa*). A clustered-stem palm from southern China, family *Palmae*. It is much desired as a tub specimen for outdoor patios in warm countries and interior plantings everywhere. It is a very durable palm, is slow-growing and produces a dense clump. It will tolerate lower temperatures than many other palms.

Rhapis excelsa differs from a less frequently cultivated *Rhapis humilis*, which has leaf segments 1⅛ inches or more wider at the middle and broader at the tip, as compared to segments less than ¾ inches wide and narrower at the tip. *Rhapis excelsa* has much coarser leaf sheaths than *Rhapis humilis* and is more robust, with stems that can grow 12 to 15 feet high and trunks of two inches in diameter. Both plants are very popular for the home and greenhouse. As decorator plants both give a bushy bamboo effect.

Propagated by division of the clump. Stems becoming too tall or crowded can be cut out at the base to make room for new stalks to grow in.

CARE AND MAINTENANCE OF PALMS

Successful maintenance of palms, as is the case for all plants, depends on a knowledge of the individual cultural requirements. The directions for handling and care of palms are listed in the table on page 103.

LIGHT AND TEMPERATURE: Palms, accustomed to growing indoors and being moved to a patio or porch in summer, must have protection from the bright sun to prevent sun scorch. Those palms that grow in a greenhouse will benefit from un-shaded glass in the winter months in cool temperate climates but must have protection of shade from the stronger sunshine in summer.

A few palms listed have proved cold-hardy as a result of habitat and experience of exposure to freezing weather for brief periods. It is concluded that these palms would be desirable for use in areas where lower temperatures exist. This includes lobbies and shopping malls.

MOISTURE: Watering is the first consideration for palms, as for other plants. As noted in the table, all palms should have moist soil. Drying of the soil ball within small containers can cause injury to the small feeder roots, which are characteristic of palms. The result is inability of the roots to supply the leaves with water. Only a few palms can withstand dry soil, as indicated in the table.

A test to make sure sufficient water is added is to see the excess water emerge from the drainage hole at the bottom of the pot. Experience will result in the application of a measured amount at regular intervals.

POTTING: A potting mixture for palms must provide good drainage, permitting aeration between waterings and letting in the oxygen that is essential for good root development. Formula A is recommended.

In the repotting of palms it is important to compact the soil very firmly around the root system. This encourages the feeder roots to penetrate into the fresh soil. A layer of drainage material in the bottom of the pot, to facilitate drainage of excess water, is essential when the potted palm is plunged inside a planter or large tub and surrounded with peat moss or other filler.

FERTILIZER: There is no special nutrient requirement for palms. A general water-soluble fertilizer applied once a month is adequate. In temperate zones, feeding should be discontinued during the cool weather and then resumed when the warm weather arrives.

INSECTS: Insect pests, unfortunately, can create a troublesome problem for indoor as well as outdoor palms. Red spider mites, mealy bugs and scale insects are the most common pests.

PRUNING: Little or no pruning is necessary for the maintenance of palms. The cutting of a cane or stem of clustered palms to thin the clumps or to reduce the height is sometimes practiced. In the natural process of growth an old leaf may turn yellow and brown and begin to droop. It can be removed by cutting rather than tearing off. Tearing the leaf sheath from the stem causes a wound, leaving an unsightly scar, and may permit fungal infection.

HANDLING AND CARE OF POTTED PALMS

Common name	Genus and species	Culture notes	Water	Temperature	Light
Fishtail palm	*Caryota mitis and *C. urens	Slightly acid potting mix.	moist	warm	high
	Chamaedorea cataractarum	Plant one or more in pot. Will tolerate lower than normal temperature.	moist (dry)	cool	low
	Chamaedorea costaricana	Retain in small pots. Will tolerate lower than normal temperature.	moist (dry)	cool	low
Parlor palm	Chamaedorea elegans	Plant one or more in a pot. Use for dish garden when small. Flowers produced when plants are one foot high.	moist (dry)	warm	low
	Chamaedorea ernesti-augusti	Requires good drainage.	moist	warm	low
Bamboo palm	Chamaedorea erumpens	Requires shade on patio.	moist	warm	low
	Chamaedorea klotzschiana	Plant one or more in a pot for effect.	moist (dry)	cool	low
	Chamaedorea seifrizii	Withstands lower than normal temperature. Ideal for outside patio in warm climates.	moist	warm (cool)	high
European fan palm	Chamaerops humilis	pH neutral potting mixture, good drainage. Suckers when young. Is a slow grower. Tolerates lower than normal temperature.	moist (dry)	warm (cool)	high
Butterfly palm	Chrysalidocarpus lutescens	Size of container regulates growth. Withstands lower than normal temperature.	moist	warm (cool)	high
Coconut palm	*Cocos nucifera (juvenile stage)	Retain in small pot to slow growth	moist (dry)	warm	low
Belmore sentry palm	Howea belmoreana	Protect from direct sun. Is slow grower. Plant three or more in a pot for effect. Withstands drafts.	moist	warm (cool)	low
Forster sentry palm	Howea forsterana	Protect from direct sun. Is faster-growing than H. belmoreana. Will resist cold, lack of light and neglect.	moist	warm (cool)	low
	Licuala grandis	Never allow potting mix to become dry. High atmospheric humidity beneficial.	moist	warm	low
Chinese fan palm	*Livistona chinensis	Is slow-growing. Avoid excessive dryness.	moist	warm (cool)	high
	*Livistona rotundifolia	Grow in small container to retain small size. Best suited for interiors.	moist	warm	low
Pigmy date palm	Phoenix roebelenii	Is a slow grower. Protect from direct sun, wind and cold. Provide good drainage in pot. Do not overpot. Neutral soil pH.	moist	warm	high
Macarthur cluster palm	*Ptychosperma macarthurii	Is a fast grower.	moist	warm	high
Broadleaf lady palm	Rhapis excelsa	Slow grower. Withstands lower than normal temperature. Usually expensive.	moist	warm (cool)	high
Slender lady palm	Rhapis humilis	Slow grower. Tolerates lower than normal temperature. Makes dense clump.	moist	warm (cool)	high
Christmas palm	*Veitchia merrillii	Avoid overpotting. Requires potting material of a neutral pH.	moist	warm (cool)	high

*Species that when young make good pot plants but will eventually outgrow containers and should be planted in large tubs or in the open ground.

Cycas revoluta

Zamia pumila

FERNS AND CYCADS

Ferns are found in their wild state all over the world. A few are native to the Arctic regions ranging southward to the equator. They grow at various elevations and number over 12,000 species. Species that grow as house plants thrive under moist conditions, moderate temperatures and are shade-loving. These are collected from tropical and subtropical areas. The species that are most widely cultivated belong to the family *Polypodiaceae*. These include, among others, Boston fern, maidenhair fern and house holly fern. These are characterized by erect underground stems having upright fronds or leaves, clustered in crowns, or by creeping stems or rhizomes with scattered leaves.

Epiphytic ferns such as the staghorns or *Platycerium*, *Polypodium* and *Davallia* have become very popular as house plants.

A group of importance to the commercial florist industry is of the genus *Woodwardia* and the leather-leaf fern *Polystichum adiantiforme*. These are marketed as cut greens throughout the United States and Canada for use in wedding work and other floral decoration.

Cycads, listed here because they are non-flowering seed plants and thus related to the ferns and their allies, are an old group of so-called gymnosperms, nine genera of which grow in the tropics and subtropics. They have fernlike leaves that form a crown at the top of a stem. Male and female cones grow at the crown but on separate plants.

Table Fern *(Pteris cretica cristata)*

A member of the family *Polypodiaceae*, comes from tropical and temperate regions. A tough, useful fern for decorative purposes, it grows from six to 12 inches high. Some fronds terminate in small forks and crests. A real dwarf form of *Pteris* is *P. multifida cristata compacta* with low, dense growth habit.

LIGHT: Medium.

TEMPERATURE: Warm. Cool nights beneficial.

MOISTURE: Moist. Withstands drier atmosphere than most ferns.

PROPAGATION: Spores. Division of clump of rhizome root growth at repotting time.

POTTING: Use mix formula A. Usually needs repotting once a year.

FERTILIZER: Feed water-soluble fertilizer once every three months. Omit during winter months.

INSECTS: Scale insects.

Pteris cretica cristata

Mother Spleenwort

(Asplenium bulbiferum)

A member of the Fern family *Polypodiaceae*. Its native habitat ranges from Australia to New Zealand and into Malaysia. This species belongs to a unique group of ferns, the viviparous group that is propagated vegetatively by the offsets which germinate from bulbils produced on the upper surface of the frond. This species grows spore-bearing fronds as well.

LIGHT: Low.

TEMPERATURE: Cool.

MOISTURE: Moist. Thrives best with moist atmosphere.

PROPAGATION: Spores, bulbils or plantlets, division. See directions on viviparous propagation, page 193.

POTTING: Potting mix formula A.

FERTILIZER: Apply water-soluble type once every three months.

INSECTS: Mealy bugs and scale insects.

Asplenium bulbiferum

Nephrolepis exaltata bostoniensis

Boston Fern

(Nephrolepis exaltata bostoniensis)

An old-fashioned parlor and conservatory fern recently gaining popularity. A member of the common fern family *Polypodiaceae*, it originates in the tropical regions of both hemispheres. The species *N. exaltata*, rarely found in cultivation today, has given way to a great number of mutants or cultivars of the variety *bostoniensis*. Foliage of the Boston type is less stiff and rigid than *N. exaltata*. They exhibit much divided pinnae, as well as more delicate, wider-spreading and gracefully drooping growth habits. Some are compact dwarflike growers with finely cut foliage. Among these are 'Fluffy Ruffles' and *childsii*. Forms like *hillii, rooseveltii* and *whitmanii* have distinctive larger foliage.

N. *cordifolia* is an unusual and distinct species with root system composed of tuberous rhizomes.

LIGHT: Medium.

TEMPERATURE: Warm. Cooler nights always benefit fern growth.

MOISTURE: Moist; a requirement of almost all ferns.

PROPAGATION: Runners produce vegetative buds and develop into plantlets. Must be pinned to the soil surface. When three or more leaves develop, cut and pot up.

POTTING: Mix A. Overgrown pot-bound ferns can be divided at repotting. Select the youngest active growing clumps and use several in a pot to make good specimens. Discard oldest coarse woody clumps.

FERTILIZER: Feed spring and summer once a month with water-soluble fertilizer solution at half strength.

INSECTS: Scale insects and mealy bugs.

PRUNING: Old grayish green-brown tips or broken fronds should be removed once a year to make room for new shoots.

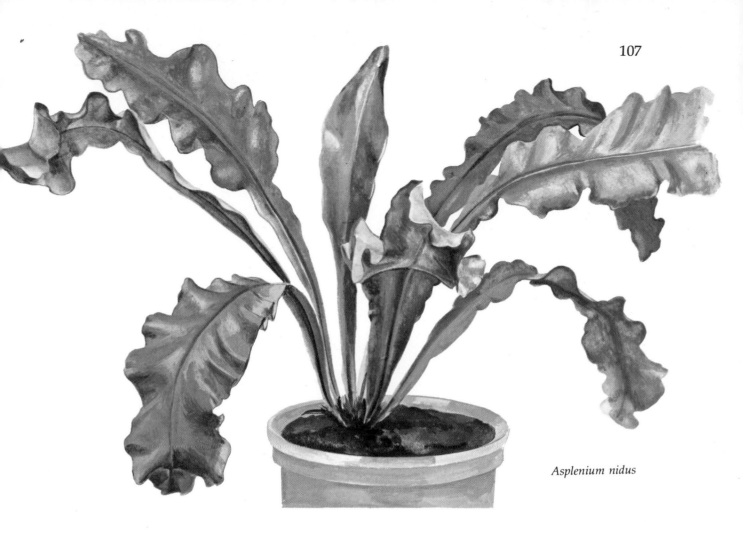

Asplenium nidus

Bird's-Nest Fern

(Asplenium nidus)

An epiphytic-type fern from Asia and Polynesia. This attractive fern produces a rosette made by its stiffly spreading, shiny green fronds of thin leathery texture, with blackish midrib and wavy margins and with black scales at the crown. The erect fronds rising from the crown produce the effect of a nest, which may be an attraction to certain species of tropical birds. Fronds of bird's-nest fern can grow to four feet long by one foot wide.

The family *Polypodiaceae* offers many ferns adaptable to home culture. Other ferns related to this genus are *A. bulbiferum* from New Zealand, Australia and Malaysia, *A. viviparum* from Mauritius. Both of these are designated as a "mother fern" because of their habit of producing bulblets that grow into plantlets. Propagation is discussed on page 191.

The epiphytic habit of bird's-nest fern will adapt to growing in drier atmospheres than those for other types.

A. nidus is an excellent plant for the outdoor patio in summer in a shady spot. Beware of slugs when outside!

LIGHT: Medium.

TEMPERATURE: Warm, with cooler nights.

MOISTURE: Moist.

PROPAGATION: Spores.

POTTING: Mix B.

FERTILIZER: Apply water-soluble type once a month in spring and summer at half strength.

INSECTS: Scale insects, mealy bugs. Snails or slugs are the most injurious. One slug alone can ruin a frond.

REMARKS: The epiphytic habit indicates caution against frequent repotting. The accumulated root system serves as a partial medium in which to grow. Do not overpot.

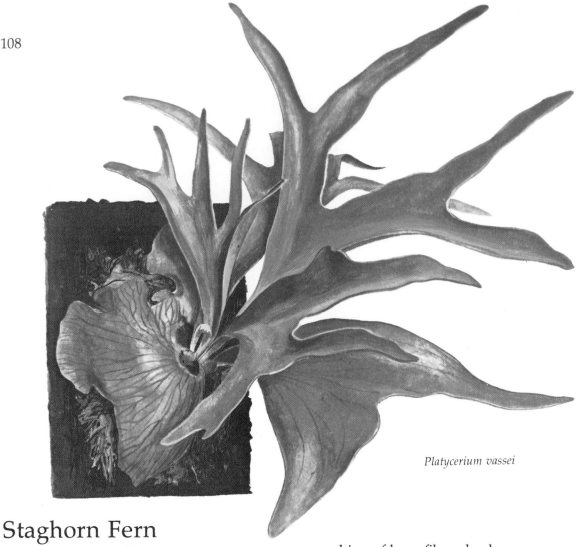

Platycerium vassei

Staghorn Fern

(Platycerium vassei)

An epiphytic fern that comes from Mozambique; other species are from tropical regions of Australia, New Guinea, Africa and the Philippines; botanically of the family *Polypodiaceae*. In their natural habitat they grow on trees. This epiphytic habit of growth renders it adaptable to growing in the home and other interior environments.

The sexual parts of the plant exist as two kinds of fronds. The sterile fronds are flat, disklike, pale green in color, and age to tan and brown at the base of the forked fronds. These serve to support the plant and accumulate organic matter that helps feed it. The forked upright or pendulous fronds are the fertile fronds that bear spores. These fronds resemble deer antlers; thus its name, Staghorn Fern.

A unique and attractive way to display and grow the Staghorn Fern is by mounting on tree fern slabs. For mounting, first place a cushion of long-fibered sphagnum moss on the slab. A tablespoonful or two of bone meal will provide some nutrition.

Tie the fern to the slab by inserting pieces of plastic-covered wire through the lower portions of sterile or basal fronds and continue through holes drilled in plaque or slab, tying at the back of tree fern slab.

LIGHT: High, exclusive of direct sunlight.

TEMPERATURE: Warm. Will tolerate cool nights.

MOISTURE: Dry. Soak about once a week, in the home.

PROPAGATION: Plantlets or ''pups'' sprout at the base of the plant. Pry out carefully and pot when small.

POTTING: Sphagnum moss mixed with a tablespoon of bone meal to a plant.

FERTILIZER: Feed water-soluble solution at half strength once a month during the spring and summer.

INSECTS: Scale insects.

Rabbit's-Foot Fern

(Davallia fejeensis)

Another epiphytic fern sometimes referred to as Squirrel's-Foot; comes from the Fiji Islands and belongs to the fern family *Polypodiaceae*. Its fuzzy, long-haired rhizome, one-half inch thick, creeps around the side of a pot or basket or on a ball of sphagnum moss.

LIGHT: Medium.

TEMPERATURE: Warm; cool at night.

MOISTURE: Moist. When moss or potting mixture feels dry, soak well with water.

PROPAGATION: Spores; sections of rhizomes.

POTTING: Balls of sphagnum moss, long-fiber type. Mix B if pot-grown.

FERTILIZER: Feed once a month in spring and summer with water-soluble solution at half strength.

INSECTS: Scale insects, sometimes mealy bugs.

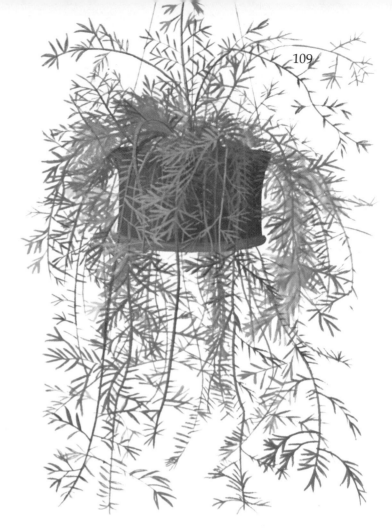

Asparagus densiflorus sprengeri

Asparagus Fern

(Asparagus densiflorus sprengeri)

A plant, not a fern, belonging to the Lily family, *Liliaceae*. It originates from West Africa and will thrive under the most adverse conditions. An easy-to-grow house plant, commonly grown by nurserymen and florists. The pendulous growth originating from tuberous roots consists of many branching sprays with light-green needles. Mature plants will often produce small, fragrant flowers, followed by bright-red berries.

LIGHT: Medium.

TEMPERATURE: Warm. Will grow at cool as well.

MOISTURE: Dry. Young plants require moist conditions.

PROPAGATION: Seed and division.

POTTING: Mix B

INSECTS: Mealy bugs.

Davallia fejeensis

Hare's-Foot Fern
(Polypodium aureum)

An excellent epiphytic fern for culture in the home or other interior environments but not often used. A native of tropical America belonging to the fern family *Polypodiaceae*. Its common name Hare's-Foot distinguishes it from Squirrel's-Foot by its very stout creeping rhizomes covered with bright rusty-brown hairlike scales. A few horticultural forms are cultivated, one of which, a sport, is known as *P. aureum mandaianum*. It possesses beautiful crested wavy pinnae or leaves of bluish-green color.

LIGHT: Medium, exclusive of direct sunlight.

TEMPERATURE: Warm; cool in winter.

MOISTURE: Moist. Can go for a week between waterings.

PROPAGATION: Division of the rhizomes.

POTTING: Mix B.

FERTILIZER: Apply water-soluble solution once a month in summer at half recommended strength.

INSECTS: Usually free.

Maidenhair
(Adiantum cun'eatum)

From Brazil, a member of the family *Polypodiaceae*. Maidenhair is an old greenhouse favorite found growing in the moist atmosphere under greenhouse benches. It survives best as a house plant in the environment of a terrarium. It grows six to 15 inches tall.

LIGHT: Medium.

TEMPERATURE: Warm. Move outdoors in summer for cooler night temperature.

MOISTURE: Always moist. Humid atmosphere.

PROPAGATION: Division. Repot in late winter, cutting fronds back to the base and dividing clumps of roots.

POTTING: Use potting mix formula A.

FERTILIZER: Feed six months after potting with water-soluble fertilizer. Repeat application in three months. Omit feeding in winter.

INSECTS: Check for hard-to-see brown scale on brownish-color stems of fronds.

Polypodium aureum

Adiantum cuneatum

Holly or Fishtail Fern
(Cyrtomium falcatum)

A tough house fern able to withstand dry atmosphere and a low light intensity. A member of the fern family *Polypodiaceae*, it is found growing in scattered areas of Japan, China and also in some parts of South Africa and Polynesia.

LIGHT: Medium

TEMPERATURE: Warm.

MOISTURE: Moist. Tolerates dry atmosphere, but ball of potting material must be kept moist.

PROPAGATION: Spores. Division of the crown when more than one appears.

POTTING: Mix A. Firm soil when repotting to encourage rooting at the crown. Do not bury crown when potting.

FERTILIZER: Feed once every two months with water-soluble fertilizer at half recommended strength.

INSECTS: Scale insects, mealy bugs.

Silver Table Fern
(Pteris ensiformis victoriae)

Also known as Victoria fern, it is of the family *Polypodiaceae*. A genus of ferns grown as greenhouse ferns and as house plants for use in dish gardens and terrariums.

An attractive cultivar from Belgium is *P. ensiformis evergemiensis*, which is smaller and more vigorous than *victoriae*.

LIGHT: Medium.

TEMPERATURE: Warm. Cool nights are beneficial.

MOISTURE: Moist.

PROPAGATION: When ferns are in need of repotting, a division of the clump will yield new plants. Also by spores. See the section on how to grow spores, page 194.

POTTING: Repotting is usually necessary once a year or whenever plants become crowded in the pot.

FERTILIZER: Feed pot-bound plants once every two to three months except in winter.

INSECTS: Scale insects.

Cyrtomium falcatum

Pteris ensiformis victoriae

BROMELIADS

The pineapple family, with its 1,800-odd species, is found growing in the American tropics. The botanists identify it as the *Bromeliaceae* family, others know the group as Bromeliads. They vary in form from a delicious tropical fruit, the pineapple *Ananas comosus*, to Spanish moss *Tillandsia usneoides*, which grows as a festoon from live-oak trees in the southern United States. Many of the species used as indoor plants are described as having rosettes of leaves arranged in cuplike forms. Most of them hold water in their tightly furled leaves.

Bromeliads are much in demand as accent plants by interior decorators for modern decor. The varieties illustrated, *Aechmea fasciata*, *Aechmea miniata discolor*, Vase Plant *Billbergia pyramidalis* and Earth Star *Cryptanthus X* 'It,' are excellent as pot or planter specimens for accent and color. Other varieties are used for tree branch and driftwood decoration.

Bromeliads are not grown for their foliage alone. Some species have very small flowers, while others have showy flamboyant blooms or leaflike bracts. The flowers last only a few days, but the colorful bracts and berries will often last for months on some varieties. Flowers and fruit may be borne on upright, arching or pendant stems.

Bromeliads can be forced into flower by the use of growth-regulator chemicals. Experiments conducted by Crop Research, U.S. Department of Agriculture, Beltsville, Maryland, and by others have established schedules for flowering. Dr. H. M. Cathey of Crop Research suggests a method for homeowner use. To cause flowering, enclose a ripening apple in an airtight plastic bag with the plant for four days. Plant will bloom in one to six months after plant and apple are removed from the bag. If plants do not respond, wait another one to two months and try again. Response depends on the plant's growth rate and its maturity; more mature plants flower more readily. Eventually most plants can be triggered into flowering.

LIGHT: High light intensity but not direct sun, which will cause leaf burn. Terrestrial kinds like *Cryptanthus* will stand as much sun as you can give them.

Special fluorescent grow lights are available that are ideal for bromeliad growing. A minimum of four parallel tubes located six to 24 inches above the plants are recommended.

TEMPERATURE: Keep bromeliads at 65° to 75° during the day and between 55° and 65°at night.

MOISTURE: Do not overwater! Some epiphytic bromeliads feed through the bases of their leaves by means of water. In nature the vaselike shape of foliage collects water and directs it to its base.

Cryptanthus zonatus

These "cups" hold and must have water at all times. The potting material that supports the plant needs water only when it is dried out. This may occur once every two or three weeks. Check cups for water weekly. Empty out and add fresh water once a month.

Cryptanthus does not hold water, and being terrestrial, needs more soil moisture. As soon as potting mix is dry, soak thoroughly.

PROPAGATION: Easily grown from seeds and offsets that form next to the parent plant. The mother plant usually dies about a year after blooming, but in the meantime the plant has put up several side shoots. When these have several leaves (which takes about four to six months), cut them off and pot on their own. Take care to remove offsets with some roots attached so young plants can get a good start.

POTTING: Use mix formula C.
(1) Put about a two-inch layer of drainage material in bottom of pot.
(2) Fill with moistened mix, leaving space on top for water.
(3) Insert offset about one to two inches deep into medium. Do not fill up over basal leaves but just over hard stubby stem that is below the green leaves.
(4) Support plant with thin sticks, if needed, until roots take hold.
(5) Water well to settle medium. Put water in cups if the species is known to need it.

FERTILIZER: Do not overfertilize! Use a complete water-soluble type at half the recommended rate. Use once a month. Empty cups a week after fertilizer application and refill with fresh water.

INSECTS: Scale insects, either black or white, may appear on leaves. They can be pushed off with fingernail or toothbrush.

Cryptanthus zonatus. This genus of bromeliad, known as Earth Stars, is a terrestrial type requiring more moisture for growing and as much sun as you can give it. *C. zonatus*, a Brazilian native, is an old-time favorite, commercially grown in large quantities. It is used as a single specimen or grown with other plants in dish gardens or similar plant groupings. The leaves are purple-bronze with golden cross bands on top and silvery ones on the underside.

Cryptanthus X 'It,' recently introduced, is grown commercially. A blazing variant of color and a slower grower than some others. A single rosette may reach 12 to 16 inches across. Bright pink along the margins of the leaf, with longitudinal pink-and-cream stripes against a center of green with pinkish overcast.

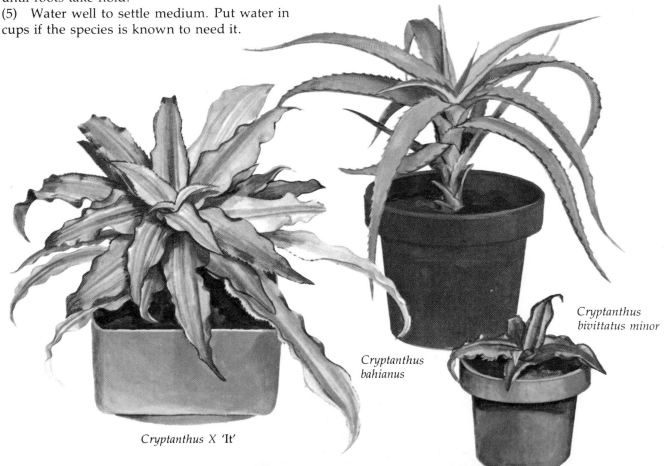

Cryptanthus bivittatus minor

Cryptanthus bahianus

Cryptanthus X 'It'

114

Aechmea miniata discolor

Billbergia pyramidalis **and** *Tillandsia ionantha*

Tillandsia cyanea

Vriesia

Aechmea fasciata

Cryptanthus bivittatus minor, also known as *roseo-pictus*, is from Brazil. It is a flattened, small, starlike, terrestrial rosette. It has satiny, olive-green leaves with two pale bands overcast with salmon-rose that turn coppery red in strong sunlight. Used in dish gardens and planters.

Cryptanthus bahianus from Bahia, more epiphytic than terrestrial, is a stiff succulent with harsh spines. A good plant for a basket. Its recurved leaves are apple-green, margins of which turn bronzy red in the sun.

Aechmea miniata discolor, also from Brazil, is one of the most popular because of its adaptability to home environments. The olive-green leaves have maroon-purple undersides. The brilliant flower cluster is composed of bluish-lilac blooms, followed by red-orange berries which last for several months.

Billbergia pyramidalis, from Peru, is an old-time favorite for collectors because of its dense head of lovely blue flowers with striking red bracts. The light-green glossy leaves form a perfect vase plant. This is easy to grow in the home.

Tillandsia cyanea, from Ecuador, is an excellent, compact, rosette-type of bromeliad. Its linear, channeled leaves are marked with thin brown lines. Its interesting flower—a broad spike—has clear pink bracts and large violet-blue flowers.

Tillandsia ionantha, from Mexico to Nicaragua, is spring-flowering. A tufted, miniature rosette not over two to four inches high, it has numerous overlapping, recurving, thick, fleshy, dark-gray-green leaves covered with silvery bristles. The violet flowers appear without stalks close to the rosette. The flush of red color at the center of the rosettes signals the flowering season.

Vriesias, with spectacular foliage and inflorescence, are a must for any collection. Their forms and varieties shape into a leathery rosette of bluish-green leaves marked with broad cross bands of brown or purple. The underside of the leaves is grayish with purple bands. The long, sword-shaped flower spikes have flattened, fiery-red bracts and yellow flowers that last for several months. More moisture and humidity required than for some other bromeliads.

Neoregelia carolinae tricolor

Aechmea fasciata is one of the oldest and most popular favorites in cultivation. A Brazilian native of which many forms have been cultivated. Its green leaves overcast with gray, some banded, are very attractive. The pink, thistlelike flower head contrasts with the gray of the leaves, making it a handsome specimen when in flower. The bractlike head lasts several months in color.

Neoregelia carolinae tricolor comes from Brazil and is an old favorite, in both Europe and America. Its straplike, shiny green leaves turn a brilliant coral color about the center of the rosette when the plant is ready to flower. The color lasts for the life of the rosette.

Billbergia nutans is easiest of all bromeliads to grow and to flower. The common name, Queen's Tears, describes the rose-bracted, nodding flowers, green petals edged with violet, and the tear drop forming on the stigma. Its silvery-bronze foliage forms a clustering rosette.

DRIFTWOOD ARRANGEMENTS: Many bromeliads grow naturally on trees. An intriguing way to promote their use is to fasten them as arrangements on driftwood.

Things to remember:

(1) Small plants of *Tillandsia, Aechmea* and *Billbergia* can be tied firmly to the wood and their roots and bases covered with a layer of osmunda fiber, sphagnum or sheet moss to prevent the roots from drying out.

(2) Do not use copper or galvanized wire for tying, because these metals will injure plants. Use plain iron nails or wire.

(3) Fasten plants securely in a vertical position, especially those which hold water in their cups. Tie tightly to prevent movement and breakage of the new roots as they form.

(4) A small hole drilled through the driftwood and florists' enameled wire will keep plants from twisting and turning. Plants with woody bases can be drilled for fine wire or nailing.

(5) Do not use treated wood or driftwood that does not have all of the salt leached out. Also avoid contact with zinc, copper or lead-based paints.

Billbergia nutans

*Brassolaeliocattleya
Norman Merkel
'Natalie'*

*Cattleya
luteola*

*Laeliocattleya
Stephen Oliver Fouraker
'Lillian Wilson'*

*Laeliocattleya
Elstead Gem
'Mem. Frank Gamble'*

ORCHIDS

Orchids first achieved horticultural popularity in the early 1880s in England, where the estates of the wealthy often possessed extensive glasshouses devoted to the care of these seemingly temperamental plants. Unhelpful legends grew up around orchids, fostered by such true events as the dramatic arrival in mid-nineteenth-century London of an orchid growing on a human skull. The prices paid for orchids in these halcyon times often equaled a king's ransom.

The tide began to turn in 1859 when Sir Joseph Paxton opened the doors to his hot and muggy glasshouses to let the cool, spring breezes in. From this time onward, orchid growers attempted to duplicate natural conditions, throwing aside the old myths of intense heat and high humidity.

Since the establishment of the first orchid firm in the United States in 1896, Lager and Hurrell, orchids have been grown with increasing frequency and even greater success, either in greenhouses, on windowsills, in a Wardian case or under fluorescent lights. Today, orchids are nearly as common in the home as begonias and as easy to grow.

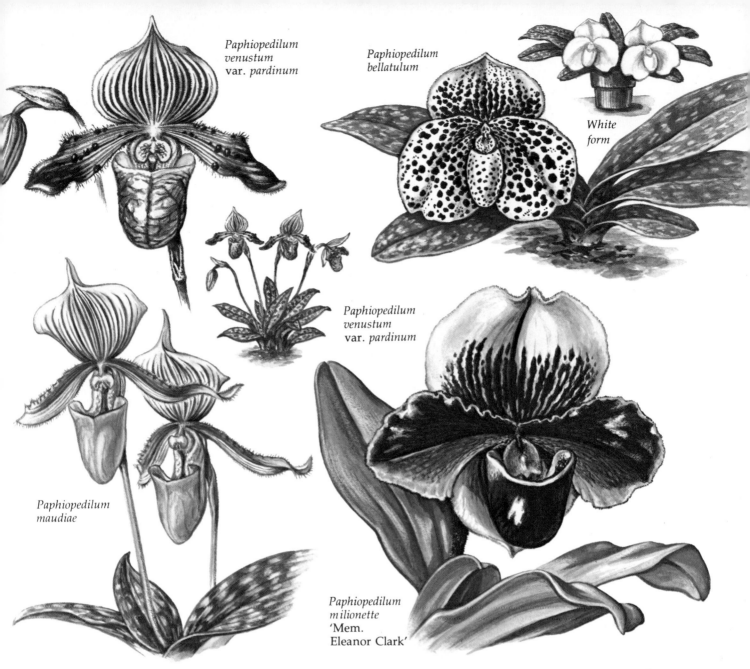

*Paphiopedilum
venustum
var. pardinum*

*Paphiopedilum
bellatulum*

White
form

*Paphiopedilum
venustum
var. pardinum*

*Paphiopedilum
maudiae*

*Paphiopedilum
milionette
'Mem.
Eleanor Clark'*

The orchid family (*Orchidaceae*) is the largest in the plant kingdom. Over 600 genera occur in nature, with more than 30,000 species. The ease with which most orchids interbreed has produced, to date, some 60,000 artificial hybrids, many of which will thrive as house plants.

Orchids are found nearly worldwide, excluding areas of perpetual snow or arid desert. While the great majority inhabit the tropical and semitropical areas of the world, growing epiphytically on rocks and trees, open to the winds, rain and sunlight, other lovely orchids can be found in the temperate regions, growing terrestrially, on the ground.

The corsage orchid, *Cattleya*, is one of many genera found throughout Central and South America, from the sea-level banks of the Amazon River in Brazil to the cool, wind-swept mountain ranges of Costa Rica, Colombia and Ecuador. The Asiatic lands of India, Burma, Ceylon and the islands of New Guinea and New Caledonia possess many *Paphiopedilum* species, while the Philippines are the home of the "Moth Orchid," *Phalaenopsis*. Orchids even flourish on the Serengeti plains of Africa or in the vast hinterlands of Australia, and some 200 species exist in North America, including the pink "Lady's slipper," *Cypripedium*, growing in the pinewoods of the Northeast.

Orchids as House Plants: Orchids can no longer be considered difficult to grow, provided that certain basic principles are followed (pages 122–23). While the variety of shapes and colors may initially bewilder the home grower, he should make his first plant purchases from among the species and hybrids within the genera illustrated in the text: *Paphiopedilum, Phalaenopsis, Cattleya, Miltonia* and *Oncidium*. Orchid plants may be obtained from numerous nurseries at a reasonable cost today.

The following orchids have all been flowered repeatedly under home conditions by orchid growers everywhere. All require low to medium light intensities and a predominantly intermediate temperature range, as described on pages 122–23, with a 40–50 percent relative humidity. Maintain the proper humidity in a windowsill collection by placing plants on a wire-mesh platform above a bed of pebbles kept continually wet. The evaporation of the water will create a suitable microclimate, particularly if a small, oscillating fan blows across the surface of the water. Ventilation is equally important. Orchids should have fresh air on all but the coldest of days. Avoid extreme hot or cold drafts directly on the plants.

A large, fluorescent light set-up—a plant cart or benches built in the cellar or study—can duplicate greenhouse conditions. Enclose the entire area in clear plastic sheeting and install a small home humidifier.

ORCHIDS FOR HOME CULTURE

Kind	Color	Temperature	Light	Time of Bloom
Brassia caudata	yellow-green	intermediate	medium	fall
Brassolaeliocattleya hybrids	rose, pink, purple	intermediate	medium	various
Cattleya mossiae	lavender	intermediate	medium	Easter
Cattleya luteola	yellow, greenish-yellow	intermediate	medium	various
Sophrolaeliocattleya hybrids	lavender to red	intermediate	medium	various
Laeliocattleya hybrids	lavender, orange, yellow	intermediate	medium	various
Brassocattleya hybrids	lavender, green, pink	intermediate	medium	various
Cycnoches chlorochilon	lime-green, yellow	intermediate	medium	spring
Gastrochilus dasypogon	yellow, dotted red	intermediate	medium	various
Haemaria discolor	white flowers, lovely velvet-green leaves with gold veining	intermediate–warm	low–medium	winter
Miltonia spectabilis	white, purple	intermediate–cool	low–medium	spring
Miltonia vexillaria	pink	intermediate	medium	spring
Miltonia hybrids	white, pink, red, yellow	intermediate	medium	spring
Oncidium cheirophorum	yellow	intermediate–cool	low–medium	winter
Oncidium ornithorhynchum	pink	intermediate	medium	winter
Oncidium varicosum	yellow	intermediate	medium	winter
Oncidium hybrids	yellow, brown, orange, reddish	intermediate	medium	various
Paphiopedilum insigne	yellow, brown, reddish	intermediate	medium	various
Paphiopedilum callosum	green, purple, white	intermediate–cool	low–medium	winter
Paphiopedilum hybrids	all colors save blue	intermediate–cool	low–medium	various
Phalaenopsis amabilis	white	intermediate–warm	low–medium	various
Phalaenopsis lueddemanniana	white, purple	intermediate–warm	low–medium	various
Phalaenopsis schilleriana	pink	intermediate–warm	low–medium	winter
Phalaenopsis stuartiana	white, dotted brown	intermediate–warm	low–medium	spring
Phalaenopsis hybrids	white, pink, yellow	intermediate–warm	low–medium	various

*Miltonia
vexillaria*

*Miltonia
Celle
'Wasserfall'*

*Oncidium
ornithorhynchum*

*Oncidium
varicosum*

*Cycnoches
chlorochilon*

Phalaenopsis
'Christopher Lynn'

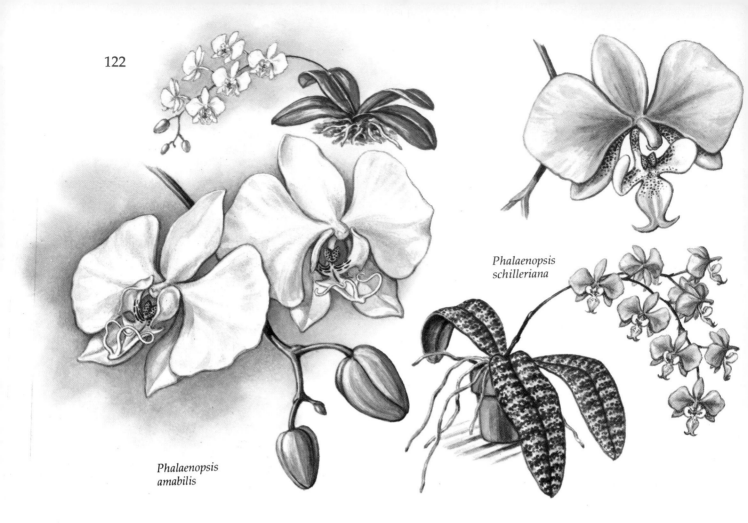

*Phalaenopsis
schilleriana*

*Phalaenopsis
amabilis*

LIGHT: Diffused, indirect sunlight is essential for orchids. Any window exposure except directly north will be suitable. The main light categories are: *high*—nearly direct sunlight; *medium*—early morning or late afternoon sunlight; *low*—shaded conditions. Orchids also flower successfully under a bank of four 40-watt fluorescent tubes. Summer your orchids out of doors, in relatively shaded conditions, if possible.

TEMPERATURE: The main temperature ranges are *warm*—75° day, 65° night; *intermediate*—70° day, 60° night; *cool*—65° day, 55° night. A five- to 10-degree drop in temperature at night is critical for good flowering. Many orchids, however, will grow well in more than one temperature range.

MOISTURE: Most orchids are epiphytes; their roots, in nature, are quickly dried by the winds. Such orchids as *Cattleya*, *Oncidium* and *Miltonia* should approach dryness prior to rewatering. Terrestrial orchids such as *Paphiopedilum* or moisture-loving ones such as *Phalaenopsis* require some moisture at all times at their roots. This does not mean a soggy medium!

PROPAGATION: Orchids may be started from seed, using the asymbiotic culture method (without fungus fertilization) in an agar medium in a sterile environment. However because special equipment is required, this method is not usually practiced by home growers. Most orchids take four to six years from seed before they reach flowering size. Orchids may also be divided, as shown in the illustrations. Keep all cutting tools sterile by flaming after each cut.

Certain orchids may also produce "keikis" or offsets, which may be potted once they have produced their own root system.

POTTING: Various potting media are available at greenhouse supply firms. Fir bark in varying grades is used, often in combination with perlite and sphagnum moss. The dense roots of Osmunda fern may also be used, but water sparingly.

Orchids should be repotted when the old medium has decayed, when the newest growth reaches outside the pot, or if the root system is unhealthy. Repot while the orchid is in active growth, usually as it is producing a new set of roots.

Clay or plastic pots are used for most orchids, although some species may grow better on cork or tree fern slabs.

FERTILIZER: Though nutrient requirements vary within the orchid family, most orchids require less fertilizer than other plants. A water-soluble fertilizer that balances the nitrogen, phosphorus and potassium and has trace elements, applied in dilute solution once a month, is adequate for home culture. Orchids in active vegetative growth utilize fertilizer; those in a dormant or resting stage require none. Apply all fertilizers sparingly.

INSECTS: Orchids, like other plants, have their share of insect pests, even in the home. The rare attacks of fungus or of mealy bugs, aphids or scale insects, can be remedied with a combination spray of Benlate (fungicide) and Malathion (insecticide). Use all pesticides and fungicides with extreme caution.

REMARKS: In summation, give most orchids good but diffused light, water them well but do not permit the medium to become soggy, and provide a five- to ten-degree drop in temperature at night. Orchids are normally very vigorous plants and will flourish with a minimum of care.

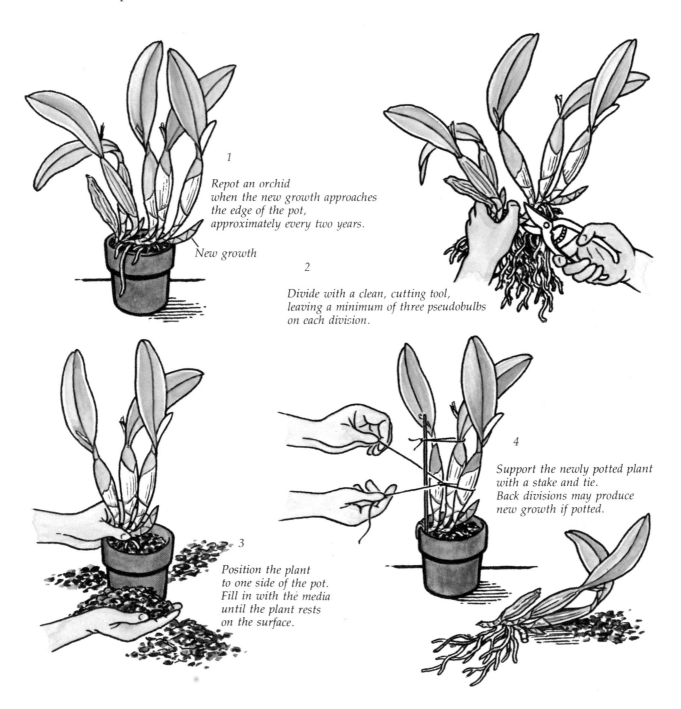

1

Repot an orchid when the new growth approaches the edge of the pot, approximately every two years.

New growth

2

Divide with a clean, cutting tool, leaving a minimum of three pseudobulbs on each division.

3

Position the plant to one side of the pot. Fill in with the media until the plant rests on the surface.

4

Support the newly potted plant with a stake and tie. Back divisions may produce new growth if potted.

Punica granatum nana

FRUIT BEARING PLANTS

Dwarf Pomegranate
(Punica granatum nana)

A dwarf form of the pomegranate tree native to the Mediterranean region. It is a conversation piece for pot-plant culture in the home. The family *Punicaceae* is small, possessing only one genus and two species. *P. granatum* is cultivated in warmer climates for its ornamental edible fruits. The species bears fruits as large as an orange.

LIGHT: Very high; direct sunlight beneficial, especially in winter.

TEMPERATURE: Warm, but cool during semi-dormancy period, which occurs in winter.

MOISTURE: Moist, with good drainage. Dry during semirest.

PROPAGATION: Seeds and cuttings.

POTTING: Mix A.

FERTILIZER: Apply water-soluble fertilizer once a month in summer at half strength.

INSECTS: Mealy bugs and spider mites.

PRUNING: Occasional trimming to make desirable shape.

REMARKS: A deciduous tree by nature, it will drop some leaves in winter, at which time less frequent watering is needed.

Calamondin Orange
(Citrus mitis)

An ornamental pot-plant orange cultivated and popularized as the miniature orange plant. It is a member of the rue family, which is known botanically as *Rutaceae*. A most attractive plant in containers, it bears flowers followed by bright orange fruits that last for months afterward. Flowers and fruits often occur together. It is offered at holiday time and used as a gift plant. Though it is really a sour orange and not good for eating, the skin and flesh nonetheless make good marmalade.

Usually citrus plants do not make good plants for home culture indoors. Their need for sunshine in order to grow into a healthy plant is a characteristic not to be overlooked.

Citrus meyeri, a semidwarf, almost thornless, has very fragrant flowers and produces lemons of table quality the year round.

LIGHT: Very high. Full sun, especially in winter, or very high under fluorescent lights. Should be grown out of doors in summer for benefit of direct sun.

TEMPERATURE: Warm; does not grow well below 55°.

MOISTURE: Moist; good drainage important. Roots are injured if grown in compacted water-saturated mix.

PROPAGATION: Cuttings. Plants from seeds are slow to fruit.

POTTING: Mix B with acid-soil reaction. Small, purchased plants in two-inch pots should be shifted to a six-inch pot as soon as possible. Use of plastic pots best to avoid frequent drying out.

FERTILIZER: Apply water-soluble fertilizer at half strength once a month when growth is apparent. Omit fertilizer after pruning until new shoot growth occurs.

INSECTS: Red spider mites. Will cause foliage and leaf drop.

PRUNING: Potted citrus become leggy in the home due to inadequate light. Plants may be pruned back to two-thirds size to encourage bushiness.

REMARKS: Occasional sink-spraying of leaves gets rid of dust and helps prevent infestation.

Citrus mitis

Persea americana

Avocado *(Persea americana)*

The alligator pear. A tropical fruit, its native habitats are the warmest parts of North and South America. For residents of temperate regions, it is a "fun" plant to grow. After you have enjoyed eating its delicious fruit, you can grow an avocado tree from the seed.

LIGHT: High. Place the potted avocado where it will get several hours of sunlight or artificial light each day.

TEMPERATURE: Warm.

MOISTURE: Moist. Always water plant with tepid water.

PROPAGATION: From seed. Wash the seed in warm water to remove all of the pulp. Cut off the pointed end of the seed and insert the broad end into a water-filled jar. To support, press three toothpicks into the top of the seed. Add enough warm water to cover about half an inch of the seed. Place the glass out of direct sun, adding water to compensate for evaporation. A mature seed should sprout in two to six weeks. When the main stem is six to eight inches high cut it back to about half size. This forces branches to form. When the roots are good and thick and the stem is leafed out, it is ready for potting. As you move the plant to the pot from its jar of water take care not to injure the root system.

POTTING: Put in rich, peaty potting mixture, like mix A. Leave the seed half exposed in the mix when planted. Use a pot that is 10 inches in diameter. When the plant is 15 inches high, place a small stake in the pot and tie the stalk to it for support.

FERTILIZER: Apply a water-soluble fertilizer solution once a month.

INSECTS: Red spider mites, mealy bugs, aphids and scale insects.

REMARKS: It is doubtful that your avocado plant will flower and produce fruit. Grow it for its leafy treelike appearance. When the plant becomes pot-bound shift it to a larger pot. This will keep it growing. Shape the plant by pruning the branches. If it gets too tall, prune it back to a desirable height. Its response to your tender loving care will delight and amaze you.

Ananas comosus

Pineapple *(Ananas comosus)*

The pineapple comes from tropical America. The experience of tasting a fresh pineapple is a treat many people look forward to. Amateur gardeners find the fun of growing this tropical fruit a challenge.

PROPAGATION: When buying a pineapple to start a plant choose one that has a deep orange color and a strong pineapple fragrance. If slicing for food preparation, cut off the top with about one inch of the fruit attached. Then cut away the meaty part, being careful not to injure the stem at the center. Set it aside to dry for a couple of days. When dried, suspend in a glass of water so that one-half inch of water covers the base of the stem. In a few weeks roots will appear and it should be potted in a mix. Add just enough mix to cover the base of the plant. Use potting mix B. Alternatively, set the top in a small pot of sand and keep warm and humid. Transfer to mix B when rooted.

FLOWERING AND FRUITING: Do not be disappointed if the first top does not root. Any time after two years it should be old enough to flower.

Ethylene, the well-known pollutant gas, when released in the crown area of the plant will trigger flowering.

To encourage flowering, ethylene gas can be produced as follows:

Step 1. If your plant appears healthy, producing new leaves, put it in a polyethylene bag and also put in two or three apples. The apples give off ethylene. Use good apples that you can eat afterward. Close the bag and set it aside in indirect light for four or five days.

Step 2. Open the bag, check the plant for water. If the treatment worked, you should be able to see some red color in the center of the leaf rosette and new leaf growth. Small rows of buds will appear and will grow into a pineapple.

LIGHT: Very high. Place plant in a sunny window.

TEMPERATURE: Warm.

MOISTURE: Water only enough to keep potting mix barely moist for a few weeks. When roots are established, keep mixture moist.

FERTILIZER: Apply a water-soluble plant food once a month.

Citrus limon 'Ponderosa'

Ponderosa Lemon
(Citrus limon 'Ponderosa')

'Ponderosa' is a curiosity, grown for ornamental rather than for food value. A member of the family *Rutaceae,* it is listed as a Maryland hybrid of 1887. It bears huge fruits with a thick coarse skin. Individual fruits weighing two pounds each are not unusual; they are not of table quality. The main crop is produced in winter.

LIGHT: Very high. Does best as an outdoor plant in warm regions.

TEMPERATURE: Warm. Outdoor temperatures below 40° are likely to be harmful.

MOISTURE: Moist.

PROPAGATION: Cuttings.

POTTING: Formula B. When repotting, take care not to disturb roots.

FERTILIZER: Water-soluble type every two months to established plants.

INSECTS: Spider mites and scale insects.

PRUNING: Potted plants become leggy. To control, prune heavily by cutting entire top back.

Coffee *(Coffea arabica)*

The well-known breakfast beverage of peoples around the world. It is a member of the family *Rubiaceae.* The original species came from Ethiopia and Angola. It is known for its shiny dark-green foliage on willowy branches. The flowers are pure white, fragrant and borne in clusters in the axils of the leaves. Half-inch brilliant crimson berries with a sweet pulp develop after flowering.

LIGHT: Very high.

TEMPERATURE: Warm. Cool temperature essential for flowering and fruiting.

PROPAGATION: Seeds; also cuttings, with difficulty.

POTTING: Potting mix formula B. Shift seedlings to larger pots to provide room for root growth.

FERTILIZER: Water-soluble fertilizer once a month for mature plants.

INSECTS: Mealy bugs and spider mites.

PRUNING: Prune out top growth.

Coffea arabica

Eriobotrya japonica

Chinese Loquat

(Eriobotrya japonica)

A member of the rose family and relative of the apple. Outdoor trees produce a pear-shaped fruit, yellow to orange in color, one to three inches long. The fruit is eaten fresh or may be used in the making of jelly, preserves, pies and the like. Loquat jelly is of superior quality. Outdoors the tree grows 20 to 30 feet tall, but it is much favored as an interior decorator's plant of tree-sized proportions. Its height and shape are easily controlled by pruning. It may also be used as a patio container plant for shady spots in the summer. It can be espalier-trained for indoors or out.

Its attraction lies in its big, leathery, crisp leaves which are stoutly veined and netted, measuring six to eight inches in length and two to four inches in width. The leaves are glossy green above, with rust-colored wool beneath. Flowering takes place in fall, but when pruned to control growth it may lose its potential for flowers and fruits.

LIGHT: Very high. Plants moved to patio in summer; need shade from direct sun.

TEMPERATURE: Cool.

MOISTURE: Moist.

PROPAGATION: By seeds, air layering and grafting.

POTTING: Potting mix formula A.

FERTILIZER: Established plants need feeding with a water-soluble fertilizer once a month.

INSECTS: Aphids, red spider mites, and scale insects.

PRUNING: Prune to shape and control growth for ornamental purposes.

Musa acuminata
'Dwarf Cavendish'

Dwarf Banana

(Musa acuminata 'Dwarf Cavendish'*)*

The Cavendish is of Chinese origin and a member of the family *Musaceae*. It is a stout-stemmed dwarf type that reaches a height of five to seven feet at maturity. Fruit production is entirely possible when given good culture indoors. The fruits are six to eight inches long and weigh four to five ounces. They are of good quality, and if harvested seven to 14 days before ripening, hung by the bunch in a shady, cool place, they will develop flavor and nutritive value as completely as if allowed to ripen on the plant. Cut the bunch down when the individual fruits are well rounded in cross-section, including a portion of the stem to facilitate handling. The terminal flower buds should be cut off at the same time.

LIGHT: Very high.

TEMPERATURE: Warm.

MOISTURE: Moist.

PROPAGATION: By divisions of the underground rhizome. Each division should contain two buds. Or by suckers detached from base of parent stem. Take suckers when two to eight months old.

POTTING: Potting mix formula A. Use tubs for final containers at least 18 to 36 inches wide. A large container is necessary to feed a plant sufficiently for flower production and fruiting. Bury rhizome sections and suckers six to eight inches deep.

FERTILIZER: Bananas are gross feeders. Apply water-soluble fertilizer solution once a month. The development of fruit depends on a constant supply of nutrients.

INSECTS: Red spider mites.

REMARKS: Fourteen months from planting a good-sized sucker to flowering.

Ficus carica

Common Fig *(Ficus carica)*

Of the family *Moraceae* and native to western Asia, whence it undoubtedly spread into the Mediterranean region. A related species of the genera of ornamentals used as house plants, namely *Ficus benjamina, Ficus elastica decora* and *Ficus lyrata.* It is used as a pot plant in shopping malls and also in the home. Its aesthetic value comes from its artistic habit of growth and its large mulberry leaf shapes. A decorator's dream plant in every way; a very effective plant for patio growing. Potted specimens growing outdoors in frigid winter climates can be moved inside an entryway or garage for protection and dormant storage. Because it is a deciduous tree it will normally drop its leaves once a year.

For outdoor culture in sheltered locations trees are bent to the ground and covered with several inches of earth, plus a mulch, to avoid the effects of freezing and thawing. Stems are sometimes wrapped with insulation cloth before severe cold arrives. Figs may survive temperatures to 10° F. before branches will freeze.

Common figs bear fruits on one-year-old stems in the axils of the leaves.

LIGHT: Very high.

TEMPERATURE: Warm; cool for winter storage and dormancy.

MOISTURE: Moist. Dry during storage.

PROPAGATION: Cuttings, air layering.

POTTING: Mix formula A.

FERTILIZER: Once a month during growth.

INSECTS: Mealy bugs, red spider mites.

PRUNING: To create desired shape.

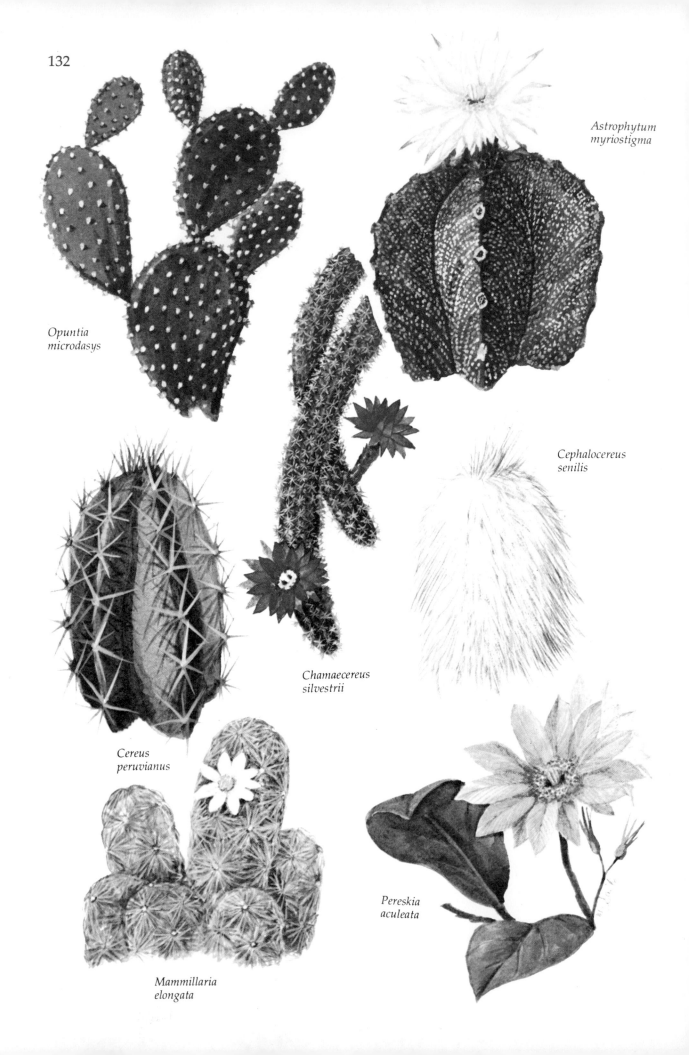

132

*Opuntia
microdasys*

*Astrophytum
myriostigma*

*Cephalocereus
senilis*

*Chamaecereus
silvestrii*

*Cereus
peruvianus*

*Mammillaria
elongata*

*Pereskia
aculeata*

CACTI AND SUCCULENTS

CACTI (from the Greek word *kaktos*, meaning spiny plant) are succulentlike plants belonging to only one family—*Cactaceae*. The family is large; it includes about 2,000 species, all being perennials with fleshy growth and most without leaves (the exception is *Pereskia aculeata* and its closely related species). If any leaves are produced during the growth stage, they soon fall off. Most cactus plants have spines, although there are a few without them. The fruit is a one-celled berry with many seeds. Another characteristic of botanical significance is the areole, which is a specially modified bud from which shooots and flowers can emerge; it usually bears hairs, bristles, spines or wool.

Some well-known cacti are illustrated. Bunny Ears (*Opuntia microdasys*) is an old favorite; the flattened oval stems known as pods are dotted with areoles covered with golden-yellow glochids (barbed bristles). It is a plant to be handled with caution because the tufts of glochids stick to the skin at the slightest touch. The growing of all species of *Opuntia* is illegal in Australia because of the damage wrought by *O. ficus-indica.*

Old Man Cactus (*Cephalocereus senilis*) is a venerable cactus with snow-white hairs, and it is one of the favorites. It grows very slowly and may reach 20 feet in 100 years. Found growing on the dry hillsides of Mexico, it is called *Cabeza de Viejo*, or Old Man's Head. It is nocturnally flowering.

Peanut cactus (*Chamaecereus silvestrii*) is easy to grow, likes some moisture and sun or partial shade. Flowers in spring and produces many stems in a season.

Bishop's Cap (*Astrophytum myriostigma*) is a popular, spineless, easy-to-grow type. Flowers freely all summer long. Takes sun or semishade. Requires some moisture.

Golden Star (*Mammillaria elongata*) is a fast-growing cactus, producing many stems in one season. Each plant is a bright mosaic of golden and harmless spines.

Barbados Gooseberry (*Pereskia aculeata*) is grown like a shrub in pots. Occasionally it needs a pruning to restrain its vinelike branching. Glossy-leaved branches with showy pink, lemon-scented flowers, *Pereskias* are living examples of nonsucculent primitive cacti from which the succulent spiny types evolved.

Hedge Cactus (*Cereus peruvianus*) is possibly native to Brazil and Argentina. Typical columnar upright branching shows near the base. Young branches with six to eight flat ribs are light green and change to blue with age. It has needlelike spines in starlike clusters of five to ten at areoles. Nocturnal flowering. Branch cuttings root easily.

SUCCULENTS. What is a succulent? The term applies to plants differing from cacti in that they have juicy, fleshy, soft and thickened leaves, stems and tubers. Succulent plants come from arid or semiarid climates. Such climates influence the evolution of plants and bring about physiological structural changes, thus creating reduction of body surfaces, modification of stomata and shallow-rooting habit. These characteristics are important to limit water loss from the plant. Such changes thus have provided plants with structures specifically adapted to survive long periods of drought. It is these resistant qualities that classify them as succulents.

Succulent types of plants are found in many families. Among them are *Aizoaceae, Amaryllidaceae, Agavaceae, Asclepiadaceae, Bromeliaceae, Compositae, Crassulaceae, Euphorbiaceae, Lilaceae,* and *Portulacaceae.*

Some well-known succulents:

Panda Plant (*Kalanchoe tomentosa*) is an elegant plant, its leaves covered with soft silvery plush, stained at margins with red-brown. It likes a fertile mix, some sun and moisture. Propagated by leaf cuttings.

Jellybean plant (*Sedum pachyphyllum*) has round, club-shaped leaves with red tips and yellow flowers. Each leaf provides a new plant for propagation purposes.

Lithops dorotheae

Aloe variegata

Gasteria verrucosa

Kalanchoe tomentosa

Sedum pachyphyllum

Sempervivum tectorum

Mother-in-Law's Tongue (*Gasteria verrucosa*) is a large genus of more than 50 species native to South Africa. *G. verrucosa* is one of the best known, with leaves of about six inches long, in opposite rows. The surface of the leaf is roughened, with small, crowded tubercles, giving the leaves a distinct gray appearance. Propagation by leaf-cutting section.

Partridge-breasted Aloe (*Aloe variegata*) requires special culture for successful growing. For potting, cover loose potting mix with one inch of pebbles and merely firm plant down, taking care to keep base of rosette of leaves above potting mix. When watering, keep moisture off crown of plant. Never permit soil to stay wet. Give plenty of sun. Propagated by offsets only.

Hen-and-Chickens (*Sempervivum tectorum*) is so called because of the miniature rosettes sprouting from the base of the larger plant. Easily propagated by removing rosettes and potting.

Stone Plant (*Lithops dorotheae*) is an amazing replica of pebbles and small stones. Since it is without spines, to protect it from being eaten by animals it resembles a group of stones. Provide good drainage, giving no moisture in winter. Grow at a temperature above 50° and provide fresh air and some sun when possible. Be sure to let potting mix dry out before each watering.

Culture of cacti and succulents

LIGHT AND AIR: For successful growth and coloration of cacti and succulent plants, fresh air by means of ventilation and plentiful sunlight are most important. If natural daylight is not available, fluorescent or "grow" lights may be substituted. At least 1,000 footcandles of light energy for a 14-hour period are required.

Some succulent plants will take low light or partial shade. Among these are the orchid cactus, *gasteria* and *haworthia*.

Cacti thrive when grown in a sunny place. A warm, sunny, south window is the best location.

TEMPERATURE: Warm temperature is conducive to growth. However, during the winter months a rest period should be provided for by cool tem-perature conditions: 50° to 60° is desirable. The rest period at this temperature may last for one or more months, depending on the species. The plants will give an indication as to this duration by the appearance of new shoot growth, thus calling for a warmer temperature and more frequent watering.

MOISTURE: Too much water is the main cause of fatality in succulent plants. The amount of water depends on time of year, temperature, age of plant and the species. During winter or dormant period, plants should be kept as dry as possible and temperature kept at 50° to 60°. Resist temptation to water. If one wishes the plant to flower, this dormant period is most important.

PROPAGATION: Cacti and other succulents may be grown by seed, cuttings, budding and grafting. Succulents are among the easiest plants to be propagated by cuttings. A good rooting mixture is peat moss and perlite or sand. It is important that cuttings be allowed to heal over before being set in mixture. This may take several days or weeks.

POTTING: Use mix C. Transplant or repot *only* in the spring, using small pots. Cacti and other succulents do not grow in pure sand as is sometimes thought. Even in arid desert regions there is much decomposed vegetation that, with the rains, becomes available as food.

FERTILIZER: Generally, cacti and succulents are not demanding in their food or fertilizer requirements. However, more healthy and vigorous plants are produced when properly supplied with nutrients.

A water-soluble type of fertilizer applied once every two months at half strength in summer is beneficial. A dry garden fertilizer or a controlled-release type applied once in the spring will give like results. *Do not apply any fertilizer in the winter.*

INSECTS AND DISEASES: Cacti and succulents are susceptible to root rot, black spot, root mealy bugs, scale insects, mealy bugs, red spider mites, aphids, and nematodes.

REMARKS: In warm weather, it is good to take plants outside. A gravel bed or wire mesh should support them.

Do not put aloes, haworthias or any small cacti outside in strong sunlight in the summer unless protection by a roof is provided to keep off direct sunshine and rains.

Snake Plant or Mother-in-Law's Tongue

(Sansevieria trifasciata laurentii)

From the Congo, of the family *Agavaceae*, it has the reputation of being one of the toughest house plants of all. It will survive under the most adverse conditions of low light and dryness, though not extreme cold. The variety *laurentii* is more desired because of its stiff, sword-shaped, yellow-margined leaves.

S. trifasciata is similar in growth habit but has zigzag gray markings.

S. trifasciata hahnii, a sport of the above (U.S. patent 1941), is known as "Bird's-nest sansevieria." It is different in habit, forming a low-spreading growth with leaves slightly reflexed, cross-banded with lighter green. It suckers freely from the base.

LIGHT: All intensities of light.

TEMPERATURE: Cool to warm.

MOISTURE: Dry.

PROPAGATION: Division of clump. Sectional leaf cuttings. Exception: *S. trifasciata laurentii* reverts back to green form; therefore, use division of clump method.

POTTING: Mix B. Repot only when pot-bound.

FERTILIZER: Water-soluble or slow-release feeding only once in three to four months.

INSECTS: Mealy bugs.

Sansevieria trifasciata hahnii

Sansevieria trifasciata laurentii

Jade Plant *(Crassula argentea)*

Of the family *Crassulaceae* from South Africa, the largest-growing *Crassula*. In mild climates and in its native home it may attain a height of eight to 12 feet. It is better known 'as. a smaller plant today grown more extensively for dish gardens and as a pot plant than any of the other succulent plants. When given good cultural conditions it will flower in midwinter. Its flowers are a dainty pink, turning white with age. The leaves are a glossy jade-green, thick and fleshy, rounded on the top side, flat on the underside, and turn reddish along the edges in the sun. *C. argentea minima* is of more compact growing habit; its dark green leaves turn red at the apex when grown in the sun.

Another species, *C. arborescens*, is a large-leaved, shrubby species, even more attractive than *C. argentea*. Its leaves are silvery with a red margin marked with tiny spots.

LIGHT: Very high.

TEMPERATURE: Cool, best for growing and flowering.

MOISTURE: Dry; more moisture than cacti.

PROPAGATION: Leaf and terminal cuttings. Let cutting dry overnight before inserting into medium. Apply little moisture during rooting period.

POTTING: Mix formula C. Repot in spring. Do so only when pot-bound. Use three-quarter size pots. Do not overpot.

FERTILIZER: Apply water-soluble fertilizer once every two months in summer only.

INSECTS: Mealy bugs.

PRUNING: Sometimes needed to attain a shapely plant.

Crassula argentea

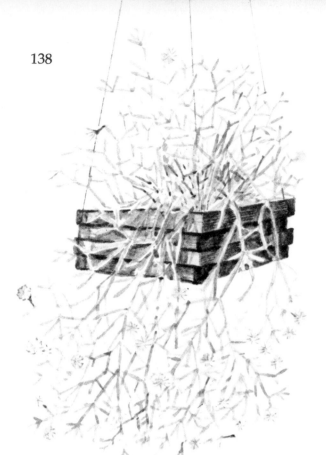

Rhipsalis cereuscula

Rice Cactus *(Rhipsalis cereuscula)*

An epiphytic type of cactus found growing from Uruguay to Brazil. It grows in crotches of trees, forming erect clumps. The pencil-sized stems and branches are crowned by short-angled twigs that carry tiny bristles in the areoles. Pink to white flowers are produced at the top of branches. Fruits develop looking like the white berries of mistletoe, which is characteristic of most *Rhipsalis*. A related species is the mistletoe cactus, *R. cassutha*, which grows on trees and rock cliffs and hangs downward as far as 3 feet or more. The cream-colored flowers are followed by mistletoelike fruits.

LIGHT: Very high.

TEMPERATURE: Warm.

MOISTURE: Dry.

PROPAGATION: Stem cuttings; seeds.

POTTING: A mixture of sphagnum moss and perlite (50-50) plus fertilizer.

FERTILIZER: Monthly application of water-soluble fertilizer in summer.

INSECTS: Mealy bugs.

Crown-of-Thorns
(Euphorbia milii; Euphorbia splendens)

Of the family *Euphorbiaceae*, it is identified by its milky sap. *E. milii* is a spiny shrub with thick spiny stems and tiny oval-shaped leaves of bright green that are shed in winter. In spite of the loss of leaves, flowers continue to develop to some extent all winter. Leaves appear on the plants again in spring.

To keep rampant growth of its stout spiny stems under control it can be trained to a trellis.

LIGHT: Very high.

TEMPERATURE: Cool.

MOISTURE: Moist, but allowed to dry between soakings.

PROPAGATION: Cuttings, allowed to dry overnight before inserting.

POTTING: Potting mix formula B.

FERTILIZER: Apply water-soluble fertilizer once every two months except in winter.

INSECTS: Mealy bugs and red spider mites.

PRUNING: To control undesirable branching.

Euphorbia milii

Epiphyllum oxypetalum

Night-Blooming Cereus
(Epiphyllum oxypetalum)

It belongs to an epiphytic group of cacti that climb into trees by means of aerial roots. They are not parasitic, because they use the tree for support only. *Epiphyllums* are found growing throughout Mexico, Central America and into Brazil. They are very easy to grow and look best when supported by stakes or a trellis, rather than being left to pursue their rampant growth habit. *E. oxypetalum*, also called Queen of the Night, is the best night-blooming species for home culture. Flowering takes place through summer and autumn. Its large, fragrant white flowers measure six inches or more across. Flowers start to open early evening and close when the sun rises. Flowers develop from areoles along the margin of the flattened stemlike leaf. True leaves are lacking. Fruits develop after flowering and are edible. Flowering takes place from growth made the previous summer season, not on present year's wood.

LIGHT: Very high; direct sun part of the day.

TEMPERATURE: Cool place of 50° for winter.

MOISTURE: Dry. Dry in winter when stored cool. Water when surface of soil is dry.

PROPAGATION: Cuttings.

POTTING: Potting formula C. Do not overpot.

FERTILIZER: Feed established plants once a month in summer. Omit in winter.

INSECTS: Mealy bugs.

PRUNING: Undesirable growth may be pruned and new plants started from cuttings.

Epiphyllum ackermannii

Schlumbergera gaertneri

ORCHID CACTUS *(Epiphyllum ackermannii)* is found growing naturally in tropical America and Mexico at an altitude of 6,000 to 8,000 feet. Its huge, glowing red blossoms are like water lilies and measure as much as ten inches in diameter. Their flowering period extends from early spring into summer. Its branches are usually flattened, sometimes three-angled. Hybridizers have created many cultivars with glowing satiny petals that display a rainbowlike iridescence. Its vivid and clear colors are shining reds of all shades, scarlet to deep crimson, as well as bright pinks, salmon, orange, snowy white, white and gold. More beautiful, if possible, are the bicolors with scarlet outer petals and radiant violet throats.

A hint for culture: Orchid cacti are found wild in tropical forests and not on dry, hot deserts. They are usually found growing as epiphytes in trees.

EASTER CACTUS *(Schlumbergera gaertneri)* The species *gaertneri* is a tree dweller, an epiphytic Brazilian cactus with stiff, spreading branches of long flattened joints, dull green in color, with purplish margins; the end joints have a tendency to droop and have a few bristlelike hairs. The flowers are tubular with radiating petals, two to three inches in length, dark red in color, and appear in spring. A variety, *S. gaertneri makoyana*, known as Cat's Whiskers, has bluish-green branches and purplish margins with yellowish-brown whiskerlike bristles at the tips. Starlike light orange-red flowers occur in spring.

Like the *Epiphyllum*, these plants do not resemble the cactus. They also come from the same tropical forests in which one finds orchids and bromeliads growing side by side. Culture is similar to methods used for orchids and bromeliads.

Schlumbergera truncata

Schlumbergera bridgesii

THANKSGIVING or CRAB CACTUS (*Schlumbergera truncata*) differs from the Christmas cactus in that the margins of the joints are saw-toothed, the teeth point forward, and the anthers are yellowish. Flowers are usually orange, but hybrids come in various shades of color. Flowering occurs earlier than for Christmas cactus, appearing to be less dependent on critical cool temperatures and short days.

The plants are propagated by taking cuttings consisting of two or three joints and placing them in pots of sphagnum moss for rooting. Water is withheld until rooting occurs or signs of wilting appear. When established as rooted plants, resume practice of feeding.

The plants respond to simple cleft and scion grafting on *Selenicereus* stock. Growth is much more rapid, and standards or treelike forms are developed.

CHRISTMAS or CRAB'S CLAW CACTUS (*Schlumbergera bridgesii*). Formerly known as *Epiphyllum truncatum* and also as *Zygocactus truncatus*, it is correctly identified by taxonomists as *S. bridgesii*.

The Christmas cactus has jointed stems that are flattened and leaflike, with rounded teeth on the margins, and four- to six-angled or winged, purplish anthers. Growers of cactus list color variations including whites and shades of pink, red and orange.

The Crab's Claw Cactus is classified as a short-day plant for flowering—that is, its flowering is usually assured when short days of nine hours occur normally or are induced by positioning the plant in a dark closet and when the night temperature drops to 60° or below. Exposure to this combination of factors for a period of about five weeks will bring flowers in ten to 12 weeks from the start of these culture conditions.

142

Tulipa
gesneriana

Hyacinthus
orientalis

Crocus
species

Muscari
armeniacum

GROWING BULBS

The revival of forcing hardy bulbs or tender tropical bulbs, corms or tubers takes its place among current ideas for indoor gardeners. A most rewarding experience is to bring flowers into your home during the winter months.

Three classes of bulbs for winter flowering:

1. *Hardy types* are daffodils and hyacinths, which can be forced for Christmas, and crocuses, hyacinths and tulips for later forcing. Also included with this group is lily-of-the-valley.

2. *Half-hardy bulbs* that grow at cool but not freezing temperatures include freesias, ixias and ornithogalums. Temperature requirements of these bulbs are difficult to manipulate in the home, so these should be left for nurserymen to grow.

3. *Tender tropical or subtropical bulbs* such as amaryllis, veltheimias and caladiums (for their foliage) are easily handled by the home gardener.

TULIP *(Tulipa gesneriana).* This is the most common of the lily family. It originated in the Mediterranean region, in Asia and Japan. Early flowering and extremely dwarf species are from the species *T. suaveolens.* Many other species and varieties are grown in gardens. For best results choose single-flowered early varieties from catalogues. Pot five or six bulbs in a five-inch bulb pan. The outside bulbs in the pan are set with the flat side to the inside wall so that the first leaf developed will hang over the edge of the pan. Store the potted bulbs at 46° to 48°. Plants started in September to October will flower in January and February. The storage period usually runs eight to ten weeks. After storage grow as cool as possible.

CROCUS *(Crocus vernus;* hybrids). A vari-colored early-flowering bulb, the crocus is one of the first harbingers of spring. Original species came from Europe, and it belongs to the iris family. Like hyacinths, crocus bulbs will grow in water. Specially designed vases of crystal glass about 3½ inches tall have a cuplike depression for holding one bulb so that the base of the bulb sets just above the water. Once started, keep in a cool, dark place for roots to develop. Then bring into a well-lighted room to flower. Crocus pots looking like so-called strawberry jars are also ideal for starting crocus bulbs. Most all varieties of crocus can be forced. Plant in shallow containers so that the top of the bulb is just covered with a mix. Store at 48° to 50° for eight to ten weeks and force at a cool temperature for flowering. Bulbs of the autumn-flowering crocus, *Colchicum autumnale,* which belongs to the lily family, are purchased for planting in the fall and can be forced. Place in a container without potting medium or moisture, supporting bulb with pebbles or sand. After flowering, the bulbs are planted permanently in the ground.

HYACINTH *(Hyacinthus orientalis).* This plant belongs to the lily family and is a native of Syria, Asia Minor and Greece. Roman hyacinths are of the variety *albus* and are cultured mainly for forcing. So-called prepared hyacinths are used for forcing. Specially designed hyacinth glasses hold a hyacinth bulb so that the base of the bulb is at the water level for rooting. No storage is needed as for other bulbs. However, starting at a cool 60° in the dark to promote rooting is beneficial. Hyacinth bulbs treated for forcing in pots are started in the early autumn. Normally three large bulbs are planted in a six-inch bulb pan. Fill with mix so that the necks of the bulbs are just showing. Store at 48° to 55° for about ten weeks.

GRAPE HYACINTH *(Muscari armeniacum).* The simplest of all bulbs to force. Save a few bulbs out of your autumn planting and plant in a shallow pot, using any good potting soil, in late autumn. Move to a cool place, 40° to 50°, for at least two months. Water about once a week until foliage sprouts. Then move to a sunny window and enjoy a bit of blue sky in your home.

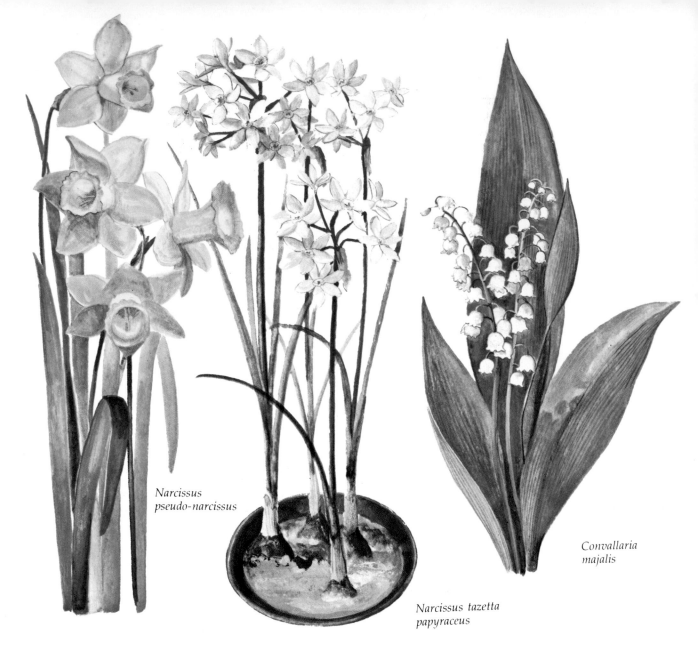

Narcissus pseudo-narcissus

Narcissus tazetta papyraceus

Convallaria majalis

DAFFODIL *(Narcissus pseudo-narcissus).* The large trumpet type with the common yellow color is one of the first of spring flowers to appear as cut flowers in flower shops or supermarkets. Bulbs for forcing are sold in early autumn as pre-cooled early flowering varieties. 'King Alfred,' 'Beersheba' and 'Rembrandt' are a few of the good varieties. Miniature daffodils are also available for forcing, are much smaller and are preferred by many gardeners.

For forcing, select double-nosed bulbs with undamaged tips. Using mix B, place five or six bulbs in a five- or six-inch bulb pan or azalea pot. Set bulbs so that the tips of bulbs are one inch below the rim of the pot. Fill with mix to that level. Potting time in the Northern Hemisphere is September to December, the earlier the better. Store pots of bulbs for six to eight weeks. Remove from storage when roots come through the drainage hole at the bottom of the pot and when the tops have started to grow. When first removed from storage, place in a cool basement window or spare room. When shoot growth has taken on green color move to a forcing temperature of about 60°. High light and cool temperatures are then essential for producing a good quality flowering plant.

PAPER-WHITE NARCISSUS *(Narcissus tazetta papyraceus).* A tropical bulb originating from the Canary Islands; a member of the amaryllis family. Bulbs are available in autumn from garden stores and flower shops, are ready to pot and grow to flowering. No cool storage treatment is required. The best temperature for quality is 50° to 60°, but they will flower at living-room temperature. Bulbs can be planted every two weeks to give a succession of bloom. Plant the bulbs in shallow dishes, filling to the neck of the bulbs with pebbles, florists' shredded styrofoam or other water-holding material. Store at room temperature before planting. Flowering will occur in four to six weeks. The later the time of starting, the shorter the time for flowering. Other varieties available are the Golden Paper-white narcissus, N. 'Soleil d'Or,' and the Chinese sacred lily, N. *tazetta polyanthos*.

LILY-OF-THE-VALLEY (*Convallaria majalis*). This is favored everywhere for its sweetly fragrant, dainty flowers in the spring of the year. A member of the lily family, it is native to Europe, East Asia and North America. It can be forced into flower at any time of the year. The "pips" prepared by specialists by cold-storage treatment can be purchased ready to flower at most any time of the year. Purchased pips are planted in sphagnum moss and kept well supplied with water. Closely spaced in the container, they can be forced at a temperature of 75° to 80° in low light intensity until flower stems are well started. Flowering takes place in high light, as is the case for Paper-white narcissus. Approximate time for forcing to flowering is 21 days.

General Cultural directions

LIGHT: High light intensity is desirable for final stages of flowering bulbous plants. Full sunlight is beneficial for paper-white narcissus and for lily-of-the-valley.

TEMPERATURE: Storage temperatures averaging 48° are generally recommended for most bulbs. Fluctuation can be expected where a controlled-temperature room is not available. A discussion of outdoor storage is included under "Remarks." An exception to low-temperature storage is for *prepared* hyacinths and crocuses that are placed at 60° for a short time for root formation. The paper-white narcissus requires no storage at low temperature.

MOISTURE: Moist. *Never drying out* is a must for bulb culture. Be sure all bulbs are thoroughly watered after potting, during storage and thereafter. Pots of bulbs placed in a cold basement or garage can be wrapped in black polyethylene to keep them moist and provide darkness.

POTTING: Bulbs for forcing have enough stored food to bring them into flower. Generally, fertilizing is not needed. Thus the requirement of a potting medium is for support and to retain moisture. A mix containing soil, peat and sand or a mixture of peat and perlite in equal parts will answer the potting requirements. Packaged mixes may need the addition of perlite or sand to give them better drainage. It is emphasized that good moisture retention of the mix is important for the storage and forcing period.

INSECTS: Aphids on tulips can be troublesome.

REMARKS: The provision of storage where an adequate temperature can be maintained is an obstacle to home forcing of bulbs. Outdoor storage can be provided in a cold frame, a pit or trench in the ground. Another method is the above-ground arrangement (see illustration).

Soil temperatures for the first few weeks during the time bulbs are buried outside may be 50° to 55°, which is conducive to root growth. It is expected that a drop to 45° will take place and, eventually, possibly to 32° to 35°. The temperature should not go below 32°. The moisture content of mix for potted bulbs should be checked before freezing weather sets in. A sheet of polyethylene may be added to give additional protection. A snow cover is excellent insulation.

BULB PLANTING PROCEDURE

1. Fill the container to within 1¼ to 1½ inches of the top of pot with loose, slightly moist planting medium.

2. Place the bulbs gently on top of the soil mix. The bulbs should never be pushed into the pot or flat since this compacts medium directly beneath the root plate.

3. Cover the bulbs with the planting medium up to about one-eight to one-fourth inch below the top of the container. This is done so that watering will have to drain through, not flow over the sides. The planted containers are then labeled and placed in the storage location.

DISH GARDENS

A dish garden is like a garden in miniature, and has become popular as an indoor gardening activity, particularly among those who live in city dwellings. Combinations of small tropical foliage plants, of woodland plants and of desert plants in varieties of form, color and texture are planted in containers to make dish gardens. A well-planted garden uses the principles of good floral design and compares with a pleasing arrangement of cut flowers and foliage.

Choice of container. The size of the container in relation to the size of the plants is considered. The container must be at least three inches deep and not more than eight inches high and should hold enough potting mixture for three to four or more plants.

Ceramic containers of dark or dull colors are more desirable than light colors. Containers made of brass, copper, pewter, iron and glass are used. Metal containers should be coated with plastic on the inside or lined with polyethylene (polythene) sheeting to prevent corrosion of the metal by nutrient salts contained in the potting mix. Ceramic containers depicting frogs, turkeys, Santa Claus, and all sorts of creations are available.

Selection of plants. It is logical that plants of tropical origin be chosen for dish gardens because they are best adapted to today's interiors with modern heating and lighting.

Only a few of the plant materials used for dish gardens are really dwarf varieties. The plants used together in a dish garden should have the same water requirements—that is, "moist" or "dry." It is foolish to think that cactus or peperomia will survive when planted in the same dish with ferns.

Dish-garden plants should be fairly slow-growing types. This qualification limits selection. Plants may be purchased or selected from the woodland. Plants purchased growing in 1½–2½-inch pots are best for transplanting to an area as small as a dish garden.

Use plants of different heights and colors to avoid massing of green foliage. Create a center of interest by the use of ceramic figurines, ducks, birds, lichen-covered rock, pieces of driftwood or shelf fungi.

In general, there are three different dish-garden types: 1) tropical gardens, 2) desert gardens, 3) woodland gardens.

Planting the dish garden. The potting mixture for dish gardens is found under heading for potting mixes.

Steps to follow in planting the gardens

Step 1. Place a one-half to one-inch layer of small pebbles or aquarium gravel in the bottom of the container for drainage.

Step 2. Arrange the plants for landscape effect.

Step 3. Fill between the plants with the potting mix. Firm the mixture about the plants with a blunt stick. Allow one-half inch below the rim for catching water.

Step 4. A top dressing for "ground cover" may be used. Sheet moss, florist wood moss or marble chips are suitable. However, it is difficult to watch the moisture content of the mix when these materials are used.

Watering the dish gardens. The tropical and woodland plants will need to be checked for water at least twice a week. Because there are several plants in one container, water is used up faster than with one plant in a pot.

Desert plants will need water less frequently. Check for water every two to three weeks.

DO NOT FORGET: If there is no drainage hole in the bottom of the container, there is danger of *overwatering.*

An efficient method of watering is to submerge the container in a bucket of water. When air bubbles stop appearing, remove. If plant is overwatered, place the dish on its side for about 20 minutes for excess water to drain off.

The finger-touch method for checking moisture content described in the chapter on moisture, page 176, may be used here also.

Dish-garden planters need optimum light conditions exclusive of direct sunlight and a temperature of normal living rooms.

If foliage wilts after planting, spray with atomizer or place planter in a large polyethylene bag for a day or two until plants recover from transplanting. Supplemental lighting with a table lamp will prolong the plant life of a dish garden. Control growth if necessary by occasional pruning or a soft pinch.

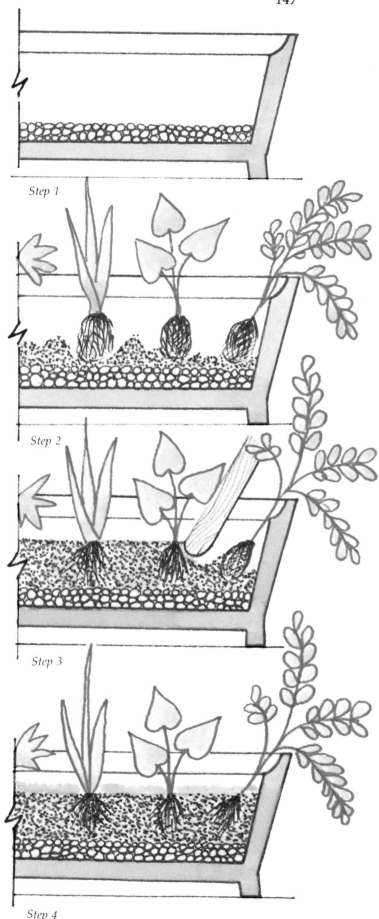

Step 1

Step 2

Step 3

Step 4

SELECTED PLANTS FOR DISH GARDENS

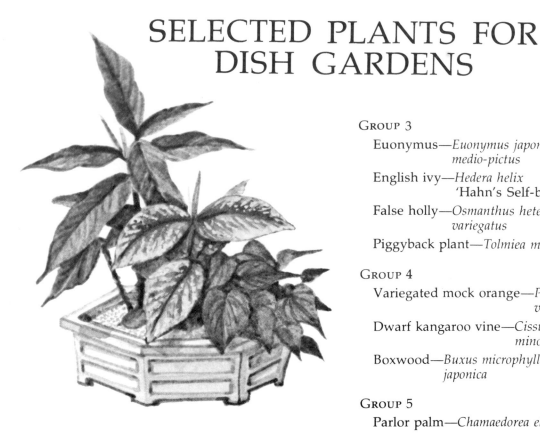

Listing of plants for these gardens is by groups that have similar growth requirements and thus go together. Any group of plants may be planted together to make a single garden or used in combination, if desired.

Plants for tropical gardens (Culture requirements are moist soil and medium light).

GROUP 1

    Chinese evergreen—*Aglaonema modestum*

    Gold-dust dracaena—*Dracaena godseffiana* 'Florida Beauty'

    Heart-leaved philodendron—*Philodendron scandens* subsp. *oxycardium*

GROUP 2

    Parlor palm—*Chamaedorea elegans*

    Marble-leaf pothos—*Pothos aureus* 'Marble Queen'

    Pteris fern—*Pteris cretica albolineata*

    Ardisia—*Ardisia crispa*

GROUP 3

    Euonymus—*Euonymus japonicus medio-pictus*

    English ivy—*Hedera helix* 'Hahn's Self-branching'

    False holly—*Osmanthus heterophylla variegatus*

    Piggyback plant—*Tolmiea menziesii*

GROUP 4

    Variegated mock orange—*Pittosporum tobira variegata*

    Dwarf kangaroo vine—*Cissus antarctica minor*

    Boxwood—*Buxus microphylla japonica*

GROUP 5

    Parlor palm—*Chamaedorea elegans*

    Arrowhead vine—*Syngonium podophyllum*

    Pink fittonia—*Fittonia verschaffeltii*

    Ardisia—*Ardisia crispa*

GROUP 9

Mother-in-Law's Tongue—*Sansevieria trifasciata*
Buddhist Pine—*Podocarpus macrophyllus maki*
Prayer Plant—*Maranta kerchoveana*
Aluminum Plant—*Pilea cadierei*
English Ivy—*Hedera helix* 'Needle Point'

GROUP 10

Asparagus Fern—*Asparagus plumosus*
Coral Berry—*Ardisia crispa*
Parlor Palm—*Chamaedorea elegans*
English Ivy—*Hedera helix* 'Jubilee'

GROUP 11

Euonymus—*Euonymus radicans gracilis*
Peperomia—*Peperomia floridana*
Pink Fittonia—*Fittonia verschaffeltii*
Baby's Tears—*Helxine soleirolii*

GROUP 12

Chinese Evergreen—*Aglaonema modestum*
Umbrella Plant—*Cyperus alternifolius gracilis*
Table Fern—*Pteris ensiformis victoriae*
Devil's Ivy—*Epipremnum aureum*

GROUP 6

Sander's dracaena—*Dracaena sanderiana*
Natal plum—*Carissa grandiflora* 'Bonsai'
English ivy—*Hedera helix* 'Maple Queen'
Chinese evergreen—*Aglaonema commutatum* var. *maculatum*
Devil's ivy—*Epipremnum aureum* (*Scindapsus aureus*)

GROUP 7

Sander's Dracaena—*Dracaena sanderiana*
Mother-in-Law's Tongue—*Sansevieria* 'Golden Hahnii'
Earth Star—*Cryptanthus* 'It'
Heart-Leaved philodendron—*Philodendron scandens* subsp. *oxycardium*

GROUP 8

Mother-in-Law's Tongue—*Sansevieria trifasciata laurentii*
English Ivy—*Hedera helix* 'Hahn's Self-branching'
Peperomia—*Peperomia floridana*
Gold-Dust Dracaena—*Dracaena godseffiana*

DESERT GARDENS

Desert gardens are planted in attractive shallow ceramic containers and in glass, such as terrariums. The author identifies glass containers of cacti and succulents as "desertariums." In this glass treatment no cover is used as with terrariums. Cacti can be combined with a few species of succulents such as the liliaceous *Haworthia*. Haworthias are small rosette-forming plants that resemble century plants and agaves of the American desert. Sedums and kalanchoes are to be avoided, for they tend to become "leggy."

Cacti can be arranged to represent really effective desert scenes by following examples of pictures in popular magazines. Use of a miniature Mexican or a thatched hut and burro figurines may be added to complete the picture. Well-placed stones to represent boulders and mountains are really the only accessories needed in cactus-planted "desertariums."

For planting, drainage is the most important consideration. Place gravel or sand to the thickness of one inch at the bottom of the container. Add potting mix (refer to potting mix formula C, page 180) to the center in a pile and line the glass with a shell-like thickness of sand. Continue to add mix and sand liner alternately until the desired planting depth is attained. Colored sand may be used in a process called "sand casting" to create rainbow effects.

Choose small plants or slow-growing types from the list on page 151. For handling, to prevent picking up spines with the fingers, use a strip of brown wrapping paper to grasp the plant. After planting tamp mix with a dowel to settle plant in place. When planting is completed, cover surface with a layer of sand or fine gravel. Gravel that is used for fish aquariums may be found in pet shops. An assortment of colors is available, if desired. Gravel at the base of plants keeps the stems dry and also helps to prevent rot diseases.

Finally, clean glass inside and out. Use a small brush to remove dirt or gravel that adheres to plants. Carefully moisten the garden by measuring a tablespoonful or two of water to each plant. Size of the plant will determine amount. Plants that have been bruised in planting should not be watered for three or four days.

A watering once a month usually supplies enough water for plants in a desert garden.

An alternate method of planting is suggested. When the container is large enough, the cactus plants in clay pots may be left in their pots and plunged into the medium; cover the rims so they are not visible. This avoids root disturbance that could cause a weak plant to be lost.

Plants for Desert Gardens

Group 1
Variegated Wax Plant—*Hoya carnosa variegata*
Peperomia—*Peperomia floridana*
Variegated Snake Plant—*Sansevieria trifasciata laurentii*
Jade Plant—*Crassula argentea*

Group 2
Umbrella Tree (seedling)—*Schefflera actinophylla*
Moses-in-the-Cradle—*Rhoeo spathacea*
Spotted Gasteria—*Gasteria maculata*
Jade Plant—*Crassula argentea*

Group 3
Hen-and-Chickens—*Sempervivum tectorum*
Zebra Haworthia—*Haworthia fasciata*
Bird's-Nest Sansevieria—*Sansevieria trifasciata hahnii*
Star Flower—*Stapelia variegata*

Group 4
Any species resembling cactus—*Euphorbia*
Variegated Peperomia—*Peperomia scandens variegata*
Sansevieria—*Sansevieria trifasciata*
Wax Plant—*Hoya carnosa* (any variety)

1. *Dracaena sanderiana*

2. *Pilea cadierei*

3. *Podocarpus macrophyllus maki*

4. *Saintpaulia*

5. *Selaginella kraussiana brownii*

6. *Chamaedorea elegans*

TERRARIUMS

What is a terrarium? *Terra* comes from the Latin meaning *earth* and *-arium* is borrowed from *aquarium*, which is a home for aquatic plants and fishes. Put together, we have a home for land creatures or plants. The forerunner of the terrarium was a glass box, called a Wardian Case. It was devised by Dr. N.B. Ward (1791–1868) and used by plant collectors to protect plants from adverse environmental conditions during transportation by sea.

When a terrarium is carefully planted the enclosure becomes a balanced ecological system comparable to a well-balanced fish aquarium.

Containers

The true terrarium is made of glass or plastic, a container of any shape or size, with the opening covered by a loose-fitting lid for ventilation. The most important requirement is transparency of the container (with no color tint). Glass is preferred to plastic because it does not scratch easily and will not discolor, as do some plastics.

Many designs have been invented. Old fish bowls, water jugs, humidors, large goblets and even glass-top coffee tables are used as terrarium containers. Expensive leaded glass and artfully designed wall hangers have invaded the terrarium market.

Planting design

Terrarium planters can be attractive and interesting when designed to reproduce a miniature landscape. The same principles of design used to create an outdoor garden are followed. Do not crowd plantings. Create open areas suggesting meadows. Build hills, low spots and grottoes. Install natural rock coral and driftwood for naturalistic effect. Use coarse white sand or natural-color aquarium gravel to simulate beaches or garden paths. Pieces of mirror or clam shells may be placed to imitate pools of water.

Miniature figurines of animals, birds and sets of Japanese houses, lanterns and bridges are available.

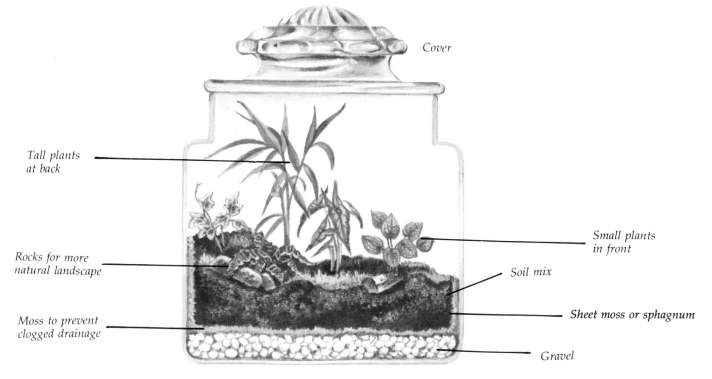

Cover

Tall plants at back

Rocks for more natural landscape

Moss to prevent clogged drainage

Small plants in front

Soil mix

Sheet moss or sphagnum

Gravel

A glass-covered aquarium used as a terrarium

Plant selection

A large variety of plants have been grown in terrariums. Some species have proven satisfactory, but a greater number have not adapted to the environment of the terrarium.

Plants selected survive under like environmental conditions and are subdivided into: 1) tall or treelike, 2) medium or shrublike, 3) low or ground cover and 4) flowering plants.

The plants are selected because of their slow growth habit. However, in the ideal environment of a terrarium they will grow and eventually crowd the container. Pruning directions are suggested under the section on "Maintenance."

Purchased plants for transplanting should not be larger than 2¼-inch pot size for small terrariums. Plants growing in nutrient blocks of peat moss are ideal. Well-rooted cuttings transplant into terrariums without difficulty.

IMPORTANT: Carefully inspect all plant material for evidence of disease and insects. If in doubt, treat with appropriate spray.

A planting mix formula is suggested in the chapter on potting soil formulas.

Drainage material

A fine grade of aquarium gravel is placed in the bottom of the container to serve as a well and to help avoid the error of overwatering.

Granulated charcoal (aquarium grade) may be added to a planting mix but is not necessary. It is recommended as an additive to mixes using garden soil as a component.

Add the planting mix and drainage material to a terrarium container, as outlined in the section on how to plant.

Plants for Terrariums

A. *Tall (treelike)*
  Variegated aglaonema—*Aglaonema commutatum maculatum*
  Parlor palm—*Chameadorea elegans*
  Dwarf umbrella plant—*Cyperus alternifolius gracilis*
  Sander's dracaena—*Dracaena sanderiana*
  Dwarf winter creeper—*Euonymus fortunei radicans gracilis (variegatus)*
  Classic myrtle—*Myrtus communis microphylla*
  Chinese podocarpus—*Podocarpus macrophyllus maki*

B. *Medium (shrublike)*
  Dwarf Japanese
  sweet flag—*Acorus gramineus pusillus*
  White-striped Japanese sweet flag—*Acorus gramineus variegatus*
  Maidenhair fern—*Adiantum cuneatum*
  Dwarf asparagus fern—*Asparagus plumosus nanus*
  Mother fern (plantlets)—*Asplenium bulbiferum*
  Dwarf natal plum—*Carissa* 'Bonsai'
  Dwarf natal plum—*Carissa grandiflora* 'Boxwood Beauty'
  Gold-dust dracaena—*Dracaena godseffiiana*
  Red-nerved fittonia—*Fittonia verschaffeltii*
  Silver-nerved fittonia—*Fittonia verschaffeltii argyroneura*
  English ivy—*Hedera helix* 'Jubilee'
  English ivy—*Hedera helix* 'Needlepoint'
  English ivy—*Hedera helix* 'Pixie'

Prayer plant—*Maranta leuconeura kerchoveana*
Spurge—*Pachysandra terminalis*
Variegated spurge—*Pachysandra terminalis variegata*
Hare's-foot fern—*Polypodium aureum undulatum*
Hedge fern—*Polystichum setiferum*
Dwarf serissa—*Serissa foetida variegata*

C. *Low (ground cover)*
  Creeping fig—*Ficus pumila (F. repens minima)*
  Gill-over-the-ground—*Nepeta hederacea variegata*
  Creeping pilea—*Pilea depressa*
  Panamiga (Friendship plant)—*Pilea involucrata*
  Dwarf club moss—*Selaginella kraussiana brownii*
  Spreading club moss—*Selaginella kraussiana*
  Creeping selaginella—*Selaginella uncinata*

D. *Flowering plants*
  Miniature eyelash begonia—*Begonia boweri*
  Dwarf begonia—*Begonia* 'China Doll'
  Dwarf begonia—*Begonia ficicola*
  Dwarf begonia—*Begonia* 'Rajah'
  Miniature gloxinia—*Sinningia pusilla*
  Miniature gloxinia—*Sinningia* 'Baby Doll'
  Miniature gloxinia—*Sinningia* 'White Sprite'
  Dwarf African violets—*Saintpaulia* (dwarf varieties, cultivars)

Cryptanthus X 'It'

How to plant

Step 1. Wash all containers aseptically clean to prevent the growth of molds and fungi. Clorox, Jeyes Fluid or a proprietary fungicide are suitable sterilizing agents.

Step 2. For a first-class job, line the inside wall of the glass with a thin layer of sheet moss to hide the planting mix. Sheet moss can be purchased from a florist or garden shop. Dyed florist moss is to be avoided.

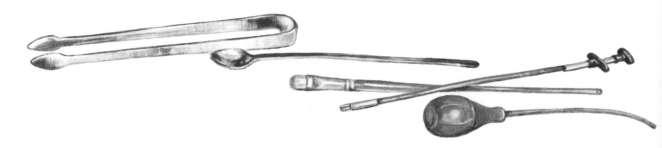

Step 3. Place drainage material in bottom and add mix according to chart. Design or lay out surface of the mix. Make hills, valleys and pathways.

Step 4. Select plants, giving thought to height and texture. Choose figurines and accessories that adapt to them.

Step 5. Dig holes with a spoon and plant as you would out of doors. Backfill each plant and pack mix with a one-half-inch wooden rod. Lightly water each plant with a syringe, wash bottle or bulb baster.

Step 6. Position accessories simultaneously with plants to complete landscape.

Step 7. When planting job is completed tamp surface to make firm.

Step 8. Cover exposed planting mix with moss, if desired. Cover some areas with gravel for paths and beach scenes. Mosses help hold moisture.

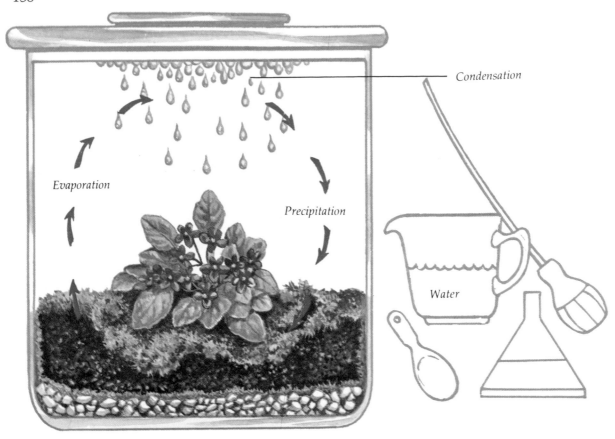

Evaporation

Precipitation

Condensation

Water

Watering and ventilation

When the right amount of water is added to a terrarium, a rain cycle is established. It is a natural thing for tiny droplets of water to form on the inside of the glass.

When the tiny droplets are no longer in evidence, additional water may be needed.

Look at the moss liner for dryness. Remove a section of moss and check the surface mix for dryness. If water is needed, add water a tablespoonful at a time until you see moisture in the gravel or on the moss.

A heavy condensation of water or fog on the inside of the glass indicates an overbalance of moisture. A drop in temperature will cause fogging of the glass. To remedy this, wipe out the excess moisture. Leave the top off overnight or longer and replace when the glass is dry.

Some manufactured containers have a built-in ventilating system that helps prevent fogging.

MAINTENANCE AND CARE

LIGHT: Bright light near a window or a table lamp is the best location. *Do not* put your terrarium in *direct sunlight*; the sun's rays can actually burn your plants.

TEMPERATURE: Generally, plants in a terrarium are tropical and will do best at 65° to 75°.

PRUNING: A program of pruning should start at planting time. The fast-growing plants such as *euonymus, fittonia* and English ivy can be soft-pinched at the growing tip. This will slow growth and encourage branching. In the ideal environment plants will grow and crowd the container. Periodically, snip off the top or side branches with sharp scissors. Cut back to just above a node or leaf joint.

DISEASES AND INSECTS: Use of clean containers, clean plants and sterilized planting mixes minimizes troubles.

Aerosol sprays recommended for insect control under the sections "Insects" and "Diseases" will take care of most problems.

Various containers used as terrariums

TERRARIUM TOOLS: Designed by the home operator, they include long-handled iced-tea spoons, stiff wire hooks (from coat hangers), funnel, wooden dowels and a long-handled artist's paintbrush. A bulb baster or a laboratory wash bottle is useful for applying water to the plants of the terrarium.

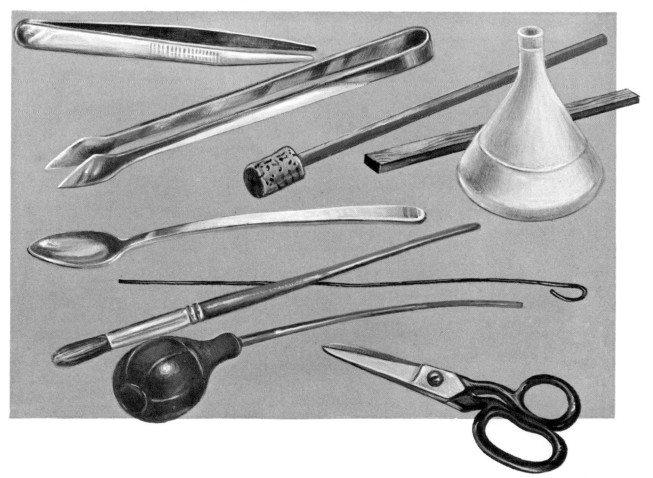

Literati

Group planting

Rock planting

Informal upright

Broom

Cascade

Upright

Slanting

M. Saito Multiple trunk

Miniatures

BONSAI

Bonsai (pronounced **bone-sigh***) is a Japanese art of growing miniature trees in small-sized containers. To achieve traditional bonsai, one combines a sense of art with a knowledge of horticulture. The ultimate goal is to produce a miniature specimen that possesses all of the characteristics of a mature specimen growing in a naturalistic setting.*

The art of bonsai originated in China and was later developed by the Japanese. Old Japanese garden books of the seventeenth and eighteenth centuries illustrate and describe bonsai. Wild trees dwarfed in nature were first used. When a supply became difficult to obtain, Japanese gardeners began to culture more readily available plant materials.

Standards and rules governing shape and design were set by Japanese horticulturists, and, through the years, guidelines for classic bonsai styles have been established.

American bonsai developed with a much freer concept of growing dwarfed plants as miniatures and the use of many tropical plants as well as some hardy varieties. Thus indoor cultivation of bonsai came about.

In comparison, the Japanese use hardy conifers and deciduous trees and shrubs; and, because of cultural requirements, the plant specimens are grown outdoors most of the year. These are brought indoors for a short period for display but returned to the outdoor environment for year-round survival.

Selection of plant material

Tropical trees, shrubs and some vines can be trained to grow as bonsai. The culture directions for growing each particular plant must be followed for successful results. The application of principles of design and culture of bonsai is essential to achieve a miniature plant. The tropical bonsai must be kept indoors unless outdoor temperatures fill the plant's requirements. In northern climates with cold winters, plants will benefit from outdoor culture on the patio in summer.

Some characteristics to look for in choosing plant material for training are: 1) small leaved, 2) short internodes (distance between leaves), 3) attractive bark, 4) stoutness of main stalk, 5) a habit of branching for good twig formation, and 6) all parts of plant in scale.

For a beginning, purchase healthy young plants from a two-and-a-half-inch to a four-inch pot size. Larger potted specimen plants may be used if desired. Check to see that the plant has a healthy root system and is free from insects and disease.

Choose a basic style

Decide on the final shape you wish to create before you start. Use one of the styles illustrated. Work with a single trunk as your basic design. This is simplest and best for a beginning.

The five basic styles are: 1) formal upright, 2) informal upright, 3) slanting, 4) cascade and 5) semicascade. These are determined by the over-all shape of the tree and the

Good tools make work easier

*The art of bonsai employs
the choice of a compatible container*

direction or angle the trunk slants away from the main axis.

The formal upright style is the basis for all bonsai forms. It is easiest to develop because it avoids the necessity for wiring and bending. In this form the tree has an erect leader with horizontal branches. There should be a lower branch extending farther out from the trunk than the others. Two of the lowest branches should come forward to the front side, with one set higher than the other. There should be a single branch at the back, extending between the two forward branches, to give the tree depth. Trim off small branches too close to the trunk or presenting clutter at the base.

Pot up specimen of formal upright style in an oval or rectangular container, placing the plant about a third of the distance from one end.

The informal upright style is similar to the formal upright style but with the top bending toward the front. This gives an illusion of motion and displays more informality. Glance down on the tree from above. If the angle is not correct, the tree may be lifted and the root ball reset to provide the correct angle. Trim branches to give proper balance.

Select an oval or rectangular container and place the plant a third of the distance from the end.

The slanting style places the trunk at a more acute angle than does either of the previous styles. The lowest branch should spread in the direction opposite to which the trunk slants, with the top bending forward slightly. Lower branches arranged in groups of three should start at a distance of one third of the way up the trunk. Slanting trees have the look of trees in nature which have been bent by prevailing winds. Prune out small branches to display distinctive placement of groups of branches.

Plant this style in the center of a round or square container.

The cascade style is representative of a natural tree grown over a cliff edge or down an embankment. Plant in a container a branch or branches with most of the foliage hanging below the surface of the soil. This style should be displayed on the edge of a table or on a shelf.

This type takes longer to train than do the others. Train so that an uppermost branch is vertical and the remainder extends forward and downward. A round or hexagonal and deep container is used for this style.

The semicascade style has a main trunk that extends away from the container and drops downward but not below the pot, as does the cascade style. Most of the branches are trained toward the front, with the shorter branches left closer to the trunk. This style looks best planted in a low hexagonal or round container that is shallower than the pot used for the cascade style.

Other style variations according to size, how planted, number of trees, number of trunks, root system, etc, are: *Miniature bonsai (under six inches); rock planting; twin planting; literati; driftwood; broom style; group planting (forest); multiple trunk; windswept; sinuous.*

Containers for bonsai

The style of the bonsai plant usually determines the pot. This is the first consideration and must be decided on. Generally containers come in round, oval, hexagonal, square and rectangular shapes; shapes usually come in sets of three sizes. The color of the container should harmonize with the color of the foliage, mostly earthy colors of dark brown, dark red, dark purple, gray and black. Evergreen conifers are usually grown in dull white or brown containers; colorful fruit or flowering plants in green, tan or white. Having better moisture retention, glazed containers are best for indoor bonsai.

The container should be just large enough to accommodate the root system after careful pruning has been done.

Training

When planting your bonsai, keep in mind your chosen theme and how it will look in the container. Like people, plants have a "best profile." Decide which is the front of the tree and then shape it. Branches should look balanced and exhibit a floating habit. Branches should not crisscross. Look down from above to make sure an upper branch does not overshadow a lower branch. Next in procedure is the basic and timely operation of pruning, nipping or pinching and wiring. For this procedure basic tools are needed: a pair of hook-and-blade pruning shears, a narrow garden trowel, blunt sticks (dowels), a pair of sturdy wire cutters and copper wire of various sizes, as well as a small watering can.

Pruning to control growth, to remove dead-wood, to remove crisscrossed branches and excess foliage is accomplished first. Prune to encourage branches to grow toward open space. Do not do all of the pruning at one time. Do it as undesirable shoots develop.

Nipping or pinching is a continuous process with tropical bonsai plants. Pinch back new growth or thin out before it becomes too thick.

Wiring is the final step. Copper wire is used because it is flexible. No. 8, the heaviest, is used for the main trunk, while No. 16, the smallest, is used for soft branches. Start wiring from the lowest point and work upward. Anchor the wire by pushing end into soil. Wire loosely. After limbs to be bent are wired, bend by hand to the desired angle or direction. Wires may have to remain in place for a year before removal.

Potting and repotting

Fast-growing trees like weeping fig, citrus or hibiscus will need repotting and root pruning at least twice a year; slower-growing types like classic myrtle and jade plant only once a year. The plant should be carefully removed from its container and an inch or more of surface soil of the ball removed. Loosened roots are trimmed back to the ball of soil. Thin out thick root masses. Heavy roots supporting top branching should be saved to establish a balance of physiological relationship.

Potting media and fertilizer recommendations coincide with those for potted house plants. Soilless mixtures are good bonsai mixes. Fertilizer is necessary to maintain the good health of the plants. It is recommended that a feeding of water-soluble type be applied during the active growth months of spring and summer. Feed once a month at half strength. Omit feeding for the month following a repotting operation. An application of slow-release type fertilizer in spring and fall is ample.

Watering, as with all cultural directions, is even more critical with bonsai than other house plants. Most tropical bonsai will require daily watering, depending on house temperature and exposure to light. When outdoors in summer on the patio, watering twice a day may be necessary. The succulent types like jade plant will need less frequent waterings. Bonsai-trained tropicals in small, shallow containers are naturally going to take more water than other house plants.

Cascade

Semicascade

Semicascade

Formal upright

Slanting

TROPICAL PLANTS FOR TRAINING

Acacia—*Acacia baileyana*

Aralia—*Polyscias balfouriana*
   Polyscias fruticosa
   Polyscias guilfoylei

Birds-eye Bush—*Ochna multiflora*

Camellia—*Camellia japonica*
   Camellia sasanqua

Cape Jasmine—*Gardenia jasminoides radicans*
   Gardenia jasminoides

Cherry, Surinam—*Eugenia uniflora*

Citrus (Calamondin, Kumquat, Lemon,
 Lime, Orange and Tangerine)—*Citrus* species

Cypress, Arizona—*Cupressus arizonica*

Cypress, Monterey—*Cupressus macrocarpa*

Fig, Mistletoe—*Ficus diversifolia*

Herb, Elfin—*Cuphea hyssopifolia*

Hibiscus—*Hibiscus rosa-sinensis cooperi*

Holly, Miniature—*Malpighia coccigera*

Jacaranda—*Jacaranda acutifolia*

Jade Plant—*Crassula* species

Jasmine—*Jasminum parkeri*

Jasmine, Orange—*Murraya exotica*

Jasmine, Star—*Trachelospermum jasminoides*

Laurel, Indian—*Ficus retusa*

Myrtle, Classic—*Myrtus communis*

Oak, Cork—*Quercus suber*

Oak, Indoor—*Nicodemia diversifolia*

Oak, Silk—*Grevillea robusta*

Olive, Common—*Olea europaea*

Orchid Tree—*Bauhinia variegata*

Pepper Tree, Brazilian—*Schinus terebinthifolius*

Pepper Tree, California—*Schinus molle*

Pink Shower—*Cassia grandis*

Pistachio, Chinese—*Pistachio chinensis*

Plum, Natal—*Carissa grandiflora*

Poinciana, Royal—*Delonix regia*

Pomegranate, Dwarf—*Punica granatum nana*

Popinac, White—*Leucaena glauca*

Powderpuff Tree—*Calliandra surinamensis*

Sago Palm—*Cycas revoluta*

Serissa—*Serissa foetida*

Shower Tree—*Cassia eremophila*

Weeping Fig—*Ficus benjamina*

RAPID-GROWING TROPICAL TREES

Brazilian Pepper—*Schinus terebinthifolius*

Jacaranda—*Jacaranda acutifolia*

Kafir Plum—*Harpephyllum caffrum*

Pink Shower—*Cassia grandis*

Powderpuff Tree—*Calliandra surinamensis*

Weeping Fig—*Ficus benjamina*

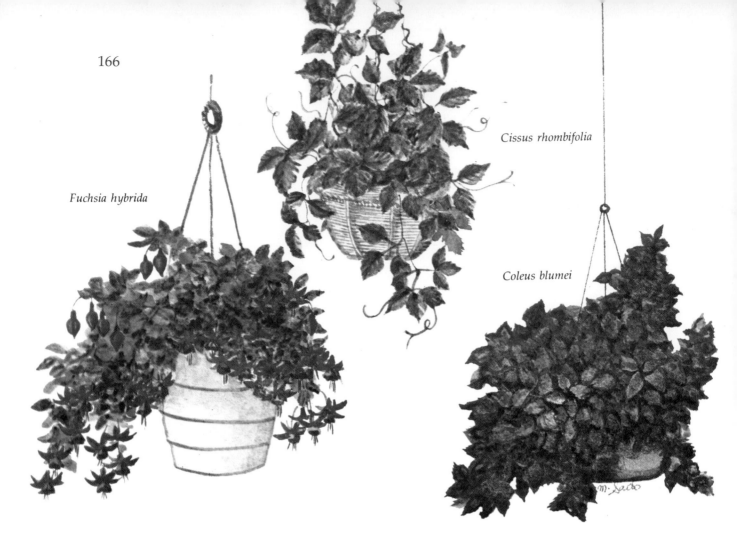

Fuchsia hybrida

Cissus rhombifolia

Coleus blumei

HANGING BASKETS

Many plants have a trailing or climbing habit of growth that is difficult to control when a container rests on a table or even on a bench in a greenhouse. In recent years the renewed interest in cultivating plants in hanging containers has solved this problem.

Lists of plants now include species that have never before been tried as hanging plants. Flowering annuals, perennials, foliage, herbs and even vegetables are used now. How convenient to have a hanging basket of ripe tomatoes within reach from your kitchen window!

The selection of plants for containers may be based on personal preference, yet there are plants which, because of growth character and ease of handling, make better specimens than others for hanging baskets.

Containers

How does one select? Any type of hanging basket will do. However, the weight of the basket, its size, color and proper provision for watering and drainage should be considered. A basket of open-weave construction is desirable because it is light in weight and durable. This kind may be lined with black plastic, burlap fiber or long-fibered sphagnum moss. Wire baskets can be lined with the same materials. Similarly, in the lightweight classification are containers made of plastic and styrofoam. Color also is a consideration. Green, tan or white are attractive with plants bearing brightly colored flowers or fruit. Brown, gray or terra cotta look best with most foliage plants.

Watering

To take care of the watering/drainage/drip problem, it is practical and efficient to move the container to the kitchen sink for a copious watering. Add water until it flows freely from the drainage hole at the bottom. Sau-

*Begonia tuberhybrida
pendula flore pleno*

*Nephrolepis
exaltata bostoniensis*

*Bougainvillea
glabra*

cers clamped or permanently fastened to the bottom serve to catch drip only after watering, not irrigation water. A cork plug may be inserted into the drainage hole to stop after-drip. Plants left at the sink overnight will have ceased all dripping by the next morning. Baskets that are lined with a porous material such as sphagnum moss are best irrigated by submersion in a pail of water. When air bubbles cease at the surface, the container may be lifted for draining.

Supports for containers

Various methods for hanging containers are provided by link chain, nylon cord and an arrangement of uniquely designed fiber knotted into a harnesslike support known as macramé. Macramé may be used to give support to clay pots that can be lifted out easily for a watering. Wire pot hangers used by orchid growers simply clamp onto the rims of clay pots and serve as convenient hangers for plants on the patio.

Other culture

The same rules for culture of potted plants apply to hanging plants. Flowering plants and cacti can take advantage of sunlight if hung from a window casing. Care must be given to foliage thus exposed by moving out of direct sun in spring and summer.

Bougainvillea, not ordinarily grown in the house, will survive in a sunny window and usually rewards its owner with brightly colored flower bracts. Pruning or cutting back long shoots of bougainvillea in summer will control growth for hanging-basket culture. Other rank-growing vines will need cutting back and pinching to control growth and promote bushiness. Three plants set together will provide a quick display in a container of full dimension. Potting mixes recommended are suitable for hanging plants as well as potted specimens.

When plants are watered they should be inspected for insect pests and, if these are found, treated as recommended in the chapters on insects and diseases (pages 200–203).

PATIO PLANTING

Most house plants are benefited by a "vacation" outdoors on the patio in summer. The outdoor environment offers optimum light, cooler night temperatures and fresh air, which results in healthier, more normal-looking plants by autumn.

Cultural needs of plants growing outdoors become more critical than for inside growing. To maintain healthier, attractive plants requires more attention to watering, fertilizing and insect and disease control.

Containers

When house plants are moved outside they should be set into beds of peat moss or sunk into oversized containers that are decorative or are designed to enhance the architecture of the building or patio structure.

Placing the potted plant within a larger tub or container of peat moss prevents the plant from being toppled over by wind or stray animals. Less frequent watering is accomplished by this arrangement.

A "pot-within-a-pot" method for patio culture is described in "Pots and Potting," page 184.

Tubs are generally made of redwood, cypress or cedar. Some are fashioned from fiber glass. All tubs should have a drainage hole from three-fourths to one inch in diameter. Tubs must stand on feet or cleats to facilitate drainage of water. The size and height of the plant should determine the shape of the container. For example, a square tub may be used for an azalea and a taller or round tub for palms or podocarpus.

Watering

More water will be needed when plants are outside because of the bright light or direct sun and the warmer temperatures of midsummer. Air movement also contributes to drying out. A simple way to water is to wait until the surface of the potting medium becomes slightly dry. Then add water until it comes out at the base of the container. Never let the potting mixture become so dry that it pulls away from the sides of the container. When heavy rains have created a moist situation, watering is needed less frequently.

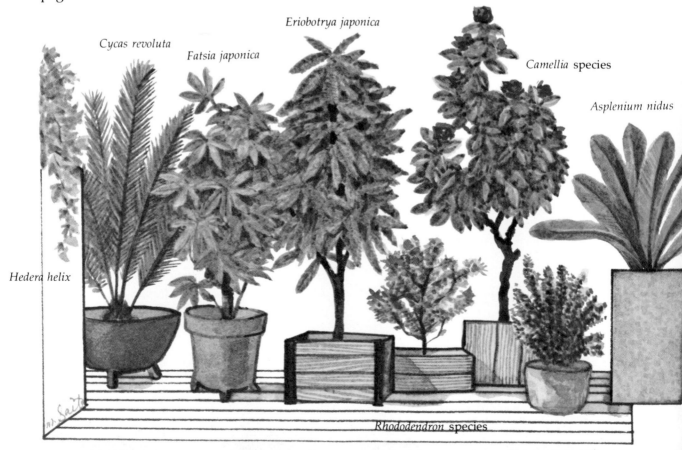

Hedera helix

Cycas revoluta

Fatsia japonica

Eriobotrya japonica

Camellia species

Asplenium nidus

Rhododendron species

Buxus sempervirens

Fertilizer

Apply a complete type of fertilizer one month after repotting. Subsequent feedings with a water-soluble fertilizer solution each month while outside are beneficial. If a slow-release type of fertilizer is used, only one application will be necessary.

Repotting

The time when plants are moved to an outdoor patio is a good time to repot or move to a larger container.

Conditioning

Caution is advised regarding the moving of tender plants outside. Do not move plants until the danger of freezing temperatures (32° or lower) is past. Tender plants that have been growing in low-light intensity should be exposed gradually to brighter outdoor light conditions. Brown blotches will appear on foliage if exposed to direct sun. Place the plants in the shade of the roof, under a tree, or provide lath shade to pre-vent such damage. Most house plants will survive very well without direct sunlight, but flowering species like the geranium, petunia and *Begonia semperflorens* do better in some sunshine.

A few plants for patio growing (to be moved inside for the winter):

Azalea (florists' type)—*Rhododendron* species
Camellia—*Camellia* species
Citrus—*Citrus* species
Coleus—*Coleus blumei* cultivars
Common (English) Boxwood—*Buxus semper-virens*
Fuchsia—*Fuchsia hybrida*
Geranium (zonal)—*Pelargonium X hortorum*
Ivy—*Hedera helix*
Japanese Fatsia—*Fatsia japonica*
Japanese Pittosporum—*Pittosporum tobira*
Japanese Privet—*Ligustrum japonicum*
Loquat—*Eriobotrya japonica*
Petunia—*Petunia hybrida*
Sago Palm—*Cycas revoluta*
Tuberous-rooted Begonia—*Begonia tuberhybrida*
Vinca Vine—*Vinca major variegata*
Wax Begonia—*Begonia semperflorens* and hybrids

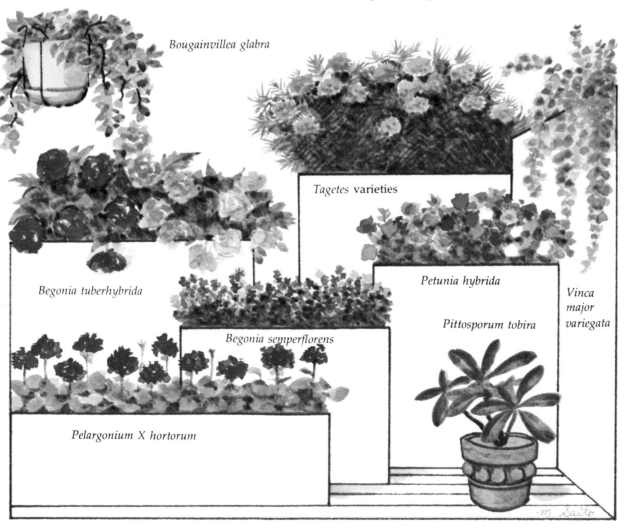

Bougainvillea glabra

Tagetes varieties

Begonia tuberhybrida

Begonia semperflorens

Petunia hybrida

Vinca major variegata

Pittosporum tobira

Pelargonium X hortorum

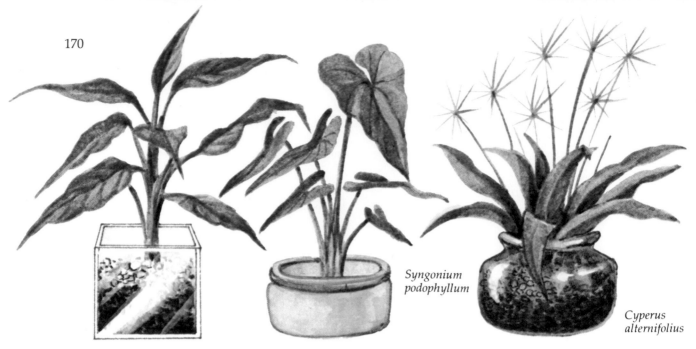

Aglaonema
modestum

Syngonium
podophyllum

Cyperus
alternifolius

PLANTS IN WATER

An old-fashioned yet practical method of starting plants in a tumbler of water or a bottle is still in use today.

A sophisticated and interesting development of this practice is "miniature water gardens" or "bottle gardening."

Any plant that roots easily in water may be cultured and adapted to a landscaped, attractive-looking water garden. Many plants have embryonic root systems at each node on the stem. When separated from the parent plant and placed in water, they develop roots in a short time.

Plants started in water survive better when transplanted to a water garden than do those transplanted from soil.

Planting media

Washed gravel, coarse sand, sea shells (washed) or pearl chips (as used in aquariums) will serve as support to the rooted plants. Charcoal granules purchased from a pet shop and added to the medium will keep the water "sweet-smelling."

Plant food

A water-soluble fertilizer diluted to one-fourth the strength indicated on the package will serve as needed nutrition.

How to plant

Step 1. Choose the container and wash it with soap and water to discourage the growth of bacteria.

Step 2. Place a small quantity of support material in the bottom of the container; add one or two tablespoons of charcoal. Arrange the gravel so that it supports the plants.

Step 3. Prepare fertilizer water in a separate vessel and add to half the depth of the gravel base. Maintaining a shallow amount of solution allows for the oxygen supply necessary for rooting and for healthy plant growth.

Step 4. Install landscape features such as figurines, pieces of driftwood, bridges, rocks and other objects of interest.

Maintenance and care

Experience will teach you how often to add clear water to maintain the proper water level.

Change the water-fertilizer solution once a month to help prevent salinity problems and the growth of algae.

Take the container of plants to the kitchen sink, tip and drain, holding your opened hand as a screen for the gravel base.

Plants for Miniature Water Gardens

Arrowhead Plant—*Syngonium podophyllum*
Chinese Evergreen—*Aglaonema modestum*
Coleus—*Coleus blumei*
Corn Plant—*Dracaena fragrans massangeana*
Croton—*Codiaeum variegatum pictum*
Devil's Ivy—*Epipremnum aureum*
Dumb Cane—*Dieffenbachia picta*
Dwarf Umbrella Plant—*Cyperus alternifolius gracilis*
English Ivy—*Hedera helix* varieties
Hurricane or Swiss-Cheese Plant—*Monstera deliciosa*, seedlings
Jade Plant—*Crassula argentea*
Japanese Sweet Flag—*Acorus gramineus*
Malaysian Dracaena—*Pleomele reflexa*
Moses-in-the-Cradle—*Rhoeo spathacea*
Painted Drop Tongue—*Aglaonema crispum*
Parlor Ivy—*Philodendron scandens* subsp. *oxycardium*
Sander's Dracaena—*Dracaena sanderiana*
Silver Evergreen—*Aglaonema commutatum maculatum*
Spathe Flower—*Spathiphyllum 'Clevelandii'*
Swedish Ivy—*Plectranthus australis*
Ti Plant—*Cordyline terminalis*
Umbrella Plant—*Cyperus alternifolius*
Variegated Screw-Pine—*Pandanus veitchii*
Variegated Wandering Jew—*Tradescantia fluminensis variegata*
Wandering Jew—*Zebrina pendula*

Tradescantia fluminensis variegata

Senecio mikanioides

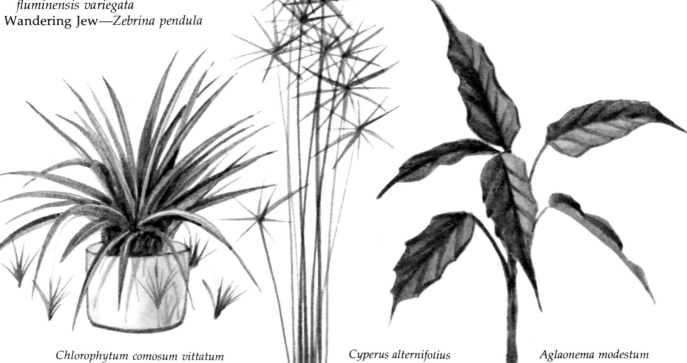

Chlorophytum comosum vittatum   *Cyperus alternifolius*   *Aglaonema modestum*

HOW TO GROW HOUSE PLANTS

The use of plants in the home or the landscape dates back to Egyptian times. Trees were grown in large containers carved from rock. One of the earliest reports of nursery practices dates back to 3,500 years ago when frankincense trees were transplanted in containers from the Somali coast, to be grown in the gardens of Europe.

Today, tropical plants large and small from the jungles near the equator are cultured and conditioned by nursery men for growth in our homes and offices. They are adaptable to living-room temperatures of 65° to 85° Fahrenheit. Some plants prefer 55° to 70°, as in the cool lobby or entryway.

Flowering plants and cacti prefer sunny locations and can be grown on the sun porch or window sill, while others, such as palms and ferns, prefer the low light areas of a room corner. Plants like *cyperus* and *spathiphyllum* find a pool in a solarium duplicates their native habitat along the banks of a tropical stream.

Light

There are three major environmental factors that limit the growth and well-being of plants: light, temperature and moisture. The foremost of these is light.

The importance of adequate light cannot be overemphasized for growing indoor plants. A plant's survival depends on available water and nutrients, proper temperature and energy. House plants derive energy from some source of light. That light is the most critical of the house plant's needs. Sun is the dominating natural source of light, yet many of our foliage plants that come from our shaded jungle habitats will survive in the dimly lit interiors of our homes and public buildings. When light is transmitted to the leaf of a plant it energizes the chloroplasts which in turn convert to chemical energy. In the process energy is used to combine carbon dioxide from the air with water in the cells to form carbohydrates (starches and sugars) and oxygen. This is the food manufacturing process called photosynthesis. The carbohydrates produced are translocated throughout the plant to grow leaves, stems and roots.

Where light is very poor or nonexistent there would be no photosynthesis, no production of carbohydrates and consequently no growth, and eventually the plant dies.

Hence, there are three important light factors that affect the survival of plants: 1) *intensity*, 2) *quality* and 3) *duration*.

Intensity

Intensity is the controlling factor of food manufacturing; with more light, more food is produced. Many of our foliage house plants, being natives of our tropical rain forests, are injured (sunburned) when placed in full sun. Thus, it is necessary to know the light requirements of your plants. Adequate light is often available near windows. Where a natural light source is not enough, it must be supplemented with artificial light or the plant must be grown in artificial light alone.

The intensity of light is measured in several ways. Horticulturists measure indoor light in terms of footcandles. A footcandle is

General Electric Model 214

a unit of illumination on a surface that is one foot from a uniform point source of light of one candle and equal to one lumen per square foot. It can be measured with a direct reading meter such as General Electric model 214. The new type 214 pocket light meter has three scales: 10 to 50, 50-250 and 200-1000 footcandles. Scale selection is made by a three-position switch located on the side of the meter. Readings from 20 to 50 fc and from 100 to 250 fc are accurate within plus or minus 10 percent; all other readings within plus or minus 15 percent. The new pocket model is color and cosine corrected. Meter is available through General Electric lamp distributors and lamp sales offices.

Light intensity readings are taken at the plant level. When light intensity is known one can increase or decrease the lighting to meet a plant's requirements.

Quality

The quality of light is the second important factor. This is measured in millimicrons or angstrom units (10 angstrom units = 1 millimicron). Growth response in plants is due primarily to red and blue wavelengths of light. Incandescent bulbs produce a larger proportion of red light spectrum while fluorescent lights produce predominantly blue. These factors are important when growing plants under artificial light alone. Most plants will flower under fluorescent lighting using cool white or a combination of cool white and warm white. Horticultural tubes are in use which supply both red and blue in a wide spectrum. For maintenance of foliage, cool white light gives the highest intensity that is beneficial.

Duration

Duration of light is a measurement of the total number of footcandles of light received. This is the product of the intensity reading of footcandles times the number of hours light strikes the plant. The longer the time the plant receives light, the more food is produced. When plants are grown in low light areas they should be lighted for longer periods to counteract low light intensity.

Most plants will maintain fairly well with twelve to fourteen hours daily of artificial light intensity in footcandle requirements of a species.

A portable light cart for starting and growing plants

174

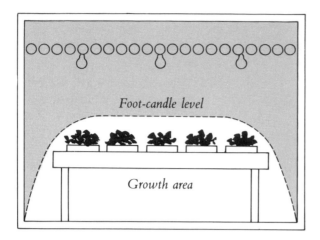

With lamps mounted crosswise over bench, footcandle level drops off at ends, where light is absorbed by walls.

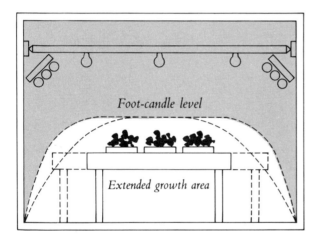

With lamps mounted lengthwise over bench, light falls off at ends. Extra rows of lamps near the walls provide more uniform lighting and increased growing area.

Supplemental plant lighting

Additional light is often desirable and necessary to bring the light requirements up to the preferred footcandle reading. This can be supplied from either fluorescent fixtures of various design or incandescent sources. Other introductions of light may be scheduled. A plant on an end table receiving light from a large window can be rotated a quarter turn a month or at each watering.

REFERENCE: Plant Growth Lighting: Bulletin TP 127 General Electric Co.

This maintains well-developed leaves on all sides. Plants moved from low to high light areas and vice versa will benefit likewise. Plants may be left for a month without harm, then exchanged to their former location. Plants can be moved to a table or floor lamp for supplementary evening lighting. Incandescent floods or reflector spots may be installed for supplementary lighting. Distance from plants is considered because of heating effects. A 150-watt flood lamp is placed not less than four feet from the plant. A 150-watt spotlight must be at least eight feet from the foliage.

Light levels for house plants

The following list of light levels is expressed as readings in footcandles and as approximate light source locations in a building. Light references listed under culture of individual species are corresponding terms of **low, medium, high** and **very high.**

150-watt floodlamp placed at least four feet from foliage

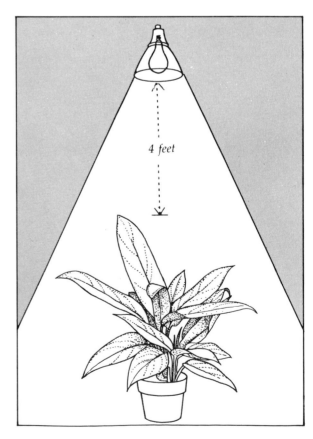

4 feet

Low—A minimum light level of 25 foot-candles and a preferred level of 75-200 footcandles (locations more than eight feet from large windows with no direct light).

Medium—A minimum of 75-100 footcandles and a preferred level of 200-500 footcandles (an average well-lighted area four to eight feet from large window).

High—A minimum of 200 footcandles and a preferred level of 500 footcandles (areas within four feet of a large window facing south, east or west).

Very high—A minimum of 1,000 footcandles and a preferred level of over 1,000 footcandles (on or at a sunny window sill facing south).

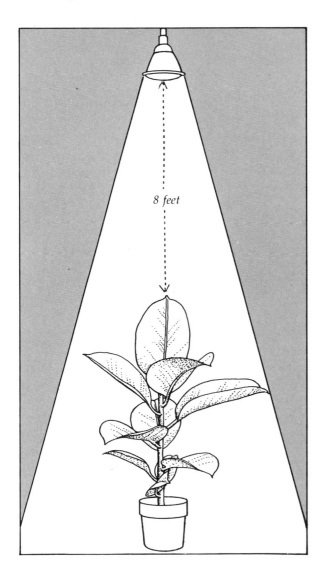

Temperature

Tropical plants, because of their geographical locations, are thought by some to require high temperatures. Many of our best house plants grow at high altitudes and thrive best with cooler minimum temperatures of 45° to 50° F., while plants growing in lower elevations grow best at 75° to 85°.

Desert plants accustomed to hot, bright days thrive best with cooler nights. When the physiology of the plant is understood, we realize that the cooler temperatures of our living quarters are beneficial for plants. Cool nights are needed for the translocation of manufactured sugars from the leaves to the roots and other growing parts.

It is a practice of commercial growers to set the night temperature of their greenhouses to run 10° Fahrenheit lower than day temperature.

In most situations, the temperatures cannot be changed and the plants must be happy with existing temperatures. In general, we find there are two ranges of temperature in our interior environments, **cool** and **warm**.

Warm we define as 75° Fahrenheit, with variations from 60° to 85°. These conditions are found in our homes and offices.

Cool we define as 60° Fahrenheit, with variations from 50° to 70°. Such conditions are found in lobbies and enclosed sun porches.

For the purpose of general reference and classification of the plant's requirements in this book, we will indicate the temperatures as follows:

Warm: day, 70° to 85° Fahrenheit
        night, 60° to 65°

Cool: day, 60° to 70° Fahrenheit
        night, 50° to 55°

Degrees Fahrenheit to degrees Celsius (Centigrade) conversion factor: $(°F. - 32) \times 5/9 = °C$.

150-watt spotlamp placed at least eight feet from foliage

WATERING HOUSE PLANTS

Overwatering is the greatest cause of plant problems. Many plants are lost because of overwatering. A plant's roots require air as well as water. Saturated soils exclude oxygen, causing the roots to rot. The plant is no longer able to take up nourishment.

Underwatering or drying out of the plant can be almost as serious. It is easier to detect this problem, because the leaves wilt readily. When the soil becomes too dry, the roots are injured and can no longer take up water. This occurs because the nutrient level becomes concentrated or too high and a burning effect upon the roots takes place. Free water must always be present to keep the nutrients dissolved for uptake by the plant.

It is not easy to decide how much to water or how often. Some plants like palms and ferns must never dry out, while peperomias and wax plants require a drier soil. Plants like *cyperus* and *acorus* need a constantly wet soil. It can be safely stated that all plants need moisture of varying degrees.

The moisture requirements also depend on the soil mixture, the porosity of the pot, the temperature of the room and the kind and amount of light it receives.

For a practical solution and for the purpose of classification of a plant's need for water in the text, the following terms will be used:

Wet indicates plants will probably need water every other day. These plants must have a constant supply of water in the growing medium at all times. One occasion of drying out usually means damage to the leaves. Example of plants needing wet soil are *cyperus* and *acorus.*

Moist indicates plants probably need watering every three to six days. Example: palms and ferns. These kinds of plants have a fine root system that is severely injured if the soil dries out. The surface soil should not become dry between waterings.

Dry indicates plants probably need watering every eight to fourteen days. These kinds of plants have coarse roots which are adapted to dry conditions. As a result they grow slower, thus delaying the development of plant parts. The surface soil layer should always feel dry before watering. Examples are peperomia, *hoya,* cacti and succulents.

The finger test

An old rule of thumb that has withstood the test of time is: *Water when the surface of the soil feels dry to the touch*. If you have any doubt, go a little further and dig into the top a half inch. If it is dry, by all means apply water. Consider your plant's moisture requirements. Is it in the **wet**, **moist** or **dry** group? If in doubt, let it go another day. Another factor to remember is that modern soilless potting mixes are designed to drain well in a short time, allowing air to come in and yet retaining enough moisture to support plant growth.

Close observation and some note-keeping will help. Mark the calendar and put on a measured amount. A little record-keeping will in time reveal how often and how much. Experience is still the best teacher. Many home gardeners find that most of their plants need water once a week. When a regular frequency is established, most plants will acclimate to it. Above all, when you water fill the pot to the rim.

The type of container will affect the matter of watering. Containers with drainage holes at the bottom are watered until the excess water drains out and away. If a saucer is provided, this drainage water is discarded because few plants can sit in water continuously. Containers without drainage holes must have a layer of gravel in the bottom to collect excess water. To check these containers lay them on their sides in a sink so the excess can run out.

Many plants die as a result of a wet, soggy potting soil condition.

PLANTS FOR INTERIOR DECORATION

Most homeowners or apartment dwellers are pleased to have a plant growing indoors; it is a challenge to select a specific plant that can contribute to the decorative scheme of the room. The chart on the next two pages lists many plants suitable for decorating the home or office. You will find on these lists the common name of the plants, their scientific names, and the sizes of the mature plants, as well as the water and light requirements of each listing. This will assist in the selection of useful plants that will add interest, color, and charm to your home.

Small or table plants are suitable for placement on a table, chest or windowsill. Many of these smaller plants are adaptable to use in terrariums, dish gardens and hanging baskets. Table or desk plants are available in four-inch to eight-inch pot sizes. These are often used singly but can be set into a planter box to simulate a planted-out effect.

Floor plants are those plants available from two to six feet tall. They are used as individual specimens or in planter groups.

Tall plants are designated as tree plants. Some grow with a single trunk and may be grouped in a container to produce a multiple stemmed specimen. Tree plants are available from a minimum of four feet to a maximum of ceiling height. Tall plants may need to be air-layered or trimmed to maintain desired heights.

Sleek modern rooms with bold severe spaces call for plants that are dramatic. Specimen plants of tree or floor size can be used as living sculpture silhouetted against a wall.

Table-sized plants should be used singly or in groups to make an interesting arrangement. These groupings may be flowering plants, green plants, ferns or cacti. Just one beautiful begonia, orchid or bromeliad may be startling in its simplicity. Use table plants in place of, or in combination with other small accents such as books, figurines and porcelains to liven up the decor. An occasional change of plants, particularly those that are in flower, gives an added sparkle to any room.

In conventional or traditional settings, plants should be used as accessories rather than as features. Study the period of the room and select and arrange the plants in the spirit of the room. Palms, Java fig and rubber plant provide form and bulk which are often useful in dramatic groupings or room dividers. Corn plant, dragon tree, hurricane plant or Norfolk Island pine are used as floor plants and provide colorful accents.

PLANTS FOR INTERIOR LANDSCAPING

Common Name	Botanical Name	Mature Size	Light Level	Water Requirement
African Violet	*Saintpaulia* species	table plant	high	moist
Aglaonema	*Aglaonema* 'White Rajah'	table plant	low	moist
Asparagus Fern	*Asparagus densiflorus sprengeri*	table plant	medium	moist
Bamboo Palm	*Chamaedorea erumpens*	tree, floor, table plant	low	moist
Begonias	*Begonia* species and hybrids	table plant	high	moist
Belmore Palm	*Howea belmoreana*	tree, floor plant	low	moist
Boston Fern	*Nephrolepis exaltata bostoniensis*	table plant	medium	moist
Bromeliads (many species)		table plant	medium	moist
Calamondin Orange	*Citrus mitis*	table plant	high	dry
Cast-Iron Plant	*Aspidistra elatior*	table, floor plant	low	dry
Chinese Evergreen	*Aglaonema commutatum*	table plant	low	moist
Coleus	*Coleus blumei*	table plant	very high	moist
Corn Plant	*Dracaena fragrans massangeana*	floor, table plant	low	wet
Devil's Ivy	*Epipremnum aureum (Pothos aureus)*	table plant	medium	dry
Dragon Tree	*Dracaena marginata*	tree, floor plant	medium	wet
Dumb Cane	*Dieffenbachia amoena*	floor, table plant	medium	moist
Dumb Cane	*Dieffenbachia exotica*	table plant	medium	moist
Dwarf Date Palm	*Phoenix roebelenii*	floor, table plant	medium	wet
English Ivy	*Hedera helix*	table plant	medium	moist
False Aralia	*Dizygotheca elegantissima*	floor, table plant	high	moist
Fiddle-leaf Fig	*Ficus lyrata*	tree, floor plant	medium	moist
Flame Violet	*Episcia cupreata*	table plant	very high	wet
Geranium	*Pelargonium* hybrids and cultivars	table plant	very high	dry
Gloxinia	*Sinningia* species and cultivars	table plant	very high	wet

Grape Ivy	*Cissus rhombifolia*	table plant	medium	moist
Green Dracaena	*Dracaena deremensis*	floor, table plant	medium	wet
Green Pleomele	*Pleomele reflexa*	floor plant	medium	wet
Hurricane Plant	*Monstera deliciosa*	floor plant	high	moist
India Laurel	*Ficus microcarpa (retusa nitida)*	tree	medium	moist
Jade Plant	*Crassula argentea*	table plant	very high	dry
Japanese Loquat	*Eriobotrya japonica*	tree	very high	moist
Kangaroo Vine	*Cissus antarctica*	table plant	high	moist
Lady Palm	*Rhapis excelsa*	tree, floor plant	medium	wet
Mock Orange	*Pittosporum tobira*	floor, table plant	high	dry
Norfolk Island Pine	*Araucaria heterophylla*	tree, floor table plant	high	moist
Orchids (many species)		table plant	very high	moist/dry
Parlor Palm	*Chamaedorea elegans*	floor, table plant	low	moist
Impatiens	*Impatiens wallerana*	table plant	medium	moist
Peperomia	*Peperomia caperata*	table plant	medium	dry
Peuter Plant	*Aglaonema roebelinii*	table plant	low	moist
Philodendron, Common	*Philodendron scandens* **subsp.** *oxycardium*	table plant	low	dry
Philodendron, Self-heading	*Philodendron* hybrids	floor, table plant	medium	moist
Philodendron	*Philodendron selloum*	floor plant	low	dry
Podocarpus	*Podocarpus macrophyllus maki*	tree, floor, table plant	high	moist
Prayer Plant	*Maranta leuconeura kerchoveana*	table plant	medium	moist
Rubber Plant	*Ficus elastica decora*	tree, floor, table plant	medium	moist
Umbrella Plant	*Schefflera actinophylla*	tree, floor, table plant	high	dry
Wax Plant	*Hoya carnosa*	table plant	medium	dry
Weeping Java Fig	*Ficus benjamina exotica*	tree	medium	moist
White Flag	*Spathiphyllum 'Mauna Loa'*	table plant	medium	moist
White-striped Dracaena	*Dracaena deremensis warneckei*	table plant	medium	dry

The temperature requirements of plants listed are generally those of room temperature: 60° to 75° Fahrenheit at night and 65° to 85° during the day. Any differences are cited in the comments on individual plants. Temperatures of up to 10° lower than the limits set here are tolerated for short periods.

POTTING-SOIL FORMULAS

FORMULA A

For those plants that need a growing medium with high moisture-retention characteristics. Plants having a fine root system are included in this group. Recommended for the following plants and others of similar culture: African violet; *aglaonema; aphelandra; begonia; cyperus; dracaena;* fern; *ficus;* helxine; palm; *spathiphyllum; tolmiea.*

Material

Sphagnum peat moss ....two parts
Vermiculite or soil ....one part
Perlite or sand ....one part

Fertilizer ingredients
for four quarts of mix*

Garden fertilizer ....two teaspoons
    (5-10-5, or 6-12-6, or 10-10-10)
Superphosphate ....two teaspoons
Ground limestone ....three teaspoons

*Four quarts equal two six-inch standard-size pots. All ingredients are measured in level teaspoonfuls.

FORMULA B

For general potting. For plants that require good drainage and aeration but must not dry out completely between watering. Use for the following plants and for others with similar requirements: *Achimenes; aeschynanthus; cordyline; columnea; dieffenbachia; episcia; hoya; monstera; nephthytis; philodendron; pandanus; peperomia.*

Material

Sphagnum peat moss ....one part
Vermiculite or soil ....one part
Perlite or sand ....one part

Fertilizer ingredients
for four quarts of mix

Garden fertilizer ....two teaspoons
    (5-10-5, or 6-12-6, or 10-10-10)
Superphosphate ....two teaspoons
Ground limestone ....three teaspoons

FORMULA C

For desertlike plants and some succulent plants with a root system that will withstand periods of dryness between watering. Plants having coarse tubers or rhizomatous roots are in this category. Following are recommended and others with similar culture requirements: *Aloe; astrophytum;* bromeliads; *cereus; crassula; gasteria; kalanchoe; lithops; mammillaria; opuntia; sedum; sempervivum.*

Material

Sphagnum peat moss ....two parts
Perlite (coarse) ....one part
Sand (coarse) ....one part

Fertilizer ingredients
for four quarts of mix

Garden fertilizer ....two teaspoons
    (5-10-5, or 6-12-6, or 10-10-10)
*Superphosphate ....two teaspoons
Ground limestone ....three teaspoons

*When mixing for cactus, use two teaspoons of bone meal instead of superphosphate.

FORMULA D

For seed sowing.

Material

Sphagnum peat moss ....one part
(screened with a one-fourth-inch mesh sieve)
Vermiculite ....one part

Fertilizer ingredients
for four quarts of mix

Ammonium nitrate...........one teaspoon
Superphosphate ....two teaspoons
Ground limestone ....three teaspoons

Alternatively, one can use some of the wide range of proprietary potting soils or seed-sowing mixes. In Britain the John Innes potting and seed-growing composts can be recommended, or any of the all-peat formulations.

Soilless mixtures are recommended for house plants. Garden soil formerly used in potting mixtures for plant growing is becoming scarce. Its composition varies with each source, and it usually needs sterilization to get rid of weed seeds, disease and insects.

Soilless mixes can be purchased from garden stores and plant shops. The mixes come in packages of assorted sizes and are packed in polyethylene (polythene) bags for convenient storage. They are mixed with nutrients, ready for use. Some are formulated for foliage plants, for African violets, for cacti, for other plants and for seed sowing.

Hints for home mixing:
1. *Peat moss should be moistened two to three days before mixing.*
2. *Peat moss and other ingredients should be thoroughly mixed together.*
3. *Fertilizer nutrients should be carefully measured and mixed together.*
4. *All materials should be spread on a clean surface and turned with a scoop shovel. The pile should be turned at least five times to ensure thorough mixing.*
5. *Mixes may be stored for future use in polyethylene bags or plastic trash cans with covers.*

Fertilizer Quantities for Large Amounts of Mixes

Material	*For one bushel*	*For one cubic yard*
Ammonium nitrate	3 tablespoons	2 pounds
Garden fertilizer (5-10-5, or 6-12-6, or 10-10-10)	6 tablespoons	5 pounds
Superphosphate (0-20-0)	2 tablespoons	2 pounds
Ground limestone	10 tablespoons	10 pounds
Bone meal	2 tablespoons	5 pounds
*Potassium nitrate (13-0-44)	2½ tablespoons	1 pound
or		
*Calcium nitrate (15.5-0-0)	2½ tablespoons	1½ pounds
*Fritted trace elements	½ teaspoon	2 ounces

Add these fertilizer ingredients to soilless mixes (without soil) in addition to garden fertilizers, superphosphate and ground limestone. Dolemite limestone, containing magnesium, is preferred to ground limestone if available. Use at the same rate.

METRIC SYSTEM CONVERSION GUIDE

Dry material weight
1 ounce (avoirdupois) = 28.4 grams (gm)
1 pound (lb) = 453.6 grams

Volume
1 bushel (bu) = 1.24 cubic feet = 35.2 liters
1 cubic yard = 27.5 bushels = 765 liters

Capacity
1 dry quart = 0.908 liters

Length
1 inch = 2.54 centimeters (cm)
1 foot = 0.31 meters (m)

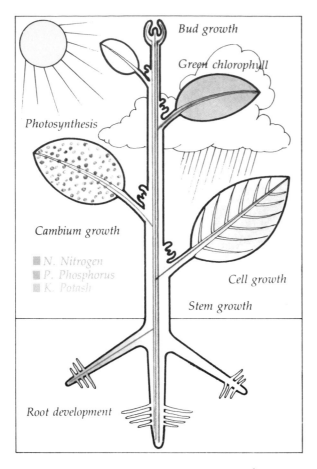

The role of plant food for the growing plant

Labels in figure:
Bud growth
Green chlorophyll
Photosynthesis
Cambium growth
■ N. Nitrogen
■ P. Phosphorus
■ K. Potash
Cell growth
Stem growth
Root development

FERTILIZERS

"N.P.K." stands for the *major* plant nutrients used by growing plants. "N" is for nitrogen, which makes green color and growth. "P" is for phosphorus, which gives the plant sturdy growth, and "K" is for potash, which furnishes energy for over-all plant development.

There are also *minor* elements, numbering about fifteen in all. These include chemicals like iron, magnesium, boron, zinc, etc.

A package of fertilizer marked 5-10-5 expresses the percentage of each of the major elements, i.e., 5 percent nitrogen, 10 percent phosphorus and 5 percent potash.

Minor elements are usually included in most fertilizer formulas and may not be indicated by chemical names or percentages.

Water-soluble forms of plant food are the most common and convenient to use for house plants, such as a 20-20-20 formula. They are sold as a powder, liquid or in tablet form. It is important to follow the manufacturer's directions for mixing. But apply only at one half the rate recommended.

Dry-granular garden type, such as a 5-10-5, 6-12-6 or 10-10-10.

Controlled-release fertilizer such as Osmocote (14-14-14 or 18-9-9), MagAmp (7-40-6) or Peters (14-7-7) are favored by commercial plant growers, and some brands are now available in consumer-size packages. These formulas are designed so that one application will last from four to ten months, depending on formulation.

Water-soluble type: Potted plants growing in soilless potting mixes need more frequent applications than plants growing in potting mixtures containing soil. The design of soilless mixes affords better drainage and aeration, requiring more frequent watering, which results in faster leaching or loss of nutrients.

Artificially lighted plants may be fertilized once a month with a *water-soluble fertilizer;* plants under normal indoor light conditions, every two months. These are general recommendations. For individual plant recommendation, refer to culture.

Dry-granular type: Apply once every four months regardless of light conditions. Use at the following rates of application:

A scant one third teaspoon per four-inch pot

One level teaspoon per six-inch pot

One level tablespoon per eight-inch pot

Controlled-release type: Read the recommendations on the package before using. Where light intensity is high or a greenhouse is used for growing, it may be necessary to supplement with a water-soluble type.

A fertilizer is not a cure-all for plant trouble or a substitute for problems of water or light. An overdose of fertilizer or an application too often will damage or kill your plant.

If in doubt—DON'T FERTILIZE.

PRUNING, TRAINING AND CLEANING

Pruning: Prune, trim, pinch—any way to accomplish the desirable shape for your plant. Judiciously exercising one of these techniques gives your plant the characteristics which are typical of its variety.

Pruning will remedy stretching for light, promote branching and provide cuttings for starting more plants.

Prune to remove large sections if necessary, to maintain shape and desirable height. Prune to remove dead branches and diseased parts. Most plants produce new growth by being cut back to six or eight inches from the soil to get rid of legginess.

Plants not prunable are single-stem palms; cluster-type palms are pruned by removing tallest shoots from the base of the plant, if necessary.

Pinch to remove the very tip of the shoot. This will control height and induce branching. Pinch the tips with the fingernails or with scissors. Pinch just above a leaf joint or node. Start when plants are young, not over six inches tall, and pinch regularly as growth progresses.

Plants that branch naturally, such as African violet, Boston fern, gloxinia and watermelon peperomia, require no pinching. Aluminum plant, geranium, coleus, fuchsia and tuberous begonia are pinched occasionally because they will grow into a single stem without a pinch.

Disbudding of side buds on flowering plants increases the size of the main flower buds. This technique is used to produce show material for exhibitions. Tuberous begonia responds well to this practice. Pinch out the buds as soon as they are large enough to handle.

Disbranching, like disbudding or pinching, removes side branches of flowering plants like geranium and fuchsia. It is used to train plants to a single trunk or tree specimen. These are called "standards." An example illustrated in this book is classic myrtle. Plants are started from cuttings and allowed to grow until they reach the desired height. The trunk is formed by a periodic removal of side branches.

Training plants is another technique used for climbing plants and for developing shapes. Philodendron, ivy, *scindapsus, hoya,* passion vine and others need support or special treatment to display their normal growth habits. The support should be inconspicuous and of such design as maintains the plant in its natural shape. Some of the materials used are cork bark, driftwood and tree fern, which are suitable for foliage types like philodendron. Trellises made of wire, steel rods or green vinyl-covered fencing are used for climbing vines and bulbous plants like the glory lily.

Shape plants by rotating from time to time. Plants will grow to be one-sided if light falls on one side of a plant continuously. Start practice when plants are small.

Cleaning: Good housekeeping means dust-free, insect-free and even disease-free plants. Cleaning plants removes the dust. Pick up dead leaves, check for insects, trim off diseased leaves or stems to produce healthy plants.

Wash foliage: Don't use milk, olive oil or liquid wax for cleaning foliage. These substances leave an oily deposit on the leaf which then collects dust and, if used on the under side, may clog the breathing pores.

Use a sink spray or bathtub shower with warm water. In summer take outdoors and use the garden hose and a fine-nozzle spray, or let the rain bathe the plant.

A generally safe recommendation is to use a few drops of a dishwashing detergent in warm water with a soft sponge to remove the dust. Holding a leaf in hand and carefully sponging the under side of the leaf helps control red spider mites.

184

When to repot

In winter, house plants slow down in growth and appear to be dormant. This is due to the reduction in light intensity and the shorter days. Because of these conditions, spring and early summer, when growth is resumed, are times to repot.

Plants growing under artificial lights for twelve to sixteen hours a day are in a condition of active growth and may be repotted when needed.

A plant should be repotted to a larger-size pot when its roots form a close mesh surrounding the ball of potting mix. This is referred to as a pot-bound condition.

A plant also may be repotted when it appears unhealthy. Repotting is done to replace the potting mix to improve drainage and aeration.

Shifting seedlings from small pots to the next larger size will assure continuation of growth.

How to repot

STEP 1. To remove the plant, place your fingers on the soil surface, grasp the pot with the other hand, turn to inverted position and jolt the rim against the edge of a workbench until the plant slips free of the pot.
STEP 2. Remove a thin layer of surface soil at top of ball. Loosen roots at bottom and break away drainage material. If roots are excessively coiled, trim away about one third of roots at bottom. When roots are heavily meshed on the sides of the ball, lightly cut vertically by shallow slashes in three places with a sharp knife. This will encourage branching of roots which will grow into the fresh media.
STEP 3. The pot size chosen should permit one-half inch or more space between the ball and the inside wall of the pot. The larger the pot the more space for potting mix. If a large amount of mix is removed, you can repot in the same size or smaller pot, although normally you would shift to the next larger size.

When new clay pots are used, soak in water for a day or so before use.

For pots with a drainage hole, place a few pieces of broken crock over the hole, starting with the six-inch size. A crock for smaller pots is not needed. If there is no drainage hole, follow the procedure of building a well as discussed on page 187.
STEP 4. Accomplish the repotting job by back-filling with the mix, tamping with a potting stick to prevent air-pockets.

Set the plant low enough so that the finished surface is lower than the rim of the pot in order to hold ample water.

Surface space for water:

Pot size	Depth of space
3-inch	¼ inch
4-inch	½ inch
5-, 6-, 7-inch	¾ inch
8-inch	1¼ inch
9-, 10-, 12-inch	1½ inch

A clay pot may be installed inside a larger decorator-type container. A well to catch excess drainage water is constructed in the bottom of the larger container. The depth of the drainage material is determined by the location of the pot rim at the top. It should set just below the rim of the larger container. The space between the walls of the two containers is filled with peat or sphagnum moss.

Water is applied to the moss and seeps through the clay pot to give the plant a constant supply of water, but a limited amount which will restrain the growth of the plant.

Choosing pot size: The question is—"Do I use a shallow pot, a three-quarter size or a standard-size pot?" Clay pots are made in shallow pans, used for small bulbs and creeping plants; three-quarter size for bulbs, ferns, etc.; and the standard size for general potting. A pot's size is designated as the diameter of its top rim.

The character of the root system determines the depth of the pot used. Where roots run to the bottom of the ball, it is evident that a standard-size pot is required. If the roots are few and congregate in the upper soil mass, use a shallow container.

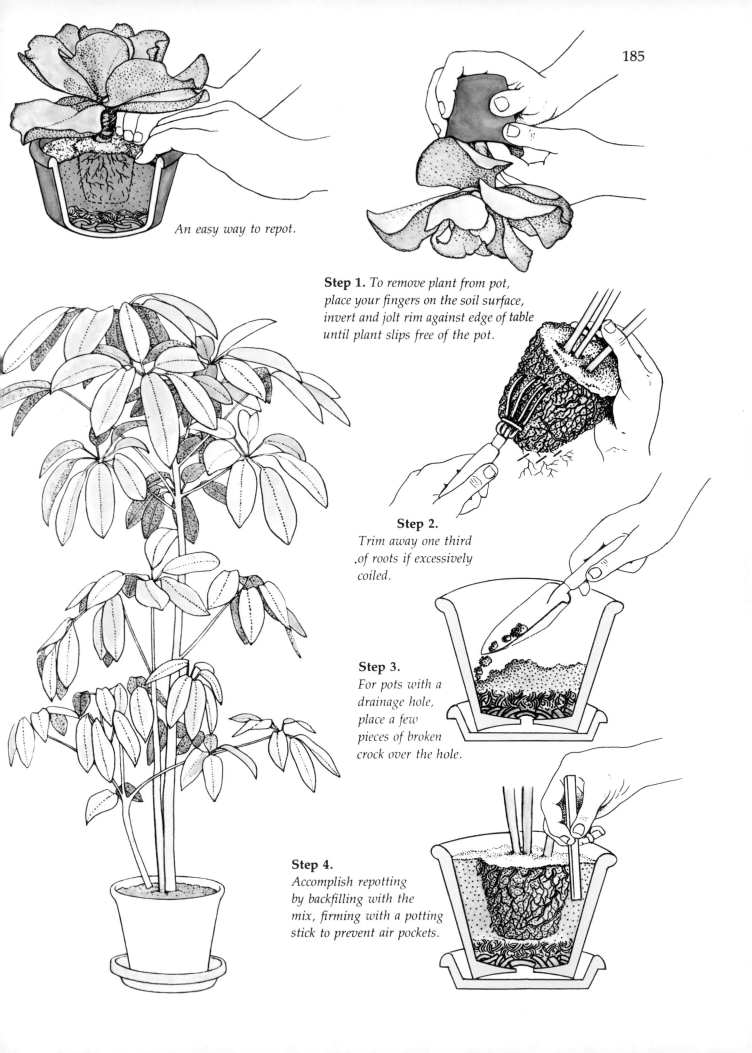

An easy way to repot.

Step 1. *To remove plant from pot, place your fingers on the soil surface, invert and jolt rim against edge of table until plant slips free of the pot.*

Step 2. *Trim away one third of roots if excessively coiled.*

Step 3. *For pots with a drainage hole, place a few pieces of broken crock over the hole.*

Step 4. *Accomplish repotting by backfilling with the mix, firming with a potting stick to prevent air pockets.*

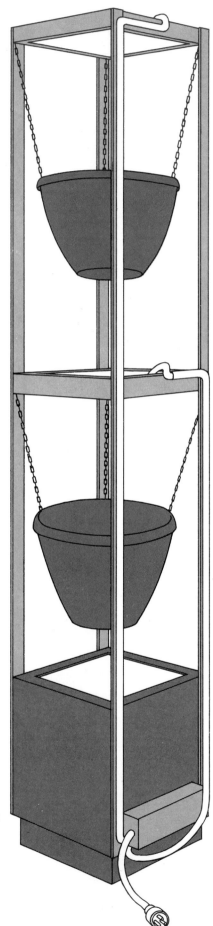

*A light rack
for hanging baskets*

POTS

Kinds of pots

Clay pots, plastic pots, ceramic containers, polystyrene and glass vessels provide receptacles for growing house plants.

Clay pots come in sizes ranging from a thimble to fourteen inches in diameter, or even larger if you don't mind the cost. Clay pots are preferred by many because the porosity of the clay allows air to move in and out.

Plastic is popular because the plants do not dry out so rapidly, thus cutting down on the need to water frequently. When a well-drained and aerated mix is used, plants do as well in plastic as in clay.

Saucers made of plastic or rubber are placed under pots to catch runoff of water.

Driftwood for growing epiphytic type and other plants

Creative designs of plant containers vary in form, color, texture and basic material. For interiors, select a type best suited to your decor.

Ceramic, polystyrene and fiberglass containers usually are without drainage holes. A ''well'' must be constructed to receive the drainage water. To do this, put one-half inch or more gravel (the larger the pot, the more gravel needed) in the bottom. Cover the gravel with a layer of long-fibered sphag-num moss to prevent filtration of the potting mix. The mix should be placed on top of this.

Other growing structures: Tree-fern slab and cork bark are practical supports for orchids, bromeliads and epiphytic ferns. These plants are tied to the supports, using a cushion of sphagnum moss for moisture.

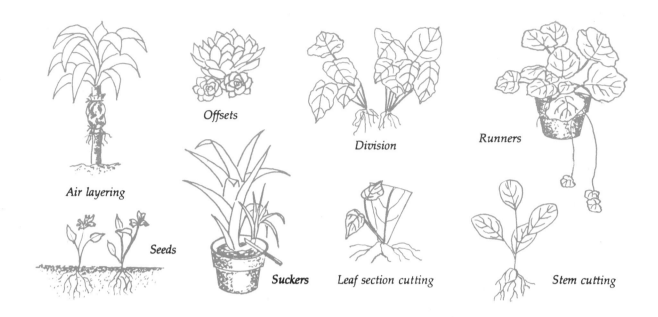

Air layering

Offsets

Division

Runners

Seeds

Suckers

Leaf section cutting

Stem cutting

STARTING NEW PLANTS

Methods of Propagation

Starting of new plants from older plants is called propagation. In many species new plants are started from seed. Seed, however, is not always viable, and since seed plants do not always resemble their parents, it is desirable to propagate by other means—namely, cuttings. Other methods also used for starting house plants include division, runners and suckers, air layering and a more skillful operation, grafting and budding.

Cuttings are selected from healthy plants free from insects, disease and nutritional problems. Plants in flower are generally not used because blossoming may inhibit rooting. The best time to take cuttings is spring and summer. Take cuttings from plants growing under artificial lights at any time of the year.

Rooting media: Choose a medium that will provide good drainage and aeration with good water-holding capacity. For general use a good grade of sand will serve well. Excellent media are perlite, a volcanic ash, and vermiculite, an expanded mica, sold under the name of Terralite.

Propagation structures: A clay or plastic pot or tray made of styrofoam or plastic that will hold about three inches of medium is suitable. Enclosing the container within a polyethylene bag will prevent loss of moisture and facilitate watering care. The cover may be removed in a week or left on until cuttings are rooted.

Planting and watering: When cuttings are prepared, stick two to three inches deep into the rooting medium and press firmly. Water well and keep moist but not saturated. The main problem is to keep the cuttings from wilting.

Chemical aids: Chemicals known as growth regulators or rooting hormones are used to hasten the rooting of hard-to-root plants. Cuttings from plants such as English ivy, *acuba* and citrus will root better if so treated. Softwood cuttings of coleus, geranium, begonia and others should not be treated. Great care should be used to follow the directions of the manufacturer.

Care after rooting: When roots have formed one-fourth to one inch long, the cutting is ready for potting. After potting ample water is needed to keep the plant from wilting.

Terminal cuttings

Consists of terminal growing point of the stem with one or more nodes below. Sectional cuttings use a portion of the stem with two or more nodes without the terminal growing point. Examples: coleus, ivy, peperomia, philodendron and begonia. Make a cutting three to six inches long, using a sharp knife. Cut through the stem below a node or leaf joint. Trim off one or two leaves from the bottom of the cutting and insert in the rooting medium. The more leaves left on the top portion, the more surface for food manufacture.

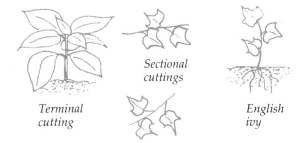

Sectional cuttings

Terminal cutting

English ivy

Leaf cuttings

Consists of one leaf only, used for propagating rex begonia, *sedum* and *sansevieria.*

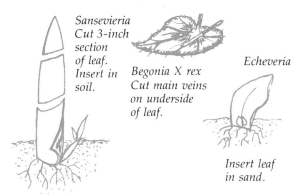

Sansevieria Cut 3-inch section of leaf. Insert in soil.

Begonia X rex Cut main veins on underside of leaf.

Echeveria

Insert leaf in sand.

Leaf-petiole cuttings

Use a stem with leaf attached for starting plants of tuberous-rooted begonias, gloxinia, peperomia and African violet.

Peperomia root in soil

African violet root in water

Leaf-bud cuttings

Consists of a piece of stem and one or more nodes for propagation of English ivy, wax plant, *nephthytis,* philodendron, German ivy and *cissus* vine.

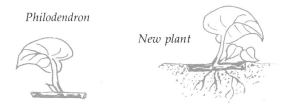

Philodendron

New plant

Leaf sectioning

Leaf sectioning is a method used mainly to start new plants from large-leaved fibrous begonias and peperomias

Select large, healthy, mature leaves, not the oldest ones. Cut off a leaf from a plant and remove the stalk or petiole. Make pie-shaped pieces of the leaf. With a sharp knife cut from the main center vein, but between the radiating leaf veins, to the outer edge of the leaf. Sections of leaf root best if a piece of a large vein remains attached to the pointed end of the pie-shaped section.

Insert the sections to a depth of half an inch (pointed end down) into the potting medium. Place at 45° angle and give support by positioning a wooden plant label at the back side. This will help excess moisture to drain from leaf and prevent the leaf section from collapsing on the moist medium.

A new plantlet will develop at the base of the cutting when two or three leaves have formed. Pot and cut away the old leaf, which is no longer needed.

Begonia X rex leaf

Plant in moist atmosphere.

Cut wedge-shaped leaf sections with part of the large vein.

Sand or peat

190

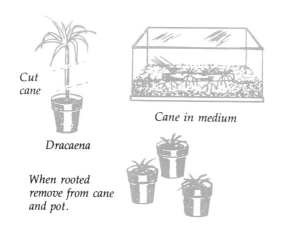

Cut cane

Dracaena

Cane in medium

When rooted remove from cane and pot.

Cane cuttings

A method of cutting leafless stems or canes of tall, leggy plants like dracaenas, *dieffenbachia* and *cordyline* into four- to six-inch stem sections for rooting. Cut canes and dry overnight to callus the ends. The next day place them on a propagation medium horizontally and cover to keep moist. Buds or "eyes" on the canes will sprout in one to two months, producing roots. The cane may be planted upright or cuttings removed and planted to develop into plants with their own roots.

Fern

Cut or gently pull apart rootstalk or rhizome.

Division

Division is the separation of the crown of the plant into one or more growing points. To accomplish this, remove the plant from the pot and cut through the root stalk or rhizome of the plant. It is advisable to leave more than one growing point to a plant. Pot and water thoroughly. Kinds which are started by division are cast-iron plant, *Cyperus*, piggyback, spider plant, fern and others.

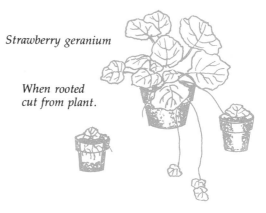

Strawberry geranium

When rooted cut from plant.

Runners

Runners are vinelike cords originating from the base of the main plant. These cords or stems usually have nodes with the ability to root and produce a new plant. The strawberry geranium, *episcia* and Boston fern are some of the house plants that have runners producing plantlets. These plantlets can be cut off and potted like a cutting or rooted in a pot of mix alongside the parent plant while attached. When rooted, it is cut from the parent plant and shifted to a larger pot when needed.

Hen and chickens

Twist or slightly pull offset, then pot.

Offsets

Offsets are similar to runners, but, instead of the new plants occurring on vinelike stems, they are produced close to the base of the parent plant. Hen-and-chickens of the rock garden is an example. Century plant, aloes and screw-pine are some house plants that make offsets that are used for starting new plants. A twist or slight pull removes offsets, which then become new plants when potted.

Suckers

Suckers are secondary growth that originates from ground level or below, from adventitious roots or underground rhizomes. As an example, bromeliads produce these growths which can be cut or broken off, then potted to grow as normal plants. Staghorn fern produces suckerlike growths alongside and close to basal female fronds.

Sucker growth should be of a good size, with some mature leaves or stems, when it is separated from the parent plant. It is likewise desirable to have a few roots in evidence at the base of the section.

Bromeliad

Cut or break off sucker at base of plant.

Root in peat moss, then pot.

Bulbs

There are two kinds. One type is like the hardy bulbs of narcissus and tulips, with thick layers wrapped around the bud; the other is like the Easter lily, with separate overlapping scales. Most bulbs produce tiny bulblets between scales or layers that eventually form new or offset bulbs. A method of using separated scales is also used. Most plant people purchase new bulbs, like the amaryllis, and grow them year after year rather than take the time and patience required for propagation, which is a slow process. Bulbous plants are also raised from seed.

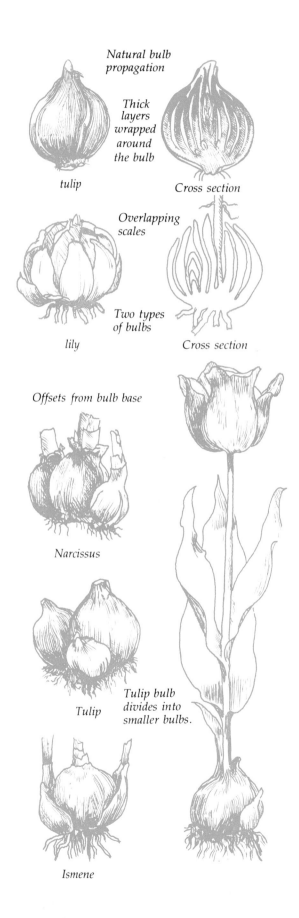

Natural bulb propagation

Thick layers wrapped around the bulb

tulip

Cross section

Overlapping scales

Two types of bulbs

lily

Cross section

Offsets from bulb base

Narcissus

Tulip

Tulip bulb divides into smaller bulbs.

Ismene

Tubers

Tubers are underground roots or stems, cylindrical, oblong or rounded in shape, made up of fleshy or woody tissue. Stem tubers may bear several tiny scalelike leaves with buds or eyes capable of sprouting new plants; root tubers have buds at the crown or upper end only, where they are attached to the stem. Stored food in the tuber supports a new plant until it grows feeding roots. The potato is a common example of a stem tuber, the dahlia of a root tuber. Many house plants grow from tubers. *Caladium* can be divided by cutting the tuber into sections, each containing a bud or eye. Cut when new shoot growth occurs, which is usually in late winter or early spring. Large-sized sections make the largest plants. Cut surfaces of tubers are dried overnight and dusted with ferbam or sulfur before being potted. Glory lily is best repotted after the foliage dies down and old and new tubers are sorted out by detaching at the stem ends. New tubers showing a growing tip are best for starting. Tuberous begonias are propagated by cutting the tubers into sections at the time new shoot growth becomes apparent. Gloxinia and *rechsteineria* are started by the same method as tuberous begonia.

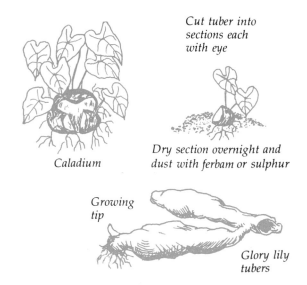

Cut tuber into
sections each
with eye

Caladium

Dry section overnight and
dust with ferbam or sulphur

Growing
tip

Glory lily
tubers

Tubers with
growing tip are best
for starting new plant.

Separate old
from new end tubers.

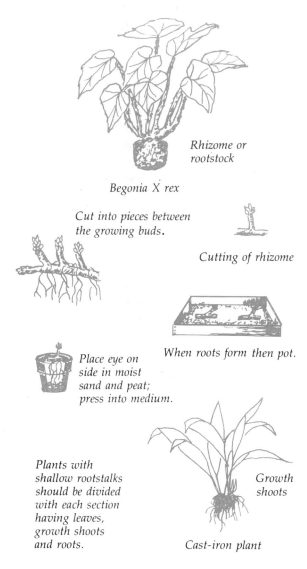

Rhizome or
rootstock

Begonia X rex

Cut into pieces between
the growing buds.

Cutting of rhizome

Place eye on
side in moist
sand and peat;
press into medium.

When roots form then pot.

Plants with
shallow rootstalks
should be divided
with each section
having leaves,
growth shoots
and roots.

Growth
shoots

Cast-iron plant

Rhizomes and propagules

A rhizome or rootstock is a thickened underground stem but is sometimes found on the surface; it consists of buds or eyes which produce shoots and grow roots to take up food. Some rhizomes are large and robust like those of Rex begonia. Others are small and scaly like those of *Achimenes*. In *Achimenes* these are sometimes found as structures in the axils of leaves; since they do not appear underground they do not fit the definition of the term *rhizome*. Instead scientists use the word *propagule*—a term used for any unspecified unit of propagation.

Methods of propagation

Germination of seeds or bulblets which are attached to the plant is one of nature's ways of starting new plants in the survival pattern. Small plants take shape and grow while attached to the parent plant. Succulents like *kalanchoe* produce plantlets along the margins of leaves. Piggyback plantlets are produced on top of the leaf blade at the petiole or stem. *Cyperus* produces plants in the axils of the leaf whorl. Small plants of *kalanchoe* are easily removed and transplanted to pots, many with roots already started. The piggyback is started from a leaf and petiole inserted in the propagation medium so that the base of the leaf is close to the medium. Roots are produced at the base of the leaf to nourish the new plantlet. When potted the old leaf is trimmed away.

Ferns are reproduced by viviparous propagation. *Asplenium viviparum, A. bulbiferum,* *Polystichum setiferum (angulare), P. aculeatum, Woodwardia radicans, W. orientalis,* commonly known as mother ferns, are capable of producing bulblets from which small plants arise. The small fern plants are found growing on the upper side of a frond, usually at the axil of the leaflet (pinnae) and rachis (stalk). To start these plantlets on their own a frond is hooked onto the surface of a tray or pot of sand and peat moss. When roots are well developed, remove to individual pots. A method used by the author is to remove the plantlet to a Jiffy 7 peat pellet. These are placed in a polyethylene bag or a glass enclosure in which humid atmosphere is maintained. In a glass case provision for a crack of air and occasional spray with an atomizer is beneficial. Growth is rapid and plantlets are ready to be transplanted to pots in about six to eight weeks. Lighting with fluorescent lights of 800 to 1,000 footcandles for 14 to 16 hours greatly accelerates growth.

Piggyback plant

Viviparous propagation

Mother fern

Tray of sand and peat

Plant in "Jiffy 7" peat pellet.

Leaf and a petiole inserted in medium

When rooted, cut old leaf away and pot.

Place peat pellets in polythene bag until well rooted.

Good-luck plant

Miracle leaf

Transplant to pots.

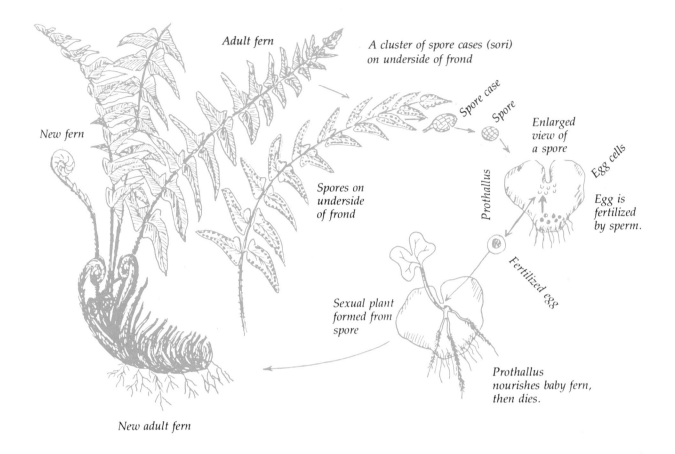

Adult fern

A cluster of spore cases (sori) on underside of frond

Spore case

Spore

New fern

Enlarged view of a spore

Egg cells

Prothallus

Egg is fertilized by sperm.

Spores on underside of frond

Fertilized egg

Sexual plant formed from spore

Prothallus nourishes baby fern, then dies.

New adult fern

Spores

Spores cause sexual reproduction in ferns. Seeds are developed by flowering plants, but ferns, mosses, lichens, fungi, algae and mushrooms depend on a microscopic organ called a spore for starting new plants. On the under side of fern fronds are found groups of orange or brown dots or lines called spore cases, which hold spores. When a spore drops into an environment of water, warm temperature, nutrients and air it grows into a small flat greenish heart-shaped plantlike structure with hairlike roots. About a year is needed for it to develop into a mature fern capable of producing spores of its own. However, this is the first of two cycles in its life cycle. This plantlike organ is called a prothallus and it bears reproductive organs on its lower surface. In the presence of a drop of moisture, male and female organs mate and the germ cell develops into the second stage, a true

fern plant. For a while the fern plant is nourished by the prothallus, which eventually dies, leaving the fern to grow as an independent plant.

Fern spores are easily collected from the under side of a frond. Careful observation with a hand lens will reveal the time when spore cases split open. When this occurs, remove the frond from the plant and place on white paper to dry. In a day or two the paper will be covered with millions of spores. For further drying and storage, place in a paper envelope and sow any time after two weeks. Early spring is excellent for sowing spores.

Several methods of sowing have been used. The important factor is sterilization of media and other utensils used. Some gardeners with access to laboratory facilities attain success using agar medium. Others use the inverted clay pot in a tray of water. Some

METHODS OF SOWING SPORES

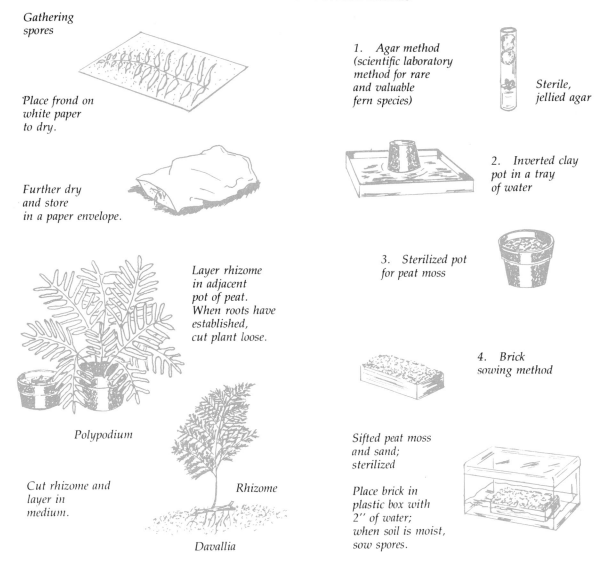

Gathering spores

Place frond on white paper to dry.

Further dry and store in a paper envelope.

Layer rhizome in adjacent pot of peat. When roots have established, cut plant loose.

Polypodium

Cut rhizome and layer in medium.

Rhizome

Davallia

1. Agar method (scientific laboratory method for rare and valuable fern species)

Sterile, jellied agar

2. Inverted clay pot in a tray of water

3. Sterilized pot for peat moss

4. Brick sowing method

Sifted peat moss and sand; sterilized

Place brick in plastic box with 2″ of water; when soil is moist, sow spores.

sow on a sterilized pot of peat moss. A brick method is described by Arno and Irene Nehrling in their book *Propagating House Plants*. A building brick is spread on its upper surface with a layer of sifted peat moss and sand, then sterilized in an oven at 250° F. for half an hour. Place the brick in a container such as an oblong plastic food box with two inches of water added. When the sand and peat mix is moist, sow the spores on the surface. Replace cover and shade from direct light. When spores germinate and prothallia appear crack the lid to admit air and remove the shade. If fluorescent lights are available, adjust to 300 footcandles for a 16-hour period. Advance intensity to 800 or 1,000 footcandles as growth progresses. When plants are large enough to handle transplant to small, then to larger pots.

Other methods of fern propagation

Davallia and *Polypodium* are propagated by spores, but a faster process is by layering the rhizomes in adjacent pots of peat or sphagnum moss. Fasten rhizome with hairpins or tie to a ball of sphagnum moss. When roots are firmly established plant can be cut loose. Another way is by cutting rhizomes into pieces two to three inches long and laying in a propagating medium.

Air layering

A method of propagation used for hard-to-root or large-foliage plant varieties like rubber plants.

Select vigorously growing healthy shoots from pencil size up to shoots one half inch in diameter.

Remove leaves and twigs three to four inches above and below the cut to be made. The location of the cut is usually 12 to 15 inches below the top of the stem.

Two methods of making the cut are illustrated. Either one will produce satisfactory results.

(1) Make two cuts through the bark, completely encircling the twig, about one inch apart. Remove the bark between the cuts to expose the wood. Be sure the cambium, a light-green area beneath the bark, is completely removed to prevent new bark from forming.

(2) For this method, make a long slanting cut upward, about halfway through the stem. Keep the incision open by inserting a small chip of wood to prevent cambium layer of the stock from healing.

After making the cuts, enclose the exposed areas with a ball of moist sphagnum moss. Soak and squeeze the excess moisture from the ball of moss before applying to the cut. Wrap moss snugly around the twig and enclose with aluminum foil or a square of polyethylene. Tie top and bottom to prevent loss of moisture.

After roots have formed in several weeks, depending on the variety, cut just below the ball of roots and transplant to a pot. Leave moss attached but make sure moss is moist before potting. Enclose entire plant in a polyethylene bag for a week or so to insure survival.

A chemical rooting hormone has been found beneficial in hastening the rooting process for hard-to-root varieties. Only a light dusting of hormone powder need be applied to the cut surfaces.

The sphagnum ball should be checked for adequate moisture from time to time.

Besides rubber plants, species responding to the air-layering method are philodendrons, dracaenas and dieffenbachias.

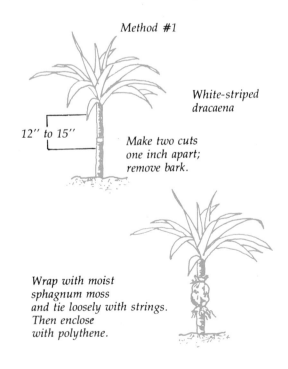

Method #1

White-striped dracaena

12" to 15"

Make two cuts one inch apart; remove bark.

Wrap with moist sphagnum moss and tie loosely with strings. Then enclose with polythene.

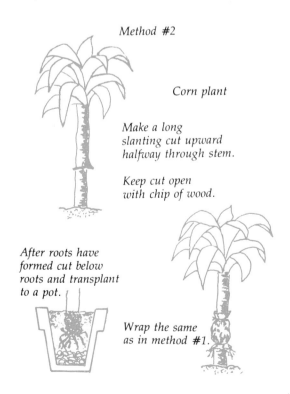

Method #2

Corn plant

Make a long slanting cut upward halfway through stem.

Keep cut open with chip of wood.

After roots have formed cut below roots and transplant to a pot.

Wrap the same as in method #1.

PROPAGATION UNITS FOR SEEDS

Units:

*Wooden flat:
can be covered
with polyethylene*

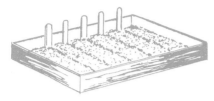

*Mixture of sterilized sand, milled sphagnum moss
and vermiculite*

Glass

*Tin can with
drainage holes*

*Clay pot placed
in plastic bag*

Watering:

*Enclosing seeds
in glass, plastic
or polyethylene helps
seeds germinate.*

*1. Before sowing seeds,
wet soil mixture
in a container
placed in a
pan of water.*

Plastic bread box

*2. After seeds have
germinated, water
with a water-soluble
fertilizer half strength.*

*True
leaves*

Seed leaves

Seedlings:

*When first true leaves develop,
transplant.*

*Cut seedlings
from flat
in cubes.*

*Growing point;
do not bury.*

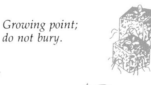

*Handle by
true leaves.*

Seeds

Media for germination of seeds may consist of any of the following: sterilized sand, milled sphagnum moss or vermiculite. A combination of any of these may be used with good results. When the seedlings have germinated, a water-soluble fertilizer solution mixed at half strength should be used to water the medium. Nonfertilized water is used for subsequent watering.

Watering

To obtain good germination, thoroughly wet the mix by placing the container of mix to soak in a shallow pan of water. When the top of mix is moist, remove and sow the seeds. After sowing the seeds, enclose the container in a polyethylene bag until they have germinated.

Temperature and light

Place the container in a room where 65° to 70° F. can be maintained. Artificial lighting with fluorescent tubes spaced six to eight inches above seedlings should be scheduled for 14 hours a day, usually from 8:00 A.M. to 10:00 P.M.

After germination, when the first set of true leaves develops, transplant to individual pots for growing on. Seedlings should be gradually acclimated to natural light and day length over a three- to four-day period.

PLANT PROBLEMS

Many common house-plant problems are a result of faulty culture.

Common Symptom	Possible Cause	Solution
LIGHT		
Leaf wilt	Excessive heat from lights or direct sun.	Move plants farther from light source.
Foliage has a yellow color; leaves drop.	Excess light	Pull curtains for sun shield
Yellow to brown patches on leaf	Sunburn	Take out of direct sun from March to October
Weak, thin and soft growth; oldest leaves drop	Insufficient light	Increase light intensity or lengthen light period
WATER		
Leaf wilt	Roots injured (rotting) from plant sitting in drainage water (consequent lack of oxygen) also Roots injured because of lack of water (high salt content in soil mass)	Provide drainage in bottom of pot, using crushed stone or broken pieces of crock; discard drainage water after watering Water more frequently to maintain a moist soil
Brown leaf tips, brown leaf margins	Dry atmosphere; also insufficient water	Keep potting mix moist
Leaf curl and leaf drop	Too much fertilizer, wind burn, drafts	Avoid drying out between waterings; avoid drafts

TEMPERATURE		
Weak, thin and soft growth, new leaves small; bud drop	High temperature, especially at night	Reduce night temperature by 10°
Yellow leaves, leaf drop, spots; bud drop	Low temperatures (also air pollution, gas fumes)	Increase room temperature
Rapid growth	Temperature not suitable for plant species	Check culture for recommendation

NUTRITION		
Stunted plant, leaves small, yellow-green color	Nitrogen deficiency	Apply a complete fertilizer of water-soluble type, according to the manufacturer's directions on the package When deficiency is corrected, apply only at infrequent intervals; once every two to three months is recommended to maintain growth
Stunted plant; small leaves; leaf margins yellow, sometimes purple, sometimes gray	Phosphorus deficiency	
Leaf margins yellow, then brown; lower leaves affected first, often with purplish cast	Potash deficiency	
Chlorosis or yellowing leaf between veins, with veins remaining green; young leaves affected first	Iron deficiency	Apply a chelated iron compound at manufacturer's directions

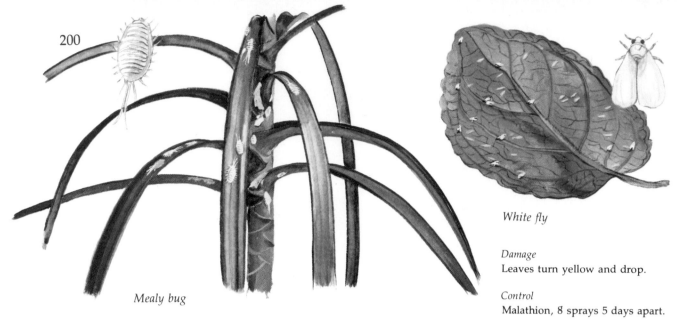

200

Mealy bug

White fly

Damage
Leaves turn yellow and drop.

Control
Malathion, 8 sprays 5 days apart.

Damage
Leaves turn yellow and die. Plant becomes stunted.

Control
Malathion, 2 sprays 7 to 10 days apart.

INSECTS

House-plant pests are best controlled by sprays or dips. Sprays are applied to plants with one- or two-gallon compressed-air sprayers or by hand·atomizers, such as a common pressure-spray bottle. Some plants are more difficult to wet than others. If the solution does not spread and wet the foliage, add only a few drops of a mild household detergent to one gallon of the solution.

Sprays or dips should be stirred frequently and vigorously to maintain uniform strength during application.

Recommended aerosols are very efficient and practical. Aerosols containing the ingredient Malathion in combination with Pyrethrum, Rotenone or Methoxychlor are fairly effective when used properly.

Pest aerosols for household or garden should not be used on house plants. They will burn foliage and often kill plants.

It is sometimes more practical to dip a plant. Mix the solution in a pail large enough to accommodate the plant. Turn the plant upside down, agitate to wet the stems and leaves thoroughly. A crumpled newspaper held by hand over the potting mix will prevent it from falling out.

Prevention control: Practice good housekeeping with plants. Inspect all plants and cut flowers brought into the home for "bugs." Isolate new plants for a month and look for bugs to develop.

Sterilize pots and potting mixtures to prevent infestation of soil-borne insects. Put pots and a container of potting mixture in the kitchen oven and heat to 180° for 30 minutes.

Wash foliage at least once a month to help remove mealy bugs, scale and spider mites. Soapy water used in place of pesticides is effective in removing most plant insects.

Hand-pick bugs with tweezers or toothpick when first discovered. A cotton swab dipped in rubbing alcohol will effectively kill mealy bugs and aphids on contact.

A word of caution: Pesticides used carelessly can be injurious to man, animals and plants. Always take time to read the label and follow directions. Use *only* pesticides that are labeled and carry directions for home and garden use.

SOME COMMON INSECTS OF HOUSE PLANTS

	Damage	*Control*
	Aphid Sucks plant juices. New growth stunted; foliage curls. Sticky honeydew secreted that is a host to sooty-mold disease.	Malathion, 2 sprays 7 to 10 days apart
	Snail **Slug** Feeds on flowers, leaves, stems and roots. Leaves a glistening trail of slime wherever it crawls.	Hand-pick at night; look under pots. Use baits containing Metaldehyde. Shallow dishes of beer near pot are partially effective
	Millipede May feed on seedlings, roots, tubers, bulbs or fleshy stems of plants, but mostly eats decaying organic matter.	Eliminate hiding places and excessive organic materials. Drench soil surface with Malathion, Sevin or Diazinon
	Red spider mite Yellow or brown specks on foliage; plant may become stunted and die.	Kelthane, 2 sprays 5 days apart
	Scale Plant becomes yellow and slowly dies. Sticky honeydew may be present.	Malathion, 3 sprays 7 to 10 days apart

DISEASES

Some Common Diseases of House Plants

Disease	Plant
Root knot nematode disease (caused by *Meloidogyne* species)	African violet, tropical foliage plants
Leaf nematode (*Aphelenchoides* species)	African violet, peperomia, gloxinia, Rieger begonia, gardenia and tropical foliage plants
Powdery mildew (airborne fungus *Oidium* species)	African violet, begonia
Crown rot (caused by *Pythium* species)	African violet, philodendron, pothos and other tropical foliage plants
Damping-off (a complex of several diseases)	Seedlings
Leaf spot (caused by *Septoria phlytaenioides* and *Cercospora* species)	Clerodendrum
Bacterial blight (caused by *Xanthomonas pelargonii*)	Geranium
Botrytis blight (caused by airborne fungus, *Botrytis cinerea*)	Geranium, begonia, azalea
Bacterial blight (caused by *Xanthomonas begoniae*)	Begonia (Rieger begonia very sensitive)
Sooty mold (caused by fungus growth on honeydew secreted by insects)	Any plant

Overwatering, poor ventilation, use of unsterilized potting mixtures, dirty pots and failure to control insects help propagate plant diseases.

NOTE: For rates of application of recommended fungicides, follow the directions on the package.

Symptoms	Control
Infected plants appear stunted and unhealthy; wilt on warm days; root galls appear as nodules on roots	Discard infected plants and soil
Yellowish leaf spots or brownish areas that turn almost black on underside of leaf	Discard plants; control materials are unsafe for homeowners
Whitish, powdery mildew growth on surface of leaves, sometimes on petals of flowers	Spray with Karathane or Actidione
Black, wet rot that makes roots look hollow and collapse, induced by cold, wet soil	Drench soil with Truban or Dexon; sterilize potting medium (discard plants) and used pots
Pre-emergence seed decay; rot of seedling at soil line	Purchase treated seed; sterilize seed-sow medium
Small, yellow, circular or irregular spots	Spray with Captan
Limited basal rot; black die-back of growing points in older plants and ultimate wilting	Grow only in sterilized potting mixture and pots; discard sick plants
Brown rotting and blighting; fuzzy, grayish spore masses	Remove old flowers and destroy infected parts; avoid excessive moisture
Small, circular blisterlike spots on leaves; yellow-greenish spots on leaf margins and ultimate wilting	Keep water off leaves; subirrigate
Charcoal-like fungus appears as black coating on stems and leaf surfaces	To prevent, control insects

GLOSSARY

Adventitious roots are those that arise from aerial plant parts, underground stems or from relatively old roots

Areole, in cacti, a clearly defined small area that may bear felt, spines, glochids, flowers or new branches

Anther, the pollen-bearing part of the stamens

Annual, a plant that completes its life cycle in a year or less

Blade, the extended part of a leaf or petal

Bulbet, a small bulb arising in a leaf axil

Callus, a term applied to the mass of parenchyma cells that develops from and around wounded plant tissue

Calyx, the circle of floral parts, composed of sepals

Chlorosis, an abnormal plant condition in which leaves turn yellow, particularly between the veins

Clone, a group of plants derived by vegetative propagation from one original plant

Cultivar, a plant of hybrid or mutant origin that is maintained only in cultivation

Cuttings, parts of a plant, usually stems, leaves or roots, prepared and used for propagation

Deciduous, a plant or tree that sheds all of its leaves annually

Division, the portion of a plant used for propagation; also the act of preparing such a division

Dolomite, a form of limestone containing magnesium, prepared for agricultural use

Epiphyte, an air plant growing nonparasitically on another plant or elevated support

Espalier, a tree or shrub with branches trained in a flat herringbone pattern on house walls, fences or trellis; a fence or trellis upon which such a plant grows

Eye, an underdeveloped growth bud that ultimately produces a new plant or new growth; eyes at joints of a rooted cutting will produce new growth

F₁ first-generation progeny from hybridization or plant breeding

Flat, a shallow tray used in greenhouses to contain small pots, propagation media and to transport numbers of plants conveniently

Floret, technically a minute flower; applied to the flowers of grasses and composites (daisy family)

Forcing, hastening a plant to maturity or other usable state

Frond, a leaf, once applied to leaves of ferns but now to leaves of palms

Genus, a designation of the first part of the scientific name of a species

Glochid, a thin barbed bristle, produced in the areoles of cholla, prickly pear and other cacti

Hardy—when used in connection with temperate zone plants it means frost- or freeze-tolerant

Hybrid, a plant resulting from a cross between parents that are genetically distinct

Inferior, beneath, below; said of an ovary situated below the apparent point of attachment of stamens and perianths (sepals and petals)

Iron chelate, a chemical that is added to the soil to treat plants with iron chlorosis; a combination of iron and a complex organic substance that makes the iron already in soils more available to plants

Leaflet, a small leaf, several of which make up a compound leaf (e.g. of the ash tree)

Mutant, the result of a sudden variation in an inherited characteristic

Node, a joint where one or more leaves or other vestiges are borne on a stem

Offset, a small bulb or other portion of a plant that can be detached for propagation

Ovary, the ovule-bearing part of a pistil

Peat moss, peat formed from partial decomposition of sphagnum moss, reeds, grasses or sedges; sphagnum peat moss is considered as best for mixing with potting soils

Perlite, a mineral expanded by heating to form white-colored, very light kernels used for lightening soil

Perennial, a plant that lives more than two years

Petiole, the supporting stalk of a leaf

Pinna, the leaflet of a compound leaf, mainly of ferns; the primary divisions (pinnae) attached to the main stem or midrib of the frond

pH—the term "pH" is a measure of the degree of acidity or alkalinity of a soil. The values range from 0, which is the most acid, to 14.0, which is most alkaline. The neutral point is 7.0. Soil reaction as measured by pH is important because it has a direct relationship on the availability of nutrients for plant growth

Pinnate, refers to a compound leaf with leaflets or segments along each side of a midrib or stalk

Pips, terminal root stocks of certain flowering plants, especially lily of the valley; also seeds of certain fruits

Pistil, the unit of the female element of a flower, comprised of ovary, style and stigma

Rachis, axis, main stalk or midrib bearing pinnae of a fern or palm frond

Rhizome, a thickened underground stem that spreads by creeping

Root-bound (or pot-bound), a condition that results from a plant remaining too long in its container

Rosette, a cluster of leaves arranged in an overlapping circular pattern, somewhat like the petals of a rose

Runner, a slender stem that grows along the surface of the ground and bears young plants, such as that of the strawberry

Seed, the ripened ovule

Sphagnum, a group of mosses native to bogs; collected in whole pieces, fresh or dried; pieces of sphagnum moss are used for air layering and lining wire baskets or totems

Spore, a simple type of reproductive cell that is capable of producing a new plant; mosses and ferns reproduce by spores

Sport, a plant that shows a marked change from the parent stock; a mutation

Standard, a plant that does not naturally grow as a tree, and which is trained into a small, treelike form

Stomata, the minute orifices or pores in the epidermis of a leaf

Subirrigation, application of water to a plant by capillarity from below

Sucker, any unwanted shoot; may come from underground or the lower part of a plant

Surfactant, wetting agent that makes water wetter by lowering its surface tension, enabling water to wet soil components more quickly

Tubercle, a miniature tuber; tuberlike body or projection

Tuberous root, a thickened underground food-storage structure that is technically a root

Variety, a third word in a botanical name that indicates a variant of a species

Vermiculite, a mineral that is heated and exploded to form spongelike, lightweight kernels; useful in conditioning soils and as a medium in which to root cuttings

Whorl, three or more leaves, branches or flowers that grow in a circle from a joint or node on a stem or trunk

"Delight... struggle to do right by her sister and the hero makes for a story of misguided sacrifice and shines a light on the winning power of love."
—*RT Book Reviews* on *His Most Suitable Bride*

"A charming love story with a mystery that keeps readers on their toes. The characters are amazing, bound to each other by their unbreakable love for each other."
—*RT Book Reviews* on *The Lawman Claims His Bride*

"Ryan delivers a great love story. Her characters come from the heart and readers will not be forgetting them anytime soon."
—*RT Book Reviews* on *Heartland Wedding*

Praise for Louise M. Gouge

"The ways the atrocities of the Civil War are shown to affect people years afterward, and their struggle to forgive, is heartrending and well done in this first Four Stones Ranch story."
—*RT Book Reviews* on *Cowboy to the Rescue*

"A sweet love story set during wartime, when everything is up in the air and people are trying to live their lives as normally as possible. The characters are wonderful and are willing to go to the ends of the earth to make their dreams come true."
—*RT Book Reviews* on *At the Captain's Command*

"An enjoyable blend of mystery, romance and political intrigue."
—*RT Book Reviews* on *A Lady of Quality*

RENEE RYAN

Renee Ryan grew up in a Florida beach town where she learned to surf, sort of. With a degree from FSU, she explored career opportunities at a Florida theme park, a modeling agency and even taught high school economics. She currently lives with her husband in Nebraska, and many have mistaken their overweight cat for a small bear. You may contact Renee at reneeryan.com, on Facebook or on Twitter, @ReneeRyanBooks.

LOUISE M. GOUGE

Florida author and college professor **Louise M. Gouge** writes historical fiction for Harlequin's Love Inspired Historical series. In addition to other awards, she has received the prestigious Inspirational Readers' Choice and the Laurel Wreath Awards. When she isn't writing or teaching her classes, she and her husband, David, enjoy visiting historical sites and museums. Please visit her website at blog.louisemgouge.com.

RENEE RYAN

LOUISE M. GOUGE

A Western Christmas

⬡ **HARLEQUIN**® LOVE INSPIRED® HISTORICAL

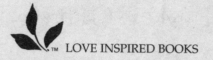 LOVE INSPIRED BOOKS

Recycling programs for this product may not exist in your area.

ISBN-13: 978-0-373-28331-6

A Western Christmas

Copyright © 2015 by Harlequin Books S.A.

The publisher acknowledges the copyright holders of the individual works as follows:

Yuletide Lawman
Copyright © 2015 by Renee Halverson

Yuletide Reunion
Copyright © 2015 by Louise M. Gouge

www.Harlequin.com

Printed in U.S.A.

CONTENTS

YULETIDE LAWMAN

Renee Ryan

To my twin sister, Robin Anderson, for all the good times we shared growing up and the support you've shown me as an adult. I'm proud to call you my family, even more honored to call you my friend.

Wait on the Lord; be of good courage, and He shall strengthen your heart; Wait, I say, on the Lord!
—*Psalms* 27:14

Chapter One

December 1, 1879
Thunder Ridge, Wyoming

Ellie Wainwright pulled her cloak tightly around her and hurried across the wide street that curved through the center of town. Cold air swirled, nipping at her cheeks. She quickened her steps, careful to avoid hidden patches of ice.

Winter had blown into Thunder Ridge, Wyoming, with enough snow to guarantee a white Christmas this year.

Ellie paused a moment to take in the pristine winter wonderland of her beloved hometown. A smile tugged at her lips, the first since she'd come home two weeks ago, mortified, humiliated and more than a little disillusioned.

Wreaths decorated most of the doorways along Main Street. Gold ribbon and red bows draped hitching rails and horse troughs. Garland hung from the rooftops of homes and businesses, while the occasional redbrick chimney boldly punched into the crisp, blue sky.

The festive decorations helped soothe Ellie's melancholy.

She was home. She was safe. She was among people who knew the details of her family's disgrace and accepted her anyway. Besides, she told herself firmly, a failed courtship wasn't the worst calamity to befall a young woman of twenty-two.

Next time, she would be wiser. She would fall for a man who could look past her family's shame and love her anyway. In the meantime, she would find another teaching position and give her attention to her students and—

A movement off to her right caught her attention. Her gaze landed on a lone rider and his bay-colored horse approaching from the west. With his hat slung low over his face and his collar pulled up against the wind, there was no easy way to identify the rider. Oh, but Ellie knew that silhouette.

She knew that man. Caleb Voss.

The widowed town sheriff had once been her brother's closest friend and the center of Ellie's secret girlhood admiration.

As if sensing her watching him, Caleb reined in his horse and turned his head in Ellie's direction. She could make out only a portion of his face and the patch of light brown hair burnished copper from the sun beneath his wide-brimmed hat.

"Hello, Ellie."

The low, husky voice sent a spattering of nerves tripping down her spine and nearly knocked her backward. "Hello, Caleb."

With two fingers, he shoved his hat off his forehead, the gesture giving her a better view of his magnificent face. Unable to move, to speak, to *think*, she simply stared up at him.

He stared back, brows arched, eyes soft.

That look. It made her think of girlhood dreams from long, long ago. Ellie stopped breathing altogether. She simply stopped breathing. Worse, she couldn't seem to tear her gaze away from that strong, square jaw, those moss-green eyes and the arresting features that had transformed from boyishly appealing to ruggedly handsome.

Caleb's eyes crinkled around the edges, the precursor to a smile. "Cold out this morning."

He wanted to talk about the weather? For some reason that made her even more uneasy.

"It's…why, yes." She forced her lungs to work one breath at a time. *In, out, in, out.* "It is rather chilly today."

"Better get inside. Wouldn't want you catching cold." His voice was low and gravelly, with a touch of concern that sounded entirely too brotherly for Ellie's way of thinking.

Holding back a sigh, she reached for the doorknob behind her. "I'm heading in now."

A tug on the brim of his hat, a slight movement of stirrups, and that was the end of their very odd, all-too-brief conversation.

Heart pounding wildly against her ribs, she twisted the doorknob and stumbled inside her friend's dress shop, Kate's Closet, named for the owner.

"Well, well, well," came the sly, knowing voice of the woman she'd come to meet. "That was certainly interesting."

Releasing another sigh, Ellie frowned at her friend.

Katherine Riley—Kate to everyone who knew her—was a petite brunette with pretty, waiflike features that included a pert nose and sparkling brown eyes, eyes that were full of amusement at Ellie's expense.

She attempted a nonchalant tone. "I don't know what you're talking about."

But, of course, she did. She'd been riveted by the sight of Caleb riding tall in the saddle of his beautiful horse, even more so when he'd stopped to speak with her.

"Ellen Marie Wainwright, I'm ashamed of you. As the daughter of our town's most revered preacher, you should know better than to fib to your closest, dearest friend." With a teasing twinkle in her eyes, Kate shook a scolding finger at her. "You and Sheriff Voss just had a…*moment*."

"We did not have a moment. Caleb and I are old friends, nothing more. He's practically like a brother."

It was the simple truth. After his mother died, and his father turned to alcohol to drown away his grief, Caleb had become an honorary member of the Wainwright family.

Even if Ellie had secretly longed for him to see her as more than his friend's little sister, Caleb had never looked at her that way. He'd been too smitten with Lizzie Covington, who he'd made his wife not long after becoming town sheriff.

Tragically, Lizzie had died in a freak wagon accident ten months ago, leaving Caleb to raise his five-year-old twins by himself. Hannah and Grace were such sweet children. Having lost her own mother, Ellie felt a strong connection to the little girls, nearly as powerful as the one she'd felt for Monroe Tipton's daughters.

She shook away the thought.

Kate's voice came at her again, a speculative note in the words. "I wonder if Mrs. Jenson will have success finding our good sheriff a woman to marry."

Ellie's shoulders tensed. "I'm confident she will."

It was no secret Caleb wanted to marry again, for his children's sake. Understandable, yet something inside Ellie rebelled at the notion of him seeking a mail-order bride. She couldn't imagine him taking vows with a woman he didn't know, or love. But perhaps that was the point.

Perhaps Caleb couldn't bear the idea of anyone replacing Lizzie in his heart and thus wasn't averse to marrying for his children's sake at the sacrifice of his own.

Depressing thought.

Despite her recent heartbreak, Ellie still believed in love and marriage. Her parents had modeled the joy that came from a godly union. The memory of their genuine affection for one another would always be with her, and was what drove Ellie's desire to marry for love, only love. Her disastrous experience with Monroe had only managed to solidify her view.

Fortunately, her father had found love a second time around and would soon marry again. Betsy Anderson was yet another connection Ellie had with Caleb. The woman her father would marry on New Year's Eve was currently serving as Caleb's housekeeper. Betsy was a kind woman and good to Ellie's father. She truly made him happy and that made Ellie happy.

The thought of her father reminded her of the one

task he'd charged her with this morning. She'd been so caught off guard by Caleb's attempt at conversation that she'd inadvertently avoided her duty.

She slipped a quick glance out the window. Her gaze landed on the handsome sheriff climbing off his horse and she felt a jolt of…something in the center of her heart. Ellie was going to have to seek him out and speak to him again today.

If not now, when?

"I'll be back in a few minutes." She left Kate gaping after her.

Shaking his head over the inexplicable compulsion to stop and speak with Ellie Wainwright—about the weather, no less—Caleb swung Gideon's reins over the hitching rail outside the jailhouse. He reached inside his jacket pocket for the carrot he'd brought with him. As he fed the horse his morning treat, Caleb stroked a hand down the animal's majestic neck and took a quick inventory of the activity around him.

People hurried about their business, their breaths pluming in frozen puffs around their heads. Horses whinnied, dogs barked, children laughed, a door slammed in the distance.

Drawing in a long pull of air, he breathed in the scent of freshly fallen snow and pine. Instead of calming him, the aroma sparked a renewed surge of urgency. Today was the first day of December and he still hadn't found himself a wife.

Time was running out if he wanted to provide the twins with a stable home by Christmas. They'd only known upheaval and heartache in their short lives and would face another one in a month when Caleb's house-keeper, Betsy, married Reverend Wainwright.

The proverbial clock was ticking. Caleb wouldn't rest until he was able to give the twins the kind of safe, calm atmosphere he'd experienced as a guest at the Wainwright home.

Nostalgia washed over him, increasing his previous resolve. After his mother died and his father disappeared into the nearest saloon, the reverend had reached out to Caleb and his four brothers. Perhaps his friendship with Everett Wainwright had played a role, but only Caleb had accepted the pastor's kindness. His untamed, out-of-control brothers had preferred living life on the edge, free to do what they pleased with no adult supervision or guidance.

Those wild, rebellious boys had grown into even wilder, undisciplined men, not outlaws, precisely, but certainly not upright citizens either.

With his brothers scattered all over the West, Caleb didn't keep in touch with them. He felt sad about that. His children had never met their uncles. They certainly didn't know Lizzie's family. They—

"Caleb?" A soft, feminine voice cut off the rest of his thoughts. "Do you have a moment?"

Warmth spread through him at the low, lush request.

Smiling fondly, he looked down at Everett's little sister for a second time in a handful of minutes. "For you, Ellie, always."

Big blue eyes fringed with long thick lashes blinked up at him. In the same manner as when he'd spoken to her only moments earlier, words backed up in his throat and an inexplicable jolt of awareness prickled down his spine.

When had little Ellie Wainwright grown up?

When had she become such a beauty?

Even with her doll-like features scrunched in an earnest expression she was unspeakably fetching. Slender and willowy, her head barely came up to his chin. Adding to the lovely image, several caramel-colored wisps of blond hair had slipped from a messy knot at the back of her neck and now flowed against her pinked cheeks.

As he stared down at her, surprisingly unable to speak, he realized she was staring right back at him, equally speechless.

The awkward moment stretched into two.

In the silence that hung between them like a heavy mist, Caleb wondered what had brought Ellie back to Thunder Ridge at this time of year. Schoolteachers usually worked from September to June, which led him to believe her return hadn't been entirely her decision.

Had someone hurt her? Something dark moved through him and a protective instinct took hold. If someone had done Ellie harm, Caleb would find them and make sure they understood—

He cleared his throat. *Not your place.* "What can I do for you, Ellie?"

She startled at the question. "Oh, I…" She swallowed, saying, "I forgot to mention earlier, I mean, when we spoke I meant to ask if you and…"

Her words trailed off and she pressed her lips tightly together. A second later, as if gathering her fortitude, she lifted her chin and threw back her shoulders in a familiar show of female bravado. Caleb smiled at the gesture. He'd always liked Everett's little sister.

Not so little anymore.

"I…" She forced a smile. "That is, my father wanted

me to ask if you and the twins would like to come over for Sunday dinner after church this week."

The earlier feeling of nostalgia dug deeper still.

Caleb had missed Sunday dinner with the Wainwrights. He'd stopped the tradition soon after his marriage to Lizzie. Now, her voice slid across his mind, reminding him why he'd avoided the Wainwright home. *You're nothing but a charity case to the pastor and his family.*

Caleb frowned at the memory. "That's a nice offer, Ellie, but tell your father that I—"

"Please, Caleb, don't say no." She touched his coat sleeve with her gloved fingers. "My father will be so disappointed."

The remark sparked a wave of guilt. Reverend Wainwright had always been good to him, better than he deserved. Yet, Caleb had all but turned his back on the man in recent years.

At first, he'd kept his distance because Lizzie hadn't liked his friendship with Everett or any of the man's family. Then, after her death, Caleb hadn't known how to make things right. His inability to help Everett in his friend's greatest hour of need had added to his reticence.

Then, there was his guilt.

Though he knew Reverend Wainwright didn't hold him responsible for Everett's incarceration, Caleb felt as if he'd let the man down by not trying harder to keep his son from falling in with a bad crowd. It had been a sad day when Everett ended up killing a man in order to a save a woman's life.

He'd done the right thing but in the wrong way.

Unfortunately, the judge had taken a hard stance

and sentenced Everett to seven years in the Wyoming Territorial Penitentiary.

As if sensing his hesitation, Ellie tightened her hold on his arm. "Say yes. It'll be like old times."

They both knew that wasn't true. The easy days when he'd shared Sunday dinner with the Wainwrights were long gone. A lot had changed since then.

Everything had changed.

Caleb thought of Hannah and Grace, of the steady, stable life he wanted to provide for them. Until he was able to do just that, the Wainwright home was the next best thing.

"Tell your father that the girls and I would be happy to dine with you on Sunday."

Chapter Two

Caleb studied Ellie's face, trying to read her reaction to his acceptance of her father's invitation. Her expression was wide-eyed, slightly flustered and utterly adorable.

An uncomfortable sensation moved through him, the kind reserved for a boy conversing with a girl for the first time.

This is Ellie, he reminded himself. He wasn't supposed to feel uncomfortable around her. Nor was he supposed to be this aware of her.

Yet the sensation persisted, digging deeper, causing his breath to hitch and his mind to empty of all coherent thought.

What were they discussing again?

Mildly amused at himself, he felt a laugh bubble inside his chest. When was the last time he'd laughed?

He couldn't remember. A sad commentary on the current condition of his life. Even with help, raising twin daughters was hard work. But also the best part of his day. When he wasn't at the jail, he put all his focus on caring for his daughters. That left little time for much else. He hoped that would change once he got married again.

"Anyway, that's all I came to say." The tentative smile that accompanied Ellie's words reached inside Caleb's chest, grabbed hold of his heart and squeezed hard. "I guess I'll see you at church on Sunday."

Staring into those big, expressive eyes, everything in him softened. "Yes, Ellie, you *will* see me there. Perhaps even before then."

"Sounds lovely." Her smile wavered ever-so-slightly. "Well, um, bye."

"Bye, now."

He watched her walk back the way she came. She looked left, then right, then hurried across the street. Twice, she slowed her pace and glanced at him over her shoulder, her lower lip caught between her teeth. Both times, when their gazes met and melded, Caleb felt an unexpected ping in the pit of his stomach.

There were logical reasons for his physical reaction to the girl—no, scratch that, not a girl. A woman. Ellie Wainwright was a full-grown, beautiful woman. She was also his friend's treasured little sister and the daughter of the man Caleb considered a second father. That made her family, the sister he never had.

Except...

After their unusual, albeit brief interchanges this morning, Caleb wasn't feeling very brotherly toward her.

He lifted his hand in a responding wave to match the one Ellie tossed at him.

His lips curved in a genuine smile.

Ellie was a reminder of everything good in his past,

the quintessential example of the stability he craved for his girls.

Stopping yet again, this time at the door leading into the dress shop, she gave him one last glance over her shoulder before disappearing into the building.

Ping.

Caleb swallowed. He swallowed again. And one more time for good measure.

Taking advantage of his inattention, Gideon rooted around for more treats, searching Caleb's coat pockets with a warm, nuzzling nose.

Giving in to the none-too-subtle demand, he fed the horse another carrot. "What," he asked in a strained voice to the tune of the animal's munching, "just happened?"

Gideon had no answer.

Neither did Caleb.

At the moment, he didn't know much of anything, except that he was wasting valuable time staring at a closed door.

Banishing Ellie Wainwright from his mind, he gave Gideon one last pat then entered the jailhouse. With efficient movements, he divested himself of hat, gloves and long coat before turning his gaze onto his deputy.

Feet propped up on the lone desk in the room, Prescott Kramer eyed him with the affable nonchalance that defined him. "Morning, Sheriff."

Caleb nodded. "Deputy."

Younger than Caleb by five years, Prescott was nearly his same height, a full inch over six feet, but broader in the shoulders and back. His eyes were a startling pale blue and he sported a head of thick, jet-black hair. The combination seemed to make the man popular with the ladies.

No arguing that women liked Prescott and Prescott liked women. That didn't mean he wasn't a fine lawman. He had lightning-quick reflexes and a calm head in tough situations. Caleb had hired him eighteen months ago and had yet to regret the decision.

Flashing a row of perfectly aligned, sparkling white teeth, the deputy slowly rose to his feet and ambled over to the coffeepot sitting atop the potbellied stove. He filled two tin cups with the thick brew they both preferred, kept one for himself and then handed the other to Caleb.

Chilled from his time outdoors, Caleb took a grateful sip of the steaming liquid. "Any problems arise overnight I need to know about?"

"Nope." Prescott shook his head. "All quiet. Took the opportunity to read."

Caleb nodded again. The one pursuit Prescott loved nearly as much as getting to know a new woman in town was reading a good novel. "Glad to hear you spent your time productively."

Prescott could have taken a short nap last night and it wouldn't have mattered much. Although Thunder Ridge was a regular stop on the Union Pacific rail line, with its no-saloon ordinance and a strong Christian presence, it was also a peaceful community.

Not that there weren't concerns that arose on occasion.

Caleb and Prescott dealt with random cases of vandalism, scuttles that came from high tempers and, of course, the occasional dispute over property lines. But the jail cells remained mostly empty. And now that Caleb's brothers were scattered all over the West, there was even less trouble in town.

Most days, his job was boring, exactly the way he liked it. He'd had enough chaos for one lifetime, first from his unpredictable childhood and then from his volatile marriage.

"Want me to take the ride through town this morning?" Prescott asked, referring to their daily routine check-in with the local businesses.

"I'll do it." Caleb had already performed an initial inspection of the outlying ranches before coming in to work. Once he rode through town and spoke with the shopkeepers individually, he'd take Gideon to the livery for a much needed brushing and rest. "You can go on home, Pres."

"Don't have to tell me twice." The deputy drained his coffee then set down his empty cup next to the stove.

With more enthusiasm than usual, he shoved his arms in his coat then jammed his hat on his head. Instead of heading out, he paused at the doorway. "Hey, Sheriff, got a question I've been meaning to ask you for a while now."

That sounded ominous. "Okay, shoot."

"Just how well do you know Ellie Wainwright?" A speculative gleam shone in the deputy's eyes. "Well enough, say, to make an introduction?"

Caleb's blood ran cold at the obvious masculine interest in the question. Prescott was nothing if not predictable. In truth, Caleb wasn't all that surprised by the deputy's inquiry, only that it had taken the man an entire two weeks to ferret out information about Ellie Wainwright.

Still.

"Don't go getting any ideas." A burst of temper spiked his tone to a near guttural growl. "Ellie's off-limits."

The warning only seemed to stir the man's interest further. "Why? Somebody already courting her?"

Not if Caleb had anything to say about it. "She's not available for an introduction and that's the end of it."

"You sure about that?" Prescott scratched a hand across his jaw, his eyes taking on a thoughtful light. "I haven't seen her with any man since she came home."

True. Nevertheless...

Caleb wasn't introducing Ellie to Prescott. Or, for that matter, any other unmarried man in town.

He told himself he was acting on Everett's behalf. He owed it to his friend to keep an eye on the man's little sister while he was in prison. This wasn't personal. It was simply the right thing to do.

Keep telling yourself that, cowboy.

"You can't meet Ellie."

"Why not?"

Caleb ground his teeth together so hard his jaw ached. "She's a churchgoing woman with a strong set of Christian values and impeccable integrity."

Prescott's eyes narrowed to tiny slits. "You implying I'm not good enough for her?"

That about covered it. "*No one's* good enough for Ellie."

Now Prescott smiled, a big toothy grin that set Caleb's teeth on edge. Clearly he wasn't getting through to the hardheaded deputy.

He changed tactics. "She's too young for you."

Which, to be fair, sounded as irrational in his head

as it did out loud, especially since Ellie and Prescott were the same age, give or take a few months.

"Ah, I get it." The other man let out a low, amused whistle. "You got your eye on the preacher's daughter."

"I don't have my eye on Ellie." That would be wrong on so many levels.

Although…

Now that Caleb worked the idea around in his head…

Ellie was sweet and warm, caring, and excellent with children. She was the kind of woman a man made promises to, the kind of woman a man cherished and—

He cut off the rest of his thoughts.

Even if Ellie wasn't Everett's little sister, she deserved far more than Caleb had to offer a woman.

Yes, he needed a wife. And, yes, Ellie was available, or so he assumed, but approaching her with the idea of marriage seemed inappropriate because of his history with her family.

Best to look elsewhere for his future bride, or at least wait a little longer for Mrs. Jenson to find her for him.

As if to contradict his decision, an image of his daughters crystallized in his mind. They deserved a good, loving mother, a sweet and warm, caring woman who would provide them with a calm, stable home life.

With few available women left in town that he hadn't already approached, and less than a month before Christmas, Caleb was getting desperate to find the twins a mother. So desperate, in fact, that he'd even agreed to let Mrs. Jenson contact potential mail-order brides from other parts of the country.

Now, he wondered if he'd been too hasty with his acquiescence on the matter. Perhaps his future wife was closer to home. Perhaps she was already in Thunder Ridge.

Perhaps she was right across the street.

Ellie reentered Kate's shop with a pounding heart and an annoying case of trepidation. Considering her rapid exit, and her subsequent conversation with Caleb out in plain sight, her friend would surely want to know what they'd said to each other. And why she'd approached him this morning, instead of waiting until after her meeting with Kate.

How was Ellie supposed to explain something she didn't fully understand herself?

Her discussion with Caleb had been brief, not much more than a question asked and an answer given. Yet, because of the long looks and inexplicable tension between them, Ellie wasn't sure what to think.

What came next?

Mulling over the question, she stood just inside the store's threshold, unable to move deeper into the room because she needed every scrap of energy to process the past few minutes she'd spent in Caleb's company.

Kate's eyebrows lifted in silent question, clearly waiting for an explanation.

Ellie pretended not to notice.

"Fine." Kate held up in her hands in a show of mock surrender. "I won't ask. Never let it be said that Kate Riley doesn't know how to mind her own business."

Ellie felt her mouth drop open. "Since when?"

"Ha-ha." Her friend sniffed in feminine outrage. "I'll have you know, you're looking at the new and improved version of me. I no longer stick my nose where it doesn't belong."

"Uh-huh," Ellie hummed in response.

"Now that you're back inside," Kate continued as if she hadn't responded, "shall we get started?"

"Absolutely." Taking several steps forward, Ellie dug inside the medium-sized reticule hanging from her wrist and pulled out the script for the Christmas play her father had insisted she direct this year.

She figured he'd assigned her the task with the express purpose of giving her something to do with her days, and to keep her mind off her troubles. As he was so often fond of saying, "Nothing helps redirect our gloomy thoughts better than focusing on others."

It was good advice that Ellie intended to act upon from this point forward. No more feeling sorry for herself. No more wondering what might have been. "I have some initial ideas for the costumes."

"As do I."

A jolt of fear moved through her. With just over three weeks until Christmas, Ellie wasn't sure she could pull off the production to her father's satisfaction. Or her own.

Lowering her head, she exhaled a small, soulful sigh of remorse. "Last night's rehearsal was a complete disaster."

"Don't you think you're being a bit dramatic?" A pair of smart-looking, female, lace-up boots moved directly into her line of vision. "It's a children's play, Ellie, one you've directed many times in the past."

Well, yes.

But that had been years ago, before she'd left for the teaching job in Colorado Springs.

Releasing another sigh, Ellie lifted her head. "Oh, Kate, I have exactly twenty-three days to put together a Christmas production that will make Thunder Ridge proud and I'm already off to a miserable start."

"I was there last night. It wasn't that horrible."

Were they talking about the same event? "The children ignored me completely."

One well-defined black eyebrow shot up in obvious skepticism.

Point taken. "All right, they didn't ignore me *completely*."

It had only felt that way.

Her inability to command a room full of rambunctious boys and girls was disturbingly new. Ellie used to be good with children, a requirement of any schoolteacher. But her confidence had vanished ever since she'd lost her job, which had been right after Monroe had withdrawn his marriage proposal because Ellie had told him about her brother's incarceration.

"What if I lose control again tonight?" There. She'd voiced her fear aloud.

Instead of gaining sympathy, the comment seemed to make her friend's smile widen. "Weren't you the one who once told me first rehearsals are always disasters?"

"I'm pretty sure I never said any such thing." *This year*.

Kate laughed. "Well, no matter what happens Christmas Eve, at least you can comfort yourself in the knowledge that the costumes will be spectacular."

Her friend punctuated the remark with a wink.

Finally, Ellie smiled, as well. Kate was her assistant, her costume designer and the reason for this early morning visit to the dress shop her friend had inherited from her grandmother.

"Ellie." Kate took her hands. "You aren't alone in

this. I'm right in the middle of the muddled fray with you."

It was exactly what she needed to hear.

"You and me," Kate said, winking again, "working side by side on the play, why, it'll be just like old times."

Just like old times.

Nearly the same words she'd spoken to Caleb moments earlier. They'd seemed appropriate at the time, but now Ellie felt foolish having uttered them.

Things could never be as they once were; too much time had passed. But maybe, just maybe, that wasn't such a bad thing.

Chapter Three

Later that afternoon, just as Ellie feared, play practice turned into an unruly mess. She willed back the tears that would have formed in her eyes had she given them a chance.

Not that any of the children would notice if she gave into her silent despair. At the moment, they were engaged in a rousing game of tag, weaving in and out of the pews, laughing and chattering so loudly Ellie could hardly think over the ruckus.

The only children paying her any attention were Caleb's beautiful five-year-old twins. Hannah and Grace Voss were fast capturing Ellie's heart as they followed her around the interior of the church like two little miniature shadows. They'd stuck close to her ever since their housekeeper had dropped them off fifteen minutes ago.

Ellie smiled down at the girls, taking in their identical sweet, tiny features, light brown hair and big green eyes the same color as their father's. They each looked up at her expectantly, clearly waiting for her to tell them what to do.

Two down, she told herself firmly, only thirteen to go.

"When are we going to get started?" Hannah asked.

"Soon," Ellie replied. "So stay close to me."

"Okay," the girls said in unison.

Smiling, Ellie put a hand on each of their shoulders and pulled them near.

High-pitched squeals rent the air. The game had heated up, boys against girls. Someone was going to end up hurt.

Enough. "Everyone, please, settle down."

Her request was promptly ignored.

For a woman who'd spent almost two years in a schoolroom of twenty-five boys and girls—ages six to fifteen—Ellie was supposed to be an expert at maintaining control in the midst of chaos. Well, of course she was an expert.

With the Voss twins following hard on her heels, she moved to the front of the church and did what she was trained to do.

She took control.

"Boys and girls." She clapped her hands once, twice, three times. "Everyone gather around. It's time to get started."

When they continued to ignore her, she whistled, loudly, a technique she'd mastered in her first months in the classroom.

Half of the unruly children abruptly froze. Ellie repeated her request. They obeyed, probably because they'd grown bored with chasing one another.

With quick, concise words, she directed the group to sit on the floor at her feet then repeated her previ-

ous order, raising her voice to be heard over the bois-
terous laughter.

Another five children joined the others at the front
of the church. Three mutineers remained, two boys and
a girl, all of similar ages, somewhere between nine and
eleven. They continued chasing one another around the
perimeter of the room. Ellie bodily inserted herself in
the middle of their game, forcing them to either stop
or ram straight into her.

They stopped.

Wide-eyed and shifting from foot to foot, they
seemed unsure what to expect from her. She took advantage of their uncertainty. "Now that I have your attention, please join the rest of us."

Her tone brooked no argument.

The three dutifully complied. "Yes, Miss Ellie."

The moment she returned to her spot at the front of
the church, the various whispered conversations drew
to a halt.

Ellie quickly organized the children into two groups,
the older ones with speaking parts and the younger
ones who would sing three separate songs during the
play.

Kate chose that moment to rush into the building.
"What did I miss?"

Ellie smiled at her friend's flushed face and somewhat wild hair. "Nothing much, we're only just getting started."

"Wonderful." With a pointed, I-told-you-so grin,
her friend swept her gaze over the children. "I see you
have everything under control."

Ignoring Kate's smug tone, Ellie put her to work.
"If you could run through the play with the older chil-

dren, I'll teach the little ones the first song they'll be singing."

"Sounds good to me." Script in hand, Kate collected her charges and escorted them to the back of the church.

Ellie settled on the floor between Hannah and Grace Voss. The twins sat on either side of her, so close they practically crawled into her lap.

As a teacher, Ellie wasn't supposed to pick favorites; she knew this, knew the dangers of getting too close to any one child—or in this case *two* children. Yet she was already falling for the twins. She wondered if her fondness for them had something to do with her connection to their father.

Ellie shook her head at herself. Had she not learned her lesson in Colorado? Her affection for Monroe's daughters had only led to heartache. Saying goodbye to them had been the hardest thing she'd ever done, maybe even harder than hearing Monroe retract his offer of marriage.

Yet, here she was, already growing attached to another widower's young daughters. Not a wise move, considering their father was actively seeking a woman to marry solely to take on the role as their mother. Caleb wasn't looking for love. And Ellie wasn't looking to act solely as a mother to his or any man's children. She wanted a real marriage and a family of her own.

Don't get too close, she ordered, even as her arms wrapped around the girls' shoulders.

Realizing what she'd done, Ellie quickly returned her hands to her lap and focused on the entire group of children. "Who wants to learn the first song we'll be singing Christmas Eve?"

Seven tiny hands shot in the air.

She soon discovered that most of the boys and girls were familiar with the tune that accompanied the song "What Child Is This?" But they were shaky on the words. Repetition would be the key to their success, besides keeping to a single verse, maybe two if they learned the first one quickly.

She sang the first two lines then had the boys and girls repeat after her. "Well-done," she praised. "Let's try that again."

On the second time through, she looked over at Kate with the other children. A quick headcount told her that one of the older boys had disappeared from the group. She was just about to alert her friend to the problem when Brody Driscoll reappeared, a mischievous grin on his face.

Ellie's heart dipped. She'd seen that look on too many young faces not to recognize that trouble lay but a heartbeat away.

Proving her gloomy forecast accurate, a frightened female screech cut through the children's singing, which was followed by several more shrieks—also female.

Ellie sighed as the girls, still screaming at the top of their lungs, scrambled away from Brody. They hopped up on the pews, dancing from foot to foot.

The older boys howled with collective laughter.

Kate, her face drained of color, eyes filled with panic, called for Ellie's assistance. "Come quick!"

Ellie tried not to sigh again. But really, how disappointing. Everything had been going so well up till now.

"Stay here." She quickly rose to her feet.

With a hand gesture, she indicated Kate join her in the middle of the church. "Tell me," she whispered.

Kate hissed two monosyllabic, oh-so-troubling words. "Dead. Mouse."

But of course.

At least Brody hadn't brought in a live rodent. That would have brought a whole separate set of issues, namely chasing down the scurrying creature.

Stifling a grin—because, well, boys were after all *boys*—Ellie bypassed the screaming girls and shoved into the gang of laughing boys, who were taking turns slapping Brody on the back.

A quick glance to the floor and, sure enough, the dead mouse lay poised on its back, claws up, head lolled to one side.

Ellie disregarded the boys pressing in around her and focused solely on Brody Driscoll. He was a good-looking kid, probably about eleven or twelve years old, with dark, wavy hair and eyes nearly the same color.

He held her gaze almost defiantly, but Ellie saw the desperation beneath the bravado, as if he was determined to get a rise out of her and yet afraid he'd get exactly that.

Face blank, eyes still locked with the boy's, she leaned over and picked up the mouse by the tail. "I believe this belongs to you?"

Brody's earlier boldness faltered.

"I…" He glanced at his friends, all still snickering, then, emboldened once again, jerked his chin at her. "Maybe it's mine and maybe it isn't."

More snickers from the other boys. She'd expected no less.

Just as Ellie opened her mouth to respond, a deep,

masculine voice cut her off. "Outside, Mr. Driscoll. And bring your rat with you."

Ellie spun around, her gaze connecting with Caleb's. Except he was no longer the Caleb she knew. He was big bad Sheriff Voss, the dedicated lawman who kept order in Thunder Ridge. The man *nobody* challenged, especially not a mischievous boy at a children's play rehearsal.

Ellie tried to gain Caleb's attention, to let him know she had the situation under control, but his gaze was locked with Brody's. "I said outside, now."

Shoulders slumped, Brody took the mouse from Ellie's fingers and headed toward the exit, Caleb one step behind.

No. Oh, no, no. Although sweet and certainly well-meaning, Ellie could not let Caleb rescue the situation. Yet she couldn't question his authority in front of the children, either.

A quandary to be sure, but Ellie needed the children to know *she* was in charge.

She trotted after Caleb and Brody, caught up with them in the vestibule. "Cale—I mean, Sheriff Voss." She gripped his sleeve. "A quick word, if you please."

Caleb hesitated at the warmth that spread from Ellie's fingers, past his coat and straight into his forearm. "Now? You want to speak to me, now?"

"Yes, Caleb. Now."

Impatience surged. Whatever Ellie had to say couldn't be more important than taking care of Brody's willful disobedience.

"Please," she pleaded in the soft, sweet voice that did strange things to his gut. "It'll take only a moment."

Frowning, he dropped his eyes to Ellie's hand still curled around his arm, then raised a questioning eyebrow. "I'm in the middle of something pretty important here."

"As am I." She dropped her hand and favored Brody with a stern, no-nonsense glance.

"Sheriff Voss will meet you outside in a moment. I suggest you spend the time alone thinking about what you've done and, of course, taking care of that." She looked pointedly at the mouse.

"Yes, Miss Ellie." Mouse tail clamped between his thumb and forefinger, Brody headed for the door.

Caleb stopped him. "Stop right there. Don't you have something to say to Miss Ellie?"

The boy sighed, his shoulders now drooping along with his head. "I'm sorry for disrupting play practice."

"You're forgiven," she said, her tone full of the graciousness inherent in her character. "But don't ever pull a stunt like that again. Are we clear?"

"No, ma'am. I mean…yes, ma'am." Sighing heavily, Brody lifted a frustrated shoulder. "I mean, no, I won't."

She patted him fondly on the arm. "That's all I ask."

Brody smiled at her.

She smiled back. "Go on outside, now."

"Yes, Miss Ellie." The boy's eyes were full of remorse as he exited the building.

Caleb had always known Ellie was a steady sort. Now he also knew she had a large store of patience. He attempted to follow her lead, though it called for great effort on his part. "I'm listening. What's on your mind?"

"I appreciate your assistance with Brody, but you must understand. I had the situation under control."

No argument there. "Yes, you did."

When he'd walked into the church he'd watched her retrieve the mouse from the floor. *I believe this belongs to you,* she'd said without a hint of inflection in her voice, or fear in her eyes. Caleb nearly smiled at the memory. Despite Ellie's diminutive stature, she was no delicate, fragile woman.

He liked that about her. "Your handling of the situation was quite impressive."

A frown formed between her eyes. "Then why did you step in?"

"For Brody's sake."

Her frown deepened. "I don't understand."

"His mother is sick, Ellie. Dying actually. She may not make it to Christmas. He's not been coping well with the prospect of losing her. This isn't the first time he's disrupted a gathering."

"Oh, Caleb. I didn't know, didn't realize." Ellie drew in a tight breath, her gaze filling with understanding. "That certainly explains his behavior this afternoon."

In a word. "Yes."

"Under the circumstances, you're the best person to talk to him."

He nodded, forever grateful Ellie knew his past. He didn't have to go into detail about how his own mother had died around this same time of year when he'd been nearly Brody's exact age. Caleb only wished Ellie wouldn't look at him with sad memories in her eyes. He didn't want her sympathy for himself, but for Brody. He turned to go.

"Don't be too hard on the boy," she called after him.

"Only what the situation requires." He found Brody waiting for him on the front steps of the church, his foot digging into a pile of freshly fallen snow mixed with mud.

"What were you thinking?" he asked the boy in a stern tone. "You know better than to bring a dead mouse into the church."

The boy looked him straight in the eyes. Tears shimmered in his gaze, but he heroically swallowed them. "I'm sorry."

Caleb didn't doubt Brody's sincerity, but he suspected the sorrow in the boy's eyes had little to do with the mouse incident. "How's your mother feeling?"

"Not good. She's so weak and can hardly get out of bed anymore. I hate seeing her suffer."

"I didn't realize her illness had progressed that much since I stopped by last week."

Why hadn't Betsy told him? His housekeeper had ample opportunity and would surely know Caleb would understand if she needed to spend more time with her dying sister.

"It's not fair," Brody said, battling tears. "Christmas is Mama's favorite holiday."

Caleb's throat seized. He understood the kid's pain, felt it deep in his own soul. He had to blink several times to keep memories of another Christmas at bay, his mother's last. "I'm sorry to hear she's growing worse."

The boy kicked at the snow, sending white puffs circling around his foot. "Aunt Betsy is sitting with her now, reading to her."

"Tell me about the mouse."

The kid shrugged. "I thought it would make everyone laugh. I didn't mean to scare the girls or Miss Kate."

"But you did."

"I know and I'm really sorry."

Caleb's throat seized again, painfully. Brody didn't have a lot of family. He had only his mother and his aunt Betsy, who worked as Caleb's housekeeper during the day and was due to marry Reverend Wainwright in a month. What would happen to the boy when his mother died? Surely, his aunt and her new husband would take him in.

But what if they didn't?

"Is Miss Ellie going to kick me out of the play?"

Like most boys his age, Brody was concerned with the immediate future, not months down the road. "Not my call. You'll have to ask her."

"But I'm playing Joseph."

"Then you better get back inside and speak with Miss Ellie."

"Yes, sir." Shoulders squared, Brody hurried up the steps.

Caleb ambled into the building behind him. Graciousness itself, Ellie welcomed the boy with a smile and a clasp on his shoulder. She whispered something to him that made him laugh. The boy nodded vigorously before rejoining his group.

Ellie's mother had been equally kind to Caleb during his darkest days. For one brief moment, he let the memories come, let them remind him why he was so determined to establish a stable home for his daughters.

Left to raise themselves, Caleb and his brothers gained a well-deserved reputation as wild and out of control, primarily due to the flagrant lack of adult supervision.

Thanks to his friendship with Everett, Caleb soon began spending more time at the Wainwrights' house than his own. He'd seen firsthand the difference a loving mother brought to a household. She brought a gentleness of spirit and a warmth that no single man could ever hope to achieve on his own.

Now, with his mind poised somewhere between past and present, he watched Ellie sit on the ground and the twins lean in against her, snuggling close.

He felt it again, the ping, followed by a surge of longing for something so far out of reach he couldn't put a name to it. He waited a beat, struggling with an onslaught of emotion and possibilities. Suddenly, the future became a clear, distinct picture in his mind.

Caleb knew what he had to do. If all went as planned, his family would be complete by Christmas.

Chapter Four

After the pandemonium over the mouse incident died down and order was once again restored, the rest of play practice went smoothly.

Ellie would like to think the children's obedience was due solely to her skills as a teacher, but she knew better. Caleb's watchful presence from the back of the church was a powerful inducement for good behavior, as was the glint of his nickel-plated badge.

Despite her best efforts to ignore him, Ellie's gaze continually wandered to where Caleb stood with his shoulder propped against the back wall. Each time she glanced in his direction, her breath caught in her throat. He looked so handsome, so impressive bathed in the afternoon sunlight that streamed in from the long skinny window on his left.

Each time their eyes met, the muscles in her stomach tightened and Ellie had to force herself to remain calm, to act normal, nonchalant.

A nearly impossible feat.

She was far too aware of Caleb in every fiber of her being, aware of his strength, of his reliable masculinity. It would be all too easy to imagine him as her husband, all too easy to dream of evenings sitting by a toasty fire with their children, the twins plus at least three more. And—

Stop right there, warned her better judgment.

She could not—would not—allow herself to view Caleb in any role other than friend, not even in the privacy of her own mind.

She forced her gaze back to the children in her group and caught two of them poking at one another. Shoving would soon follow. Were they the only ones growing antsy? Ellie took a fast assessment of the entire room and immediately noted the telltale signs of boredom in shifting feet, wandering gazes and general inattentiveness.

With the idea of preempting the inevitable, she called an end to rehearsal. "We'll pick up where we left off next Monday afternoon, same place, same time."

A mass rush to gather coats and gloves accompanied this announcement. Goodbyes were tossed between the children. Feet pounded toward the exit. Soon, the only people left in the church besides Ellie were Kate, Brody, Caleb and his daughters.

After a none-too-subtle nudge from Caleb, Brody apologized once again to Ellie and Kate. "I'm sorry for bringing a dead mouse into the church."

Although Ellie had already forgiven the boy, she did so again.

Kate wasn't so quick to excuse Brody's behavior. "Your shenanigans certainly got my blood pumping, and I don't mean that in a good way."

Brody sheepishly repeated his apology, then added, "I didn't mean to scare you, Miss Kate."

"Apology accepted. However," she said, ruffling the boy's hair with a little more force than necessary, "you will leave all rodents and other critters outside where they belong. Are we clear on this?"

"Yes, ma'am."

The incident now settled between them, the boy gallantly offered to walk Kate back to her shop and she graciously accepted.

Then there were four.

Hannah and Grace crowded around Ellie, asking if she needed someone to walk her home, too, and maybe they could do it, with their father's assistance, of course.

Ellie's first response was a rush of longing, the kind of achy wistfulness she didn't dare allow to take hold.

She was already dangerously enamored with Caleb's daughters. More time spent in their company would only make it harder to watch another woman eventually become their mother.

"While I certainly appreciate the offer, there's no need. I live right next door."

"Nevertheless," Caleb interjected before his daughters could respond. "The girls and I would very much like to escort you home."

Something about the set of his shoulders, the look in his eyes—a sort of decisiveness she didn't know quite how to interpret—made Ellie's blood vibrate with nerves. "But my house is out of your way."

"Not that far."

He was right, of course. Caleb and his daughters lived on the other side of the street, barely a half block to the north. Ellie could see his front door from her father's porch. She really had no reason to resist the kind offer.

Yet, resist she did.

Her inner conflict was so intense, so tangled with tempered hope, that heat surged into her face.

"It's settled," Caleb declared, taking advantage of her silence. "While you gather your belongings I'll help the girls into their coats."

Ellie capitulated. Arguing any further would only make her appear ungrateful. Besides, a few extra moments with Caleb, and his daughters, would be a treat worth savoring for many days to come.

"Thank you," she said. "I'll only be a moment."

Over the next two days, Ellie made a concentrated effort to avoid the entire Voss family. She managed to do so easily enough, primarily by sticking close to home. But her self-imposed isolation came to an end Sunday morning. Church beckoned, as did the promised dinner with Caleb and his daughters, a meal Ellie was looking forward to more than was probably wise.

The day dawned clear and cold. The sky was a brilliant blue that looked brittle enough to crack. Tucking her hands inside her muffler to keep them warm, Ellie stepped onto her father's porch, smiled up at the heavens, then made the short trek next door to the church.

She'd dreamed of Caleb again last night, the same dream she'd had the night before and the night before that. They'd been sitting together in front of a roaring fire, the scene playing out exactly as she'd imagined at play practice. While she read to their children, Caleb stoked the fire. The twins were there with them, plus a babe in a cradle, and...

It had only been a dream, she reminded herself, triggered no doubt by a long-ago affection for a boy who had grown into an attractive man. A man so averse to falling in love he was prepared to take wedding vows with a stranger.

Ellie would be smart to keep her distance, especially emotionally. She would see the Voss family today, and then go back to avoiding them.

As if to mock her resolve, she caught sight of Caleb and his daughters crossing the street. Her stomach performed a quick, hard roll. Caleb was handsome in all black save for his crisp white shirt. The girls were absolutely adorable all wrapped up in matching blue coats, mittens, hats and scarves.

"Miss Ellie," one of the two bundles shouted as she lifted her hand in a wave.

"Hello, Hannah," Ellie called out in return.

The child's eyes widened. "How did you know it was me?"

The little girl's surprise was understandable. Ellie doubted many people could tell the twins apart. On first glance the girls were identical. But they had very different personalities.

Hannah held herself with more confidence than her sister. She was certainly more precocious. Her smile also came quicker, with a mischievous glint in her eye.

Clearly impatient for an answer to her question, Hannah jammed two tiny fists on her hips. "Did you really know it was me or did you just guess?"

Holding back a laugh, Ellie smiled down at the gregarious child. "Actually, I can tell you apart from your sister rather easily."

"You can? That's really, kind of…" Hannah seemed to search for the right word "…amazing."

"Yes," Grace agreed, slipping in front of her sister so she could join the conversation. "Very, very amazing."

Not for the first time, Ellie felt a need to pull the two girls close. They were smart and sweet, the kind of children any teacher would be glad to have in her classroom. And that any woman would be proud to mother as if they were her own children.

Careful, her better judgment warned for the hundredth time in a smattering of days. *Remember your place.*

Hannah attempted to reclaim her spot in front of Ellie, all but shoving her sister out of the way.

Silent until now, Caleb muttered something to the girls then set a hand on each of his daughter's shoulders. The gesture was all it took to put an immediate end to their jockeying for position.

Impressed, Ellie lifted her gaze to meet his.

His eyes were dark beneath the brim of his hat, his smile a mere tilt of one corner of his mouth. Ellie thought she detected a hint of humor in his expression, and something that looked like affection. For her, or the girls, or all three?

The responding hope in Ellie's heart felt too intimate, too real. How was she supposed to remain immune to the man when he looked at her like…like… *that*?

"It's good to see you again this morning." His deep voice fell over her soft as a caress.

She swallowed back a sigh. "Good to see you, too."

Their gazes held a long, silent beat. As always, whenever he gave her his undivided attention, an unspoken message passed between them, one Ellie didn't fully understand. Right then, in that moment, she somehow felt less alone.

Which made little sense. She wasn't alone. She had her father, and would soon add his future bride, Betsy, to the ranks of her family.

And yet, with Caleb eyeing her so closely, his gaze soft and welcoming, a warm sensation moved through her. Ellie couldn't help but think of far-off dreams and a happily settled future.

"Will you sit with us during service?" Hannah asked.

Touched by the request, Ellie once again smiled down at the child. "If it's all right with your father, then, yes, I'd like that very much."

"As would I." Caleb held out his hand to her.

Ellie accepted the silent call without hesitation, then just as smoothly, reached out and grasped hold of one of Grace's hands. Caleb took one of Hannah's and the four of them entered the church linked together.

Caleb steered their tiny group to one of the middle pews. A lot of shuffling and giggling ensued as he and Ellie removed the children's hats, coats and gloves. Almost as soon as they were settled in their chosen seats, the girls between the adults, the strains of the first hymn filled the church.

As if the organist and Ellie were in cahoots—which, admittedly, they were—the song was "What Child Is This?"

Hannah and Grace launched into the tune with great enthusiasm. Grace had a better memory than her sister, but Hannah caught up at the end of each line, all but shouting the words *sleeping* and then *keeping*.

Eyes dancing in amusement, Caleb chuckled softly. Ellie glanced at him with raised eyebrows.

"I believe a bit of practice at home is in order," he whispered for her ears only.

They shared a smile over the children's heads. Other young voices joined in the song, voices that belonged to children in the play. Ellie's heart soared. Evidently her second rehearsal had been a success.

The rest of the service went quickly. Her father's sermon was on God's love given to mankind in the gift of His Son, an appropriate message for the season. After the congregation sang the last hymn, her father dismissed them all with a prayer and a blessing for the coming week.

Ellie and Caleb went through the arduous process of swathing the twins in their winter weather gear. She then escorted the Voss family around the back of the church and into the tiny room off the kitchen of the parsonage where she and Caleb once again began unraveling two squirming children from coats, gloves, scarves and hats.

A pleasant female voice rang out from the kitchen beyond. "Do I hear the sound of familiar laughter?"

"You do, indeed," Ellie called out in response.

Betsy Anderson, the woman engaged to Ellie's father and who also served as Caleb's housekeeper, stuck her head around the corner. Her light brown eyes peeked out from behind wire-framed glasses and, in what Ellie considered Betsy's no-nonsense style, her gold-streaked, brown hair hung in a single braid down her back.

Somewhere in her late thirties, maybe early forties,

the other woman's face was slightly lined, probably due as much to her worry for her dying sister as from age.

At the moment, however, Betsy's pleasantly round features wore a happy smile. Her cheeks were pink from exertion, as if she'd hurried to the house and then went to work immediately after the service, perhaps even before the final hymn was sung. She was going to make a wonderful pastor's wife.

The Voss girls squealed in delight when they were finally free of their coats and saw their housekeeper smiling down at them.

"Miss Betsy, Miss Betsy," they said in tandem. "Did you hear us singing in church this morning?"

"I most certainly did."

"Want to hear the song again?" Hannah asked.

"I do, yes." She held up a hand to forestall the impromptu concert. "*After* we eat dinner."

Their little faces fell.

Ellie quickly took control of the situation. "Come on, girls. Let's get you washed up for dinner."

Giving them no chance to argue, she guided them to the washbasin. Halfway through the room, she heard Caleb inquire after Betsy's sister.

"Her health is failing by the day."

Ellie's heart went out to Betsy, as well as the sister she loved and the woman's young son. As she helped the twins wash their hands and faces, Ellie lifted up a silent prayer for Clara Driscoll and her boy, Brody.

Lord, be with them today and always, bring them the peace that can only come from You, the peace that surpasses all understanding.

Having lost her own mother at sixteen, Ellie knew

the sorrow Brody suffered as he helplessly watched his mother die.

Heart in her throat, she looked down at the Voss twins. They, too, had lost their mother, at a much younger age than Brody. How much of Lizzie did they remember?

No woman could ever replace their mother, but Ellie prayed that whomever Caleb married would love his daughters as her own. That woman wouldn't be Ellie. Not because she couldn't see herself loving Hannah and Grace, but because she could also see herself loving Caleb.

That love would only bring her heartache. Caleb wanted a very different kind of marriage than Ellie did. No good would come from building up hope that one day he'd change his mind.

She must focus on her own future. She'd already sent out queries for another teaching position. Though jobs rarely opened up in the middle of the school year, she was confident the Lord would provide in His time. She simply needed to have faith. And patience.

She set aside the towel in her hand. "All done."

"Thank you, Miss Ellie."

The girls hugged her, then ran off to find their father and Betsy. Ellie stayed behind, her mind traveling back in time to the pain and humiliation of being judged for something her brother had done.

When she'd told Monroe the entire story of Everett's crime, she'd expected him to give her the same grace and understanding her father showed the members of his flock. Ellie had terribly underestimated the widowed preacher's capacity for forgiveness.

It was telling that she missed Monroe's daughters

more than she missed him. In fact, she missed her teaching position more than the prospect of marrying him.

Even though matters hadn't turned out as she'd hoped, Ellie's dream of becoming a wife and mother still lived in her heart. Wiser now, she promised herself that whomever she eventually married, he would love her with his whole heart.

She would settle for nothing less.

Chapter Five

Caleb stepped into the Wainwrights' living room and took in all the Christmas decorations. A sense of homecoming slipped through him, calming his soul, reminding him of the kind of home he wanted to provide for his family, not only at Christmastime but all year long.

Standing here, looking at the festive living room, he tried to recall the last time he'd been in this house. It had to be before he'd married Lizzie. Not much had changed in the years during his absence.

The furniture, positioned in the same places, still looked comfortable and inviting. If he closed his eyes, he would still be able to navigate around the overstuffed sofa, the brocade-covered chairs, the piano and various tables. He could walk to the wallpaper and run his fingers along the swirling floral pattern.

He'd spent many happy days in this house, the family treating him as if he was just another Wainwright son.

Guilt clogged the breath in his lungs.

He should have kept in closer contact with Reverend Wainwright. The man had lost his wife to illness, his son to prison and then his daughter to a job in Colorado Springs.

As if his thoughts could conjure up the man himself, the reverend came up behind Caleb and clapped a hand on his shoulder. "I can't tell you how happy I am you accepted my invitation. It's been too long since you were in this home."

"I'm sorry for that, Reverend."

"Don't be." The man's eyes held nothing but acceptance. "You're in a busy season of life, still grieving your wife and raising five-year-old daughters on your own."

"I'm not completely on my own," he countered. "Your future wife has been a godsend these past ten months, keeping my house in order and caring for the girls."

"My Betsy is a generous woman."

Too generous, he knew. She had enough of her own concerns with her nephew and dying sister, yet she still managed to help out Caleb and his tiny family.

He really needed to find a wife, sooner rather than later. After the chaos Lizzie had brought into their home, after the long absences, the not knowing how long she would be gone, or if she would ever return, Caleb was determined to restore order in his home. His daughters deserved stability. They deserved a carefully controlled, ordered life.

There could be no more unnecessary upheaval in their lives.

As if reading his thoughts, Reverend Wainwright addressed the situation directly. "I hear you've enlisted Mrs. Jenson in your search for a bride."

Caleb resisted the impulse to correct the other man.

He wasn't looking for a bride, but rather a mother for the girls.

To say as much would be splitting hairs. The important point was that the owner of the local boarding-house was on the hunt for a suitable woman for Caleb to marry. "Mrs. Jenson seems confident she'll have success soon."

The woman knew his parameters, knew he only wanted a marriage of convenience.

Would she find him a wife in time for Christmas?

The holiday was three weeks away and Betsy was marrying Reverend Wainwright on New Year's Eve. Even without the concerns with her sister, Caleb would soon be without help.

"Betsy and I have discussed your situation and we've decided she'll continue working for you until you can find a suitable bride."

Caleb blinked at the other man, humbled by the offer. Once she married Jedidiah Wainwright, Betsy would take on the role of a pastor's wife, which would require all sorts of additional tasks besides simply running his home. She would visit the sick, as well as deliver aid to the poor and less fortunate.

No matter how desperate his situation, Caleb couldn't take away from others in far greater need than himself. "If Mrs. Jenson doesn't have success soon, I'll figure something else out."

Laughter came from his left. Out of the corner of his eye, Caleb watched Ellie direct his daughters to a spot on the rug, a ball and jacks in her hand.

"The offer stands, son."

Son. The term washed over him like a warm summer rain. Caleb had done nothing to deserve this man's kindness. The words from Reverend Wainwright's sermon came back to him now. *Grace is a gift undeserved and unearned, freely given to us by our Heavenly Father.*

Caleb thought of his earthly father. Harold Voss hadn't been a bad man, just a weak one, so swallowed up with grief after his wife's death he'd had no problem abandoning his five sons to fend for themselves.

But Caleb hadn't been completely alone. This man standing before him now had modeled the Heavenly Father's love in too many ways to count.

The back of Caleb's eyes burned and his throat closed up tight, too tight to push words past his lips. He thought of Brody Driscoll, of the difficult days ahead. At the boy's age Caleb had his brothers, and Everett, and the Wainwrights.

Who did Brody have?

He had his aunt Betsy. But the boy needed a father figure, a masculine role model.

The thought had barely materialized when Betsy called her future husband into the kitchen to help her with moving chairs to the table.

Caleb attempted to join the reverend, but he shook him off with a smile. "I've got it covered. Go spend time with your daughters."

"Thank you, Reverend, I believe I will."

He found the girls still playing jacks with Ellie. He couldn't take his eyes off her. A sunbeam streamed through the window, backlighting her in golden splendor. Her pale blue eyes were thickly lashed and shimmered with good humor. She was as lovely and as bright as the sun behind her, her skin as lustrous as a pearl.

Her pink lips parted in a smile and his mind emptied of everything but her. *This is Ellie,* he reminded himself. He knew he was in deep trouble the moment she looked in his direction.

A profound ache spread from his heart and traveled up into his throat. Unable to resist her, he entered the room. The click of his heels on the hardwood floor was as familiar as the fixtures on the wall. The look and smell of Christmas was all around him.

"I love your tree, Miss Ellie," Hannah remarked in a wistful tone.

"We don't have one in our house," Grace added, looking—and sounding—as forlorn as Caleb had ever witnessed.

Regret swirled in his stomach. He'd been so focused on finding his daughters a mother he'd let the smaller, equally meaningful matters slip away from him. Just because he didn't have a wife to provide the girls with a stable home didn't mean he couldn't get them a Christmas tree.

"There's a simple solution," he said, stepping fully into the room, into the moment. "I'll cut us down a tree of our own this week."

"Oh, Papa, do you really mean it?" The restrained joy in Grace's eyes was mirrored in Hannah's gaze.

Their genuine surprise came as somewhat of a blow. "I absolutely mean it."

The girls cheered, then hopped to their feet and rushed to him. He trapped them against his chest.

"My dear sweet girls," he said in a low, choked voice. How he loved them.

"You're the best, Papa," Grace said into his shirt.

"The very, very best," Hannah agreed.

Overcome with emotion, he leaned down and buried

his face in their baby-fine hair that smelled of the lilac soap he'd bought at the mercantile last week.

He felt his chest tighten with unspeakable love so strong it nearly brought him to his knees. A soft gasp came from Ellie. On impulse, he glanced over at her. Her eyes swam with some unreadable emotion. The look made him feel somehow taller, maybe even heroic.

"If you need help decorating your tree," she said, shifting to a standing position, "I'd love to offer my assistance."

The girls stepped out of his arms and proceeded to shower their enthusiasm onto Ellie.

Caleb caught what looked like a vulnerable expression on her face. Was it a look of longing, he wondered, or was it a trick of the light?

Betsy called them all to the table. There was a festive feel to the meal. Heaping bowls of whipped potatoes, corn and preserves were passed around, while varied conversations collided over one another.

Why had he avoided this home?

Why had he denied his daughters the taste of normalcy and stability he himself had found with this family?

The meal went by in a blur.

Once they finished eating and Betsy had set aside two plates of food for her sister and nephew, the girls asked if they could sing their song. Betsy guided the twins toward the piano in the living room.

Reverend Wainwright joined them.

Caleb stood beside Ellie in the doorway and watched his daughters entertain the older couple. A silence—comfortable as only one between longtime friends could be—settled over them.

Now, he told himself, *make your offer now.*

"Can we talk?" He waited for her to swing her gaze to his to finish the rest of his request. "In private?"

The question seemed to render her momentarily speechless. She rallied a second later. "Yes, of course. Why don't we take a short walk?"

"Splendid idea."

Huddled inside her coat, Ellie fell into step beside Caleb. They walked in companionable silence for several blocks then retraced their steps at a slower pace. Not quite sure what had motivated his request to speak with her alone, she slid a covert glance his way from beneath lowered lashes.

He appeared lost in thought, and she wondered at that, wondered what was on his mind. But then she feared she knew.

"Is this about the Christmas tree?" she blurted out. "Did I overstep by offering to decorate it with you and the girls?"

"You didn't overstep." He drew to a halt and looked at her with an easy smile, prompting her stomach to twist.

She opened her mouth but shut it when she realized he wasn't through speaking. "In fact, I want to thank you for the offer. The children have never had a Christmas tree, so I'm pleased they're going to get one this year."

No Christmas tree? Ever? "But surely your wife—" She cut off the rest of the words. "Never mind, I shouldn't have brought up Lizzie."

But now that she had, she realized this would be Caleb's first Christmas without his wife, and his daughters' first Christmas without their mother.

"In answer to your unspoken question, no, Lizzie didn't decorate for Christmas." Something cheerless came and went in his eyes. "Holidays made her melancholy."

Ellie sensed there was more to the story, but she didn't think now was the time to pry. "I'm sorry, Caleb, for you and the girls."

"Thank you." He began walking again. She trotted to catch up then slowed her pace to match his.

The tension on his face told her he needed to unburden himself about something. Ellie reminded herself that above all else she was this man's friend. Friends offered one another support, no judgment, no condemnation, no inquisitions.

"Christmas isn't solely about the decorations," she began. "It's about being with family and…"

She let her words trail off, regretting opening her mouth, fearing he would misunderstand what she'd meant to say.

"I don't disagree, Ellie. Family is everything. But the girls have never experienced a real Christmas with all the trappings. I want that for them."

Those poor children.

This poor man.

No wonder Caleb wanted to remarry so quickly after his wife's death. "At least you have Betsy," Ellie offered in a small voice. "She'll make your house a home this Christmas."

"I'm sure she will." His response lacked enthusiasm.

In that moment, Ellie felt such longing. *I want to be the woman to give the Voss family a happy Christmas, all three of them.*

What was stopping her?

Nothing. Absolutely nothing was holding her back, except her own fears. And her selfish worry over what it would do to her if she allowed herself to get too close to this man and his children.

Well, this wasn't about her. This was about a family in need of something she had the ability and desire to give.

Ellie remembered what it was like to lose a mother, to experience that first holiday with the hole in the home left after her death.

"I have a proposal," she said when they arrived back at her house.

"I was going to say the same."

They shared a smile and for that brief moment a spark of hope kindled to life deep within her.

"You first," he said. "Tell me what's on your mind."

"Well. I was thinking." She paused at the foot of the porch, gathering her thoughts. "Maybe I could—"

The sound of pounding feet up the walk cut her off. She looked over her shoulder. "Brody? What's wrong, what's happened?"

Before the words left her mouth, Caleb was spinning around to face the boy.

"It's my mama." He skidded to a stop, slapped his hands on his knees and sucked in several gulping breaths of air. "She fell down and hit her head. There was lots of blood, but she made me promise not to get Doc. I helped her clean up as best I could. When she fell asleep I came here. Aunt Betsy is the only one who can convince Mama to let Doc inside the house."

"I'll fetch your aunt for you." Ellie rushed inside the house.

After a brief explanation, Betsy and Ellie's father grabbed their coats and hurried outside.

Deciding the others accompanying Brody was enough, Ellie stayed behind with Caleb's daughters. She did her best to keep Hannah and Grace occupied with a story. Their eyes drooped, a clear indication the excitement of the day was catching up with them.

As Ellie directed them to join her on the couch, she lifted up a silent prayer for Brody and his mother. *Lord, heal Clara Driscoll, bring her peace and freedom from pain, and give Brody the courage he's going to need in the coming days.*

When the girls went from tired to cranky and started arguing over who got to hold the book, Ellie settled them on each end. Covering them with a blanket, she began singing a favorite lullaby from her childhood.

Their eyes shut almost immediately. Just about the time their breathing evened out, Caleb reentered the house.

One look at his face and Ellie knew Brody's mother was in a bad way. She cocked her head toward the sleeping children, then motioned for Caleb to follow her into the dining room.

As soon as the swinging door shut behind them, Ellie broke her silence. "How is Brody's mother?"

"Better than we feared. Doc didn't appear too concerned over her injury."

"Good." She breathed a sigh of relief. "That's really good news."

"I left her with your father and her sister." Shadows swirled in Caleb's gaze, dark and worried. Wanting to offer comfort where she could, Ellie touched his arm.

He blessed her with a slight smile.

As a thought occurred to her, she slowly pulled her hand away. "Betsy will want to spend as much time with her sister as possible, day and night."

"Yes." Caleb rubbed a hand over his eyes. "As she should."

"That leaves you in a bind."

He nodded. A pensive look shaded his face, but he said nothing more.

"I'll watch the children for you." The offer came out of her mouth as natural as a breath.

Caleb eyed her speculatively. "Actually, I had a more permanent solution in mind."

Her heartbeat slammed against her ribs. Hope rose. She shoved it back with a hard swallow. This wasn't about her. It wasn't the realization of a dream, or a fairy tale. It was real life and real people in need. A woman was dying, a fractured family in pain.

"You're a good influence on my daughters, Ellie. I trust you with them completely."

Ellie sought to still the pounding of her heart. There was no reason to feel alarm. So she'd caught Caleb watching her throughout the day, his brows knit together as if working out a puzzle, or sorting through the particulars of a plan.

"You're a steady woman, smart and capable. Easygoing, and not prone to outbursts or unnecessary drama."

Listening to Caleb describe her with such bland words, Ellie didn't know whether to be flattered or insulted. *Steady, capable, not prone to outbursts.* Was she truly that boring?

That forgettable?

Did he think her lacking in the finer, feminine qualities of kindness, gentleness and, well, prettiness?

"We've known each other for years." He touched her cheek with such tenderness she thought she might cry. "I've always liked you, Ellie."

"I've always liked you, too, Caleb."

A broad range of memories swept across her mind, dragging her back to childhood when this man had been a boy, and she a young girl with stars in her eyes. He'd championed her on more than one occasion, such as the time when Everett had stuck her braid in an inkwell. It was Caleb who'd helped her wash out the black goo.

Then, on the worst day of her life, when her mother had died, Caleb had been by Ellie's side. He'd let her cry on his shoulder, had tenderly dried her cheeks with the pads of his thumbs.

"…and that, Ellie, is why I'm asking you to marry me."

What? Had she heard him correctly? Had he just asked her to marry him, while she'd been skipping down memory lane?

Surely she'd misunderstood.

Untangling herself from the past, she forced herself to focus, to recall the precise words he'd uttered. One line came back to her. *You'll make the girls a good mother.*

There'd been no mention of love.

"Well?" He touched her arm, looked at her expectantly. "What do you say?"

"Could…could you repeat the question?"

He smiled. "Ellie Wainwright," he said in a low, soft, affectionate tone. "Will you marry me?"

Chapter Six

As he waited for Ellie's answer, Caleb choked down an unexpected bout of nerves. *Say yes*, he silently willed.

Say something, he amended two seconds later. *Anything*.

Why wasn't she speaking? –

Why was she staring up at him, standing motionless, moving only her eyelashes in a quick, fast flutter?

Perhaps he'd been too abrupt with his words, too quick to get to the point.

At last, Ellie's lips parted slightly, as if she meant to say something, but then she snapped her mouth shut.

Caleb's agitation increased.

He couldn't bear her silence a moment longer. "Before you respond, let me say again—"

"You want to marry me?"

He nodded, not sure why she sounded so confused. The more he worked the idea around in his head, the more he wanted Ellie to mother his daughters.

"Why?"

"Excuse me?"

"*Why* do you wish to marry me?"

Every muscle in his body tensed. He thought he'd made himself clear. The catch in her voice said differently. "I told you."

She blinked again, three rapid flutters, then clasped her hands tightly together in front of her. "I… I think I need you to restate your reasons."

Ah, now he understood her confusion. Apparently he'd spoken too quickly. An oversight easily fixed.

"Ellie." He took one of her hands again, gently pressing his palms to hers. "You're good with the girls, patient and kind. They like you. You seem to like them… and you're frowning."

"Am I?"

He gently squeezed her hand and immediately felt a sense of calm, as if all was right in the world.

The connection didn't seem to have the same effect on Ellie. A storm of emotion brewed in her eyes, even a hint of pain.

Caleb hadn't meant to upset her with his proposal, though it seemed he'd done just that. "Tell me what I said that's made you so sad."

"I'm not sad, I'm merely confused." Her frown dug deeper. "I don't understand why you want to marry me. Is it only for your daughters' sake?"

He heard what she was really asking, but chose to bypass the loaded question. "The girls have experienced much uncertainty in their young lives. I've provided what stability I can, but they need a mother. A mother like you. You're the steadiest woman I know."

"There are other women in town who are equally steady."

"Perhaps, but you're also trustworthy, stable and reliable. And—"

"Kate Riley is all those things." Still frowning, Ellie pulled her hand free of his. "As is the local school-teacher, Lillian O'Hare. Either woman would make a perfectly acceptable mother for your daughters."

True, and he'd considered them in the past, had even approached both women. Now he was grateful they'd declined his offer.

Ellie was special. They had a history. They were friends. He cared about her, liked her. "We'd be good together."

Their home would be free of turmoil.

Sighing, she reached up and fiddled with the top button of her collar. "You don't really want to be married. You're simply looking for a woman to mother your daughters."

"That's not to say we won't enjoy a comfortable, peaceful life together. I'll keep you safe, Ellie. I'll take care of you. I'll never leave you, or allow harm to come to you."

"What about love?"

Caleb's throat seized at the question. His relationship with Lizzie had been a love match but had become tumultuous quickly, bringing only pain and disillusionment to them both.

"Love isn't what the songs and poems claim." He took his time, carefully choosing his words. "Love wanes with time. But friendship, now that, Ellie, lasts forever."

"Do you really believe friendship is better than love?"

He didn't just believe it. He knew it in the deepest part of his soul. "Yes."

The disappointment in her eyes made his shoulders

bunch again, the muscles drawing so tightly together a knot formed in the middle of his back.

"The kind of marriage you're suggesting isn't for me. I want to build a home, a future and a life on the solid foundation of love. Anything less would be nothing more than existing."

"Companionship has its advantages."

"God intended marriage for more."

Caleb had never heard Ellie speak that passionately before. As he stared into her expressive gaze, he felt a moment of regret.

"As much as I like and admire you, my answer is no. I won't marry you."

The sense of defeat that shot through him nearly dropped him to his knees.

"I understand." He sensed he'd just lost something precious, something that might have been, were he a different man.

His friendship with Ellie was strong. Even Lizzie had noticed their connection. She'd accused him of having tender feelings for Everett's little sister. Caleb had told his wife any tender feelings he had for Ellie were based on a bond that had been forged in childhood.

He'd meant what he said. They could have a built a good life together.

But she wanted more than he could give.

He'd had his chance at love. Despite dedicating all he had to making his marriage work, it had failed. Love had only complicated matters, not helped. Lizzie's constant dissatisfaction had thrown their home into chaos and his daughters had suffered. They were still suffering. He couldn't—*wouldn't*—risk their well-being again.

"I'm sorry, Caleb, truly I am." Ellie's voice went soft. "I hope we can remain friends."

"Always."

"Then in the spirit of friendship, I have a counter-offer. A compromise, if you will."

The shyness in her voice was downright adorable. Caleb found himself smiling in response. "What did you have in mind?"

"Let me take over for Betsy while she focuses on her sister. I'll keep your house and watch your daughters until you find another solution, or—" She paused, before continuing, "a woman to marry, whichever comes first."

Now that he'd allowed himself to think of Ellie as more than Everett's little sister, Caleb couldn't imagine anyone else in his home but her. Unfortunately, they wanted different arrangements. "That's kind of you, but—"

"You need me, Caleb, and I'd really like to provide your daughters with a nice Christmas, one they'll not soon forget."

The smile she gave him radiated from the goodness of her heart.

He desperately wanted what she offered. For the girls. "It won't be an imposition?"

She waved the question away with a flick of her wrist. "Until I find another teaching position, my days are relatively free of obligation."

Her words caught him up short. "You're planning to leave town again?"

The thought weighed heavy in his gut. The sensation felt like grief.

"I can't stay in Thunder Ridge indefinitely, especially since the only teaching position is already taken.

I've sent out a half-dozen queries. No replies yet, but I'm sure I'll hear something soon."

He thought he heard a note of humiliation in her voice. Not for the first time he wondered why she'd left her job in Colorado Springs.

"You truly want to leave Thunder Ridge?"

"It's not that I want to go, but once my father marries Betsy I'll be in the way."

"Neither would want you leaving town on their account."

"Perhaps you're right, but newlyweds deserve time to themselves. I want them to enjoy one another and find their rhythm as a couple without me around. So you see. I'm perfectly available to step in for Betsy, at least temporarily."

He'd rather her in his home on a permanent basis. It wasn't meant to be.

"What do you say?" Ellie's smile shot through him like a sharp knife slicing through gristle. "Will you allow me the honor of watching over your daughters and giving them a Christmas with all the trappings? One they won't soon forget?"

Under the circumstances, he really didn't have much of a choice. "We can give it a try."

What could possibly go wrong?

"Oh, Caleb, I won't let you down." She beamed as if he'd given her a treasured gift.

She'd never looked more beautiful. Her pull was strong, more powerful than he'd previously understood.

A crack split open in his heart, giving him all sorts of reasons for regretting his decision. Not a single reservation had to do with his daughters.

"Unless you can think of a reason I shouldn't start

immediately, I'll arrive at your house first thing to-morrow morning."

He could think of a hundred things that could go wrong with this plan. Starting with the fact that he and Ellie were at cross-purposes, with no chance of resolv-ing their differences.

Despite his misgivings, he found himself saying, "That'll be fine."

The night's chill still clung on the air when Caleb greeted Ellie at his front door the next morning. De-spite the early hour and the heavy mist swirling around her feet, she looked eager to begin the day.

As was becoming a regular occurrence, her smile did something to his gut. The sensation wasn't alto-gether awful. Just being near Ellie made Caleb think of better days ahead, of endless possibilities, of hope for the future.

Problem was he'd given up on hope a long time ago, at least in terms of himself. For his daughters, that was another story. He had countless dreams for them. It was a real shame Ellie wanted a love match, while he only wanted friendship.

"Good morning, Caleb."

"Good morning." He stepped aside to let her enter his house. A blast of cold air followed in her wake.

He quickly shut the door. After a cursory glance over the main living area, then a peek in the kitchen, Ellie focused her blue-blue eyes on him. "Where are the girls?"

"Still asleep." He hitched his chin toward the hall-way behind her. "They were so excited about the prospect of spending the entire day with you that I had a hard time getting them settled last night."

Her widening smile suggested this piece of information pleased her.

"Probably best to let them rest. I have big plans for us today. I even brought supplies." She showed him the large carpetbag slung over her shoulder. "You won't recognize your home when you return tonight."

Curious, he leaned over and attempted to glimpse inside the large tote. "What do you have in there?"

"A little of this, a little of that, all of which will require eager hands and resourceful minds."

"Sounds fun."

"That's the general idea."

He laughed. She joined in, and for the first time in months Caleb's chest felt less tight, his heart beat easier in his chest.

"How about giving me a quick introduction to your home?"

"Follow me." He dedicated the next ten minutes to showing her around the house, pointing out various places of interest.

Lastly, he escorted her into the room off the kitchen where the family's coats hung on pegs.

Tour complete, he reached for his hat. "I'll try to come home before sunset."

"You're leaving? Now?" She circled her gaze around the kitchen, stopping at the stove tucked in the early morning shadows. "But you haven't eaten breakfast yet."

"I'll grab something at the Whistle Stop Inn."

"Are you certain? I could make oatmeal."

He was tempted, but decided to stick to his regular

routine. No good would come from relying too much on Ellie, even for something as simple as an early morning meal.

"I need to get to the jail and relieve Deputy Kramer," he said by way of excuse.

Two minutes later, dressed for the cold weather, Caleb trekked through the biting wind. His first stop was the livery stables three blocks south of where he lived.

Gideon greeted him with a toss of his regal head and a whinny that shook the rafters.

Caleb was just as pleased to see the horse.

The rest of the day went as expected. He ate a quick breakfast, checked on nearby ranches, then stopped in at each of the local businesses.

In the afternoon, he broke up a heated argument between the cooper and blacksmith that had begun over signage. Near the end of his shift, just as Prescott arrived to take over for him, Caleb dragged Skeeter Quinn, the town drunk, out of an empty horse trough, where the grizzled old man had decided to "take a little lie down"—Skeeter's words.

Skeeter was far from pleased over his interrupted nap and proceeded to make his displeasure known at the top of his lungs.

His own temper turning dark, Caleb decided to lock up the blustering old coot in a jail cell to dry out. As expected, Skeeter turned even more belligerent the moment the door clanked shut. He continued ranting for a good five minutes then wore himself out and promptly passed out on the lone cot.

Caleb rubbed a hand across the back of his neck and studied the snoring form. Sprawled out on the cot, his head listing to port, Skeeter looked—and sounded—entirely too much like Caleb's father in his final days.

"Keep an eye on Skeeter," he told Prescott. "I'll hunt down his son and send him over to collect him."

"No problem, Sheriff."

Skeeter snorted in his sleep, then took to mumbling over some incomprehensible grievance.

Caleb headed for the door.

"Hey, Sheriff," Prescott called after him, a curious note in his voice. "I was wondering if you knew whether or not Ellie Wainwright had any plans for—"

"She's unavailable." To punctuate his point, Caleb turned and scowled at the deputy.

Prescott's amused gaze held his. "How do you know?"

"I know."

The deputy chuckled low in his throat. "You really aren't going to introduce me to her?"

"No, I'm not."

"Come on, Sheriff. I heard she's sweet. Word around town is that no one's officially courting her. Surely she would want to meet—"

Caleb slammed the door on the rest of whatever Prescott had to say.

His temper escalating yet again, he set out north of town where Skeeter's son, Billie, lived. A block into his journey, he heard his name. "Sheriff Voss, Sheriff Voss, I have news."

Glancing in the direction of the voice, he caught sight of Mrs. Jenson waving a letter high above her head.

Trepidation marched along his spine. Nevertheless, Caleb crossed the street with clipped strides and greeted the woman with a tentative smile.

Short, scarecrow thin, with gray-streaked black hair twisted in a knot at the nape of her neck, she wore too many ruffles, layers upon layers of lace and a self-satisfied smile.

"Good afternoon, Mrs. Jenson. You're looking rather…" He searched for the proper adjective. "Glee-ful."

"That's because *this* arrived in the post today." She lowered her hand and proceeded to wave the small stack of papers beneath Caleb's nose. "You'll be happy to know I've found your bride."

This was the exact information he'd been waiting for, yet Caleb couldn't drum up any real enthusiasm.

His silence didn't seem to deter the woman. "Her name is Sadie Taylor."

He didn't know what to say. But the look of expectancy on Mrs. Jenson's face suggested she was waiting for him to respond. "That's a…ah, nice name?"

This earned him a nod of approval. "Isn't it?

"According to her letter…" The older woman skimmed the front page a moment. "She's twenty-two years old, recently widowed, with no children of her own. She lives in Blue Springs, Missouri, and is a schoolteacher."

Caleb's mind went straight to another schoolteacher, the one back at his house taking care of his daughters and providing them a "Christmas with all the trappings, one they won't soon forget."

"There's only one concern." Mrs. Jenson's tone filled with distress. "Mrs. Taylor won't be able to make the journey to Thunder Ridge until after the school year is complete."

Caleb couldn't tell if the hitch in his breath was disappointment or relief. Probably a little of both. "I'd hoped to marry before then."

"Yes, I know, dear." Mrs. Jenson patted his forearm. "But I warned you these things take time."

He frowned.

"Now, now, my boy, there's no cause for despair. Of all the letters I've received in response to my advertisement, Mrs. Taylor is the most suitable and has agreed to your stipulation of a marriage in name only."

Caleb considered this vital piece of information. Sadie Taylor of Blue Springs, Missouri, sounded perfect for his future bride.

Where was the relief? The pleasure?

"And here's a bit of heartening news." Mrs. Jenson looked up from the letter. "Mrs. Taylor's father is a preacher in their small town."

What were the odds?

The woman who supposedly suited him best was a twenty-two-year-old schoolteacher whose father was a preacher. Sounded exactly like someone else Caleb knew, save for one glaring difference. Ellie wanted more than a marriage of convenience.

"Well, then." Mrs. Jenson folded the letter in half. "Shall I continue my search? Or should I tell Mrs. Taylor to make the journey to Thunder Ridge?"

Caleb thought of his daughters, of the disorder they'd suffered most of their lives. Hannah and Grace needed a mother. Sadie Taylor fit his requirements.

Under the circumstances, there was only one answer to Mrs. Jenson's question. "Tell her to come as soon as possible."

Chapter Seven

Later that afternoon, Ellie knew the exact moment Caleb entered the house through the back door. Her awareness had nothing to do with the amount of noise he made banging snow off his boots. The very air in the kitchen changed.

"Papa's home, Papa's home," Grace announced at the top of her lungs.

Hannah repeated the mantra, her voice pitched an entire octave higher than her sister's.

The urge to join the girls in their happy, squealing enthusiasm came alive inside Ellie. She resisted, barely.

Setting aside the spoon in her hand, Ellie looked over her shoulder. In walked Caleb, dressed in black from head to toe, his face red from the cold, his hair attractively mussed from a recent finger-combing.

Ellie's heart raced. Her palms went damp. Her brain emptied of thought. *Oh, my.*

Bouncing on their toes, Grace and Hannah vied for their father's attention, each attempting to tell him about their day.

Caleb divided his attention between both girls. He

even made comments and asked questions, somehow able to discern their fast chatter.

As Ellie watched him interact with his daughters, she fell a little in love with him. He was such a good man, a devoted father. Her knees wobbled. They actually wobbled.

Would she ever grow used to that handsome face, that tall, lean frame, that bronze, sun-kissed hair? Surely, in time, the sight of him would become familiar enough that her stomach would no longer roll and dip whenever he was near.

Caleb's gaze shifted from his daughters to Ellie, his fatherly attentiveness replaced with something far more adult, something solely for her.

Oh, my.

Pulse roaring in her ears, she quickly looked away, but not before she caught the boyish grin he flashed in her direction. "Something smells good."

"We made soup," Hannah announced.

Footsteps sounded on the kitchen floor. "What kind of soup?"

This time, Grace answered his question. "Vegetable."

"No kidding?" He approached Ellie, coming so close she was forced to look up. The air in the kitchen suddenly felt thinner, her head lighter.

"Vegetable soup is my favorite."

"I remember," she managed to say past the tightness in her throat.

The look of pleasure in his eyes transported her back in time, to the many days Caleb had spent at her house, to the thrill she'd experienced whenever her mother told her to set an extra place at the supper table for him.

Her heart skipped a beat as memories collided into one another. She nearly rolled her eyes at herself. This was Caleb. Everett's childhood friend.

Her friend, too, the man who'd asked her to marry him because of their history and longtime acquaintance.

Friendship lasts forever, he'd told her. Perhaps that was true, but it wasn't enough for Ellie, not nearly enough.

Why couldn't he love her, just a little?

"Supper will be ready in a few minutes," she said, relieved her voice came out smooth and steady.

Smooth and steady. That was her, all right. Steady Ellie.

She thought she might cry.

Obviously unaware of her inner turmoil, Caleb peered over the edge of the pot. "What can I do to help?"

"I have everything under control here." Well, of course she had everything under control, seeing as she was so *steady.*

"Can we show Papa what we did today?"

Happy for the interruption, Ellie smoothed her hand over Grace's light brown hair. "That's a wonderful idea."

Back to battling for their father's attention, each girl took one of Caleb's hands and, together, they tugged him toward the living room.

Wanting to see his reaction, Ellie followed the trio, her eyes solely on Caleb.

Barely three steps into the room, his feet ground to a halt. He looked left, then right, then left again. "You've been busy." At the sound of wonder in his voice Ellie's stomach hit her toes.

Trying to take in the room from his perspective, she moved in beside him. "We still have more to do, but we've made a good start."

"It's so much more than I imagined."

No longer fighting with one another, the twins took turns narrating the events of the day.

"We cut out paper snowflakes and stars, which took *all* morning, and then we made those." Hannah pointed out the paper decorations on the wall and the green sprigs that lined the mantelpiece.

Grace hurried to the center of the room and showed off the three large washtubs they'd filled with branches, pinecones and sprigs of holly.

When the girls finished giving the detailed story behind each decoration, Caleb came up to Ellie, took her hand and gave it a gentle squeeze. "Thank you."

The simple gratitude made her knees wobble again. Stupid knees. "It was my pleasure."

She couldn't make herself look away from his handsome face.

They were having *a moment*, and Ellie thought she might lose her breath completely. How was she supposed to remember they were friends when Caleb looked at her with such affection, such warmth?

Ellie had a desperate, all-consuming need to make this man happy, to fill his life with joy and laughter. And love. Most of all, love. She had so much to give.

She quickly broke eye contact; it was either that or sigh wistfully.

Releasing her hand, Caleb sent the girls to wash up

for supper. Clearly reluctant to leave, they exited the room at the speed of snail.

Ellie tried not to let her heart fill with love for them. Had she learned nothing from her experience with Monroe? She'd failed to keep up her guard. Already, she adored the twins more than she should. They were sweet and eager to please and had so much of Caleb in them.

"You're a good father," she said once they were alone.

The smile he gave her transformed his face, softening the bold lines and angles. Caleb was already ridiculously attractive. That smile only made him more so.

Ellie gave in to that sigh after all. "We'll string popcorn and cranberries tomorrow. I was thinking of baking cookies the day after that, and then," she said as she swung her gaze back to his, "there's the matter of a tree."

"I'll take care of cutting one down this week."

"That would be lovely." She clasped her hands together at her waist. "Speaking of trees…"

She hesitated, hoping she wasn't overstepping, then reminded herself he'd put her in charge of giving his girls a happy Christmas.

"Go on," he urged.

"What do you say about possibly, maybe, entering the annual tree-decorating contest in town?"

The event had been a tradition in Thunder Ridge since Ellie was a young girl. In her mind, the contest, with its cheerful feel and good-natured competition, marked the beginning of the Christmas season.

"The children and I have never entered the contest."

"Never?"

He shook his head.

Oh, Caleb. Sympathy squeezed in Ellie's heart. This man and his daughters had missed out on so much. It was as though they'd lived in Thunder Ridge, yet not really been a part of the community.

"There's nothing quite like competing for the gold star." The winning family received a beautiful topper for their tree at home.

"The contest is tomorrow evening. I would think it's too late to enter at this point."

"It's never too late," Ellie said, her voice softening, her heart opening a little more to this man.

She thought of the time Caleb had joined her family in the contest. She'd been seven, he twelve. Caleb had lifted Ellie onto his shoulders so she could put ornaments on the highest branches. They hadn't won the contest that year, but Ellie hadn't minded. She'd been too thrilled that Caleb was there.

So many of the happy memories from her childhood included this man.

"There's no official entry process," she said, determined to focus on the present rather than the past. "Families simply show up at the center of town and are assigned a tree. It's no more complicated than that."

He looked at her for a long, wordless moment.

Ellie had to set her jaw against the quiver of impatience racing through her. "Well? Do you want to enter the contest with the girls this year?"

"Will you be joining us?"

She grinned at the absurd question. "Goes without saying."

Another wordless moment passed between them. "Why not? Could be fun."

"Is that a yes?"

Caleb smiled, slowly, devastatingly. *Oh, my.* "It's a yes."

The next evening, a light southern breeze rippled through the center of town, bringing with it a break from the bitter cold. A full moon hung in the cloudless sky, providing a soft, pale glow over the town. Strategically placed torches added additional light.

Nearly two dozen pine trees lined the town square.

With a critical eye, Ellie studied the tree assigned to her and the Voss family. The girls stared up at her, waiting for her to tell them what to do. Caleb was also silent, evidently allowing Ellie to take the lead.

She considered a few options.

The sound of several different conversations filled the air, a sure sign that other contestants were contemplating their strategy. In an effort to keep the competition fair for all, no one was allowed to start hanging ornaments until seven o'clock sharp.

Several of the more jolly groups sang Christmas carols.

Ellie hummed along while her mind debated two distinct plans of attack. She really wanted to win this year, for Caleb and the girls. And maybe even for herself.

Her failure in Colorado Springs still stung. She desperately needed to accomplish something good, something positive.

Tapping her finger to her chin, she caught sight of her father and Betsy at the refreshment table. They would soon be handing out cups of hot cocoa. The older couple had enlisted Brody Driscoll's help. Ellie figured it was a nice distraction for the boy.

She made a mental note to assign him special duties at play practice this week. She would also figure out a time to visit his mother. Maybe she and the girls would bring over a batch of Christmas cookies tomorrow.

Tonight, they had a tree-decorating contest to win.

"What time is it?" she asked Caleb, her gaze still on the tree, sliding over branches from tip to trunk.

"Five minutes to seven."

Ellie circled the tree, assessing the unadorned branches. There were several bare spots that would require special attention, but overall, they'd been given a good, hearty blue spruce.

She and the girls had prepared for this moment all day, stuffing their finished decorations in the carpet-bag now resting on the ground at their feet.

"I should warn you," she said to Caleb as she returned to her original spot. "I'm feeling terribly competitive."

A low rumble of appreciation sounded in his chest. "That makes two of us."

The teasing note in his tone didn't quite match the serious look in his eyes. Tonight was important to him, Ellie realized, perhaps more than he realized.

Determined to make the evening memorable for him and his daughters, she decided on a strategy. "All right, girls. I need you to organize our decorations in separate piles. You'll want to sort them by color."

While the twins worked, Ellie smiled up at Caleb.

His eyebrows lifted in inquiry. "I take it you have a plan of attack?"

"Absolutely." She circled the blue spruce again,

Caleb matching her step for step. The scent of pine filled her with happy memories of Christmases long, long ago. "Help me turn this around."

Together, they repositioned the tree by reaching for its bucket, twisting it until the fullest section faced outward.

Ellie stepped back, nodded her head in satisfaction. "Much better."

The moment the words left her mouth the bells on the church steeple began chiming the top of the hour. "That's our cue to begin."

As one, she and Caleb dropped to their knees beside the twins.

"All right, we only have thirty minutes," Ellie informed them. "Caleb and Hannah, you'll work as a team, while Grace and I will work together."

Three heads bobbed in agreement.

Ellie continued her instructions. "Each team will hang ornaments on the tree according to color, remembering to space them out so no one color dominates any section. You two will focus on the red, blue and gold decorations." She pointed to Hannah and Caleb. "Grace and I will focus on the others."

"Efficient," Caleb muttered in approval.

Ellie grinned. "We'll work on opposite sides of the tree, moving from top to bottom, left to right. Any questions?"

None were voiced.

"Excellent. Let's get started."

Chapter Eight

Caleb gave Ellie a mock salute. Focused and intent, she was a little scary and utterly adorable. He liked this side of her, liked it a lot.

"Here's a red one," Hannah said, raising her little hand in the air.

He took the ornament. "Ready for this, pumpkin?"

"Ready!" Head down, she dug into the pile once again and pulled out another red decoration.

For the next few minutes Caleb worked with his daughter on their side of the tree, top to bottom as Ellie had instructed. When the branches were sufficiently adorned, they moved to their right.

Another few minutes passed and they shifted again. Soon, they were back where they'd begun. They started the whole process again, this time focusing on the blue and the gold ornaments.

After the second pass, Caleb stepped back to admire their handiwork.

"Five minutes," yelled Mayor Pritchett from his perch on the church steps. "You only have five minutes to finish decorating your assigned tree."

Ellie poked her head around the now full branches. "How you two doing on your side?"

"Nearly done." Caleb handed the last decoration in their pile to Hannah, then picked her up and perched her on his shoulders. Giggling, she placed the handmade snowflake on a bare branch near the very top of the tree.

"All right, let's have a look." Ellie and Grace came around to their side of the tree. In silence, the four of them studied their creation.

Caleb tried to be objective. He really tried. But he just couldn't pull it off. Their decorations might not be the best made. In fact, some were actually rather poorly done. Yet every paper ornament, snowflake and star, every lopsided cloth doll constructed out of cotton batting, had been fashioned by his daughters' tiny hands.

"It's perfect," Caleb declared.

"Can we take it home?" Hannah asked.

Caleb started to respond, but Ellie beat him to it. "These trees remain in the center of town for everyone to enjoy all season long."

Two identical scowls formed on the girls' faces. "Oh."

Ellie placed a hand on their tiny shoulders. "Not to worry. We'll recreate everything again on our tree at home."

Home, the word had rolled off Ellie's tongue naturally, leaving Caleb wanting…something…more.

"One minute," came the final warning from Mayor Pritchett.

"All that's left is to put the angel on top." Ellie reached into the bag and pulled out the last decoration.

He recognized the Wainwright family tree topper.

"Will you do the honors?" Ellie asked, the ornament stretched out in front of her.

An image flashed in his mind, a memory from another Christmas, when he'd lifted Ellie onto his shoulders so she could put the angel atop the tree. After he'd set her back on the ground she'd peered up at him as if he was her hero.

He'd felt strong that day, special, as if he mattered.

"Thirty seconds."

He took the tree topper from Ellie. Their fingertips brushed lightly during the handoff. It was nothing more than a brief touch, but he suddenly yearned for something he could never have. Something he feared only she could provide.

"Hurry," she whispered. "Time's almost up."

Time *was* almost up, at least for them. But not yet, not tonight. Tonight they were a family.

With swift movements, Caleb reached up and placed the angel on the very top of the blue spruce.

He was just pulling his hand away when the mayor yelled, "Time!"

"Now comes the hard part," Ellie announced to the children. "Waiting for the results."

Grace's eyes widened. "Do you think we'll win?"

"I think we have a wonderful chance." Hands on hips, Ellie made a grand show of studying their collective effort. "Our tree has a little bit of all of us in it and that makes it—"

"The most special tree of all," Caleb finished for her.

"Yes," she whispered. "The most special tree of all."

He recognized the longing in her blue eyes, primarily because it was the same sensation that washed through him. Unable to stop himself, he stepped in beside her and took her hand without overthinking the move.

They stood linked together for one beat, two, then the girls moved in between them and Caleb was forced to let Ellie go.

Betsy arrived with a tray of mugs filled with hot cocoa. Brody was barely a step behind her. Excited to show off their first effort at decorating a Christmas tree, the twins begged the two to take a look.

"Have you seen the other trees?" Brody asked the girls after giving theirs a good, long scrutiny.

They shook their heads.

Brody looked over at Caleb. "Is it okay if I take them around the square?"

He agreed, then added, "Keep hold of their hands."

The twins chattered without taking a breath as the three headed off.

While the judges moved from tree to tree, a flurry of children chased each other in circles or tossed balls. As Caleb looked over so many familiar faces, his thoughts drew loops from past to present. Gathered in the town square were generations of young and old alike, individuals bound by friendships and shared experiences. Some families were in the midst of triumphs, others—like Brody's—were facing tragedy this Christmas season.

"He's such a good boy and so very brave." Wiping at her cheek, Betsy watched Brody as he guided the twins from tree to tree.

The boy reminded Caleb of himself at that age, desperate for a sense of normalcy, for days free of pain and sickness and fear. Brody was at a critical age, where his choices, good or bad, would stick with him. He could head down the wrong road just as easily as the right one.

Caleb had been poised on the edge of a similar threshold one long-ago Christmas. He'd been given the gift of Reverend Wainwright's guidance. Would the older man step in with Brody as well?

You know what he's going through, Caleb. You could guide him. The thought pushed him to ask the question on all their minds. "How's Brody's mother?"

Betsy's eyes immediately filled with tears. "Not well. I fear she won't make it to Christmas Day."

How will the boy take the loss? Caleb wondered.

"I'm so sorry," Ellie said, pulling her future stepmother into a fierce embrace. "What can I do? Whatever you need, say the word and it's done."

"Pray. Clara and Brody need your prayers most of all."

Ellie stepped back and took Betsy's hand. "Of course."

Betsy looked out over the crowd. "It's a shame Clara's missing tonight's festivities. Christmas is her favorite time of year and this contest has always been one of her most cherished events."

A murmur of sympathy slipped out of Ellie. Caleb's sentiments exactly.

The judging committee arrived and began circling their tree with grave, unreadable expressions. Betsy left to deliver hot cocoa to other families.

Eyes on the judges, Ellie moved in beside Caleb.

They stood shoulder-to-shoulder, both holding silent as the committee made notations in tiny notebooks they carried with them.

The moment they walked away, Ellie whispered, "How do you think we did?"

"No idea."

"Oh, Caleb." She turned wide blue eyes in his direction, the long, silky black lashes a stark contrast against her pale skin. "I know it may seem trivial in light of Clara Driscoll's suffering, but I really want our tree to take the grand prize. The girls worked so hard on the decorations."

Caleb nodded in agreement. He wanted to win for his daughters, as well. The twins had lost their mother only ten months ago. Lizzie's death had come as a shock.

Finally, the judges made their decision. The mayor climbed the church steps and called for quiet.

Brody returned with the girls just as a collective hush fell over the crowd.

"Third place goes to the Johnson family."

Cheers and applause erupted, then slowly died down when the mayor raised his hands in the air. "Second place goes to Miss Kate Riley. And the winner is…" He held the pause for effect. "Our very own Sheriff Caleb Voss and his family."

The children squealed in delight. "We won! We won! We won!"

The backs of Caleb's eyes stung at their reaction, his heart aching with love for them. Hannah and Grace hadn't been this excited about anything in a very long time, maybe never.

Why had he held back from entering events such as these? Even without a wife, he and the girls could have—

"Caleb, didn't you hear the announcement? We

won." Ellie leaped into his arms, cutting off all coherent thought, save one startling revelation.

Here, wrapped in his embrace, was exactly where Ellie Wainwright belonged.

Embarrassed by her impulsive act, Ellie quickly stepped out of Caleb's arms. "Sorry, I let my excitement get away from me."

"Perfectly understandable." Caleb chuckled, his eyes warm and full of masculine satisfaction. "We won."

"We did." Ellie wanted to linger in the moment. She wanted to bask in Caleb's smile, in simply being with him and the girls. But it seemed everyone in town rushed over to offer up their congratulations.

The girls beamed under all the attention.

"Thank you, Ellie," Caleb said in a low, heartfelt tone. "Thank you for making tonight special for the girls." He held silent a moment, before adding, "And for me."

Beneath the glow of the torches, Caleb's green eyes looked several shades darker, almost black. He was so attractive, so full of charm and sincerity. When he leaned his head slightly closer to hers, Ellie's lungs forgot to work. She could feel the heat coming off him in waves, could smell his familiar scent, a mix of pine, spice and bergamot.

"Ellie," he said on a long, masculine breath. "You're beautiful."

The declaration was so spontaneously tender Ellie struggled to think clearly. Would he kiss her next?

Surely not in front of all these people, and especially not in front of his daughters, who weren't paying them any attention. Hannah and Grace were too busy showing off their tree and explaining—in great detail—how they made each and every one of the winning decorations.

Friends, Ellie told herself firmly, *you and Caleb are only friends*.

Oh, but friends didn't stare at each other the way Caleb was looking at her now. Friends didn't feel this strong connection that went beyond words.

Compelled by some unknown need to be near him, she leaned in close to Caleb. Closer, closer…

Her friend Kate ran over, forcing Ellie to step back or embarrass herself.

"I can't believe you beat me. *Me*." Kate parked tightly balled fists on her hips. "I haven't lost this contest in years. Everyone knows I'm the most imaginative in town."

Ellie laughed. "And the most humble, too."

Kate made a face then spun around to stare at the winning tree. "I suppose I can see why you won," she admitted, her tone holding a grudging note. "Your tree does have something special. Well-done, Sheriff."

"Thank you, Miss Riley, but Ellie was the mastermind behind our success." He gave her a smile. "She's a marvel."

Kate laughed. "I couldn't agree more."

For the next few minutes the three spoke of nothing in particular. The moment Kate wandered off, a tall man with black hair, broad shoulders and a smile so white Ellie felt momentarily blinded arrived at their tree. The tin star pinned to his coat suggested he was a lawman like Caleb.

"Congratulations, Sheriff."

Caleb responded with an odd glare and a muttered word of thanks, his tone bordering on slightly rude.

The other man seemed perfectly unaffected by his boss's cold response. "Aren't you going to introduce me to your friend?"

Shoulders tense, expression tight, Caleb blew out a slow hiss. "Ellie, this is my deputy, Prescott Kramer. Pres, this is Miss Ellie Wainwright."

"Miss Wainwright." The deputy nudged Caleb aside and focused his pale blue eyes on Ellie. "It's a pleasure to meet you at last. I've heard a lot about you."

Not quite understanding the tension between the two men, Ellie took the extended hand. "And you as well, Deputy Kramer."

He started to say more, but they were interrupted by another group of well-wishers.

Each time someone complimented their effort, Caleb deflected the praise back to Ellie and the girls. "They did all the work."

Blossoming under the attention, the twins regaled everyone who would listen with how they'd made each decoration with Miss Ellie's help.

A half hour later, Caleb, in his role of town sheriff, declared the event over. He and his deputy skillfully herded people off to their homes.

While Caleb completed his duty, Ellie guided the girls to a bench out of the main stream of traffic. Winding down from the day's excitement, they snuggled in on either side of her. It wasn't long before they dozed off.

Happy to sit for a moment, Ellie watched Caleb. He moved with such competence, his love of the town inherent in every step he took, in every moment he paused to speak with individual townspeople. So caught up in watching him, she didn't hear her father approach.

"Congratulations, my dear." He sat on the edge of the bench, careful not to disturb the girls. "Your mother would have loved your tree."

"She's been on my mind all day." Every activity she'd introduced to Hannah and Grace, her mother had first done with Ellie.

Momentary sadness washed over her, a feeling very similar to homesickness. Not only was she missing Mother, but also the other family member absent.

"I wish Everett was here."

Her father let out a weighty sigh. "He loved this event as a boy, but he didn't have much use for it once he grew into a man."

They both knew why. Everett had fallen in with a rough crowd. He'd turned wild, but not so undisciplined that he'd completely lost his inherent sense of integrity, as evidenced by his actions the night that had landed him in prison.

He'd been protecting a woman from her own husband. His interference had saved her life. That piece of information had only partially swayed the judge in Everett's favor, giving him a shortened sentence of seven years.

Ellie's eyes burned with sorrow for her brother. "He did what was right, Pa. He acted on an innocent woman's behalf."

Her father nodded.

As if by silent agreement, the conversation turned back to the evening's tree-decorating contest. They laughed about the way Kate howled in outrage over coming in second, and how Rufus Butterfield's ancient hound dog, Dexter, kept jumping up on Mrs. Jenson's tree, much to her vociferous dismay.

When they fell into a companionable silence, Ellie caught Caleb's eye and waved. He waved back then went to work dragging Dexter off Mrs. Jenson's tree yet again.

"I haven't seen Caleb smile this much in years." Her father nodded at the man in question. "It was kind of you to step in and help him out so Betsy can focus on her sister."

"I think I need the Voss family as much as they need me," she admitted before she could censure herself.

Her father shifted in his seat. "Won't you talk to me about what happened in Colorado Springs and why you came home in the middle of the school year?"

"Eventually, yes, but—" she dropped a pointed gaze on the children leaning against her, and said "—not tonight."

Her father knew the very basic details of her broken engagement, but Ellie had made a point of avoiding the particulars. The humiliation of being rejected so completely still hurt too much to put into words. She just wasn't ready for a thorough retelling of the events.

He opened his mouth as if to respond, but then closed it just as quickly.

Betsy strolled over with another tray of hot cocoa. "Any takers?"

"None for me," Ellie whispered.

"Me, either, but here, let me have that." Her father rose and reached for the tray. "I'll help you with cleanup."

After a brief goodbye, the couple left Ellie alone

with the girls. She pulled them closer, watching her father and his future bride pick their way around the decorated trees. They looked good together, she decided.

Their ease with one another was evident in their bent heads and genial manner. Her father had found love twice, while this was Betsy's first time. She'd told Ellie she was glad she'd waited for just the right man to come along at just the right time.

Betsy's happy ending gave Ellie hope.

She thought she'd found her happily-ever-after with Monroe, but he hadn't been the right man. She hadn't really loved Monroe, she knew that now. With hindsight, Ellie wondered if her initial attraction to the widowed preacher had been influenced by her feelings for his daughters.

Grace stirred, yawned loudly, then slowly opened her eyes. "Is it time to go home yet?"

"Soon."

Hannah woke next. "Will you read to us before we go to bed, Miss Ellie?"

Caleb chose that moment to return.

She looked at him before answering. "If it's all right with your father I'd very much like to read to you tonight."

"Of course it's all right with me." He drew her to her feet. "Come, let's go home."

Ellie and Caleb each took a child's hand and guided them the block and a half to his home. The evening was cold, but not unbearable. The crunching of snow beneath her feet was one of Ellie's favorite sounds in the world.

A second later, she heard another of her favorite sounds. The children giggled as their father told them how Dexter the hound dog, at the ripe old age of seventeen, was quite skillful at toppling Christmas trees.

Ellie joined in their laughter. *Him*, her heart whispered.

Caleb Voss was the one.

Instead of joy, sorrow filled her. The man she would love until the end of her days only wanted to be her friend. He wanted a marriage of convenience and was willing to take vows with a stranger, a mail-order bride he'd never met.

He deserved so much more. Ellie thought her heart might break for him. For herself. For the family they would never have.

Chapter Nine

Caleb noticed a change in Ellie a block away from his house. She'd grown unnaturally quiet, almost withdrawn, as if intentionally holding a portion of herself separate from him and the girls. He couldn't think what had occurred to make her pull back. One moment she was laughing, the next her face went taut and her eyes registered sorrow.

Baffled at her shift in mood, he opened the door that led to the tiny room off the kitchen and stepped back to let the girls enter ahead of him. While Ellie helped the twins off with their coats, Caleb moved through the darkened house, lighting lanterns, then the wall sconces.

By the time he returned to the living room, Ellie had already settled Hannah and Grace on the couch. She looked up and held his stare. Her fathomless blue eyes reflected the lantern light, the flame flickering deep within their depths. It struck Caleb without warning how precious she was to him, how beautiful.

She took his breath away.

Hannah tapped her shoulder. "Miss Ellie? Will you

read to us from our new book? It's called *A Christmas Carol.*"

Ellie lifted a single eyebrow.

He pointed to the side table. "We're on the second chapter."

Retrieving the book, she sat between the twins and flipped to the proper page. Caleb noticed how her fingers shook ever-so-slightly, but she firmed her grip and began reading. "'When Scrooge awoke, it was so dark, that looking out of bed, he could scarcely distinguish the transparent window from the opaque walls of his chamber.'"

Ellie's sweet, musical voice brought the scene alive.

Riveted, Caleb sat in the overstuffed chair facing the couch and listened to the cautionary tale.

Watching Ellie read to his girls was an image Caleb would treasure for years to come. The scene was already etched in his heart and mind forever. When she was living in another town, teaching a roomful of students who couldn't possibly adore her more than Hannah and Grace did now, Caleb would pull out this memory and once again feel the warmth of the moment.

If only he could keep Ellie here forever. If only he could give her the marriage she wanted, the life she deserved. It was an impossible hope. He'd tried with Lizzie and had failed.

Twice she'd run off, deserting her family for something more, something Caleb couldn't give her, only to come back for another try at marriage.

They would be happy for a while. She'd be a doting mother and loving wife. Then she would grow dissatisfied and disappear once again.

The last time she'd strayed from home she'd died in a fatal wagon accident. Whether she'd been leaving town that day or returning home, Caleb would never know. All he knew was that he'd let Lizzie down, and now she was dead.

He absently rubbed his chin, feeling the stubble of a late-day beard. A rush of frustration surged.

He tore his eyes away from Ellie and focused on his daughters. Both girls valiantly fought to stay awake, but Caleb recognized a losing battle.

When Ellie paused to turn the page, he seized the opportunity to put an end to her reading. "That's enough for tonight."

She startled at his abrupt tone. He hadn't meant to speak so sharply. Softening his voice, he tried again. "You can read more of the story tomorrow evening."

"That sounds lovely." She closed the book and set it on the table beside the couch.

Around a yawn, Grace asked, "Will you tuck us in, Miss Ellie?"

She lifted another questioning look in Caleb's direction.

He nodded.

"I'd like that very much." She drew the girls to their feet.

Five minutes later, after faces were washed and nightgowns had replaced their day dresses, Caleb and Ellie tucked the twins into bed.

As if in silent agreement, both girls clasped their hands together and squeezed their eyes shut for evening prayers.

"Thank You, God, for Miss Ellie," Grace said, peeking one eye open then slamming it shut when Caleb caught her. "Thank You for letting her come take care of us. We wouldn't have won tonight without her."

Hannah picked up where her sister left off. "And please, God, let Miss Ellie stay with us forever and ever because we love her and Papa, too."

Caleb pinched the bridge of his nose between his thumb and forefinger. His daughters were already attached to Ellie. What would her leaving do to them?

Clearly, he hadn't thought through the ramifications of bringing her into his home. What other choice had he had?

"Amen," Hannah and Grace said in unison. Both sets of little eyes remained closed, exhaustion winning the final battle of the night.

Caleb bent over and kissed each of his daughters' foreheads. "I love you," he said, his voice hoarse with emotion.

Avoiding his gaze, Ellie took her turn kissing each girl. They were asleep seconds later.

Heart weighing heavy with emotion, Caleb motioned for Ellie to follow him out of the room. He couldn't have spoken had he tried. In the matter of two short days, Ellie had turned his house into a home and had given his daughters a taste of family.

How was he supposed to marry another woman? After having Ellie in his life, watching what she gave his daughters, Sadie Taylor of Blue Springs, Missouri would surely fall short of expectations.

Caleb caught Ellie watching him with moist blue eyes.

His throat closed shut.

She was so pretty, standing in the soft light of the wall sconce above her head. Her hair glittered with a dozen shades of gold. Compelled, he took a step toward her. It was a small move, yet Caleb felt as if he'd crossed an invisible line.

No turning back.

He cleared his throat. Barely able to suck in a decent breath, he was suspended between past and present, between surrender and battle, between joy and regret.

Ellie gave him a shaky smile.

"I'd like to take the girls to see Clara Driscoll tomorrow." She spoke in a voice no louder than a whisper. "We'll bake cookies then bring her a plate. Unless, of course, you object."

He couldn't come up with a reason why he would. Clara wasn't contagious. She merely had a weak heart that was giving out on her. She could probably use the company and it wouldn't hurt the girls to learn how to give of their time to someone in need. "I have no objection."

Ellie sighed. "Betsy says her sister is growing worse by the day and there's little the doctor can do to stop her decline."

"It's a rough situation."

Ellie sighed again. "Poor Brody, to lose his mother during the holidays, it's so sad."

Yes, it was. "The town will rally around the boy."

"Of course they will." Her blue eyes softened with emotion. "Because you'll make sure of it."

Caleb nodded, relieved he didn't have to say more on the subject. With Ellie, he didn't have to explain how he'd lost his own mother a week before Christmas.

With Ellie, he didn't have to explain *anything.*

He took another step toward her, desperately wanting to make promises he feared he couldn't keep.

She was the steadiness he craved, the stability he'd never known. But none of those things were what drove him to close the distance between them.

"Ellie." He reached up to cup her cheek, then dropped his hand before making contact. "I want you to know that I—"

His mind went blank. He couldn't remember what he'd meant to say. All that was left was a deep, painful longing. Reaction overruled judgment.

Emotion replaced logic.

He pulled her into his arms.

Whispering his name on a soft, lilting sigh, she leaned into him. It was all the encouragement he needed. He lowered his head.

The kiss was brief, as gentle as a summer breeze, nothing more than a quick meeting of lips. Yet, as Caleb lifted his head and stared into Ellie's stunning face, he experienced the sensation of coming home.

After years of searching, of yearning, of wanting something always just out of reach, he was home at last.

With Ellie. His Ellie.

The affection he'd always felt for her morphed into something stronger, something lasting. Was it…love?

No. He couldn't allow himself to love her. Love hurt. Love brought pain and disappointment and chaos.

She didn't deserve that torture.

There could be only affection between them, only friendship.

He set her away from him.

She blinked, pressed her fingertips to her lips. Faint shadows of confusion shimmered in her eyes.

Caleb needed to apologize. Not for kissing her—he

wasn't sorry for that—but for being unable to give her what she wanted, what she deserved.

"Ellie—"

"No, Caleb, please don't say a word, not one word. The moment simply got away from us."

Their kiss had been more than that. He knew it. Her soft, dewy expression said she knew it, too. But she wanted to pretend nothing special had happened. He wasn't sure he could change her mind. He wasn't sure he should.

Just yesterday he'd given Mrs. Jenson the go-ahead to tell Sadie Taylor to make the journey to Thunder Ridge. His mail-order bride would arrive in a matter of months.

"It's getting late," Ellie said. "I should head on home."

"I'll see you out."

They walked toward the back of the house in silence, each lost in their own thoughts. Caleb helped Ellie into her cloak, then put on his own before escorting her out the back door.

Under the giant yellow moon, he surveyed her face, recognized the discomfort he himself felt. "I didn't mean to cross a line."

She reached up and placed her gloved fingers on his cheek. "It's over and done with now. There's no need to speak of it again."

She was letting him off the hook. He hadn't earned such kindness.

Her hand dropped from his face, her warmth replaced by a cold blast of arctic air.

"Good night, Caleb." She turned to go.

He called after her. "Ellie, wait."

She paused, looked over her shoulder, but didn't turn back around. "Yes?"

"Still friends?"

She smiled. "The very best."

Without another word, she hurried across the street, climbed onto her porch and then disappeared inside her father's house.

For several moments, Caleb stood alone, motionless, gazing up at the star-speckled sky.

Ellie was everything he wanted for his daughters. She was respectable, stable, with a generous heart and an endless capacity to love. She was goodness itself.

It had been wrong to kiss her. Why, then, had the moment felt so right?

The next afternoon, following a long visit with Clara Driscoll, Ellie put the twins down for a nap. They'd protested, but had settled down once she started reading from *A Christmas Carol*. Two pages into Ebenezer Scrooge's adventures and they'd drifted off to sleep.

Now, as she watched them slumber from the doorway, Ellie thought her heart might burst with love. Hannah and Grace had become precious to her. She adored them as surely as if they were her own. She felt the same connection with their father.

He claimed he wanted only friendship, but his kiss had said otherwise. She reached up and placed her fingertips to her lips, to the very spot where his mouth had first touched hers.

Whether he returned her feelings or not, Ellie was in love with Caleb. No use pretending otherwise. As she padded soundlessly down the hallway and into the living room, she realized the love she felt for him now was much stronger than what she'd experienced as a young girl. It was deeper, more powerful and all the scarier for its intensity.

Sighing, she picked up a stray toy and put it in the basket where it belonged. She looked around the room and smiled at its transformation, now so festive, so full of Christmas cheer.

"Gorgeous," she whispered.

"Yes, you are."

"Oh!" Her hand flew to her throat and she spun around. "Caleb. You're home early." Really early.

A long, indefinable pause seemed to shiver between them.

"There was a disturbance out at the Potter ranch. Turned out to be a stray dog rummaging for food." Shaking his head as if reviewing the incident in his mind, he gave a short laugh. "A hearty meal in the animal's belly and now Mrs. Potter has a lifelong friend who won't be leaving her side anytime soon."

He removed his hat, splayed a hand through his hair and shook his head again.

Ellie could only stare. Caleb had always been too attractive for his own good. That hadn't changed with time. If anything, age and experience had made him more appealing. "Are you home for the day?"

"Afraid not." He rolled his shoulders, seeming tenser than usual. "I thought I'd stop home on my way back to the jail to say hello to you and the twins."

"The children are napping," she said. "We spent half the morning baking cookies, the other half visiting with Clara Driscoll."

He dropped his hat on a nearby table. "How'd it go?"

"Very well. She seemed a bit stronger when we left."

"I'm glad." He shifted, the motion practically stirring the air with his essence, his masculine scent. "Any of those cookies stay close to home?"

"Of course." She led him into the kitchen and presented the plate of freshly baked cookies.

Grinning like the boy she once knew, Caleb snatched a molasses bar. He finished the treat in two bites and yanked up a sugar cookie.

When he grabbed for a third confection, she playfully slapped his hand. "Save some for later."

"Come on, Ellie." He gave her a pitiful look that fooled no one. "Wrangling stray dogs is hard work."

"You can have one more."

Eyes glittering with mischief, he took two.

Laughing, Ellie set the plate back on the table. Needing something to do with her hands, she began sorting cookies by shape and color. Even with her back to him, she could feel Caleb's eyes on her.

"Stop staring at me," she said without glancing his way.

"I like looking at you."

His voice was filled with good humor and something far more intense. She risked a glance in his direction. A mistake. He was watching her in the same way he had the other night. Right before he'd kissed her.

How she wanted him to kiss her again.

Ellie thought she'd learned her lesson with Monroe. She'd promised herself she would only fall in love with a man who could love her back.

Still, her heart wanted Caleb.

"You're so beautiful."

He'd called her beautiful. Not stable or steady or reliable, but beautiful. The compliment did strange things to her insides. "Thank you."

"I've made you uncomfortable again."

Why deny the truth? "Maybe a little."

Without a moment's hesitation, he pulled her into his arms. He held her gently against him, resting his chin atop her head. "I don't ever want to hurt you."

She pressed her face into his shirt, breathing in his scent, a lovely mix of winter air, cedar and pine. "Oh, Caleb, you could never hurt me."

But he already had, by refusing to open his heart, by allowing himself to feel only friendship for her. If only she knew what kept him from wanting a real marriage. Why was friendship so important to him? Had his love for his wife been so strong there was nothing left for anyone else?

How tragic. Ellie's father had found love twice so she knew it was possible.

Slowly, reluctantly, she stepped out of Caleb's arms. "I need to check on the girls."

"Let me." He smiled softly, placed a kiss on her nose. Then he was gone.

Moments later, high-pitched, little-girl squeals of delight merged with Caleb's masculine laughter.

Ellie's heart lurched at the sound. She would miss this family when their time together was up, which would be here all too soon. Mrs. Jenson was on the hunt for Caleb's bride. The woman's previous success rate told its own story. Caleb would be married come spring, if not sooner.

Ellie could already feel the Voss family slipping away from her.

"Please, Lord," she prayed. "Let Caleb's future wife be worthy of him and the girls."

Chapter Ten

Not long after the twins woke from their nap, Caleb went back to work. He'd stayed longer than he should. Every moment in Ellie's company put in him grave danger of falling in love with her—something that must not happen.

He pushed into the jailhouse with more force than necessary. Prescott met him at the door, his lips pressed tightly together in what appeared to be an attempt to hold back a grin. "You have a visitor, Sheriff."

Caleb moved deeper into the building and spotted the boy. "Brody? Did we have an appointment?"

The kid didn't respond right away. He merely shifted from foot to foot, looking wildly uncomfortable. "No, I, uh," he muttered, as he shot his gaze around the room, "need a favor."

"Shouldn't you be in school?"

"Miss O'Hare said I could leave early."

"Is that typical?"

"No." The boy scuffed his foot on the wood plank beneath him. "I might have told her my mother needed me."

"And yet you're here instead of at home."

"Yeah, well." Brody shrugged, still refusing to meet Caleb's eyes. "That's because I need your help."

Caleb shared a look with Prescott. The other man lifted his hands in the air, palms facing outward, as if to say he had no clue what the boy wanted. "What can I do for you?"

"I want to buy Mama a Christmas present. But Mr. Snodgrass said I can't come into the mercantile without an adult." Brody heaved a sigh. "He said I can't be trusted, seeing as I have a reputation around town for causing trouble."

Something dark moved through Caleb. He hadn't been allowed in the mercantile at Brody's age for much the same reason. Caleb had carried a reputation for causing trouble well into his teen years. Some of the distrust in him had been earned, some of it not. Brody was no different.

However, considering the fact that he'd come to Caleb—the town sheriff—was proof that the boy wanted to make the right decisions. Something Caleb didn't take lightly. "What did you have in mind for your mother?"

"See, that's the other problem." Brody strained to contain his agitation, but it showed in his reddened cheeks and fidgeting feet. "She's a girl. I don't know what to get a girl."

"Maybe together we can figure it out."

Brody's eyes lit with relief. "That's what I was hoping you would say. Can we go over there now?"

"Now works for me." Caleb swung his gaze to Prescott's. "You're in charge while I'm gone."

"No problem." The deputy settled in behind the desk and picked up his book.

Caleb escorted Brody outside.

It didn't take long to make the short journey to the mercantile. Like other businesses in town, the store was decorated for Christmas with garland, bows and a large wreath on the front door.

Brody led the way inside, with Caleb a step behind. He breathed in the scent of oats, spices and burlap.

Halfway through the store, he caught Mr. Snodgrass's eye, a man as wide as he was tall with a shock of unruly white hair and small, black eyes that reminded Caleb of a rat. The old man was anywhere between seventy and a hundred and had owned the mercantile since before Caleb had been born. In fact, the store was as much an institution of Thunder Ridge as the Whistle Stop Inn and the train station on the Union Pacific line.

"Good afternoon, Mr. Snodgrass."

"Sheriff Voss." The older man smiled at Caleb then frowned when he caught sight of Brody studying a display of colored perfume bottles.

Caleb had once been on the end of that very same look. Instinct had him setting a protective hand on Brody's shoulder. "Mr. Driscoll and I are here to find his mother a Christmas gift."

"That boy is not allowed—"

"I'm hoping you can help us find the perfect item." Caleb shot Snodgrass a warning glare.

Nose tilted at a haughty angle, the proprietor straightened his waistcoat with a hard snap. "Of course, Sheriff, it would be my pleasure to assist you and the boy."

His tone said otherwise.

"How much money do you have, Brody?"

The boy pulled out a handful of coins, mostly pennies, and spread them out on the counter. "Will this be enough to get a really good gift? Maybe one of these pretty bottles?"

Mr. Snodgrass frowned. "That's barely enough for a few pieces of candy."

"Oh." Tears gathered in the boy's eyes.

"Brody," Caleb said. "Why don't you shop around while I speak with Mr. Snodgrass?"

Drawing in a tight breath, Brody reluctantly did as he requested.

Caleb waited until he was out of earshot before speaking again. "Whatever he chooses for his mother I'll pay the difference."

"Do you think that's wise?" Censure filled the store-owner's voice. "Isn't it sending him the wrong message?"

"What message would that be?"

"How will he learn to fend for himself if you pay his way?"

Fend for himself? Caleb's vision tinged red. "He's still a boy."

"Plenty old enough to learn to take responsibility for himself. You, of all people, know what his life will be like when his mother passes. You should be teaching him—"

The man broke off. Eyes narrowed, he released a feral hiss. "What is that boy up to now?"

Caleb turned in time to see *that boy* pilfer one of the perfume bottles. It was a gutsy move, and about as stupid as they came, but Caleb understood Brody's desperation.

He'd once been that desperate.

He started out.

At the same moment, Mr. Snodgrass bellowed, "You there!" His face pinched in a sour expression. "Put that back this instant."

The man scrambled out from behind the counter, moving as fast as his large girth and ancient bones would allow.

Caleb beat the other man to Brody by precious seconds and stuck out his palm. "Hand it over."

Eyes not quite meeting his, the boy did as requested without a single word of complaint or hesitation. He started to speak, but Caleb cut him off with a shake of the head. "I'll deal with you later. For now, keep your mouth firmly shut. Understand?"

The boy nodded, his face drained of color, his expression forlorn and full of guilt.

Spinning back around, Caleb shot out his free hand to stop Snodgrass's pursuit.

"We'll take this one." He passed off the blue-tinted bottle before Mr. Snodgrass could argue and added, "We would like it wrapped in special Christmas paper with a pretty red bow on top."

The older man's mouth worked but no words came out, just a high-pitched squeak of outrage. "But, but… I saw him put this in his pocket."

"It's in *your* hand now."

A satisfying lurch of silence fell over the store.

"There's still the matter of payment."

Caleb dug out his wallet then handed over a banknote. "That should cover it."

Five minutes later, his mother's gift tucked beneath his arm, a very silent Brody followed Caleb out of the mercantile.

The sky had turned a dingy gray, and the threat of

snow hung in the air. A block out, Brody's silence broke like a poorly constructed dam over a rushing river. "I'm sorry, Sheriff. One minute I was looking at the bottles, wishing I could buy one for Mama, and the next thing I knew I was putting one in my pocket."

Regardless of understanding the boy's motives, Brody had made a very poor error in judgment, one that could have ended very differently had Caleb not been in the store. "Stealing is still stealing, Brody."

"I've never done anything like that before."

"That's no excuse."

"I'm sure I would have put it back before we left."

"Maybe you would have," Caleb said. "And maybe you wouldn't. The point is that your intention was to take something that didn't belong to you."

"I'm sorry."

"I believe you are, but you're not out of trouble yet. I expect you to work off the cost of your mother's gift."

The boy hung his head. "Yeah, okay."

"You'll start this afternoon, at the jail, cleaning out the wood-burning stove."

It would be hot, dirty work and would take all day. Caleb hoped the lesson stuck.

The alternative was too depressing to contemplate.

Later that afternoon, when play practice was winding down, Ellie's gaze landed on Brody Driscoll. He'd been unusually obedient. He even offered to help organize the younger children during song practice instead of taking a recess with his friends.

It was during the first of the two songs that Brody told Ellie the entire tale of what had happened in the mercantile earlier that day. Once he started, his words tumbled over one another, making Ellie's head spin as she tried to keep up.

"And then Sheriff Voss paid for the gift and insisted Mr. Snodgrass wrap it up real pretty-like, with a red bow and everything." Brody took a quick breath. "But when we were out on the sidewalk, he told me I was still in trouble and that I had to work off the cost of my mom's gift, which was really fair of him, don't you think?"

Ellie ruffled the boy's hair. "I do, indeed."

None of Brody's story surprised her. Not the part about Caleb covering for him, or the part about him paying for the gift and insisting the boy work off the cost.

Caleb took care of his town like family. He carried their burdens effortlessly and without complaint.

Who carried his burdens? Who did he lean on when life got tough? Who kept him company and talked to him about his day?

Oh, Caleb.

He needed someone to share his life with him, not just a friend, but a helpmate, someone who cared about him, who loved him. If only…

"…and it was really dirty, with lots of soot and grime. It smelled real bad, too, but it wasn't too terrible."

Realizing Brody had continued the conversation without her, Ellie attempted to file through the information he'd imparted. "Sounds as if you like hard work."

"I suppose." The boy lifted a shoulder. "It sure beats getting in trouble."

Ellie couldn't argue with that.

The song came to an end. She gathered all the children at the front of the church. "We made excellent progress today, but the play is in less than two weeks. I expect everyone with speaking parts to know your lines by the time we meet again. You'll perform without scripts."

A groan rose up from the older children.

"Don't worry. I'll prompt you if you forget your lines."

The next ten minutes passed quickly. The older boys and girls went on their way. Parents arrived to retrieve the younger children. Some took a moment to thank Ellie for her work on the play, while others hurried out of the church in an effort to beat the bad weather brewing in the sky.

Kate said her goodbyes, adding a reminder about their meeting at her dress shop the following evening for final wardrobe decisions.

And then...

There were only three children left—Caleb's daughters and Brody. The girls hovered around the boy like bees to a flower. They didn't seem to mind that he rarely responded.

Ellie's smile came immediately as she watched their valiant effort to engage Brody in conversation.

Both girls stared up at him with stars in their eyes.

Brody, for his part, seemed completely oblivious to their female interest. The tolerant pose he struck reminded Ellie of Caleb as a boy. Had she looked at him in the same way his daughters stared up at Brody?

Had Caleb been equally unaware of her?

She had only a moment to ponder the question when the man himself arrived at the church. His grin flashed beneath the wide round brim before he reached up and swept the hat off his head.

Ellie's heart fluttered at the romantic figure he made.

He was a tall, lean man, muscular in all the right places—shoulders, biceps, chest. It was easy to see why Lizzie Covington had fallen for him. He was pleasing to look at, but his best feature, at least in Ellie's opinion, was his rock-solid character. He was a man of Christian integrity, who exuded quiet strength and confidence.

Caleb not only knew what to do in a crisis, he followed through with whatever needed to be done. A woman could lean on him in good times and bad.

Hannah caught sight of her father and rushed over to him. Grace soon followed. And so began a detailed accounting of today's play practice. When they'd exhausted that topic, the little girls prattled on about *wonderful* Brody and *magnificent* Miss Kate and their very most *favorite* Miss Ellie and how much they loved, loved, *loved* singing practice the most.

Caleb nodded his head, looking a little dazed.

Even Ellie found her head spinning. Her heart filled with affection. The girls were unusually animated and utterly delightful. Becoming too attached was a bad idea, the worst of the worst. She'd be wise to keep up her guard. *Too late*, something inside her whispered.

Too, too late.

She loved all three members of the Voss family.

Caleb crouched in front of his daughters and brushed a tangle of curls off each of their faces. "I'm sorry to hear you had a terrible time."

"No, Papa. Weren't you listening? We had a, oh—"

Hannah blew out a laughing gust of air "—you just made a joke."

Dropping a kiss on her head, he stood, then looked over at Brody. "Hey, wasn't expecting you to be here still."

"I'm heading out now."

"You could have left sooner," Ellie said, only just realizing that Brody never stuck around this long after practice.

"I wanted to wait until the sheriff showed up before leaving."

A line of confusion dug across Caleb's forehead. "Was there something you needed to speak with me about tonight?"

"No. I—" Brody pushed out a fast breath. "I didn't want your daughters and Miss Ellie to have to wait all alone inside the church."

Understanding dawned in Caleb's eyes. "You stuck around to keep them safe."

"Yeah, I guess."

"That was good of you, Brody." Caleb clapped the boy on the shoulder. "I'm here now so you can go on home to your mother."

"Yeah, okay." The boy turned to Ellie. "I can walk you home on my way."

Sympathy squeezed Ellie's heart. Beneath all the pranks, Brody was a good boy. "That's very kind of you to offer. Let me gather up my belongings. Wait here, I'll only be a moment." She quickly stuffed papers in her bag then reached for her cloak.

Caleb beat her to it. "Oh." She blinked in surprise. This wasn't the first time she'd failed to hear his silent approach. "You're certainly light on your feet."

"Necessary for my job." He wrapped her cloak around her shoulders, then drew the open collar together at the throat.

Ellie's heart took a hard thump, thump, and she told herself, *no*. Or, more precisely, *No, he can't be yours. He only wants you as a friend.*

"You all right, Ellie?"

"Yes, of course."

"You sure?" He cocked his head. "Your face is pale."

Avoiding a direct answer, she cast a quick glance to the back of the church. Hannah and Grace had returned to their one-sided conversation with Brody.

"Brody told me what you did for him at the mercantile."

Caleb was silent for so long she wondered if he'd heard her.

"You'll be pleased to know he owned up to what he did."

"He's not a bad kid." Caleb released a very masculine, if somewhat weary, exhale. "Just in need of guidance."

"He's going to be okay," she said. "He has his aunt, and my father, and you. What you did today, giving him the opportunity to make a bad decision right, will go a long way toward setting him on the proper path."

"Everyone deserves a second chance."

Monroe hadn't thought so. At least not in her—or, more to the point, her brother's—case. When Ellie told him about Everett's incarceration, he'd paused only slightly before he retracted his marriage proposal. Apparently, a preacher in charge of a flock of godly men and women couldn't have his name connected to a man in prison for murder.

If not a preacher, then who?

Ellie's father had always taught that God loved the lost. The Lord wanted to save everyone, not just the good, but also sinners.

"Ellie? Did you hear me?"

She jolted at the sound of Caleb's voice coming at her as if from a great distance. "No, I—" She sighed. "I was thinking about Everett."

Eyes filled with sorrow, Caleb rubbed the back of his neck. "I'm sorry I couldn't help him more."

"You did what you could."

"It wasn't enough."

Ellie heard the regret in his voice and worried that Caleb carried a portion of the blame over Everett's incarceration. "It's not your fault he went to prison."

"The evidence proved manslaughter, not murder." Caleb flattened his mouth into a hard, grim line. "The judge should have given him a lighter sentence. Seven years was too harsh."

Yet Everett had accepted his punishment without complaint. "Do you know what he said to me right before he was taken away?"

Caleb shook his head.

Ellie could hear her brother's voice in her head even now, two years later. "Don't cry, Ellie-bug. I have to pay for my crime. It's the right thing to do."

As she repeated Everett's words, Ellie added a few of her own. "He doesn't blame you. You shouldn't blame yourself."

She saw Caleb processing her words. It would take him time, but he was a smart man. He would eventually release his guilt.

But she wouldn't be around to witness it. Another

woman would soon be living in Caleb's home, acting as a mother to his children and a wife to him. The thought made her heartsick. For all Ellie knew, his mail-order bride was already on her way to Thunder Ridge.

She must face the truth of her situation or risk a lifetime of hurt and regret. Caleb would never be hers. She couldn't keep building up hope that he would one day change his mind about her, about them.

When his future bride arrived in Thunder Ridge, Ellie would have to say goodbye to Caleb and his daughters.

It would be the toughest thing she'd ever done.

Chapter Eleven

Sheltered with his daughters beneath the church over-hang, Caleb watched Brody take Ellie's arm and then guide her into the swirling snow. The boy kept his pace slow, making sure Ellie didn't slip on the slick mud. Watching the two disappear around the corner of the parsonage, Caleb felt a lump rise in his throat.

No denying the boy was strong-willed, with a penchant for pranks, but Brody didn't have the heart for true disobedience. His troublemaking was directly related to his mother's illness, something Ellie seemed to understand. Her treatment of the boy showed the depths of her compassion.

Something hopeful worked through Caleb, warming him in a way he didn't know he needed warming. A crack had opened in his heart sometime in the past week and Ellie had slipped through, taking up residence without even trying.

How would he find the fortitude to let her go when she took a teaching job in another town?

"Papa?" Grace tugged on his sleeve. "Are we going home now?"

Caleb registered his daughter's question, winced at his inattention, then guided both girls across the street with the same care Brody had shown Ellie.

Once they were safely inside the house, the girls unbuttoned their coats themselves and hung them on their respective hooks. Ellie's doing, no doubt. She wasn't just taking care of the twins. She was also teaching them how to manage everyday tasks.

"Miss Ellie left supper for us," Hannah announced when he simply stood there watching in mild surprise as she neatly put away her hat, scarf and gloves in the proper bin.

"She said since it was cold meats and cheeses we could fix our own plates," Grace added. "You want us to fix one for you, too?"

"I'd like that."

His little girls were growing up, he realized with a start. Hannah and Grace weren't babies anymore. Come next September they would be old enough to attend school.

They needed a mother to guide them from precious little girls to capable young women.

He prayed Sadie Taylor proved worthy. But what if she didn't? What if she brought chaos instead of calm?

Desperation gripped hold of his chest and squeezed all the breath out of his lungs.

He shoved aside the sensation and told himself to live one day at a time, one moment at a time, starting with this one right now. "I have a surprise for you."

"You do?" Grace asked, eyes wide. "What is it?"

"You'll have to come and see."

Both girls bounced and twirled around him. At the threshold of the living room, he swept his arm toward the blue spruce he'd cut down while they'd been at play practice. "Well? What do you think of our Christmas tree?"

Their delighted squeals answered his question.

"Oh, Papa, it's wonderful," Grace said between laughs.

"Will you help us decorate it?" Hannah asked.

"Try to stop me."

For nearly a half hour the girls admired their new tree and made detailed plans for decorating the branches.

Caleb was happy to simply listen to their excited chatter. *Lord, I want to do right by my daughters. Lead me to the woman You want in their lives…and mine.*

This was the first time he'd added himself in the prayer. The significance barely had time to sink in when a loud knocking yanked his attention to the front door.

"Sheriff Voss, you in there? Come quick, I need your help."

Recognizing the panic in Brody's voice, Caleb strode across the room and swung open the door. "What's happened?"

One look at the boy's face and he knew.

"It's Mama. She's real bad. Aunt Betsy sent me to get Doc, but he's not at his home or the clinic." Tears streamed down Brody's cheeks. "I don't know what to do. You gotta help me."

"Take a breath, Brody. That's it. Now another." Caleb set his hands on the boy's shoulders. "We'll find Doc, but first I want you to go to the parsonage and tell Miss Ellie I need her to come watch the girls."

"Be right back." Brody bolted across the street.

Caleb explained the situation to his daughters in calm, even tones. "I'll probably be gone most of the evening."

"That's all right, Papa," Hannah said, her eyes swimming with little-girl concern. "Brody and his mama need you."

"Yes, they do."

Grace moved in closer and patted his cheek with her palm. "Don't worry about us, Papa. We're big girls."

He'd barely had time to kiss each forehead before Ellie burst into the room, Brody hard on her heels.

"I'm here," she said between breaths, her voice packed with worry. "You can go now, Caleb. Go find Doc."

He rose. "I have no idea how long I'll be gone."

"Take all the time you need." She all but pushed him into the tiny room off the kitchen. Eyes locked with his, she took his coat off the hook and handed it to him. "I'm not going anywhere."

With her promise ringing in his ears, Caleb guided Brody out the back door and headed toward the center of town to find the missing doctor.

Twenty minutes later, Ellie watched the girls pick at their food. Their concern for Brody and his mother was evident in their unnatural silence and restless movements.

After supper, in an effort to distract them—and herself—Ellie read from *A Christmas Carol*. Whenever she turned the page she sneaked a glance at the front door, which remained fully shut. No Caleb. No news. She thought she might crawl out of her own skin.

By ten o'clock, her plan to divert the girls' attention

found success. Neither Hannah nor Grace could keep their eyes open longer than seconds at a time. Abandoning the book, Ellie herded them off to bed. They each said a prayer for Brody and his mother.

Ellie tucked the covers up to their chins, added a kiss to each of their cheeks, then returned to the living room with nothing to do but worry.

She padded around the room, ran her finger along a bookshelf, a table, the edge of a chair. She noted the addition of the Christmas tree. But, at the moment, couldn't find any real joy in what lay ahead for her and the girls as they decorated it for the season.

Detesting idle hands, she folded and refolded a blanket, found another one and repeated the process twice over.

Caleb's continued absence didn't bode well for Brody's mother.

Lord, be with Clara Driscoll tonight. Bring her Your comfort and peace in her hour of need.

She lifted up another prayer for Brody. *Give him the courage to face the loss of his mother, if that be Your will this night.*

At least Caleb was with the boy. If anyone in town understood what Brody was going through, it was him.

The clock on the mantel chimed eleven.

Frustrated with her own company, Ellie paced into the kitchen. She puttered around, cleaned dishes that weren't dirty until, finally, the back door swung open.

She rushed through the house to meet Caleb. Something in the way he held his shoulders made her heart hitch with dread. "You're home."

When he lifted his head Ellie's breath backed up in her throat.

"Is Brody's mother…? Is she…?" She couldn't make herself finish the question.

"Clara Driscoll passed several hours ago."

"No! Oh, Caleb, no."

His gaze fastened on a spot somewhere far off in the distance. He looked so lost, so full of torment.

Ellie briefly touched his sleeve. "I'm so sorry. Poor Brody."

Nodding, Caleb choked out a breath. "When it became evident his mother wasn't going to make it through the night, the boy presented her the Christmas gift he'd picked out at the mercantile this afternoon."

He paused, clearly struggling to speak.

Ellie held silent in an effort to give him the time he needed to gather his control.

"Clara was too weak to remove the wrapping, so Brody did it for her. Eyes shining with love, she gripped the blue bottle to her heart and told him he was the best son a mother could ever ask for and then…"

Caleb covered his eyes with his hand, blew out a slow, tortured hiss. "She patted his hand, settled back on the pillow and…" He dropped his hand, saying, "Breathed her last."

"Oh, Caleb." Ellie felt tears forming. She did nothing to stop them from falling freely down her cheeks.

"Brody was inconsolable in those early moments after she died. Betsy tried to ease his pain, but she was too stricken with her own grief to be of much help."

Able to picture the heart-wrenching scene, Ellie's tears flowed faster.

"That's why I was gone so long." Caleb's eyes were hot with anguish. "The boy needed someone who understood his agony."

"He needed you."

Caleb lifted a shoulder. "I would have stayed longer, but your father arrived, assessed the situation and immediately stepped in with Brody."

He didn't have to say more. "Pa will take care of him."

"I have no doubt." Caleb rolled his gaze to hers. His eyes were deep, fathomless pools of raw emotion. "He'll ease Brody through his sorrow, just as he did for me the night my mother died."

Ellie felt Caleb's sadness deep in her marrow. Her heart ached for Brody, and for Caleb, for the little boy he'd been.

Needing to give him comfort, she wrapped her arms around his broad shoulders.

For several heartbeats, he remained motionless in her embrace, as if frozen inside his own grief. Gradually, his arms came around her.

"Ellie," he said in a low, tortured voice. "Now that I know Brody is in good hands, it's as if a floodgate has opened. I can't stop the memories of my own mother's passing."

She put her hand on his snow-dampened hair, stroked gently. She was contending with her own memories and needed to receive Caleb's comfort as much as she needed to give it to him. "I understand, you know."

"I know." He sucked in a deep, audible breath, then pulled her just a bit closer, just a bit tighter.

It was on the tip of her tongue to tell him she loved him, to assure him he would never be alone in this world as long as she was in it, too. But she feared if she revealed the contents of her heart right now, he would pull away from her.

He stepped back and stared into her eyes. She was acutely aware of several things: his handsome face, his tormented expression, her yearning to soothe away his pain.

"What will happen to Brody now?"

"Betsy and your father have plans to take him in and raise him as their own."

Ellie mulled this over, thinking the idea made perfect sense.

Betsy was the boy's aunt, the only family he had left. She was about to marry a man who would love and guide the boy into a capable adult.

As if his mind had traveled along the same route as Ellie's, Caleb said, "Your father will be a good influence on Brody. Look how he changed my life."

Yes, Ellie thought, her father had made a difference in Caleb's life. He'd grown from a troubled boy into a man of uncompromising integrity. He was a wonderful, loving father now, a man who would make an extraordinary husband. If only he would allow a woman into his heart.

If only he would allow *Ellie* into his heart, she would spend the rest of her life being the wife he deserved.

Chapter Twelve

As Caleb predicted, Thunder Ridge rallied around Brody. In the week following his mother's death, the townspeople treated the boy with the compassion and love he needed to help him manage his grief. Sorrow clung to him like a second skin, but he was growing stronger by the day.

He remained living in his home, with his aunt. However, once Betsy married Reverend Wainwright the two of them would move into the parsonage. According to Ellie, Brody was shining in his role as Joseph in the children's Christmas play and hadn't brought a single rodent into the church since that first time.

The Sunday before Christmas Eve, Caleb escorted his daughters out the back door of their home. He paused and eyed the dark wall of clouds coming in from the west. Another snowstorm brewed, the second in so many days.

Caleb hustled his daughters across the street. Sunday dinner at the Wainwrights' would follow morning service, their third this month. Caleb wondered if they would continue the tradition after Ellie left town.

Depressing thought. Nothing would be the same without her.

"Hi, Miss Ellie!" Grace waved at the lone figure standing on the porch of the parsonage. Hannah followed suit.

Caleb could only stare at the beautiful picture she made. With the snow-covered mountains behind her, dressed in her blue cloak and matching hat, she looked like a winter princess.

Waving back at the children, Ellie started down the steps.

The girls ran to meet her at the edge of the walkway.

Caleb made the trek at a slower pace. His breath caught at the sight of Ellie with his daughters. She was so natural, so unconsciously affectionate.

He wasn't supposed to feel this sense of wonder over a simple interaction he'd seen a dozen times in the weeks since she'd entered his home. He wasn't supposed to feel this connected to a woman who could never be his.

It would be foolish of him to forget that Ellie was leaving town one day soon and that he'd made a tentative agreement with a mail-order bride. Anything between him and Ellie was already doomed. Yet something about her called to him. She pulled at places inside his soul no other woman had touched.

Caleb cared for Ellie. He cared so much it scared him.

But if he let himself love her, he could very well destroy her, as he had Lizzie.

When she glanced toward him, he saw the faintest sign of nerves. "Hi," she said on a rush of air.

Mouth dry as dust, he tipped his hat in response.

Hannah tugged on her sleeve, forcing Ellie to look down.

"You're sitting with us, aren't you, Miss Ellie?"

"Of course I'm sitting with you."

Hand in hand, the four of them entered the church and found their usual seats. Only after they were settled—Caleb on one end of the pew, Ellie on the other, with the girls in between—did he realize they were sitting in the same order as the past three Sundays. They'd fallen into a pattern.

As if they were a family.

He swallowed back the well of emotion rising in his throat.

The pianist took her place. With her trademark smile, Ellie handed him a hymnal.

Voice rough as gravel, he thanked her.

Three songs later, the reverend took his place at the pulpit. He looked out over the congregation, smiled kindly, then began his sermon with a bang.

"Love." He paused, caught several eyes, then added, "A simple word. A simple sentiment. Or is it?"

Caleb shifted in his seat, glanced down at his lap, back up again. Out of the corner of his eye he saw Ellie sit up straighter, her lips pressed tightly together. Apparently she was as uncomfortable as he was with the topic of her father's sermon.

"The Lord commands us to love one another as we would ourselves. But what is love?"

As he spoke, the reverend ran his gaze over his flock, stopped for a second on his daughter, then moved on to Caleb. Caleb quickly looked away, tugged on his collar, cleared his throat. It was as if the man was trying to make his point directly to him.

"Many of us confuse love with something it is not."

The entire congregation leaned forward. Caleb remained unmoving. What did he know of love? His father's love had destroyed him. Caleb had loved Lizzie, but that had ended just as tragically.

"Paul's words to the Corinthians tell us that love is patient. Love is kind. It does not envy, does not behave rudely, is not provoked."

Caleb understood that kind of unselfish love—when it came to his daughters. Not when he considered his relationship with Lizzie. Their time together had been full of strife and provocation, with not nearly enough patience and certainly not enough kindness.

"Love endures all things. It never ceases, never wavers, not even when times get hard or disappointments arise."

Caleb heard a rustle of material as Ellie shifted in her seat. He caught her gaze over the children's heads. She gave him a sweet, shaky smile.

Everything her father claimed was love also defined Ellie. She was kind. She was patient. She never behaved rudely, never provoked.

"Love is constant."

Ellie was constant.

"Love does not seek its own will, but that of others."

Ellie always put others first.

The rest of the sermon was lost on Caleb. His mind was in a whirl. All this time, he'd been defining love in relation to his experience with Lizzie.

Had he been wrong? Suddenly, the interior of the church closed in on him. Heat radiated from deep within him.

He needed fresh air, now. He leaned over his daughters and caught Ellie's attention. *Heading outside*, he mouthed.

She nodded, but said nothing. She didn't need to respond. Caleb was fully confident she would take care of his daughters in his absence.

This wasn't the first time he'd noticed how attuned Ellie was to him, and he to her. He'd dismissed their easy camaraderie to their long-standing friendship.

Now, as he climbed to his feet and made his way down the center aisle, he wondered if he'd been wrong about that, as well.

Was his bond with Ellie based on something more than friendship, something deep and lasting and constant?

Was he in love with Ellie?

Something the reverend said had him pausing at the door, looking back over his shoulder. "If love has to be earned, it isn't love at all."

Struck speechless, Caleb quickly left the church.

Ellie watched the door click shut behind Caleb. She wanted to go after him, but he'd left her in charge of his daughters.

Casting a final glance at the empty foyer, she returned her attention to the sermon.

She closed her eyes and drew in an unsteady breath. It was as if her father was speaking directly to her. Perhaps he was. Just last night she'd told him why she'd come home. She'd included all of the humiliating details, ending with her doomed relationship with Monroe.

Ellie attempted to listen to the sermon, but half her mind was on Caleb and the look in his eyes when he'd left their pew.

The sermon must have struck a chord with him,

as surely as it had with her. What else explained his swift departure?

When Caleb didn't return, not even for the final hymn, Ellie started to worry. Hoping he'd gone on ahead to her father's house, she ushered the girls outside then through the back door of the parsonage. She was helping them out of their coats when Caleb joined them.

He moved around Ellie and, without looking directly at her, greeted his daughters. In the confines of the tiny space, she was aware of his masculine presence, of the differences in their sizes—her petite frame to his taller, stronger build.

As if sensing her eyes on him, he glanced her way and gave an easy smile. Her breath snagged on a skittering rush of air.

There was something different in his eyes, something new and solely for her. Her heart burst with hope. There was also a looseness in his stance. He seemed easier in his skin.

Unable to look away, Ellie studied Caleb's face a moment longer. He really was different, freer, as if a heavy burden had been lifted from his shoulders.

Smiling into her eyes, he sent the girls inside the house.

Ellie attempted to follow but he stopped her progress with a hand on her arm. "Can we talk?"

"Of course. Here? Or somewhere else?"

"Wherever we can't be overheard."

What he had to say must be serious; she saw it in his gaze, heard it in his voice. The tiny thread of hope flared fully to life.

"The porch," she decided. Still dressed in her cloak,

she led him back outside and around to the front of the house.

He held silent on the short journey.

People bustled by on the planked sidewalk. Some waved, others called out a greeting, but most hurried on their way, paying them no mind. Ellie supposed this was as alone as they would get. If they kept their voices down it should suffice.

"You wished to speak with me?" she prompted.

"Your father's sermon today…it's gotten me to thinking."

Eaten alive with hope, yet afraid to let herself give in to the emotion, Ellie held perfectly still. "The sermon resonated with me, as well."

Caleb's eyes widened ever-so-slightly. "That surprises me."

"I don't see why."

"I always thought you knew everything there was to know about love."

She nearly snorted. "Hardly."

Swiftly, yet gently, he took her hand. "Tell me what happened in Colorado Springs."

The abrupt change in subject would have seemed ill-timed if she were speaking to anyone else. But this was Caleb. He knew her well, better than most. Of course he would make the correct leap from a sermon on love to her unexpected return home. "It's not a very happy tale."

"Ellie." Her name slipped out of him almost without sound. "Someone hurt you, a man."

Cheeks heating from remembered shame, she pulled her hand free and lowered her head. "Yes."

"Tell me what happened."

The request was so Caleb, spoken softly, and full of tenderness without a hint of judgment. The pain in her heart released ever-so-slightly.

Tentatively, she reached out and touched his broad, capable shoulder in a vague, barely there gesture. Still, her fingers tingled inside her gloves. She dropped her hand and closed it into a fist. "There was a man, a widowed preacher with three young daughters. He showed interest in me almost as soon as I arrived in town."

"You returned his feelings."

How to answer? With the truth, of course. She took a very tiny pull of air. "Not at first, no."

She went on to explain how her lack of interest hadn't deterred Monroe. He'd been relentless in his attempt to court her. "My affection for his daughters eventually spilled onto the father."

"So you grew to like him."

She nodded.

"Then why didn't you marry him?"

"He asked. I accepted. All seemed well for a time. But he withdrew his marriage proposal when I told him about Everett's incarceration. I didn't intentionally hide the information, though that's what he claimed."

In the span of a heartbeat, Caleb's expression went from confused to furious. "This so-called preacher, this man of God, took back his proposal because Everett is locked up in the Wyoming Territorial Prison?"

She fought off another wave of humiliation. "Basically, yes."

Caleb's lips flattened into a hard line. "He didn't love you."

"I realize that now. My father's sermon helped clarify my suspicions." A sigh leaked past her lips. "Now you know why I won't settle for a marriage of convenience. I want my husband to love me enough to stand by me no matter the obstacles."

"Ellie, you deserve nothing less. You deserve to be loved completely, unceasingly and without conditions."

She sighed.

"Listen to me." He cupped her cheek with his palm. His expression was unguarded, and so full of affection that Ellie lost her ability to breathe easily.

"Ellie, dear, sweet, beautiful Ellie, your husband should love you with all that he has inside him. He should stand by you always, in good times and bad, no matter what comes your way."

"Yes, Caleb, that's precisely the kind of husband I want." It was the kind of husband he could be, if he'd let himself love a woman with the same devotion he did his daughters.

Ellie nearly said as much, but Betsy chose that moment to poke her head around the front door. "Ah, there you two are. Dinner is on the table."

Hating that she'd left the other woman to serve the meal alone, Ellie headed for the door.

As he had earlier, Caleb stopped her with a hand on her arm. "Monroe Tipton didn't deserve you."

Her father had said much the same thing last night. It had taken her a while, but she'd come to the same conclusion. "No, he didn't."

She tried to head inside, again. *Again*, Caleb wouldn't let her go. "I have more to say."

"All right." With eyebrows lifted, she waited for him to continue.

He opened his mouth, but seemed to reconsider and

shut it again. "What I have to say is too important to rush through it. We'll speak again after we eat."

By the look in his eyes, she sensed whatever he had to say would change her life forever. Ellie had never been more excited, more nervous, or more impatient for a conversation to unfold.

Chapter Thirteen

Sunday dinner at the Wainwrights' had always brought Caleb a sense of belonging. In this home, he'd learned the very essence of family. He'd felt safe here, comforted. He'd done his best to replicate their example in his own home. But he'd always felt as though he'd fallen short, especially in the months since Lizzie's death.

In the past few weeks, with Ellie in his life, the possibility of having a real family, and a loving home, had become more than a far-off dream.

He knew what he wanted now.

He wanted Ellie to be his wife, in every sense of the word.

Friendship would never be enough. He'd been wrong to think he could settle for something so benign. He loved Ellie, as a man loved his wife.

"Caleb?" She leaned in close. "Are you all right?"

He was more than all right. He was free of the past. Free to step into the future with this woman by his side.

If she would have him.

Smiling, his heart bursting with love, he said, "All good on my end."

"Are you certain?" She looked pointedly at his full plate. "You're not eating."

Still smiling, he picked up his fork and shoveled in a bite of potatoes. When he finished chewing, he asked, "Better?"

She laughed softly. "Much."

Near the end of the meal, Hannah asked Brody, "Want to play jacks with my sister and me?"

The boy frowned at the question, no doubt trying to come up with an appropriate reason to avoid what most boys thought of as a girl's game. "How about tin soldiers?" he suggested.

"Whatever you want to play." Grace nudged her sister with her elbow. "Let him pick the game."

Hannah shrugged. "Okay, sure. Tin soldiers sounds... fun."

Once they were given permission to leave the table, the three sped out of the room. By unspoken agreement, Caleb and Ellie took over cleanup detail.

This, Caleb thought as he made a second pass around the table and grabbed a handful of dirty dishes, *this is the future I want, sharing Sunday dinner with the people I love.*

He would ask Ellie to marry him this very afternoon.

The moment the dishes were cleaned and put away, he took Ellie's hands in his. "Come outside with me a moment. I have something I want to ask you."

"Oh, my, that sounds ominous."

The look of amusement on her face moved through him, bringing certainty. How he loved this woman with all his heart. Why had he resisted for so long?

No more. He wouldn't let another day pass without letting Ellie know how he felt.

Following her to the back of the house, he helped her into her cloak, donned his own coat and then escorted her outside.

They walked a few moments in silence. Now that the time had come to propose, Caleb worried he wouldn't get the words right.

Even more disconcerting, what if she turned him down again?

"Ellie." He drew her to a stop and pulled her a step closer, near enough to smell the hint of wild orchid wafting off her. The scent of the woman he loved. "I'm glad I have you in my life. I never want to lose you."

Her eyes widened. "What...what are you saying?"

"I'm saying that I finally understand what love is."

"Well, of course you know what love is." She laughed, the rich, husky sound solely hers. "I've seen you with your daughters. You, Caleb Voss, have endless bounties of love in your heart. Don't let anyone tell you otherwise."

Her confidence in him brought certainty to his heart and a slice of wonder to his soul. "You've taught me that love, the kind between a man and a woman, doesn't have to hurt, or bring pain and disappointment or end in heartache."

Her eyes softened, then turned thoughtful, as if she was trying to put a puzzle together but couldn't quite make the pieces fit. "Your marriage to Lizzie... I gather it was not a happy one."

"No, it wasn't."

In a halting tone, he shared the torture of living with

Lizzie's mood shifts and her penchant for running away when matters grew tense.

"Oh, Caleb."

"Not every argument ended with her abandoning me and the girls. But the threat was always there."

Sympathy washed over Ellie's features. "That must have been incredibly stressful on all of you, especially the girls. Oh, Caleb. They must have been so worried when their mother up and disappeared."

"I tried to protect them from the worst of it."

"Surely they sensed all was not right and that it wasn't normal for a mother to leave home without warning."

"I'm not sure how much they remember."

"Probably more than they should." She shook her head sadly. "No wonder you want to provide them with a calm, stable home."

"I'm glad you understand."

"Of course I understand. Lizzie's erratic behavior is why you're seeking a marriage of convenience."

He nodded. "In my experience, which granted, is limited, love brings chaos and pain."

"That's not love, Caleb. I don't know what it is, but it's not love, not the kind the Lord intended between a husband and a wife."

"I know that now."

"I'm glad." She moved a step closer, so near that if he lowered his head just a bit their lips would touch. He wanted this woman to be his wife. He wanted to love her till the end of time.

He stared at her without blinking, half fearing if he closed his eyes, even for a split second, she would disappear. "Ellie, I want you to know I care for you deeply."

No, that wasn't what he'd meant to say.

She lifted on her toes and pressed her lips to his. When she stepped back, she gave him three simple words that were already in his heart. "I love you, Caleb."

"Ah, Ellie, I lo—"

"Wait." She placed her fingertips to his mouth. "Before you respond, let me have my say first."

He'd rather finish telling her he loved her, but this seemed very important to her. "All right, I'm listening."

"I will always consider you my friend, Caleb, but friendship will never be enough. I want so much more from you."

"I want more, as well."

"Oh, Caleb, truly?"

"Truly. Ellie, will you…" He paused, looked around, realized they were standing on the planked sidewalk in front of the church. It seemed appropriate they'd stopped walking at this specific spot.

"I need to do this right." He pulled her beneath the overhang. "Ellie Wainwright, you make me want to be a better man, the man you deserve. You make me want to live life to the fullest. I can't imagine any other woman by my side."

He took her hand, started to lower to one knee, but a movement off to his left caught his eye and he made the mistake of hesitating.

"Sheriff Voss. *Sheriff Voss*, something quite wonderful has happened."

Shoulders tense, he looked in the direction of the

voice. Mrs. Jenson was bearing down on him and Ellie. And she wasn't alone. She had a young woman with her.

"Your troubles are over."

Dread tumbled in his gut. Mrs. Jenson had her hand clamped around the younger woman's wrist and was all but dragging her across the street.

"I have brought someone you will want to meet at once."

His heart sank.

No, Lord, please, no.

In silent desperation, he studied the young woman. She was certainly the right age to be Sadie Taylor. She was pretty, to be sure, with coal-black hair, fair skin and pale blue eyes. But she wasn't nearly as beautiful as his Ellie.

Ellie had grown deathly still beside him. He cut a quick glance in her direction, winced at the stillness that had come over her. Her face gave nothing away but he could feel her sorrow. It matched his own.

Mrs. Jenson hurried up the walkway. Given little choice, her companion stumbled along after her. "Good news, Sheriff Voss. Your future bride was able to leave her position in Blue Springs sooner than expected."

Everything inside Caleb froze at the way Ellie stiffened beside him.

"I'll leave you three alone." Ellie's tortured voice sliced him at the core.

This couldn't be happening. Not now, not when he knew exactly what he wanted, and who.

"Oh, hello, Ellie." Mrs. Jenson dropped a perfunctory smile in her direction. "In my excitement, I didn't see you standing there."

"H-hello, Mrs. Jenson." Ellie dropped her gaze to her toes.

Ignoring everyone but the woman he loved, Caleb attempted to take Ellie's hand. He needed to tell her how he felt, that he wanted to spend the rest of his life with her.

She shifted out of his reach. Head still lowered, she fumbled out an excuse about her father needing her inside.

"Ellie, wait. Don't leave yet."

He was talking to her back.

He started out after her, but Mrs. Jenson was not to be deterred.

"Sheriff Voss, I'd like you to meet your bride, Sadie Taylor."

Caleb forced a smile for the young woman's benefit. His change of heart wasn't her fault.

"Mrs. Taylor." He held her gaze without wavering. "There's been a change in plans."

Ellie hurried into her father's house. She found the girls sitting on the floor in the living room, playing jacks with a clearly reluctant, albeit patient, Brody. One or both of them must have convinced him to try the game.

The three children looked like a family. They would have become a family, if Ellie had married Caleb.

She briefly closed her eyes against the sorrow pounding through her blood and swallowed back tears. She would not cry. She would...*not*...*cry*.

She'd known this day was coming. Caleb had warned her. And yet, for a brief, hope-filled moment, she'd believed all would work out. He seemed ready to propose again. This time for all the right reasons. No, he hadn't actually said he loved her, but she sensed he'd been on the verge of pledging his heart.

Now, she would never hear Caleb say *I love you.* Not in the way a husband said the words to his wife.

"Miss Ellie, are you watching us?" Hannah asked from her position on the floor.

"I am." Or rather, she was now.

"Brody is really good at jacks."

Determined to focus on the children, and not what was being discussed outside the church, Ellie forced her attention on the game unfolding on the floor. Tongue clamped between his teeth, Brody threw the ball in the air and gathered up a handful of jacks. He had fast reflexes and caught the ball before it bounced twice. "Yes, Brody is very good at the game."

"Want to play with us?"

Ellie shook her head. "Not right now. Later, perhaps." *When my heart isn't breaking.* "I have to check on something in another part of the house."

Head down, she rushed to her father's private sanctuary in the back of the house. She took a roundabout route, bypassing the kitchen where her father and Betsy were drinking coffee and talking in low tones.

Eyes damp with sorrow, barely able to see through a blurry haze of regret, she opened and then closed the door quietly behind her.

Now that Caleb's future bride was in Thunder Ridge, he could very well be married before Christmas.

How would she ever bear seeing him with another woman?

Choking on her hurt, on her terrible sense of loss,

she sank into a wingback chair and buried her face in her hands.

She wanted to sob for hours. She refrained, holding back the tears by sheer force of will.

Barely a month ago, she'd come home from Colorado Springs vulnerable and humiliated. She thought she'd experienced the worst kind of hurt imaginable. She'd been wrong, so wrong. Losing Caleb and his daughters hurt a thousand times worse.

She'd promised herself she would never fall in love with a man who didn't love her back. And she hadn't. Caleb loved her, she was sure of it. But he hadn't said the words. He probably never would. He was promised to another woman, a stranger who wouldn't expect too much from him. A woman who would accept his conditions for a marriage of convenience.

Ellie choked on a sob after all.

A pounding came at the door.

She lifted her head. The bold, hard raps of knuckles to wood continued.

"Ellie, open up, I know you're in there." Knock, knock, knock. "Let me in."

She swiped furiously at her cheeks. "Go away, Caleb."

"Not until you hear me out."

She stood, moved to the door, but couldn't gather the courage to do as he requested. She placed her hand flat on the wood instead. "I can't talk to you right now. Please, Caleb, let me alone."

"I'm not leaving."

The cloud of misery hanging heavy in her heart lightened somewhat at his determination. She pushed back from the door.

"Ellie." He'd never spoken her name with such tenderness. "Open up."

Swiftly, without hardly knowing she'd meant to do it, she twisted the knob and swung open the door in a single swoop.

Caleb reared back.

Clearly, she'd caught him by surprise.

He recovered quickly. Then gave her his slow, gentle smile, the one she'd first fallen in love with all those years ago.

"I can't do this." She turned her back to him.

"Ellie." Again, her name slipped past his lips like a caress. "I have much to say to you, things you deserve to hear."

"I'm not feeling very conversational."

"That's good." He moved around her. "Because I plan to do all the talking."

Holding nothing but Ellie's gaze, Caleb got straight to the point. "Matters aren't as they may seem."

"Are you saying that the woman with Mrs. Jenson isn't your mail-order bride?"

"Oh, she's the woman Mrs. Jenson has chosen to become my wife."

Ellie's deep, hesitant intake of air was more eloquent than words.

"But I won't be marrying her."

"You...you won't?"

"I told her there was a change in plans."

"You did?"

"She wasn't upset over my change of heart, more confused," he said, briefly reliving his surprise. "I offered to pay for her return ticket, but it seems she wants to stay in Thunder Ridge. Mrs. Jenson is already making plans for her to marry someone else. Billie Quinn's name came up, as did a few others."

"I'm sorry things didn't work out as you planned." The smile playing at the corners of her mouth suggested otherwise.

His own lips lifted. "No you're not, and neither am I."

They held one another's gaze.

"Ellie, all I've ever wanted was a normal, stable home for my daughters. I thought that was enough. Love never entered the equation. I'd had my chance at love and didn't want another try. But then you came into my life and taught me to want more, not only for the girls but also for myself."

"Love and stability don't have to be mutually exclusive. You need both to make a home."

"I know that now."

Ellie had already told him how she felt. *I love you.* She'd said the words sweetly, confidently.

It was now his turn to say them to her. "I love you, Ellie."

Her eyes filled with tears.

He smoothed a fingertip along her cheek, down her jaw. "I love you with all that I am."

"I love you, too. I have for a very long time."

The wonder of that stole his breath.

"I want you to be my wife. I want us to have a real marriage, not one of convenience but a union full of love and laughter. Ellie, will you marry—"

"Yes."

"—me?"

"Yes, yes, yes." Laughing, she leaped into his arms

and planted her mouth to his. "Yes, Caleb, I'll marry you."

He stared into her eyes. "You don't want to think about it? You'll be getting three of us."

With the softest expression he'd ever seen in her eyes, she cupped his cheek. "I want to be your wife. I want to mother your daughters as if they were my own. I want to build a home with you and the girls and any other children that may come along, God willing."

Other children. With Ellie. He couldn't think of a richer, more satisfying future.

"I want to marry you as soon as possible," he said. "And start our life together."

"I'm pretty sure that can be arranged. I happen to know a preacher who will happily perform the ceremony."

He kissed her nose. "Handy."

"Isn't it?"

He kissed her cheek. "When do you want to tell the girls?"

"I was thinking now."

"Sounds perfect to me, but first..." He kissed her lips, lingering a moment longer than any friend would dare.

"You know, Caleb," Ellie whispered in his ear. "If we work out the timing just right, we could be a family by Christmas."

A family by Christmas. "That would be the best gift I could ever hope to receive."

* * * * *

Dear Reader,

I adore creating characters searching for love, family and a place to call their own. The day Ellie and Caleb became husband and wife two special little girls gained a new mother, one who couldn't have loved them more if they'd been born to her. Now, that's what I call a happy ending.

When I was approached to write this shorter book, I never expected to embark on my own unique journey. In the process of helping Ellie and Caleb find one another, I discovered a brand-new town with a host of characters waiting for their happily-ever-after. This isn't the last time I'll be visiting Thunder Ridge, Wyoming. I certainly hope you'll come along for the ride, as well.

I love hearing from readers. You can drop me a quick note either through my website at www.reneeryan.com or on my Facebook page ReneeRyanBooks.

In the meantime, *happy reading*!

Cheers!
Renee

YULETIDE REUNION

Louise M. Gouge

This story is dedicated to my wonderful editor,
Shana Asaro, whose insights always improve
my stories; to my hardworking agent,
who wisely guides my writing career;
and, as always, to my dear husband, David Gouge,
who is my inspiration and loving support.

Walk in love, as Christ also hath loved us.
—*Ephesians* 5:2

Chapter One

Riverton, New Mexico
December 1886

At the sound of approaching hoof beats, Emma Sharp didn't bother to look up from clearing away the charred boards of her family's burned-out barn. No doubt more men were coming to help with the cleanup. The ones who'd come first thing this morning said last night's blaze had been visible in the clear, black sky from ten miles away, so she expected many good neighbors to show up throughout the day and for days to come.

Emma shoved a lock of hair from her forehead with her leather-gloved hand and blew away the fine strands that always lingered to tickle her forehead and cheeks.

The hoof beats stopped nearby and a familiar voice called out in a teasing tone, "My, my, what a pretty sight."

Emma froze. *Jared Mattson.* The last person she wanted to see, even at her best. Today, dressed in Pa's old trousers and faded flannel shirt, she cringed in spite of herself. Even two years after he cruelly played with her affections and then jilted her without any explanation, she still couldn't bear to be in his presence. She could manage to ignore him in church and at social gatherings, but now, covered from head to toe with soot, she would make an easy target for his teasing wit.

She looked up to see the grin on Jared's too-handsome face but quickly cut her gaze away from him to focus on his brother Cal, whose gray eyes exuded kind regard. "Hey, Cal. Nice of you to come over and help. Julia's inside fixing refreshments. I know she'd like to see you before you get to work."

For several weeks, Emma's younger sister, Julia, had expected a proposal from Jared's truehearted younger brother. Maybe this would be the day. It was a marriage both families approved of. In all her twenty years, Emma had never met a nicer young man than Cal. Too bad some of that couldn't rub off on Jared.

"Thanks, Miss Emma." Cal threw a leg over the pommel of his saddle and slid to the ground. All five of the Mattson brothers dismounted that way, just like Indians. And all five were entirely too good-looking with their dark brown hair, gray eyes and hardy cowboy forms. Many a gal in this part of New Mexico Territory had tried to lasso one of the four single brothers, with no success. That was, until Julia won Cal's heart.

"I'll be right back out to help." Cal led his horse to the hitching rail by the back door of the house and looped the reins around it.

Jared slithered from his gelding, posted his fists at his waist and surveyed the damage with those piercing dark gray eyes that used to make her heart beat faster. "What happened?"

She paused for the briefest moment. "The barn

burned down." She granted him a quick, cross glance and added under her breath, "Obviously." Lifting another ruined board, she tossed it into the pile to be burned in the fireplace. Very few boards could be salvaged for a new barn, meaning Pa would have to spend a lot of the profits from this past fall's cattle sale to rebuild. At least they could store up several barrels of wood ash to make soap for a long time to come.

"Do tell." He tipped his wide-brimmed hat back to expose the pale line across his forehead that most cowboys sported. "Did you knock over a lantern while milking, like Mrs. O'Leary's cow did in Chicago back in '71?" The continued grin on his well-formed face issued a challenge she couldn't resist.

"Nope. O'course, I've never been as clumsy as you." She gave him a sidelong glance. "I seem to recall having to soak my feet for quite some time after dancing with you at the harvest celebration in '84 when you stomped on them every two seconds." Back then, she'd been quick to forgive his lack of dancing skills because she'd expected a marriage proposal any day, one that never came. That was the last night he'd courted her.

"And I seem to recall—"

"Enough." She held up a hand with the palm facing Jared. "Did you come to work or to yammer?" If he were closer, she'd be tempted to swipe some of her soot over his face, no matter how improper such a gesture would be.

"Weelll." He drawled out the word slowly as he pulled on his well-worn leather gloves. "I reckon I'd best pitch in and get this job done. Sure don't look like you and the boys have put much of a dent in it."

He nodded toward the three other men who'd

showed up four hours ago and hadn't stopped working since. Half of the rubble had been cleared and sorted, so the men laughed and made a few humorous retorts. He doubtless knew these old friends didn't mind his teasing, so his comment was obviously meant to goad *her*. He'd wait a long time for her reply.

"Thank you, Cal." Julia's voice wafted across the barnyard as she emerged from the house carrying a refreshment-laden tray.

Cal insisted on taking it from her, and his starry-eyed gaze at Julia caused an unexpected ache in Emma's chest. If she were as sweet and ladylike as her sister, maybe she could win the love of a true-hearted man. But Pa needed somebody to stand shoulder-to-shoulder with him in running the ranch, and she was determined to be the one. Pa never complained about not having a son, even though he and Ma had lost three baby boys. God's will, he called it. Ma said that most folks out here in this harsh land lost a child or two, and she bore her burden of grief with grace. Emma could only admire their faith and try real hard to fill in where God had left an empty spot.

Julia poured coffee from a steaming tin pot into crockery cups, and Cal passed them around to the men. They hesitated to take the offering, each looking at his grimy hands.

"Never mind the soot on the cups, men." Julia gave them one of her glorious smiles. "It'll wash off."

Emma could see two of them melt into puddles of admiration, although not Jose Mendez, who was happily married. He and his wife, Maria—who was expecting a baby in a few weeks—had been chosen to portray the Holy Family during all the Las Posadas doings, which would begin tonight and were supposed to end up at the Sharps' barn on Christmas Eve. Emma had looked forward to being in the middle of Riverton's brand-new Christmas celebration with all of their neighbors. After all, this important event had been planned to bring the community together.

When the Denver and Rio Grande Railroad had extended their line to Espanola in 1880, Americanos like the Sharps and Mattsons had begun to move into the area to establish businesses and cattle and sheep ranches. Some communities saw deadly conflicts between the long-settled Mexicans and the newcomers. But the people who settled north of Espanola in the town they named Riverton decided to put their Christian faith into practice. Instead of trying to run off the Mexicans, they sought cooperation. Led by the pastors of Riverton's new community church and the two-hundred-year-old Spanish mission, they planned to celebrate Christ's birth by combining their traditions.

In the American tradition, folks would have Christmas trees and gift exchanges. Following Mexican customs, the community would gather at a different home, or "inn," for nine evenings to celebrate Las Posadas. For this event, "Mary and Joseph" would travel from home to home seeking lodging. Each night, a different family would welcome them with refreshments and singing. The final celebration would take place on December 24, Christmas Eve. The inspiration of the Mexican tradition rang true to the new settlers, who'd done a sight of traveling themselves as they'd moved into this New Mexico Territory. Everyone had looked forward to watching Mary and Joseph find shelter at the Sharps' large barn for the final and largest celebration. To finish it all off, they'd planned to have fireworks out in the field. Now another place would have to be chosen. Emma was particularly disappointed over having to miss the first night of the celebration, maybe every night.

As though reading her thoughts, Julia gave a soft sigh. "Looks like we'll have to find another place for our Christmas Eve party. We were so much looking forward to having everyone come and celebrate Jesus' birth here at our place."

"Who's to say you can't still do it?"

Emma had to look around to be sure she heard right. Had Jared said that? Before she could offer a tart response, Cal spoke up.

"Whadda'ya have in mind, brother?" His gray eyes twinkled, as though he already knew the answer to his question.

"Why, building a new barn, of course." He grinned that maddening grin of his that said he had everything under control. "Our pop said we could stay as long as it took to rebuild. We'll get things started and then invite folks to come over for a barn raising. Pop said y'all'd need a barn before the worst of winter arrives. Gotta protect your horses and milk cows and that prize bull and all. That's why we took so long getting here today." He waved a hand toward the pack mule Emma hadn't noticed behind their horses. "Had to pack up and bring our gear and tools so we could stay." He looked beyond Julia. "That all right with you, Mr. Sharp?"

"I'd be much obliged, boy." Pa grimaced painfully as he limped toward them, leaning heavily on his cane. He'd fought the fire right hard last night and had fallen down more than once in his desperation to put it out. Of course Ma and Emma and Julia had been right there, along with Paco, the lone cowhand in their hire who hadn't gone over to Texas for the winter. "You sure Ralph can spare you?"

Jared and Cal traded a glance and laughed.

"I think our older brothers were glad to get rid of us for a spell," Cal said. "There's not so much work around the ranch in the winter that four men and a boy can't handle it."

"I'm much obliged." Pa coughed softly, probably to clear some of last night's smoke from his lungs. "We'll put you up in the spare room."

Emma shuddered. Even though she couldn't build a barn all by herself, she also couldn't bear the thought of Jared Mattson staying in their house for however long it took to rebuild. But one look at Pa's blue eyes beaming with gratitude and joy told her she had no choice. She was stuck for who knew how long with the man who'd courted her with flowers and buggy rides for a whole entire summer. Then without a word after that harvest dance, he'd up and quit coming around, breaking her heart. Now he had the unmitigated gall to march around like a peacock as though he'd done nothing wrong.

She might have to accept his help, but she didn't have to like it. Snorting out her displeasure, she started back to work tossing boards with a vengeance, imagining all the while one of them landing on Jared Mattson's head.

Jared hadn't expected it to be easy to work around Emma. Even two years after briefly courting her, he couldn't look at her without considerable admiration for her beauty, strength and feisty disposition. But he wasn't about to let his heart go, as he'd almost done back at that harvest dance when they'd both taken turns stepping on each other's feet. That very night he'd learned that his oldest brother Rob's wife, Maybelle, had taken their baby girl and left Rob and their six-year-old son, just as Mama had left Pop and their five sons six years ago.

Maybelle wasn't the only woman besides Mama to leave her husband when life got too hard out here. It just proved what he'd always believed: Women couldn't be trusted. So he was more than just skittish about trusting his heart to one. He absolutely refused to risk it. Three of his brothers agreed, but not Cal, who was eager to marry Julia. Jared would leave the sappy, lovey stuff to him, and he would stand by him if and when his heart got broken. At twenty-one, Jared was settling comfortably into his bachelor ways.

Trouble was, being around Emma at church and other gatherings burdened him with a powerful temptation to hand his heart to her on a platter, all ready for carving. She was such a good-looking woman, and he was, after all, only a man. His sole protection against the danger was to tease her until she got riled, just like now. If she hated him enough, he'd be safe from those fine blue eyes surrounded by black lashes as soft as down on her tanned cheeks. Safe from wanting to touch that thick black hair framing her pretty oval face. Safe from wanting to run a finger down that straight, pretty nose. Safe from wanting to place a kiss on those sweet rosy lips...

Thunk! A board landed about two inches from his right foot, and he jumped to the side.

Thank You, Lord, for the interruption. He'd been falling in love again just like he promised himself he'd never do.

She sure could toss a board as easy as any of the men who'd come to help. 'Course, other than Jose, they were a sight older, closer to Mr. Sharp's age and probably not as strong as they used to be. Jared didn't even mind that Emma wore men's trousers and a rough shirt. Her younger sister looked all right in that frilly blue dress, but she wasn't out here clearing away fire damage. Probably couldn't heft more than that tray of coffee and cookies, fare that he'd yet to earn.

"Now, Emma." Mr. Sharp laughed, then coughed real hard. No doubt he still had smoke in his lungs from the fire. He bent over, and Emma patted him on the back and helped him sip some coffee. When he could finally speak, he waved a hand toward Jared. "Be careful throwing those boards. Don't injure the helpers before they even get started."

"I won't, Pa." She went back to work. "Just getting rid of the rubbish."

Ouch. That stung. Jared swallowed hard. It was also no less than he deserved. He knew he'd hurt her, but it couldn't be helped. When he'd quit courting her, he'd saved them both from a worse grief down the road.

"You're sure your pa can do without you and Cal for a while?" Mr. Sharp beckoned to Jared, and Jared stepped away from the dangerous area.

"Yessir. He said to tell you he could send over some lumber if you need it. We were gonna build an addition on the east side of the house." More than an addition. It was to be a separate house for Cal and Julia, assuming she agreed to marry him. But he couldn't tell Mr.

Sharp that until the wedding was for certain. "Pop said it can wait until spring."

Mr. Sharp's eyes got a little red around the edges, and he coughed again. Emma's jaw dropped, but even then she looked pretty as a cactus bloom. And twice as prickly, too, he reminded himself.

"We'll be much obliged, son." The old man shook his head in wonder. "I'll settle with him come spring after sheep shearing."

"That'll be fine, sir. I'll send word for my brothers to haul the lumber over tomorrow."

Mr. Sharp put an arm around Jared's shoulder. "I know you and your brothers built a barn a couple of years ago, so you know what you're doing, like most men around here. These other fellas have their own responsibilities, but they've said they'd help when they can. Since you'll be right here, I'd like for you to take charge, if you don't mind."

"I'd be pleased and proud to do that, sir." His heart felt near to bursting over the man's trust in him. With four brothers, he'd always had a hard time getting noticed, mostly because Pop was too busy to pass out praise. With Mama not there to encourage him like she used to, Jared often felt lonely in the midst of his large family. Right now he couldn't resist a glance at Emma. To his surprise, she glowered at him. Hadn't he just offered to help her pa?

"Pa, I know how to build a barn." Her cross expression didn't diminish her beauty one bit. "Put me in charge. I worked side by side with you when we built this one." She waved a hand toward the sad remains. "Don't you remember?"

Mr. Sharp chuckled. "Yep, I remember. You did a

mighty fine job for a fourteen-year-old girl, and you're doing a mighty fine job of cleaning up this mess. Tell you what. You and Jared can share the responsibilities. What do you say?"

If flames could shoot from a woman's eyes, Jared would be on fire right about now. But Emma smiled at her pa and spoke in a deceptively sweet voice. "Why, that's just fine. We can have a contest to see who's the better builder. He can build the frames for two sides, and I'll build the other two and get them ready for a barn raising."

"You do that, my gal. Get 'em all ready for a raising. We'll send out the word. I know we can count on our neighbors to help us finish the job. A little competition will make the work go faster." Mr. Sharp chuckled again. "Well, I'll leave you to it. Mrs. Sharp made me promise not to stay out here long." He hobbled away toward the house leaning on his cane, and then turned back. "If we get it built by Christmas Eve, maybe we can finish the Las Posadas celebration here after all."

Jared had sensed a heap of relief in the old man, and his heart went out to him. Mr. Sharp was getting on in years. He was forty-five if he was a day. Too old to be hit with a tragedy like losing his barn and much of his winter's supply of hay, not to mention wrenching his hip real bad. At least all the animals had survived, and hay could be bought from their neighbors. God was merciful. Jared wasn't too sure about a building contest, but what choice did he have?

Then it struck him. A contest would keep Emma and him at odds, a sure remedy to stop him from losing his heart to her. What did the Proverb say about a contentious woman? Something about constantly dripping water? Yep, that was Emma. He chuckled to himself.

"What are you laughing at?" There she stood, her face still covered with soot, her fists posted at her waist in a challenging pose, still looking mighty fine.

Jared laughed out loud. "Just thinking how much fun I'm gonna have whupping you in this contest."

"Whupping me—?"

"Emma, dear." Julia dragged Cal over to her sister's side. The two of them had been making calves' eyes at each other while Mr. Sharp had stood right there. Either the old man approved of Cal, or he was too concerned about the barn to notice.

Emma's expression softened as she gave Julia her attention. "Yes, dear?"

"Do you really think the barn will be finished by Christmas Eve? That's just eight days."

Jared suspected sweet Julia was trying to smooth the waters between him and Emma. Cal's little gal didn't seem to understand that some folks liked to bicker. As long as it didn't turn cruel, a healthy argument could fuel a man's energy for the job at hand. He and Cal would need a heap of energy if they were going to finish the barn in time for the final night of Las Posadas. The Christmas celebration was important for unifying the community, so they just had to finish.

"It'll be finished if the bad weather holds off *and* if we get back to work." Emma scowled at Jared. "That mule good for anything besides being a pack animal?"

"Yep. That's why we brought him. He can haul away the boards that can't be salvaged."

"Then get your gear into the house and get started." Emma brushed an arm over her forehead to shove back her hair, but fuzzy little baby hairs fell back into place around her face, making her look younger than her twenty years. "And don't forget to salvage the nails."

"Hold on." Annoyance gripped Jared. "Your pa put me in charge."

"Humph." How could she look so pretty with that scowl on her face? "If all you want to do is stand around chin-wagging, somebody's got to give orders." She spun away from him and marched across the barnyard toward the other men.

Jared watched her for about five seconds too long before he set about unloading old Homer, the mule. How could a woman dressed in men's clothes look so entirely appealing? And how was he going to keep from falling off of the bad side of good sense and landing smack dab *into* love with her?

Pop had five sons. He could have sent any two over to help Mr. Sharp. Why did Jared have to be one of them?

Darkness was near to falling when Emma strode over to the back porch where Ma and Julia had set up a table with hot water in porcelain basins and soap and towels on the side. Before washing her face and hands, she brushed off as much soot as possible from her clothes. It would still be a challenge to wash out the rest.

She hadn't stopped working all day except for a few minutes in the early afternoon when she'd eaten a sandwich and drunk some coffee. Now she was powerful hungry, and the smell of beef stew and fresh baked bread had wafted out across the barnyard and teased her for hours.

After that first shock of having to work with Jared Mattson, she'd managed to stay far enough away and keep busy enough to forget him. Mostly. The only problem had come earlier this afternoon when new help arrived and he'd insisted on giving them orders. To the credit of most of them, they'd looked to her for confirmation. She got a kick out of seeing the consternation on Jared's face. Whup her in this contest? Not likely. Not with most of the men wanting to please her. Not that she understood why, but as long as it got the job done, she appreciated the way they deferred to her. And unlike Jared, they spoke to her respectfully and without a hint of teasing.

Most of them could only stay for a few hours, but it helped considerably. Now where the old barn had stood, only blackened earth remained. Tomorrow they'd use brooms made of dried tree branches to clear away the rest of it. Then the rebuilding would begin.

"Save some of that hot water for us." Jared stepped up on the porch with Cal right behind him. "Although I'm sure you need it worse than we do."

Emma had promised herself she would ignore him, but once again he'd said just the right—or wrong— thing. "I doubt there's enough water in the whole Rio Grande to get you clean. That soot looks mostly ground in permanent like." She wanted to say it probably went all the way to his black heart, but decided that was just a bit too much. To forestall any comeback she glanced over at Cal, who was busy cleaning up at the third basin. "You're pretty good at salvaging those nails. That'll save Pa a heap of money."

Cal gave her a brotherly grin. "Glad to help, Miss

Emma." His gray eyes had a happy twinkle to them as he hurried through his ablutions.

Emma figured he couldn't wait to join Julia in the kitchen. Ma had told Julia to make the bread and some corn pudding, which would probably encourage Cal to propose sooner rather than later. Having learned to cook from Ma, Emma wasn't ashamed of her own skills, but this was Julia's time to shine.

Once she finished washing and drying her face and hands, she lifted the basin to dump the water in the yard. She managed to slosh just enough water onto Jared's trouser leg and down into his boot.

"Oh, I'm sorry. I didn't realize you were standing there." Lying wasn't all that bad if it was teasing, was it? Then why did she feel a pinprick of guilt? Probably because the weather was mighty cold, though not quite as freezing as it would be once night came.

"No harm done." Jared lifted his basin, and Emma knew she was in trouble. "Oops! Sorry." He gave himself away by apologizing before dumping the sooty water down her side. "Clumsy me."

Her guilt disappeared as she stifled a scream, but his crooked grin almost made her laugh. She did manage not to jump as he had. If the air weren't so cold, she'd take time to throw Cal's basin over Jared's head. "Is that a confession? You agree that you're the clumsy one?"

Before he could answer, she ducked into the house through the back door and into the warmth of the kitchen. Ma and Julia looked up expectantly from their tasks.

"Supper's almost ready." Ma tilted her head toward

the hallway. "You'd best change out of those dirty clothes before you come to the table."

"Yes, ma'am."

"Put on a dress, dear." Ma gave her a smile that seemed suspiciously sly. "And brush your hair."

Oh, no. If Ma and Julia were playing matchmakers, they'd be sadly disappointed, at least where Jared Mattson was concerned. She'd never again let him break her heart.

"Yes, ma'am."

Emma hurried down the short hallway to the room she shared with her sister to keep from having to heat two chambers. Sure enough, they'd laid out her blue dress made from the same bolt as Julia's to save money. They'd also set out the tin can of Pretty Lady's Dry Shampoo and Emma's boar's bristle brush. At first, she thought about ignoring both and going to the table in another pair of Pa's old trousers. But even at her age, when she ought to have her own children to boss around, she didn't like to disobey or disappoint Ma.

After wrapping a towel around her shoulders, she sat at the vanity table Ma had ordered from the Montgomery Ward catalog, one of her attempts to help her daughters become ladies out here in this wild country where fine manners didn't always show up. Or matter.

Usually, Emma and Julia brushed each other's hair to a fine sheen before bedtime. This time Emma had to work through the tangles of her bushy black hair by herself. Even with the hair powder, soot rained down on her white towel and the bare floor. After several minutes, though, she decided she was presentable. If not, too bad. She was hungry enough to eat a grizzly.

As much as she'd tried to hurry as she changed

clothes, she still found the others already waiting for her in the dining room. Jared and Cal had cleaned up pretty well, at least well enough to sit down at the Sharps' formal dinner table rather than eating in the kitchen. Even with their damp, slicked-back hair, they looked as handsome as ever. At least at first glance. A closer look showed nothing but kindness in Cal's eyes, while Jared's uplifted chin and arrogant smirk revealed a callous, coldhearted man.

Julia rushed over to Emma and grasped both of her hands. "Emma, Cal's asked Pa's permission to marry me! Pa said yes, and I said yes, and now we're gonna to get married two days after Christmas!"

The squeal of delight in her voice warmed Emma's heart. Sweet Julia deserved to be happy. Emma pulled her into a tight embrace. "I'm so pleased for you, my dear."

Over Julia's shoulder, she could see Jared's arrogant expression had turned to…what? He looked as if he'd chewed on a lemon. Did he disapprove of Julia, or was it marriage in general he didn't favor? Either way, Emma would make sure he didn't get in the way of her sister's happiness. Even if it meant making him miserable enough to go home. Maybe Mr. Mattson would send one of his nicer sons back to help.

That was it. Emma would make sure Jared was miserable enough to hightail it home. Who needed him and his mean ways?

How odd that the thought of him leaving sat like lead in her heart.

When Emma walked into the dining room, Jared had to grit his teeth real hard to keep from gawking at her. My, she cleaned up good. Although he could detect a few smudges around the edges, probably no more than he himself had, she looked mighty fine. He swallowed hard, puckered away an involuntary smile and lifted his chin, a pose that was sure to hide his unwilling admiration.

He was happy for Cal, maybe even wished some of that happiness would rub off on him. If their eight-year-old nephew, Robby, hadn't been crying for his mama just a few nights ago, Jared might reconsider his bachelor existence, which this woman threatened in ways he'd never imagined. But what had his brother Robert told his son about a mama who didn't love them enough to stay? Jared reminded himself of how often he'd had to hide his tears from his brothers after their own mama left. He supposed they'd all found ways to deal with it. Then there was that woman on the other side of the river who'd up and left her husband…

"Aren't you hungry?" Cal clapped Jared on the shoulder and gave him a little shove toward the table.

"Enough to eat a horse." He hadn't realized he'd been woolgathering. Taking a deep breath to hide his embarrassment, he looked to Mrs. Sharp to show him where to sit.

Naturally, she pointed to the empty spot next to Emma, 'cause Cal would want to sit beside Julia. Good thing the table was long enough so Jared didn't have to rub shoulders with Miss Prickly Pear. He sat adjacent to Mr. Sharp and across from Cal.

Another good thing was he didn't have to talk to Emma 'cause all the conversation at the other end of the table was about the upcoming wedding. Emma and Mrs. Sharp seemed as excited as Julia.

"I know we'll need to feed the men who come help with the barn." The older lady leaned toward her younger daughter. "But somehow we have to make time to finish those yellow dresses we started last summer for you and Emma, so you can wear them for the wedding."

"Oh, Ma, that sounds grand."

More chatter went on among the women at one end of the table while Mr. Sharp grinned indulgently at his womenfolk. Cal kept his eyes on Julia, and Jared knew he was making plans. Now that the wood for the small house was going to rebuild the Sharps' barn, they'd have to make room back at the Mattson ranch for the newlywed couple.

Jared needed to make some plans, too. He and Cal shared a room, so when Julia moved over to their ranch after the wedding, Jared would have to sleep in the bunkhouse until that new house was built in the spring. Or the summer. Whenever they could get around to it once their ranch work increased.

The time had come for a change Jared had been working on for a good while. One day Pop wouldn't be around, and he'd announced last spring that he'd willed his property evenly to his sons. Jared could make it easier for them all by setting out on his own so the land could be divided into four parts instead of five. As the fourth of five sons, he'd always known this day would come. While he loved his brothers, they'd never let him or Cal make important decisions. Easygoing Cal didn't seem to mind, but Jared could only tolerate it for so long.

He would talk Pop into giving him his inheritance in cash so he could leave these parts and find his own spread in Colorado. He'd heard of prime cattle land up there. He'd miss his family, but a man had to make his own way. He wanted, no, *needed* his own place. Not only would it solve the problem of Pop dividing the family's property, it would also take him away from the temptation sitting right next to him in the form of pretty Miss Emma Sharp.

Against his will, he glanced at her. The womenfolk were chattering away about the wedding dinner. That would be some feat to accomplish just a day or so after all the other festivities. For his part he aimed to make sure they could enjoy the final night of Las Posadas right here on Sharps' ranch in a brand-new barn. The community needed to join together to celebrate their common faith in the Lord Jesus Christ instead of fighting over their differences.

"So you gotta stay for Christmas with us so you'll be right here for the wedding." Mrs. Sharp aimed her comment at Cal, but a glance and a smile included Jared in the invitation.

"Yes, ma'am." Cal grinned, already the indulgent son-in-law. "We'll accept. Won't we, Jared?"

"Well…"

"Of course you will." Mr. Sharp batted the back of his hand against Jared's shoulder. "No sense in going home and then riding back ten miles for the wedding. It'll be nice to have a houseful, and you'll be available to help Cal."

More chatter erupted, this time about Christmas doings, decorating a tree, baking and such, things the Mattson men hadn't bothered with since Maybelle left. Other than the community parties and the like, Christmas was a woman's thing, but Jared did know that staying here meant he'd have to give a present to each member of the Sharp family. That would be a challenge.

After settling into bed that night and after Cal finally stopped talking about how wonderful his bride-to-be was, Jared gave some thought to those presents. He could give Cal and Julia that gold piece he'd won in an eighth-grade spelling bee back in Charleston. He'd make a quick trip home to fetch it. But what about Mr. and Mrs. Sharp? What about Emma? He'd better hurry up and figure it all out.

Most nights at home, he usually whittled until sleep took over, and he'd brought along his whittling gear just in case he had time to enjoy his hobby. If he stayed up a little while each evening, he could make a bolo tie with a wooden slide for Mr. Sharp. He'd included some green apple wood from a tree they'd cut down because it'd never produced fruit. From that he'd make Mrs. Sharp a set of spoons and maybe a fork. Old Fuzzy, Pop's cook and housekeeper, went through wooden utensils pretty fast, so Mrs. Sharp probably did, too.

For Emma he could carve a comb for that thick, bushy hair that kept falling out of her little pins. Hair that he kept wanting to brush aside so it wouldn't hide her pretty face.

Oh, it was time to move to Colorado, all right. And Christmas couldn't come soon enough for him so he could start making his escape.

Chapter Two

Emma listened through the walls to hear whether Jared or Cal snored. Not that she cared, but if they did, it would make it hard to have them sleeping in the next room for over a week. She couldn't abide snoring and had always been glad Ma and Pa's bedroom was across the house. Once Pa fell asleep, he sounded like a hog grunting while it dug for grubs.

Now all she could hear was soft scraping and scratching sounds. Ma never let the cats inside the house, so it wasn't them. The guard dogs were in the sheepfold doing their job. What were Jared and Cal up to? It wasn't as though they couldn't be trusted. She was just curious.

Oh, bother. She would not let that little sound trouble her. She had more important things to think about, such as what presents she should give the brothers. With Ma's invitation for them to stay for Christmas, which delighted Julia but annoyed Emma, manners demanded that they receive gifts. She'd already made presents for her family and now must find time in the next eight days to make two more. Nobody could ever accuse the Sharp family of skimping on hospitality.

At supper Cal had said that since there were no women to bake or decorate at their house, the Mattson men didn't make much of Christmas. That was why they so eagerly accepted the invite. But not celebrating Christmas? How sad for little Robby. Every child should get at least one present. Maybe she could buy some penny candy for the boy and give it to him on Christmas Eve. Or even make some of Ma's special taffy. But what to give the two brothers on Christmas morning when her family exchanged gifts?

She recalled earlier watching Jared tug on his leather gloves. While they were a bit stretched, they still had a lot of wear left in them. But they could use a new lining. She could knit a pair with no trouble. She might not care much for the man, but he had come to help, so she'd do the decent thing. And of course Cal would need a pair, too.

Once she had that settled, a yawn took hold of her, and she nestled deeper beneath her quilt. Best get some rest. With or without Jared Mattson in the house, tomorrow would hold more challenges than she'd ever faced in her twenty years. She dozed off and dreamed of cats scratching at the kitchen door.

She awoke before daylight and dressed quickly. Julia wasn't in her bed, so she was probably already helping in the kitchen. Emma's body ached from yesterday's labors, not to mention the night before when they'd all fought the fire. But work on a ranch didn't stop just because a body ached. She hurried to the kitchen to do her share of the chores.

As always, Ma and Pa had been up for some time

and were already busy. Ma turned griddle cakes in a fry pan on the stove while Julia removed a pan of biscuits from the oven. Pa was straining fresh milk through cheesecloth into clean jars. Even at this early hour, even with his wrenched hip, he'd completed one of Emma's chores, milking their two cows. She wished he wouldn't do that, but he always said he didn't like her going out in the dark and the cows wouldn't be happy if they had to wait until daylight to be milked. She'd make sure to beat him to the chore this evening.

"How many for breakfast?" She opened the cupboard door to get out plates. Would they have to hold breakfast until Jared and Cal got up?

"Seven." Pa finished straining the milk and set the bucket outside the door for the cats. "Paco insists on working today."

Emma nodded thoughtfully as she counted out seven of Ma's everyday plates. Their middle-aged hired hand had nearly worn himself to death while they'd fought the fire, so Pa had ordered him to rest yesterday. Paco had complained but had taken Pa's advice. It was just like the hardworking man to insist on returning to work as soon as possible.

Emma set the plates around the table. "I suppose the Mattson boys are sleeping in."

Pa gave her a long look. "No, daughter. They're out in the fields checking on the stock, making sure there's enough hay saved from the fire for our sheep and cattle, at least for a day or two."

At his chiding tone, heat rose up her neck. She knew better than to suggest that any of the Mattson men were lazy. Their hardworking lifestyle was well-known in these parts. Jared and Cal were no different from their brothers. Which was the only good quality she'd allow that Jared had.

As if her thoughts had called him inside, Jared bumbled through the door, his arms loaded with half-burned wood reclaimed yesterday from the barn. He stopped in the doorway and held one foot at an odd angle. "You let these cats inside, Mrs. Sharp?"

"Oh, no." Ma grabbed a broom and bustled over to the door to keep several tabbies from squeezing past Jared's large boot. "Shoo. Shoo."

Jared chuckled as he made it inside without any felines and dumped the boards into the wood box beside the stove. "I reckon they're looking for a new home now that the barn's gone. Another reason to get the new one built soon." He stared at Emma as if seeking her agreement.

She quickly closed her gaping mouth. Like Pa, most men would have kicked the cats out of the way, but Jared hadn't. He'd even cast a sympathetic glance at the mewing little critters. "Uh-huh. Gotta get it built real soon." She broke away from his indiscernible gaze and bent to her task of placing cutlery beside each plate. Maybe there was more to this man than she thought. He might have jilted her, but any man who got up early to see to a neighbor's livestock, who didn't kick cats, couldn't be all bad.

No! She refused to think kindly of Jared Mattson. Everybody, even outlaws, probably had some good qualities. But like an outlaw, Jared's faults outweighed his assets.

Paco and Cal came in the back door, and they all sat down at the large round kitchen table. Ma had outdone herself, serving up eggs, ham, sausage, bacon, griddle cakes, fried potatoes, biscuits and strawberry jam. Jared's manners were all right for a man who lived without a lady's influence in the home, but he filled his plate to heaping at least twice. She'd never seen a body eat so much. He'd only worked maybe an hour this morning, hardly enough labor to create such an appetite. He'd eat them out of house and home before Christmas.

Jared rarely got to eat such fine food. Beef stew last night and ham, eggs and griddle cakes this morning, and plenty for seconds served up at both meals. *Mmm.* Cal was in for some good cooking once he married. Maybe Julia would favor the rest of his family with her mama's recipes from time to time. Pop's cook, Old Fuzzy, had learned to cook on cattle drives, so his specialty was beans and fatback. Maybe Julia could teach him a thing or two. Confident that Julia would accept Cal's proposal, Pop had already said they weren't going to turn the little lady into a family servant. That's why he'd wanted to build a separate dwelling as soon as possible where the newlyweds could have some privacy. But under the circumstances, giving the lumber to Mr. Sharp was the right thing to do.

As he ate, Jared considered Emma's agreement to his comment about needing to build the barn fast. Was she as concerned about the cats as he was? If he wasn't mistaken, at least one female kitty was expecting in a few days, so she'd need a warm place to give birth as winter wore on. As much as Pop hated cats, he always said they were a necessary evil for a rancher. Otherwise field mice would eat up all the hay and grain and destroy anything made of leather.

Jared liked cats. The day Mama left for good he'd

taken refuge in the barn, where his brothers couldn't see him cry his eyes out. One little female kitty had taken up residence on his lap and had reached up to touch the tears on his cheeks, as if she knew he was grieving and wanted him to know she understood. From that moment they'd formed a bond that lasted until she went the way of all ranch animals. Then Jared had grieved all over again.

He bit into a biscuit smothered with newly churned butter and strawberry jam. My, my, this was mouthwatering. He glanced at Emma, who was busy with her own biscuit. Could she cook as well as her mama? He had no doubt she could. Maybe having a wife wouldn't be so bad.

The memory of Mama's departure filled his mind, and he stifled a bitter grunt. Having a wife would be fine...until she left. Come next spring when the work on the ranch got busier, maybe Julia would get tired of being around all the Mattson men and hightail it back to her mama and pop. Then where would Cal be?

"You about done?" Cal punched his shoulder and grinned. "Or are you gonna eat another half dozen eggs?"

Jared shook off his foolish ruminations. Cal was plum loco in love, so there was no sense in reminding him about Mama or Rob's wife leaving their families. His brother would have to learn the hard way. Best get on with the day. Jared had a barn to build.

By the time Jared, Cal, Emma and Paco had swept away the final debris from the barn site, Rob and Will had arrived with the first load of lumber. They all pitched in to unload.

After the boards were piled to the side, Rob took

charge in his usual bossy-oldest-brother way. "You need to dig out those burned corner posts before you try to put in new ones, then shore up the soil. Run a length of twine from corner to corner to make sure your walls are straight. Be sure to build the wall frames that'll face each other the same size." He carried on for another few minutes, spouting things Jared had known since they'd all built their own house and barn six years ago. All the more reason for Jared to get his own place.

He traded a look with Cal, and they both rolled their eyes. Then he glanced at Emma to see how she was taking it. He guessed her easygoing smile was hiding a small volcano. At least that would be the case if Jared were giving the orders. When Rob finished, she gave him a neighborly nod.

"Much obliged, Rob." She followed him and Will to the wagon. "You make sure we're doing it right when you come back."

"Yes, ma'am." Rob touched the brim of his hat. "We'll be back later today with another load. I'll check on your work then." He started to climb up into the wagon.

"May I ask a favor?" Emma cast a glance over her shoulder and wrinkled her nose at Jared, a clear indication she didn't want him to hear whatever she planned to say. As he took a couple of steps back, she beckoned to Rob. He bent down so she could whisper something to him.

He quickly straightened, and a gentle, uncharacteristic grin split his face. "That would be mighty fine, Miss Emma. Mighty fine. I'd be much obliged."

A tiny streak of jealousy shot through Jared's midsection. Was she trying to start something with his oldest brother? A married man? Well, separated, but still married. Naw. Couldn't be. Her manner wasn't the least bit flirty, and the friendly look on Rob's face was more fatherly than mushy. Besides, why should Jared care? He had no claim on Miss Emma Sharp. Why, he didn't care in the least who she talked to. To prove it, to himself mostly, he stomped over to the pile of boards and started to work.

Emma had no idea why Jared was throwing boards around that way. Good thing they were solid pine and not likely to break. She heaved out a sigh of satisfaction that one matter had been taken care of. Rob had given her permission to give his son some candy for Christmas. Maybe that would spur him to do more of the same for little Robby to celebrate the day. Like his pa, Rob was a good man, if a little gruff. Emma hadn't known Maybelle very well, but she couldn't imagine why the woman had taken their baby girl and left Rob and Robby two years ago. Seeing him smile at her offer to give little Robby some candy warmed her heart. Too bad some of his finer qualities hadn't rubbed off on Jared. Of course, Rob had been pretty bossy about the barn building, but no more than Pa when he was giving orders to his cowhands.

"We should divide the boards into two stacks so we both have some to work with." Jared heaved another one onto the pile on his left.

"Do tell." Emma nodded to Paco. "We can help." As they counted out the boards, she glanced at Jared. "Why don't you and Cal dig out those old corner posts?"

"I don't know about that." Jared's grin seemed

forced, but it was still cute enough that Emma had to stifle a tiny jolt in her heart. "Are you sure we can trust you not to shortchange our team?"

"I reckon you'll just have to." She brushed the hair from her forehead with the back of her hand. "You sure we can trust you to frame out your sides equal to ours?"

He gave her another grin, this one a little more relaxed. "I guess you'll just have to."

Emma turned away so he couldn't see her smile. What a rascal he was. She may not be able to trust him with her heart, but he did know how to build a barn. This competition might turn out to be fun.

With both teams organized enough to begin framing out their sides, the rest of the morning went by pretty fast. By the time Ma rang the dinner bell, Emma felt they were well on their way to a new barn. At least as long as harsher weather held off.

Gazing north toward the Sangre de Cristo Mountains, she felt a shiver go down her spine despite a morning of hard, sweaty work. The dark gray clouds hovering over those distant peaks hinted that a snowfall was in the near future. Emma prayed it wouldn't be a blizzard.

After dinner, while they waited for Rob and Will to bring a second load of lumber, she saddled her mare to ride out to check on the sheep and feed the guard dogs. Lucien, the Basque shepherd Pa had hired when they first came out here six years ago, had worked for many years for the Mexican sheep rancher who used to own this land. Lucien's experience was much needed since Pa only knew about cattle ranching. But just a week ago, Lucien's last sheepdog had died, and the shepherd had succumbed to the call of his homeland, saying he must return to Basque country on the border between Spain and France.

Until Pa could find another equally competent replacement, the family could only go by instinct on how to tend the animals, a vital part of their livelihood. Thanks to brothers Frank and George Bond, who'd established a wool business down in Espanola, the income provided many necessities and even some extras for the family. 'Course, all of last spring's wool profits and last fall's cattle sales would now have to go into rebuilding the barn. Some gains, some losses. Such was the way of ranching.

As Emma rode south along the Rio Grande, which was showing signs of nightly freezing near its low banks, she heard a horse approaching from the rear at a fast pace. Her heart jumped. Not everyone in these parts appreciated the influx of Americano settlers. Was it Indians? Mexicans? Both had settled and owned this land for centuries. Should she continue to stare straight ahead or turn around and face whoever it was? Her hand went to the rifle sheathed to her saddle.

"Hey!" Jared Mattson's unmistakable voice cut sharply through the cold December air.

For the briefest moment relief flooded Emma and her heart jumped again, this time rather pleasantly. *Oh, bother.* Her agreeable reactions to the man just had to stop. Yes, she was glad to have a man along as she rode out to check on the sheep, just not this man.

"Wait up, Emma." His horse galloped up beside hers and fell into the same cantering pace. "You lit out like a bat after a horsefly. What's the hurry?"

"Isn't it obvious?" She tossed her hair over her shoulder. It had come loose from the tiny pins that never seemed to hold it in place. Her hat hung on its leather strings down her back, but she was enjoying the cool breeze through her hair and hadn't bothered to put it on. "Gotta check the sheep."

"Yep. I know." Was that worry in his voice? "Now, I know you can take care of yourself, 'specially with that rifle you've got strapped there to your saddle. But your pop sent me to keep you company. Said you might need some help with those sheep."

Emma snorted, a sound her mother would scold her for if she were here. Emma always tried to be ladylike around Ma so as not to grieve her. "What do you know about sheep? All you have up at your place is cattle."

Jared shrugged. "That's right."

He didn't seem inclined to say more, which was just fine by her. Pa had probably sent him to look after her, and if the scowl on his face was any indication, he didn't particularly relish the chore. She didn't want to be with him either. Never mind that he'd looked quite manly all morning as he'd worked on his side of the barn. Not that she'd noticed. Well, yes, she had. The work made them all hot, and he wore a thin shirt that showed off his muscles. Who could fail to see that?

He'd seen her, too, dressed like a man, working like a man on her side of the barn. What of it? She wasn't the only woman in these parts who had to get out of the kitchen and do a man's work. Long before the barn caught on fire, she'd worked alongside Pa to keep the ranch going.

Maybe that was why Jared had jilted her. He wanted someone more girly, like Julia. But why hadn't he taken up with any of the other gals at church? At least a half dozen or more hung around the Mattson boys after

Sunday services every week, each trying to get their attention. Will and Cal seemed to be the only ones who responded to their feminine ways. Now Cal was engaged, and maybe Will would be soon, if the gal he was sweet on said yes. Emma knew without a doubt she would have said yes to Jared if he'd proposed two years ago instead of suddenly quitting his courtship. Was it her fault? Or his?

She couldn't change, wouldn't change. She was who she was. What she had to be for her family. If that meant she'd be an old maid, so be it. She had to be true to herself.

And yet part of that truth was that she longed to be loved and cherished by some fine Christian man, to be married and have a quiver full of children, as the scriptures described it. She supposed the Good Lord just had a different plan for her life.

Stubborn, prickly female, taking off on her own like that, acting like she doesn't need anybody to look out for her. Jared ground his teeth but decided not to argue with her. When he'd seen Emma ride away from the house after dinner, he'd been plenty concerned. Too many unsavory men wandered these parts, and a gal shouldn't be out alone, even in the middle of the day. Not even one who could shoot her rifle as well as Emma.

He hadn't exactly lied about why he'd followed her, but the truth was Mr. Sharp hadn't sent him. Jared offered to do it. Mr. Sharp got a funny look in his eyes and then gave Jared a crooked grin and a brief nod. Which only went to prove the old man misunderstood his concern. Jared was just doing a decent man's duty by protecting his neighbor's willful daughter.

One thing was true: Jared didn't know much about sheep. They'd seemed fine when he and Cal fed and checked them before sunrise, and so had the dogs. They'd find out in a few minutes.

The sheepfold lay on the side of a hill with barbed wire fencing all around it. A one-room adobe house stood to one side, the humble house where the Basque shepherd had lived. Nearby was a small adobe barn filled with hay. Jared felt a flash of anger toward the man for abandoning his employer just as winter was setting in. Then he recalled that the old fella had begun to show signs of the rheumatiz, so maybe he deserved to retire. Not to mention, living out here by himself probably got pretty lonely. Jared would have to be prepared for that when he moved to Colorado.

The two large brown guard dogs bounded over to the fence to greet Emma and Jared, wagging their tails as if they wanted to be petted yet still not breaching their boundaries.

Emma dismounted and went through the gate. "Hello there, Blackie, Jennie." She ruffled their thick winter coats. "What a good boy and girl you are."

Jared followed her lead. "Hey there, doggies." He knelt down and was rewarded by a couple of tongues licking his cheeks. Their lively welcome toppled him over, and he landed on his backside on the cold ground. Laughing with shock and surprise, he found himself the object of even more canine affection as the dogs pounced on him. "Hey, cut that out."

"Blackie, heel." All business now, Emma used her bossy voice to summon the dogs. "Jennie, come." She slapped her leg and gave a sharp whistle, one that many a cowboy would envy. This little gal had hidden talents.

The dogs scurried to her, wiggling and whimpering almost as if they were apologizing for something. Emma crossed her arms and stood as straight and tall as her five-foot-one-inch height would allow. The dogs sat and eyed her expectantly.

"Have you been taking care of these sheep?" She spoke to them as if she was talking to a ranch hand.

The critters tilted their heads and whined. Emma huffed out a sigh, and her shoulders slumped. "Yeah, I'm as confused as you are. I know you're used to Lucien being here, but for now you're just gonna have to take care of things for us."

Jared surveyed the flock of a hundred or so animals, and his gaze took in some men riding along a ridge maybe a half mile away. He couldn't make out who they were, and they weren't headed this way, but their appearance confirmed he'd been right to come with Emma. Not that he'd tell her that. Or even mention the riders if he didn't have to. "The sheep look all right to me."

"Yeah," Emma said. "To me, too. But the dogs seem a little anxious. I sure hope no predators have been around." She scanned the field, squinting her eyes in the early afternoon sun. "No signs of coyotes or bears. That's good. Plenty of hay." She waved a hand toward the adobe barn. "Thank the Lord we moved it down here just last week, or it would have burned up."

Jared grunted his agreement. "That's the Lord's mercy indeed."

She shot him a glance, as if surprised that he would acknowledge God's goodness. Or maybe surprised that he cared about her family's livestock. He'd never been able to figure out Miss Emma Sharp, so he'd just set those thoughts aside.

Without another word, she gave the dogs one more pat on their heads and then retrieved the bag of table scraps to feed them. That chore done, she was in the saddle and headed back to the ranch house before a man could say *tumbleweed*. Jared shook his head and followed at a more leisurely pace. That was, until he remembered why he was here instead of at home. He had a barn to build, and if Rob and Will had returned with more lumber, he needed to be there to help them unload.

As he kicked his horse into a gallop, a thought came from somewhere in the back of his mind. Those sheep were all right today, but a bear, a coyote or even a pack of wolves could come along at any time and destroy what Mr. Sharp had worked long and hard for. They needed another shepherd, and they needed him now. With his wrenched hip, Mr. Sharp wasn't in any shape to ride down to Espanola to hire one. If Jared went, he'd lose a day of competition with Emma in building the barn. More important, with those clouds hanging over the Sangre De Cristo Mountains, a blizzard could come along at any time and stop their work altogether.

Lord, there's gotta be an answer. If I can help, give me wisdom. Show me what to do.

After placing the last board on her pile, Emma rolled her shoulders to work out a cramp, which she refused to let slow her down. She mustn't stop working. If Jared kept on jawing with his brother Will over by the Mattsons' wagon, she and Paco would have a good head start on framing their second side of the barn. Of course, they couldn't raise the barn until Jared and Cal completed theirs, but she'd still have the satisfaction of beating them on this part. Rob Mattson said he'd gather other men in the community for the raising, so if Emma and Jared worked without interruption, they'd have the barn finished just in time for the Christmas Eve Las Posadas.

She'd been surprised at how glad she'd been to have Jared follow her out to the sheepfold, even happier after she'd spotted three men on the hills across the river. Of course, she hadn't pointed them out to Jared because that would have been as much as admitting she appreciated that he'd come, even though Pa had sent him. Anyway, Jared probably saw the men, too. From the shape of their wide-brimmed hats, they appeared to be Mexicans. That didn't mean they were dangerous, but one could never be too cautious.

After a long day of work followed by Ma's usual fine supper, the family and the two Mattson brothers gathered in the parlor. Last night Pa hadn't been up to reading the scriptures, but he was doing better tonight and wanted to resume the family tradition. Emma sat on the settee beside Julia and got to work knitting the gloves for Jared and Cal. Her hands ached from a day of lifting and hammering boards, but the lanolin in the unwashed wool soothed the pain, and soon the kinks worked themselves out. Then her fingers fell into the familiar rhythm of making close, tiny stitches required for comfortable gloves. She'd shorn the wool herself last spring, carded it and then spun it into yarn on Ma's spinning wheel to save for just such a project as this. Doing all that work gave her a special sense of satisfaction.

Jared and Cal sat across the room, each whittling at something, but she wouldn't be too nosy. Maybe they'd decided to make gifts, too, or maybe they just liked to keep their hands busy, a habit her family knew well. Right now, Ma and Julia were stitching tea towels for Julia's hope chest, which was just about filled with all the things a woman needed to begin housekeeping.

A bittersweet pang struck Emma's heart. This cozy scene wouldn't be the same once Julia was gone. Even at that, Emma was happy for her sister.

Holding the large Holy Bible on his lap, Pa began to read the fifth chapter of Ephesians.

"'Be ye therefore followers of God, as dear children. Walk in love, as Christ also hath loved us.'"

Emma stopped listening so she could think about that first verse for a moment.

She wanted to be a follower of the Lord Jesus Christ, but it was mighty hard with Jared Mattson in her home for nigh on to two weeks. Even though the Lord said she needed to forgive him seventy times seven for his offenses, his being here kept the remembrance of his jilting her right in front of her face. And all the while he acted as if he'd never done a thing wrong.

Pa had reached the part of the chapter about wives submitting to their husbands, and Emma understood why he'd chosen this passage to read tonight. He was advising Julia regarding her upcoming marriage. Julia wouldn't have any trouble with that. She was the sweetest, most agreeable person Emma knew. A few verses down, the scripture instructed husbands to love their wives as Christ loved the church. From the gentle look in Cal's eyes, Emma felt fairly sure he'd do just that. Like Julia, he was kind and easygoing. She figured they'd be too busy trying to make each other happy ever to argue.

Pa finished reading the chapter, his face aglow as it always was after he read the Holy Bible. He reverently placed the large, leather-bound book on the coffee table and said, "Let us pray." It was his signal to the family that bedtime had arrived and their labors must cease. "Lord, we thank You for this day, and we thank You for a restful sleep to come. Thank You for your Word. Help us to be obedient to it in all things. Now, Lord, although we don't know why You permitted our barn to burn down, in faith we thank You. We believe all things truly do work together for our good, so we'll trust in that promise. In Jesus's Name we pray. Amen."

Everyone chorused "amen" in response and then gathered their things to retire.

"Emma." Pa gave her a warm smile, the one that usually preceded some word of correction. Wasn't she too old for this? "Sit with me for a moment more."

The others said their good-nights, with Ma shooting a mysterious smile over her shoulder as she left the room. As quiet settled over the house, Emma gazed at Pa expectantly.

"Yessir?"

"Daughter, I've noticed that you're doing a fine job on that barn."

She shifted in her seat on the settee. He always gave a word of praise before telling her what she'd done wrong. "Thank you, sir."

"I've also noticed something else." His smile went

from paternal to teasing. "A certain young man on these premises admires you more than a little bit."

He couldn't have said anything more outlandish. "Oh, Pa—"

"Now, don't 'oh, Pa' me. I know he broke your heart two years ago, but I believe he's done considerable growing up since then." He chuckled softly. "Why, today when he asked to follow you out to the sheepfold, I thought sure Ma and I would have another proposal to deal with."

"What? He asked you?" Emma's mind raced. "But he said…"

"Don't know what he said, my gal, but I know what I see. If you have any soft spot in your heart for him, then just try being a bit nicer to him, and let's see what happens." He blew out a breath, and his eyes took on a troubled look. He quickly forced another smile and spoke in his usual cheerful tone. "On the other hand, if you're eager to see the last of him, then keep on being your usual feisty self. Now, get on to bed and get some well-deserved rest."

Emma kissed Pa's cheek and made her way to her bedroom. After donning her nightgown, she took care not to wake Julia as she nestled beneath the quilts, knowing all the while she'd have a hard time going to sleep.

So Jared had asked to follow her. Why? Was Pa right about him admiring her? *Nonsense*. She'd believe that when the sun rose in the west.

"Emma?" Julia turned over and faced her in the darkness. Her voice didn't sound the least bit sleepy. Obviously, she'd been waiting for Emma to come to bed.

"What, dear?"

"Cal told me something today that you need to know."

Her mind still reeling from what Pa said, Emma had a hunch about what was coming, so she didn't respond.

"Don't you want to know?" Julia sounded annoyed, unusual for her.

Emma breathed out an exaggerated sigh. "Not really, but you're going to tell me anyway, so go on."

Julia giggled, sounding more like herself. "Well, Cal said that Jared said... Well, didn't exactly *say*...but has made it really clear to Cal that he's in love... Well, he didn't say *love*, but that's what I think he means. What do you think?"

Emma pursed her lips to keep from giggling like Julia, not because of what she'd said but the way she'd said it. Her sister had no idea how funny and adorable she was. But if Emma were to make a guess, she'd say that a conspiracy was going on to put her and Jared back together. Well, it just wasn't going to happen.

"Well?" Had they been out of bed, Julia's impatient tone would have been accompanied by a tilt of her head and a perplexed look on her sweet face. "What do you think?"

"Well..." Emma drawled out her repetition of the word. "Who is Jared in love with?"

Julia gently shoved Emma's shoulder. "You, silly."

"Uh-huh." Emma rolled over to face away from her sister. "Good night, Julia."

Julia's exasperated sigh would have made Emma laugh if her heart weren't suddenly tied in knots. Jared loved her? Maybe so. Maybe not. But she wouldn't do as Pa said and start being nice to Jared just to get him to say so. Even if Pa was right about him growing up, Jared would still have to prove himself to her.

She might have to work like a man on the ranch, but she was still a woman inside. If Jared Mattson loved her, he'd have to eat some crow before she'd ever accept his courtship again. The Lord said to be kind to her enemy, even forgive his offenses, but He never said she had to marry him.

Chapter Three

After the family devotions, Jared had gathered his whittling gear and carried it to the bedroom, taking care not to let any wood chips fall out of the small canvas tarp he always spread across his lap. It had been a long, tiring day, but he still wanted to work on the Christmas gifts a bit more before settling down for the night.

Sitting with the Sharp family and hearing the verses Mr. Sharp read had stirred something deep inside Jared. His family had never gathered in the evening that way, not even before Mama left. Tonight had shown him a side of family life he'd never dreamed of, and he'd enjoyed it more than words could explain. What would it be like to have Pop and all the brothers gather at the end of each day to hear God's Word and pray together?

A quiet, private man, Pop had never read the scriptures to his sons or prayed at meals, although he did insist on them going to church. That was where Jared had learned about the Lord's salvation, and he'd accepted Jesus into his heart. Each time the pastor preached a message, Jared tried to apply the lessons to his life. He even picked up their family's Holy Bible from time to time and read it for himself, but sure not the way Mr. Sharp did, as though he understood it all. Many passages still remained a mystery to Jared.

Did Pop know about the verses in Ephesians that instructed a man to love his wife as Christ loved the church? All these years, Jared had blamed Mama for leaving her family, for not submitting to Pop's plan to settle in this harsh land. But maybe Pop bore some of the blame. Had he loved her as Christ loved the church, sacrificing himself for her? Jared would never know the answer to that, but it was something to think about if he ever planned to marry. Which he didn't.

"Say, brother." Cal climbed into the upper bunk bed, beat his pillow into shape and then fussed with his blankets like a dog circling to make its bed in the hay. "I've been meaning to tell you something important. Just haven't had a chance."

"What's that?" Jared sat on the edge of the lower bed and hunched over Emma's comb to carve the right amount away to make smooth teeth. It wouldn't do for it to snag that beautiful black hair. Beside him, the kerosene lantern on the side table cast just enough light for him to work.

Cal hung his head over the side so he could look Jared in the eye. "Julia says Emma loves you."

"What!" Jared sat up straight, banging his head on the wooden side of the bed above him. "Ow." It didn't hurt all that bad, but it gave him an excuse for venting his disbelief of Cal's dumb statement. "She does not."

"Does so." Cal rolled over and disappeared from view.

"Does not." Jared muttered the words with finality, hoping Cal would drop the subject.

Instead, Cal's annoying face popped back over the bedside. "Does so."

Jared blew out a growling sigh. They hadn't had one of these childish discussions in years, but Cal would never stop until he won, so Jared might as well give in.

"All right, baby brother, what makes Julia think Emma l-loves me?" The word was so foreign to him, he could barely stammer it out. Nobody in the Mattson house ever talked about love.

"Girls know these things about each other." Cal's smug tone further annoyed Jared.

"So she didn't actually say it to Julia."

Cal kept quiet for a few minutes. At last he said, "Not in so many words."

"That's what I thought." Jared put away his handiwork and dumped the shavings into a wastebasket near the door. He crossed the room and lowered the wick on the lantern until the flame went out before climbing into bed.

Cal's regular breathing indicated he wouldn't be arguing anymore. Jared never got used to how fast his younger brother could fall asleep. Sleep often eluded Jared because he always felt the need to set his day in order in his mind before surrendering to sleep.

His thoughts returned to this evening's family gathering. He didn't intend to marry, but...but what if he did? What would it be like to have his own wife and children sitting around at night reading scripture and praying, everyone's hands busy with necessary tasks like knitting or carving or mending clothes, maybe folks sharing the events of their day?

A strange longing settled in his chest, a longing he couldn't dispel with the usual thoughts about Mama and Maybelle abandoning their families. If Julia was right, if Emma did love him—which he was sure she didn't—maybe he should reconsider his plans to remain a bachelor.

Emma was a mighty fine-looking woman and a hard worker, doing a man's work out of necessity, which made him admire her far more than he did her pretty face. She even seemed to enjoy it. With so much of herself invested in the land, she probably wouldn't run off to the city like Mama and Maybelle. But he wasn't anywhere close to considering courting her again, not till he made up his mind to see it through to the end. He'd hurt her something awful two years ago, and he wouldn't do it a second time. If he decided to court her, and that was a mighty big if, he would treat her as Christ treated the church, loving her and giving himself for her.

But that didn't mean he had to let her win the barn-building competition.

In spite of her skeptical thoughts the night before, Emma woke up with a feeling of anticipation. If Jared loved her, she should be able to tell by the way he treated her. She wouldn't accept anything less than the way Pa treated Ma or anything less what Pa read in the Holy Bible last evening. A man who courted was declaring himself ready to be a husband, so he should behave toward his intended bride as the Lord did toward the church. For a brief moment, she let herself believe that meant Jared should let her win the barn-building contest.

But if she backed up a few verses in that chapter of Ephesians to the part about wives submitting to their husbands, she knew that a gal who planned to marry needed to be willing to submit to her husband after the wedding. All the more reason to be very careful in making that choice. But did that mean she should let Jared win? Or at least let him have more say-so about the way things were done?

Pa said Jared admired her, and he'd emphasized *admire* with a twinkle in his eyes, which meant he believed Jared loved her. Not only that, but even telling her about it meant Pa approved of Jared, like he approved of Cal. Would he really want both of his daughters to marry and move up to the Mattson ranch? If they did, who would take care of him and Ma? Who would shoulder the responsibilities around here?

By the time Emma got dressed and made her way to the kitchen, her head was spinning with these ideas, though she'd reached no conclusion on either issue, especially where Jared was concerned. It didn't help that he kept glancing at her across the breakfast table but stared down at his plate when she returned the look. She couldn't detect any admiration in those gray eyes. What was he thinking? She brushed a hand over the side of her hair and then scolded herself for the self-conscious gesture typical of some of the silly girls at church. She wasn't anything like them. No wonder Jared had stopped courting her.

None too soon for her, it was time to get to work on the barn. A light snow had fallen in the night but not enough to prevent progress. By noon the hazy sun had melted most of it and the dry breeze took care of all but a few remnants hiding in corners.

After dinner five neighbors came to help for the

afternoon. One of them, Buck Paisley from down the road, brought a wagonload of lumber.

"Me and the wife figured you might run out," he said. "This is left over from the addition we finished last September."

Pa welcomed the offer. "We'll figure out a trade one day soon."

"Fine by me."

Another man, Juan Martinez, unloaded two tin pails filled with eight and sixteen penny nails. "We'll work it out, too, *amigo*. We got to get this barn built for the last night of Las Posadas, *si*?"

"Si." Pa smiled warmly and thanked them all, but Emma could tell he was concerned about repaying all of these trades. He wasn't a terribly proud man, but he did have a healthy dose of self-respect that didn't cotton to charity.

The men gathered around him with hammers and saws in hand.

"Tell us what to do, Señor Sharp." Juan's brother, Diego, held up his hammer.

Leaning on his cane, Pa laughed. "Well, I'm not the boss of this operation. You'll have to speak to my daughter." He waved a hand toward Emma. "Or Jared Mattson over there." He beckoned to Jared, who hustled over to the group. "These two are your bosses, so choose which one you want to work for. Whichever team finishes their side first has bragging rights and gets served first at the Christmas feast."

For several seconds, not a sound was heard in the barnyard. Then laughter erupted from the five men.

"I choose Miss Emma." Patrick Ahern's green eyes sparkled with approval.

Emma felt an odd little tickle near her heart. She had no feelings for Patrick other than friendship, but it was nice—and different—to receive such admiration, which usually went to Julia. Without meaning to she glanced at Jared, who was glaring at the back of Patrick's head. The tickle near her heart turned into an oddly pleasant hitch. Was he jealous? Were Pa and Julia right about his feelings for her?

The rest of the newcomers stepped over to Emma. "We'll be on your team, too, Señorita Emma," Diego said. The others chorused their agreement.

"Hey." Jared posted his fists at his waist. "How about some help for my team?"

"All right." Emma gave him a sassy smile. Maybe this was a chance to see if he did have feelings for her. She'd send the two married men to him and keep the single ones. "Mr. Paisley, Juan, would you please work with Mr. Mattson? I'll keep these other men on my side."

Sure enough, Jared scowled for a few seconds as if he'd figured out what she was doing. Then he tipped his hat and gave her an elaborate bow. As he straightened, the smirk on his fine lips sent a giddy feeling through Emma. My, he was a good-looking man. Those broad shoulders and strong arms could heft a lot of weight, as she'd seen these past couple of days. But physical strength and a handsome face didn't mean he was husband material. And from the way he gathered his team and quickly gave them assignments, he had every intention of winning their competition. So much for a man sacrificing for his lady.

"Miss Emma." Patrick leaned against Buck's wagon and chewed on a toothpick. "I have no doubt we'll get this thing built by Las Posadas."

She eyed him briefly, seeing too much interest there. Maybe he'd been a bad choice for her team. "Not if we stand around jawing."

She marched across the barnyard and could hear her men following behind her. Paco was waiting beside her two framed sides, which lay on the ground. They briefly discussed what each of the four men would do, and the work began. Patrick acted busy but seemed to skirt around actual work. What a difference between Jared and him. On the other hand, every time she looked Jared's way, he seemed to feel her stare, because he'd look up from his work and give her a brief nod and that cute, crooked grin. And each time, she had to resist the urge to brush her bushy hair back from her face in that silly, girly way.

When Julia brought out coffee and cookies in the middle of the afternoon, Patrick sat on a stump beside where Emma stood.

"This is a mighty fine place you folks have here, Miss Emma." He gazed around the barnyard and beyond. "Mighty fine. I suppose if a man married one of you sisters, he'd gain more than a pretty bride." He waggled his red eyebrows at her and gave her a slick smile.

Emma shrugged and turned away to hide her shock at his rude comment. She'd never considered such a thing before, but as the idea sank in, she realized it was true. Julia and Cal already had their plans to live at the Mattson ranch, so that left her. Maybe she should do what Pa said and try to encourage Jared's interest, try to get him to marry her. Instead of moving to the Mattsons' place, they could stay here, if Jared agreed. Then Pa would have the son he'd always wanted even though he never said so. Then she wouldn't have to carry the burden of the ranch all on her own. Yet if Jared didn't love her, it wouldn't be a love match; it would be a business arrangement. Her heart sank like a brick in her stomach.

Without meaning to, she once again looked in Jared's direction. His scowl was a bit hard to read, but he obviously wasn't happy about Patrick's comment. The brick in her stomach lightened considerably.

She could do this. She could marry for Ma's and Pa's sakes. Maybe if she made Jared jealous enough, he really would fall in love with her. Turning a friendly smile on Patrick, one she didn't feel at all, she deliberately brushed her hair back behind her ear in that girly gesture she despised. "Now aren't you the sweetest thing talking about pretty brides? You do know Julia and Cal are promised, don't you? That leaves just one sister." She almost gagged on the words.

Patrick's smile broadened, and he winked. "Yes, ma'am. I knew that."

"Everybody back to work." Jared set his coffee cup on the tray and waved impatiently to his men. "This barn won't get built if we waste time talking."

Emma made sure he was looking her way before giving Patrick another smile.

"You sure are pounding that nail mighty hard," Cal muttered as he carried another two-by-four to Jared. "Are you wishing it was that cowboy's head?" He nodded toward Patrick Ahern.

"Humph." Jared pulled his hammer back and gave the nail one last whack. His brother read him well and probably agreed with him about Ahern. The man was a shirker, a schemer and a ladies' man, someone Jared

had no respect for. If he could sweet-talk Emma into a courtship, that would prove she didn't love Jared. Worse, it would ruin her life.

Jared had been galled by Ahern's suggestion that by marrying one of the Sharp girls, a man would eventually own this ranch. No man worth his salt would marry a good woman such as Emma just so he could have her father's land, especially if he didn't love her. If Jared married Emma—or anybody—they'd buy their own place and build it up just like Pop and Mr. and Mrs. Sharp had done.

Ahern's words also sent a thread of worry through Jared. What if the scalawag actually decided to court Emma? What if she fell for his pretty words? The only solution Jared could see was to beat him to it. Staying here in the Sharps' house gave him the advantage, so he'd best make use of it. Strange how that thought made him feel good instead of scared. Despite his unhappy memories of Mama and Maybelle, he'd begun to feel that he could risk his heart again. He'd pray about the courting first, of course. He'd vowed not to hurt Emma again, and he meant it. Yet, if the Lord gave him a sign, something to prove she cared for him, he'd jump into courting her with both feet.

By the end of the afternoon, the four side frames were ready to raise and secure to the corner posts, but it would take more than eight men to accomplish the task. The day was too far gone for them to gather more help, and Jared's other brothers couldn't come until Monday. With tomorrow being Sunday, no work would be done because everybody would go to church and rest, as the Lord instructed. Even Pop. Sunday work around the Mattson ranch was limited to seeing to the animals' needs and nothing more.

As the men left one by one to return to their homes, Jared kept an eye out for Will. Yesterday, he'd asked his brother to ride down to Espanola to search for a shepherd for Mr. Sharp, if one was to be found. The Basques who had come to New Mexico to work for the Spanish settlers had grown old, and few new ones had immigrated here to take their places. Will promised to do his best, but Jared wasn't holding his breath that he'd succeed. By sundown, it was clear Will hadn't found the right man.

After another fine supper, Saturday night baths and a peaceful evening in the Sharps' parlor, Jared spent a while whittling in the bedroom. He hadn't received a sign about courting Emma, nor had she encouraged his attentions. Unless he could count her offering him thirds of her mother's tasty mashed potatoes and gravy. She hadn't done the same for Cal, but maybe she was just being hospitable because she sat beside Jared at the dining room table. On the other hand, that courtesy was an improvement over his first day here when she'd seemed to think he was eating too much. But then…

He had to stop this crazy thinking. He needed to relax and let things happen. Then maybe the sign would come. He put away his whittling and lay down, determined to trust the Lord, only to dream of Patrick Ahern standing with Emma in front of the preacher.

Yip-yip-yip! Piercing animal cries broke the silence of the winter night.

"Coyotes!" Jared sprang from his bed and quickly donned his clothes and boots.

Cal wasn't far behind him as he dressed, grabbed his rifle and headed out of the room. Emma, fully clothed, was already heading down the hall toward the kitchen.

Mr. Sharp met them at the back door with Emma's rifle in hand.

"Be careful." Light from the candle he held etched worry lines deep into his face.

"I will." Emma took the rifle and darted outside.

"We'll take care of her." Jared patted Mr. Sharp's shoulder.

Mr. Sharp grasped Jared's arm and held on tight, his gaze boring deep into Jared's eyes. "I know you will."

The old man's confidence reinforced Jared's determination to protect her, even though he'd never tell her he was doing it. He and Cal were only a few yards behind Emma as she entered the corral. Not wasting time on saddles, they grabbed halters and lead ropes from the wooden fence, put them on their horses, mounted up and kicked the animals into a gallop. Although his emotions were gripped by the urgency of the situation, in the back of his mind he could only admire a woman who could ride bareback—and at a gallop, no less.

The half-moon spread its dim light over the landscape, and within minutes they covered the quarter mile to the sheepfold. The sheep bleated in terror as they huddled against the barbed wire fence, some entangling their thick wool on the sharp spikes. On the far side of the fence, the two brave guard dogs barked furiously to hold four coyotes at bay. The varmints paced back and forth looking for a weakness.

Emma tried to still her horse, but he turned in circles, probably spooked by the coyotes. Jared managed better and fired off the first shot at the largest one. The nasty critter yelped in pain until Jared ended its misery with a second shot. Cal fired at the remaining three as they took off across the barren winter landscape, one of them limping on three legs.

"Nice shots." Emma jumped from her horse and secured its lead rope to a fencepost. She strode toward the coyote carcass. "Let's hang this varmint on the fence to keep his friends from coming back."

Jared and Cal traded a look. They'd never been convinced the practice worked. More likely the blood would spook the sheep. But Emma seemed determined to do it. Jared shrugged and slid from his horse to help her, with Cal right behind him. Once the smelly animal was secured, they wordlessly went about loosening the sheep from the fence.

While he worked, Jared couldn't slow his racing thoughts about the determined woman beside him. If she wanted, she could stick to safer duties and chores expected of women. Or tonight she could have cowered in a corner while her father took charge. Yet she'd beaten him and Cal out the door, rushing to save Mr. Sharp from losing valuable livestock, not to mention save him a great deal of pain.

As he thought more about it, he remembered why he'd courted her in the first place. When she got all gussied up for church, she outshined every other female in the congregation. Yet in this moonlight she looked mighty fine in those dusty, oversize trousers, cooing like a mourning dove to the frightened sheep as she separated them from the barbs, taking a few minutes to commend the guard dogs and promise them steak in the morning. Tough as nails and fully feminine at the same time. She knew and loved this land and wouldn't be likely to leave it. How could a man not admire a woman like that?

At last exhaustion forced them all back to the house for a few hours of sleep before church. In the morning, chores came first, of course. Jared convinced Emma that he and Cal could take care of the sheep and guard dogs while she helped her ma. To his surprise, she accepted the offer. Even gave him a sweet smile that caused all sorts of odd feelings to tumble through his chest. Was that the sign he'd prayed for? Pop would say a man should never make a decision based on feelings. But how *could* Jared know what to do?

At the sheepfold, the dogs devoured the chunks of beef and gratefully licked the hands that fed them before settling down to gnaw on bones.

The brothers returned to the house to find the Sharp ladies had a breakfast feast spread across the kitchen table. When Emma poured coffee for everyone, Jared had to pull his lips between his teeth to keep from whistling at how nice she looked.

She wore her pretty blue dress, the one like Julia's, only different. Whereas Julia's had all sorts of lacy ruffles and ribbons like the ones most of the girls at church wore, Emma's getup looked simpler. The only decoration was a single dark blue ribbon around the high neckline. It seemed to him that Emma's dress suited her. He couldn't exactly use the word *elegant* to describe her appearance, short as she was, but *refined* seemed about right, especially when she stood up as tall as her height allowed. Nobody seeing her at church this morning would believe she'd been out in the middle of the night untangling sheep from barbed wire.

He'd never before noticed such things about a lady's appearance. After living in a house full of men all his life, his eyes had been opened to something new. Maybe this was the sign he'd prayed for. But how could he be sure?

Emma and Julia sat behind Ma and Pa in the surrey. Emma felt both sad and grateful that Pa had been able to save it from the fire. Otherwise they'd have to take a wagon, which would be harder on Pa's hip.

After they'd gotten all of the animals out of the barn, he'd gone back in to retrieve this fine buggy he'd been so proud to buy just last spring after sheep-shearing. But when it proved heavier than expected, he'd pulled too hard on the traces, fallen and twisted his leg clear out of the hip joint. Yet he'd limped out of the burning barn, pulling the surrey to safety.

The doctor from Riverton had reset his hip, yet it still pained Pa considerably, bad enough to keep him from working on the new barn. To hear Pa tell it, though, it had been worth it to save the conveyance so he could take his "girls" to church in style. She wouldn't hurt Pa's feelings by disputing what he said, so she put on her happiest smile and tugged her warm woolen cape closer around her cheeks to keep out the cold wind.

Just looking at Jared brought another kind of warmth to her face. He wore a white Sunday shirt, a black bolo tie and a blue-and-red-plaid winter jacket, and looked so handsome as he rode his horse beside the surrey. Although she hadn't told him, she was deeply grateful to him. Last night he hadn't been obliged to go out in the cold to save the sheep, yet he had. Well, and Cal, too. But he had more interest in protecting Pa's property considering he'd soon be part of the family.

As far as Emma was concerned, Jared had proved his character over these past few days. Yes, he jilted her, but maybe after those picnics and outings she'd enjoyed so much, he'd decided they weren't suited to each other. She could forgive him. Wish him well. Hope he found the woman of his dreams.

No, that was going too far. Instead, maybe she could figure out how to be that woman, so long as she wasn't expected to change too much. She couldn't mince around like the other girls. Couldn't simper and give false compliments. Winning a man's attention and admiration was an art she'd never even tried to acquire. She'd feel foolish trying now.

But then, maybe Julia was right. Maybe Jared already loved her. What could she do to get him to say so? She might not always come up to Ma's standards of ladylike behavior, but she did hold fast to one of those lessons: she wouldn't chase after any man, not even Jared Mattson. If he wasn't attracted to her, as Julia insisted he was, then it was hopeless. Her only consolation came from knowing he'd be with her family for another week. That was plenty of time for a man to decide his feelings and speak up about them.

For now, she needed to turn her thoughts toward the Lord. She and her family had a good deal of blessings to be thankful for, especially this past week. In spite of losing their barn, no animals died and Pa would heal soon. Through it all, they'd learned how much their neighbors cared for and respected them. People from both the Mexican and Americano communities had offered time and resources. Even Yankees and Southerners had put aside bitterness left over from the War Between the States, and tomorrow a passel of men would arrive for the barn raising.

Only God could bring about such unity in this diverse community, and it was all because of Pastor Daniel and Brother Miguel, the minister from the Spanish mission across the road from Grace Church. The two preachers had decided years ago it was their responsibility to bridge the gap between the longtime settlers and the newcomers. Through their wise teaching, folks had learned to respect land boundaries and one another. As

Brother Miguel often said, "Love your neighbor, as the Lord commands, and not just those who agree with you."

The surrey pulled up to Grace Church, and folks they hadn't seen since last Sunday surrounded them to offer words of sympathy and encouragement. Several ladies placed food baskets in the storage box on the back of the surrey for tomorrow.

"Much obliged." Ma blinked back a few tears. "I wondered how I was going to feed all those fellas who're coming to help with the barn raising tomorrow."

When several men expressed dismay over the fire, Pa brushed off their condolences with his usual wry humor. "Just because my Christian name is Job don't mean I've suffered more than anybody else around here. My family's all safe and well. That's what matters." Despite the strength of his words, he let Jared and Cal help him and Ma down from the surrey.

While Jared attached a lead rope to the horse's halter and tied it around the hitching post, Cal lifted Julia down. Emma scooted over, her pulse racing with uncertain hope. Would Jared lend her a hand? From the corner of her eye, she saw Patrick Ahern headed in her direction. Conviction told her not to accept his help or even grin at him as she had yesterday. If she did, she'd be no better than Jared when he'd courted but then jilted her, encouraging feelings that weren't returned. She started to climb down on her own, but Jared was there before she could blink.

"Mind if I help you?" His gray eyes held a note of doubt, but his gloved hands were already moving toward her waist. He grasped and lifted her easily with a grip so strong she hardly needed to steady herself by clutching his shoulders.

"Much obliged." To her consternation, her words came out breathlessly.

He must have noticed, because he got that cute grin on his face that made her heart trip all over itself.

To make matters worse—or maybe better—he held out his arm. "May I escort you?"

She took it gladly, could even allow that Julia might be right about his feelings for her.

"Ahern." He nodded to Patrick, and his voice dripped with triumph.

Emma huffed out a cross breath. So this was nothing more than a competition between the two of them to see whom she was partial to. Her growing happiness disappeared, replaced by cold reality. At least Patrick had been honest enough to admit he was interested in Pa's land and not her. Had Jared decided that wasn't a bad idea? Was he planning to court her again so he could get the ranch? If so, he'd be sadly disappointed.

She wouldn't shame Ma and Pa by giving him a piece of her mind right here in front of the church when she should be thinking about worshipping the Lord. But tomorrow she'd make sure her team won the barn-raising competition. After that, the day she said goodbye to Jared Mattson couldn't come fast enough to suit her.

Chapter Four

*W*omen! Jared had been right about not marrying one of 'em. Even if Emma wasn't the sort to leave her family, even if she loved the land and would stay on it if things got bad, what man could stand living with a prickly pear? One minute she was all sweet and thankful to him for helping her down from the surrey and offering his arm. The next she was as cold as the surrey wheels after traveling over two miles of frozen ground. She even ignored her mama's instructions to sit by him and moved beyond her family to the other end of the pew. What had set her off?

Two things were sure. One was that he couldn't wait to beat her in the barn-raising competition. Two, he couldn't wait to get back home so he could make plans to move to Colorado.

He nodded to Pop, who sat across the small sanctuary with Jared's other brothers and nephew. All except Will. Maybe his middle brother was still down in Espanola looking for a shepherd. Jared grunted. He'd sent Will to find help for Mr. Sharp, not to impress Emma. He had to admit, though, that he'd hoped she would look favorably on him for trying to solve the sheep problem. Now he refused to care. Even if Will was successful, she'd likely shrug it off.

"Good morning and welcome." Pastor Daniel took his place at the front of the congregation. "Please turn to hymn number one, 'Holy, Holy, Holy.'"

After that soul-lifting song, the minister invited them to bow their heads for prayer. Jared felt a guilty twinge in his chest. He'd been so focused on his troubles with Emma that he'd forgotten to prepare his mind for worship. The Lord had forgiven all his sins, but Jared wouldn't use that as an excuse for failing to worship Him. He redirected his thoughts right away, joining in the next hymn with enthusiasm.

"Redeemed, How I Love to Proclaim It!" was a new song to Jared, written by Fanny Crosby, but he managed to read the music, thanks to Mama's early teaching. If, as the third verse said, he thought of the Lord all day long, how could he go wrong? If he made the Lord's "law" his delight, the Lord would lovingly guard his footsteps. No one could ask for more. On the last chorus, he attempted to follow Mr. Sharp's bass harmony and was rewarded with a curious look from Emma. It wasn't quite a smile, but it wasn't a grimace, either, so he must have sung all right.

Maybe he'd been wrong about her mood. Maybe she'd sat so far away from him so people wouldn't think they were courting again. If so, it was a smart thing to do and protected them both from gossip. He'd noticed when they came in that several younger ladies had cast curious glances their way, then huddled together and whispered who knew what. Didn't everyone know he and Cal were staying with the Sharps to help with the barn? How could that cause gossip?

Jared had to work hard to turn his mind to Pastor Daniel's sermon, but soon the minister's words swept away all other thoughts. He preached from Galatians 3:13: "Christ hath redeemed us from the curse of the law, being made a curse for us: for it is written, cursed is every one that hangeth on a tree." Mrs. Crosby's hymn had been the perfect choice for today. Pastor Daniel spoke at length about all that the Lord's redemption meant, and Jared wished he'd brought paper and pencil to write down all those good ideas.

One Bible passage did stick in his mind and lift his heart. Hebrews 13:5 said, "I will never leave thee, nor forsake thee." He needed this reminder every day of his life. No matter who abandoned him, the Lord would never leave nor forsake him. Neither would the Almighty turn prickly or distant for no reason. According to the Word of God, Jared could count on it. So he would.

Back at the Sharp ranch, while he and Cal fed the guard dogs, sheep and other livestock, the Sharp ladies fixed a tasty fried chicken dinner. After that, they all settled in for a relaxing afternoon in the parlor, everybody busy with their handiwork and sipping coffee. Unlike Pop, who forbade anything but the most necessary chores, Mr. Sharp didn't mind his family and guests doing small jobs like mending clothes, whittling or oiling harnesses.

Jared liked that practical view of God's day of rest. Sometimes he got the idea that Pop was either mad at the Lord or trying extra hard to please Him through living a perfect life—and making sure his sons did the same. Did Pop even listen to Pastor Daniel's sermons? Had he heard the part today about being redeemed from the curse of the law? Jared prayed those holy words would seep into Pop's brain and give him some joy and peace.

Without thinking, he began to hum the sermon hymn, and soon the family joined in. Mrs. Sharp pulled out her concertina to accompany them. After they finished "Redeemed," she asked what else they'd like to sing.

"I always like 'Amazing Grace,'" Mr. Sharp said.

Julia opened a hymnal and held it so her mama could see the notes and remind everyone of the words. After that, each person requested a favorite. Emma chose "What a Friend We Have in Jesus."

Coming from a house that hadn't heard any music since Mama left, Jared felt his heart just about burst with holy joy. This was what family life was supposed to be like, and seeing Emma's love for the Lord helped him appreciate her a whole heap more. He just hoped he wasn't one of those "griefs" that Jesus bore for her, as the song said. In truth, though, he knew all too well he'd brought her grief.

When they'd been in church this morning, he'd decided to shrug off his care for her, but here in her home, he couldn't stick to that decision. Even if they didn't court again, he'd have to make sure he didn't hurt her a second time. Maybe he should let her win the barn-raising competition. On the other hand, that would let his crew down. He'd just try his best and leave the winning up to the Lord. After all, the rivalry was meant for fun. Yet he suspected winning meant more to Emma than it did to him.

Thinking back to Mr. Sharp's Bible reading that first evening he and Cal were here, Jared wondered if letting Emma win would be like sacrificing himself for her, as Christ had for the church. Of course, he'd only be sacrificing his manly pride, not his life. He could manage that, couldn't he? Especially since he'd damaged her womanly pride when he'd jilted her.

Yep, he needed to let her win but without telling Cal or any of his team. That would be the hard part, because everyone at church now knew about the competition. All those men had a stake in it now. They wouldn't take kindly to him letting them down.

"Don't push so hard, dear. Be gentle."

Across the room, Emma now held the concertina while her mama gave her instructions on how to change an ear-splitting screech into a pleasing tone. The dogged look on Emma's face was one he'd seen before. She meant to conquer the music box just like she meant to win the barn-raising competition. A mixture of admiration and consternation swept through Jared. My, this lady was feisty and determined and not a little proud. Somehow he didn't think she'd take it kindly if he let her win. He had to put out his best effort just as she intended to do. Even if it meant he lost her good opinion forever.

Lord, how did I manage to get myself into this mess?

Emma had no idea why she'd asked Mama for a music lesson in front of Jared, especially since she didn't seem to have that knack Mama had for bringing a pretty tune out of the squeezebox. Why set herself up for teasing? She still hadn't gotten over the way Jared had spoken to Patrick before church. Nor had she gotten over Suzette Pursers asking if they were courting again since they were at church together. Did Suzette want to know if it was all right to flirt with Jared? Well, she could go right ahead, even though deep down inside, Emma didn't like the idea one bit. Suzette was a short, pretty blonde, just the kind of girl all the men buzzed around like bees. Why would she need to flirt with Jared? To prove she could catch the man Emma couldn't keep, a man more than one other girl admired? Emma didn't have any trouble understanding why he got all of that attention.

He was the handsomest of the five brothers, even though they all looked pretty much alike. Well, except that his grin was cuter than the others, and those gray eyes twinkled with mischief from time to time, unlike his dour oldest brother's and their pa's. Cal was spoken for, so he didn't count. Jared enjoyed church, even seemed a tad more spiritual than any of the other Mattsons, if his enjoyment of the hymns and rapt attention to the sermon were any indication. All of that, and he was a hard worker and generous with his labor, as well.

Maybe she'd been too hard on him about Patrick. It wasn't as though he'd started a fight with the cowboy. He'd just sounded a bit too proud because she'd chosen to walk into the church with him. He'd really done her a favor by warding off an unwanted suitor. So why couldn't she spare him a kind word or at least a friendly smile?

It was his fault. If he hadn't jilted her, maybe she could trust him. But the old saying, Fool me once, shame on you. Fool me twice, shame on me, kept coming to mind. She could trust him with the sheep, trust him with his share of building the barn. She just couldn't trust him with her heart.

In the late afternoon horses' hooves sounded in the barnyard. Everyone set aside their work and hurried down the hallway, through the kitchen and out the back door. Will Mattson and two companions dismounted from their horses. Two black-and-white sheepdogs and a pack mule accompanied the dark-haired young man and woman.

"Howdy, Mr. Sharp." Will stepped over to Pa to shake hands. He tipped his hat to everyone else. "Mrs. Sharp. Ladies. Brothers." Emma didn't think his pleasant smile held near the charm as Jared's. "Let me introduce Xavier and Angelique Elizondo. They'd like to take care of your sheep for you. Here are their references." He handed a sheaf of papers to Pa.

Her own mind reeling in amazement, Emma watched Pa's jaw drop and hang loose for a full five seconds. At last he shook himself and took the papers, scanning them briefly. Then he reached out to the young man.

"Señor Elizondo, you got yourself a job." He shook the man's hand as if it was a pump handle and nodded to the young woman. "Señora Elizondo."

"Gracias, Patron." Xavier grinned broadly, while Angelique offered a shy smile. "We are grateful for the work."

"Now, none of that *patron* stuff. I'm just a humble rancher." Pa turned to Will. "Young man, I don't know how to thank you for finding these folks."

Will shuffled his feet. "It wasn't me, sir. Jared had the idea. Said you couldn't go looking for yourself 'cause of your... Say, how's your leg?"

While they jawed briefly about Pa's health improvements, Emma stole a glance at Jared. His face beamed with some fine feeling. Not pride, just honest happiness. And he'd arranged all of this. She wanted to think he'd done it for her, but in truth he would have done it for anybody in need. All the more reason to admire him. All the more reason not to take it personal.

He looked her way, catching her before she could turn away. His grin made her heart skip.

She couldn't keep from grinning back. "Thanks."

He reached up as if he meant to tip his hat, but he wasn't wearing one. He pantomimed the gesture, and they both laughed. The moment further warmed her heart, and she had a hard time stamping out the little thread of hope trying to weave through her chest.

By nightfall they had the Elizondos settled in the small adobe house near the sheepfold. Ma had provided food, a few kitchen utensils and some bedding. Jared and Cal brought wood for the small cast-iron cookstove and the fireplace that would heat their new home.

Xavier introduced himself and his sheepdogs to the guard dogs and then waited patiently while the critters sniffed each other and decided who was top dog. At that point, Xavier quickly let them know he was in charge simply by his straightened, commanding posture and a few firm Basque words. The guard dogs crouched down in a submissive but not cowering posture. The sheepdogs lay down and watched him expectantly. With a simple gesture and a few more words, Xavier ordered his dogs to enter the sheepfold and get acquainted with their new charges. The two took off and did as they were told, circling the sheep and herding them around as if they were showing off their talents.

"How does he do that?" Emma glanced at Jared.

"Beats me." Jared grinned and waggled his dark eyebrows at her. "There's a few folks I'd like to see mind me like that."

Emma gaped at him, and that cute grin of his no longer touched her heart. Did he mean her? Did he really mean *she* should mind *him*? A wife might do well to be submissive to her husband in obedience to the Lord's command. But Jared Mattson would never boss Emma around. And she couldn't wait till tomorrow to show him.

This time Jared knew exactly why Emma turned prickly. He'd tried to tease her, tried to hint that he really liked her and wanted to see where their renewed friendship might take them. He'd thought they'd gone beyond easy hurt feelings because of the laugh they'd shared back at the barnyard, but his awkward attempt at humor had failed.

Now that he thought on it, he recalled his plans of last week to tease her for the very purpose of keeping her riled so they would *not* renew that friendship. Why did he think he could tease her now and hope for a better result? Before he could figure out how to make it right, she said goodbye to Xavier and Angelique, mounted her horse and rode away. He had no choice but to mount up and follow her back to the ranch house.

The Sharp family always turned in early on Sunday to get a good night's sleep before the new week. As usual, Jared sat up for a while to whittle. He sanded between the teeth of Emma's comb to smooth out any edges that might snag her hair. He didn't want to give her a gift that would cause her pain. Didn't want to cause her any pain at all. Once was enough between any two people.

At last barn-raising day arrived, and Jared anticipated success, at least on the barn. The weather was crisp and cold, with a hazy sun overhead and dark clouds covering the Sangre de Cristos' highest peaks. By midmorning, some thirty men had arrived, along with a few women who came to help with the cooking.

While it was good for the community to come together, Jared hoped everybody would continue to get along, that nobody would want to refight the Mexican-American War or the War Between the States. Even though that last conflict had ended over twenty years ago, some Southerners carried a heavy dose of bitterness against any Yankee who crossed their paths.

Pop had fought for the Confederacy, but he never talked about it. Seven years ago when the family sold their small farm outside Charleston and packed up to come West, Jared saw Pop all misty-eyed as he briefly held his gray uniform and then firmly set it aside to be left behind. In spite of his taciturn ways, he was the first to shake hands with Mr. Sharp of Ohio's Seventh Volunteer Infantry Regiment when the Sharp family moved here shortly after the Mattsons. For these two men, the war had ended on April 9, 1865, when Lee surrendered to Grant at Appomattox Courthouse.

If only Jared's "war" with Emma could end so peacefully.

One thing was sure. They needed to finish the barn so the community could gather here in four days for Las Posadas and establish that kind of unity.

"'Morning, Jared." His oldest brother, Rob, strode over from the building site wearing an all too familiar expression. "You need to put a few more studs in those frames before you try to raise them."

"That so?" Jared tried to keep his anger down. After Mama left, Rob had gotten even bossier than any oldest brother had a right to be. It only got worse when his wife left him. Jared couldn't wait to move out and be his own boss for a change.

"Yep." Rob crossed his arms over his chest. "You don't want the walls to cave in on Mr. Sharp, do you? Take a look at the two sides Emma and Paco built. Studs shouldn't be more than twelve inches apart."

Jared frowned, aching to tell Rob he could go build his own barn if he was so smart. But concern about the success of the project outweighed his pride. "That'll set back the raising, but best to do it right in the first place."

Jared informed the workers about the need to brace up his two sides of the structure, setting into motion a flurry of activity. Rob suggested they leave the studs in place and brace them with horizontal supports. Everyone agreed that would sufficiently reinforce the two walls. Over near the corral he saw that Emma was sitting on a stump knitting, a big grin on her face, while her team of workers kept themselves busy tending livestock and other helpful ranch work to stay occupied until time to raise the sides.

"We need to keep score on each part of the building," she said. "No fair for us to have to wait while you catch up. We could have the whole barn finished before you get your part done." She tossed a long lock of that pretty black hair over her shoulder, an unconscious gesture unlike the obviously flirty way the girls at church did it. Yet the movement stirred a bit of excitement in Jared's chest. Would she like the comb? Would she—

"Hey, watch out!" His brother Will shoved him out of the way before another man with a board on his shoulder knocked into his head. "You'd better quit gathering wool and start working. This is your competition, ain't it?"

Heat rushed to Jared's face, and it intensified when he looked at Emma. Instead of the smirk he expected, her eyes were wide and her mouth open, almost as if she was scared for him. He shrugged and offered her a crooked grin. She raised her chin, gave a little sniff and then went back to her knitting. Which made him grin even more. She did like him, did care what happened to him. She was just too proud to admit it.

Emma almost had fallen off the stump she was sitting on when one of the men had come near to hitting Jared in the head with that board. The fella had been moving fast, so it would have hurt Jared pretty bad. To her chagrin, he'd caught her gaping at him. Just like any man, he'd shrugged it off and had given her one of those cute grins. Also to her chagrin, her heart had once again taken over and jumped clear up to her throat. Thankfully, she'd managed to hide her concern and return to her knitting.

These gloves were coming together nicely. Too bad she didn't have enough time before Christmas to knit pairs of socks for Jared and Cal, as well. With no woman in their home, and only Old Fuzzy to cook and clean for them, they must have a hard time with such necessities. She supposed they kept the Riverton mercantile in business with the clothing needs of six men and a growing boy. Maybe she could manage to knit some socks for Robby. That wouldn't take much time.

Thinking about the Mattsons, she chuckled to herself as she recalled how Rob had given Jared that setdown. If she'd been the one to tell Jared about the studs being too far apart, he would have laughed. She'd noticed that first day that Rob had an eye for such things, so she'd waited for him to step in. Of course, she'd also prayed. Although she didn't think it was right to ask the Lord for His favor in the competition, she did pray the barn would be built strong and sturdy and would be finished before the snows came. Those were the most important things.

Another thought edged its way into her mind. Jared had looked a bit peeved as Rob spoke to him like a scolding father, yet he hadn't argued. She respected that. Seemed Jared got along with everybody—except her. That insight downright depressed her.

Ma, Julia and the other women set out a fine spread of sandwiches, potato salad and coffee. The Mexican ladies had brought a stew they called chili, which wasn't the least bit chilly. Emma's tongue burned for quite some time after she ate a bowlful, but she had to admit it was mighty tasty. Always on the lookout for warm winter dishes, she wondered whether she could make it with a milder pepper, maybe add some beans and a few tomatoes, and serve it with corn bread. Made her hungry all over again just thinking about it.

With nine men working on Jared's team, they'd finished repairing his two sides by dinner. Now that everyone had eaten, both teams went into action. Heavy ropes were brought out and attached to the top beams of the frames. Two adjacent sides were pulled upright and secured to their shared corner post. A third side was raised and secured, and then the fourth. Finally, they raised the frame for the roof and set it in place above the sides. After the last nails were driven into the boards, Emma and Jared inspected all of the joints and agreed they were sound. A loud cheer went up from the workers, with each man turning to his neighbor to shake hands over a job well done.

While daylight lasted, the teams added siding, each finishing a good portion of their two sides. When the men began to drift away to return to their own homes and chores, Emma felt great satisfaction over all they'd accomplished. From Jared's wide-open smile, she could see he shared her joy.

Pa limped out of the house, pain evident on his weathered face, but he shook hands with each man who'd helped. As everyone said their goodbyes, Emma prayed that the weather would hold off for another few days. The barn was close to finished, but they still had the rest of the siding, the roof, interior, doors and windows to complete and only four days to do it.

After all the noise of the work, supper was a quiet affair, with everyone too tired to talk. Once Jared and Cal tended to evening chores and Pa read a Bible passage, another early bedtime seemed like a good idea. Having wielded a hammer for several hours, Emma couldn't even make her fingers hold on to her knitting needles.

Late in the night, she awakened to shuffling sounds coming from the kitchen. Determined to let Julia and their parents get much-needed rest, she considered waking Jared but decided not to waste time. She slipped on her bathrobe and shoes, picked up the poker from beside her fireplace and quietly tiptoed from the room. Light from the banked stove fire sent ominous shadows dancing across the kitchen wall, while one large black shape wavered menacingly across the wooden floor.

Emma raised the poker, prepared to strike the intruder. She peered around the doorjamb to see that dark figure hunched down by the still warm stove.

"There you go, little mama." Jared's voice!

Emma lowered the poker and laid it on the table. "What are you doing?" she asked in an urgent whisper.

He jerked around and almost lost his balance. "Emma. Sorry to wake you." He gave her a sweet smile very unlike his cute grin. "Come see what we got here."

She moved closer and saw what held his attention. The expectant barn cat lay on a burlap potato sack panting, clearly preparing to give birth. Her own heart melted at Jared's gentle care for the kitty. He scratched under her chin and cooed soothing words.

"Ma's not going to like this," she whispered.

"Aw, she won't mind, 'specially when she sees what's outside." He jutted his chin toward the back door.

Fearing the worst, Emma moved the curtain aside and peered out through the door window. Sure enough, snow drifted down and covered the barnyard with a dreamy blue-white blanket.

"At least it's not a blizzard." She let the calico curtain fall back into place over the icy window.

"At least not yet." Jared gave her a rueful smile.

Emma sighed. No sense in jawing about what they couldn't control. She pulled over a chair and sat near the stove to warm herself. "How come you like cats? I never met a man who likes cats."

He gave her an uncertain glance, as if he was deciding what to say. Finally, he stood, pulled a chair over beside her and sat. He held out his hands toward the stove. "Guess I should heat this up a bit if we're gonna be here a while."

After he added a log and stirred the fire, he sat back down and stared at the flames as if he was deep in thought. Emma had a mind to ask if he'd forgotten her question but decided to keep quiet. It was none of her business why he liked cats. For now it just felt good, felt right to be sitting here beside him while Kitty brought her babies into the world.

Jared felt that itch in his brain that warned him not to say too much. He'd never dared to tell his brothers about the cat that had consoled him after Mama left. They wouldn't only have laughed at him. They never would have let him forget it. In a family of men where sentimental feelings were considered the domain of the weaker gender, a man had to be strong, tough. Even little Robby was learning not to bellyache about anything, not even his mama leaving.

Sitting here beside Emma in this cozy kitchen, though, Jared felt a softening in his heart that outranked his brain. He bent down to pet the cat and then gave Emma a sidelong glance. The open curiosity in her pretty blue eyes seemed to say she wouldn't judge him or think him unmanly if he confessed all. He'd give it a try and pray he didn't live to regret it.

"Back when my mama left us, shortly after we came out here, I was just fifteen. Not too grown-up, I suppose." He gave her a self-conscious grin, and she returned a warm smile. "It hurts to admit it, but I broke down and cried." He chuckled. "Not a very manly thing to do, so I hid in the barn loft so none of my brothers could see me."

Just talking about it stirred up that old grief about Mama, so he swallowed hard and stared at the blazing stove. "This little gray barn cat came over and crawled up in my lap, purring like nobody's business. She reached up with her paw and touched the tears..." He choked a bit and cleared his throat. Funny how talking about it brought back such bittersweet pangs even after all these years. "She seemed to understand I was a just kid and I was hurting." He risked a glance at Emma.

Tears streamed down her sun-kissed cheeks, and he wanted real bad to add a kiss of his own. Instead, he turned back to the stove. "We were friends till the day she passed on. I've had a fondness for cats since then." More unruly emotions threatened to undo him, so he sniffed dramatically and chuckled. "'Course, she only made friends with me so's I'd favor her at milking time. She was always the first one lined up for a squirt of milk."

Emma's laugh was more of a sob. She dabbed her tears with her bathrobe sleeve. "Jared, that's the sweetest thing I've ever heard."

Another warning tickled his brain. He sat up and gave her a stern look. "Now, don't you go telling Julia, 'cause she'll tell Cal, and he'll tell our other brothers and—"

She set her small hand on his forearm and squeezed. "Your secret is safe with me."

He gave her a curt nod but added a smile so she'd know he trusted her. That was one of the many fine things he was beginning to understand about Emma: she could be trusted.

They looked down to see the mama kitty had delivered one tiny black kitten, with more sure to come. The little mama licked her baby and purred and then looked up at Jared as if to say, "See what a fine baby I have?"

"We should call her Mrs. Cat," he said. "What do you think?"

"I like it." Emma gave him one of her sweet smiles. "Say, I'll sit with her if you want to get some rest." She tilted her head toward the hallway. "If the snow lets up, we'll need to get as much work done as possible tomorrow."

"Aw, I suppose she'll do all right by herself. Barn cats have kittens alone all the time." Without thinking, he took Emma's hand. To his surprise, she let him. He stood and gently tugged her to her feet, staring into those sky blue eyes and barely able to breathe for her closeness. He did manage to whisper, "We could both use the rest."

She nodded, and her pretty black hair tumbled around her shoulders. He couldn't wait to see it secured in place with the comb he'd made. To keep from reaching out to brush it back, he let go of her hand and banked the fire in the stove to be sure no sparks would escape.

"I supposed you're right." She moved toward the hallway. "Let's turn in. Morning will be here before we know it." She glanced back over her shoulder. "I sure hope Ma won't be too upset about the cat."

Jared gave her a reassuring grin, but he wasn't so certain. He'd have to get up early and let Mrs. Sharp know he'd been the one to bring Mrs. Cat inside the house.

* * *

As much as she needed rest, Emma couldn't go back to sleep. When Jared had taken her hand, it had felt... *right*. She'd still been in the throes of deep emotion over his story about the cat that had tried to wipe away his boyish tears, and his touch had sent all sorts of feelings skittering through her. She liked cats pretty much. Had even enjoyed playing with the friendly ones in the barn. But she'd never had one reach out to her that way. What a strange, sweet thing.

Even stranger was Jared's reaction. It showed how truly tender his heart was and how deeply his mother's abandonment had wounded him. Emma could almost understand why he'd jilted her. He'd decided women couldn't be trusted. Yet by telling her his deepest secret, he *had* trusted her, which moved her in ways she never could have imagined. From watching Ma and Pa, Emma saw that his story was the sort of thing married folks whispered to each other after the children were in bed at night. Telling secrets showed trust, but it also made a body vulnerable. Emma would die before she told anyone about Jared and the cat that had befriended him.

In the morning she dressed for outdoor work and made her way to the kitchen with Julia right behind her. The sound of Ma's laughter stopped her at the door. Pa stood at the worktable straining milk from a pail into a gallon jug, while Jared wiped snow from his neck with a towel. He looked Emma's way and winked, that cute grin on his handsome face.

"Yes, ma'am, Mrs. Sharp. That's a fast way to wake a body up. Just dump a bucket of snow over his head."

Pa chuckled. "So you and Cal had your first snowball fight of the winter."

"Snow's too dry to make balls." Cal leaned against the wall, his arms crossed. "But I had to dump the snow out of the bucket so we could milk. What better place to dump it than my big brother's head?"

Emma appreciated that laughter was a good way to start the day, but had Ma even noticed the cat beside the stove? She caught Jared's eye again and questioned him with a look. He winked *again* and gave a quick nod. If he knew what those winks did to her heart, she doubted he'd have done it. A man shouldn't wink at a girl unless it meant something.

"Good morning, ladies," he said.

"'Morning," Emma and Julia chorused as they scurried about the kitchen, dodging three oversize men in their efforts to help Ma complete the breakfast preparations. No matter how much Emma promised herself she'd beat Ma to the kitchen of a morning, Ma always got there first.

Once everyone sat at the table and Pa said the blessing, Ma slid a wily glance at Jared. "You surprise me, boy. Most men don't care a whit for cats, and most barn cats steer clear of people. I appreciated your compassion on those helpless critters over there."

Emma hadn't had a chance to count the kittens, but Ma wouldn't like it if she got up from the table to check. It was clear, though, that she wasn't angry about the cat, which eased Emma's concerns.

"Weelll." Jared drawled out the word, as he often did. "Pop says cats are a necessary evil on a ranch, but I figure they're near as important as dogs when it comes to keeping down the pest population." He glanced at Emma, and a vulnerable expression crossed his eyes.

She gave him a bright smile and then glanced to the floor beyond the stove. "How many kittens did she have after we went to bed?" No use in trying to hide that she and Jared had been up together.

"Three more," Jared said.

Only Julia reacted. "Did you see them born?" At Emma's nod, she added, "Oh, I wish I'd been up, too."

Ma grunted in her ladylike way. "You've seen plenty of birthings, and you'll see plenty more."

Pa appeared too busy eating to enter the conversation, but Emma noticed a brightening in his eyes that usually hinted he did have something to say. He finished his eggs, ham and potatoes before giving his plate a little shove to indicate he was finished.

"Cal, I've been thinking." Pa's gaze flitted briefly to Jared before settling on his younger brother.

"Yessir?" Cal ate his last bite and dabbed his lips with his napkin, something Julia had taught him to do over these past days.

"That Patrick Ahern may have been out of line to say what he did about my ranch going to a son-in-law of mine, 'specially since he seemed to think he had a chance to marry into the family." Pa frowned at Emma. "But I'd sell the place before I let his sort own it."

She returned the look, cross that he'd think she would marry a loafing opportunist.

Ma poured more coffee into Pa's cup, and he took a sip before addressing Cal again.

"That don't mean it's a bad idea. For some time I've wondered what to do with the place when my daughters married and left home. Being laid up these past few days gave me time to think. I'd like the ranch to go to my sons-in-law, and so far you're the only one in sight."

His piercing glance at Emma made her stare down at her plate. Did he think she could just go out to the kitchen garden come summer and pick a husband like she picked a tomato?

"Now," Pa said, "I know your pa plans to make room for you and Julia over at his place. But do you think he'd be troubled if you moved over here for good after the wedding?"

Julia squealed and grabbed Cal's shoulder. "Oh, Pa! Oh, Cal!"

Cal's eyes got big and round, and he sat back in his chair. "My, oh my, Mr. Sharp, that's quite an offer." He punched Jared, who sat on his other side. "Isn't it?"

Jared had watched Pa with interest, but now he gave his brother a warm smile. "I'll say it is, brother. And I believe I can speak for Pop in saying he'd be pleased as punch if you accepted. He's always happy when good things happen for any of his sons."

Emma's eyes stung and then watered. Not a hint of jealousy had crossed Jared's face, just pure, open joy on behalf of his brother. She knew him well enough to know it was for real, and she admired him all the more for it.

"That's settled, then." Pa drained his coffee cup and stood. "Now let's get that barn finished."

"You sure you feel like working, Job?" Ma's voice wavered a bit.

"I do." His whole manner bespoke eagerness to return to the ranch work he loved.

Emma's eyes watered again. Pa always pushed himself. That's what caused him to wrench his hip in the first place. She'd have to make sure he didn't overdo today.

The morning wind blew bitter, but it swept away a good deal of the dry snow. The sun came out and hinted at warmth it didn't deliver. Still they managed to work on finishing the siding. Pa joined Emma's team, holding boards in place for her as she pounded in the nails.

Since they'd started building last Friday, it had galled her that she needed to strike nails about six times to get them all the way in, while Jared gave them maybe three hard whacks. But somehow today she didn't feel the same rancor she'd felt when they started this competition. Not about the nails. Not about Jared in general. Something had happened between them last night that sort of made up for their unhappy past, at least for her. Did he feel the same way? And if he did, would he do anything about it?

She made up her mind right then that if he proposed, she'd accept.

Chapter Five

That morning only a couple of men came to help, one
for each team of workers. Jared, Cal and their helper
finished putting up the boards on their sides by din-
nertime. As Jared went through the motions of building, his thoughts stayed back in the kitchen, both last
night and this morning.

He'd never felt so close to anyone as he had to Emma
last night. She'd listened to his deepest secret and then
let him take her hand. All the bitterness she'd right-
fully felt toward him these past two years seemed to be
gone. Later, as he'd lain abed, he'd wondered whether
he should forget his dream about having his own place
in Colorado and take up courting her again. This time
he wouldn't back out. He'd see it through to the end.
Then he'd offer to live with the Sharps and work this
ranch. That would be an even better alternative to Colorado because he could live near his family without
living with them. He cared for all of his brothers, but
the older ones were awful bossy, while Mr. Sharp respected him. Working for him would be a sight easier
than always having to answer to Rob.

Then this morning Mr. Sharp shocked them all with his invite to Cal. Jared was more than happy for his brother, yet if Jared courted Emma now, she might think it was so he'd get a share of the ranch. That would be worse than jilting her. He should have kissed her last night when he had the chance. Should have told her how he regretted his past actions but that he was a changed man. That he admired—well, *tumbleweed*, might as well admit it. He loved her. Would she believe him if he told her that now?

He'd been neglectful of praying about it, so he lifted a silent prayer for the Lord's direction. As they began their work on the roof and interior, he waited and waited for an answer. The Lord seemed intent on teaching Jared to be patient, so he'd try to hurry up and learn.

"If we can't go tonight, we have to go tomorrow night." Emma glanced around the table over dinner. "We've never even seen a Las Posadas celebration. How will we know what to do when it's our turn? That's just three days away."

"The barn's almost finished," Pa said. "I don't see why you young folks can't go. I'm sure you can finish it in the time you have left."

"Oh, yes. Let's go." Julia gave Cal a sweet smile. "Can we go?"

"If you want to go, we can." Cal's smile mirrored Julia's.

Emma's sting of envy wasn't as sharp as usual. She looked at Jared with expectation. "Want to go?"

"I thought we were going to work on the *farolitos* tomorrow evening." A teasing look filled his eyes.

"We can do that tonight." Emma did want to make the *farolitos*, the customary Las Posadas paper lanterns that would illuminate the path from the main road to their new barn. Ma had already bought paper bags and candles. All they needed to do was put a couple of inches of sand in the bags and secure the candles in the centers so the brown bags wouldn't catch on fire, place them along the path and then light them before "Mary and Joseph" arrived. Jared seemed eager to help make them. Maybe if he enjoyed working alongside her enough, he'd want to do it more often. Maybe even for the rest of his life.

"I don't know," Jared said. "Tomorrow Cal and I have to put shingles on the roof. That might take well into the evening."

"And Paco and I need to build the interior." Emma wouldn't let him off without a fight. "We're gonna take a few hours off tomorrow evening to enjoy ourselves. That's all there is to it."

She could hear the bossiness in her own voice, and her conscience stung. That was the old Emma, not the new one who prayed every day that Jared would give voice to the tender feelings so obvious in his eyes when he looked her way. His interest in finishing the barn showed more than neighborly care; it showed his concern for her family's well-being. *Her* well-being. That made her feel real good. Pa always protected Ma, and even though Emma had done a man's work every day of her life, she still longed to have someone look out for her that way. So she quit her argument and gave him the platter of griddle cakes along with a sweet smile like Julia always gave Cal.

Jared smiled back. "I suppose it wouldn't hurt to attend the celebration."

"Before you get started on those shingles, would you help me plan out how wide the stalls should be and where I should put the tack room?"

She already knew all that, and she knew he knew she knew. So she expected a teasing answer, maybe something about wasting his time so she could get ahead. But somehow the competition had faded away over the past few days. Ever since they'd sat up that night with Mrs. Cat.

"Ma'am, I'd be happy to consult with you on the matter." Jared waggled his eyebrows playfully.

Emma laughed. Actually, it was more like a giggle. Bother. She was starting to sound as girly as Julia. But somehow, she decided, that wasn't a bad thing after all.

All day long the Lord stayed silent, not giving Jared any direction about courting Emma other than to remind him to love her as Christ loved the church. He did notice she'd altogether quit being prickly and sassy. He couldn't say his actions brought about the changes, but he couldn't say they hadn't either. As to courting her, the Lord didn't give word *or* wisdom on the matter, no matter how many memorized Bible verses Jared recalled or how much he prayed. Maybe it was God's will for him to go to Colorado, after all. He'd have a hard time leaving Emma behind. A real hard time. Maybe Emma would agree to go with him.

That was it! The Lord's answer. He wouldn't try to horn in on Cal and Julia's blessing of inheriting the ranch. Instead, he and Emma would strike out on their own. The idea excited him so much he came near to hammering his thumb instead of the nail he held against a wooden shake shingle.

He looked down to where she was trimming a board on the sawhorse. As always, she was hard at work. My, she was beautiful. How had she felt about her father's invite to Cal the other morning? Was she pleased that her sister would still be living here? They got along real well, just like he and Cal. Maybe she wouldn't want to leave with him so they could settle in their own place. Maybe her love for her family and for this particular piece of land would keep her here.

The only way to find out was to propose to her, but when? Did he need to wait until after Las Posadas? After Cal and Julia's wedding? Just then, Emma glanced up at him and gave him that pretty smile of hers. One of Pop's favorite sayings came to mind: "There's no time like the present to get the job done."

Jared set his hammer down, clambered down the ladder and strode over to her. Of course when she looked at him with those sky blue eyes, he got tongue-tied. All he could spit out was, "Nice day."

"Sure is." She looked back at her work and kept on sawing.

"It's a good thing we didn't get any more snow."

"Uh-huh." She paused and looked at him again, and his heart leaped clear up into his throat. "Did you come down here to say something? Like you've given up the competition 'cause you know I'm winning?" Her teasing smile held a world of good humor.

"Yes, ma'am. No, ma'am."

Mr. Sharp chose that moment to come out of the barn with another board. The old man looked better every day, a tribute to everyone's prayers and the hard work he'd been doing.

"Mr. Sharp, I want to marry Emma. I know I didn't do right last time, and I made a bad mistake. Could you please forgive me and give me your permission to court her again?" Did that sound all right? Was that what he should say? Wait. Had he just said that out loud?

Mr. Sharp's eyes widened. "Why, Jared, I wondered when you'd come around. Yes, you have my permission to court Emma." He looked at her. "Is that all right with you, daughter?"

Emma stood still as a statue, her mouth hanging wide-open. Mr. Sharp reached over and lifted her chin. "Close your mouth, daughter, and answer the question." He didn't seem to notice his own contradiction, but his blue eyes twinkled.

Which made Jared feel mighty good because it meant Mr. Sharp wouldn't mind having him for a son-in-law. That idea emboldened him more than he ever could have expected.

"Emma, will you go courting with me, or should we just go ahead and get married the same day as Cal and Julia?" If she hesitated to say yes, he'd tell her about Colorado and make sure she understood he loved her, not this ranch.

Tears began to stream down her cheeks, freezing in the wind against her bright pink skin. "I'd like that, Jared."

Much relieved, he gave out a hearty laugh. "Which one? Courting or marrying?"

"Oh, you." She set down her saw and smacked his arm.

"Ow!" Through his thick jacket it didn't hurt in the least, but he hollered anyway. "If you're gonna hit me like that, maybe I'll change my mind." Uh-oh. Shouldn't have said that. 'Specially since he'd done it once and would never do it again.

She answered by snuggling under that same arm and squeezing him around his middle. "No, you won't. I won't let you."

Her sassy smile tickled his insides, and he didn't have any choice but to squeeze back, even with her father looking on.

"Let's go tell Ma." Emma stepped out of his arms, leaving him with an empty feeling. Now that he had her back, he couldn't bear the thought of losing her again.

"Sure thing." He gripped her hand, and they hurried across the barnyard toward the kitchen door. Behind them, Jared could hear Mr. Sharp's slower, uneven footfalls on the cold ground.

The moment they stepped into the room, mouthwatering aromas of fresh-baked bread and stewed chicken swept over them. Jared's belly rumbled in reply, and he and Emma shared a laugh. My, that felt good! He took off his hat to let the indoor heat warm him from the top down.

Then they saw Mrs. Sharp seated at the table, a letter in hand and tears running down her cheeks. Julia sat beside her chewing a thumbnail, a worried look on her face.

"Ma, what on earth?" Emma sat beside her mama and took her hand.

"What is it, Annie?" Mr. Sharp nudged Julia to another chair so he could sit on Mrs. Sharp's other side and pull her into an embrace.

Jared watched with concern and a good measure of interest. A husband took care of his wife, something he'd have to do for Emma, even if she cried. Mr. Sharp set a good example.

"This letter's from Maggie." Mrs. Sharp looked at Jared. "She's my baby sister. Lives in Cleveland. Her husband died last summer, and she's been struggling ever since to hold down a job and manage the house and six small children."

Jared felt a pinch of worry, but he couldn't rightly say why.

Mrs. Sharp pulled a handkerchief from her sleeve and dabbed at her tears before sliding the letter over to Mr. Sharp. "She's asking us to send Emma to help her with the little ones." She gripped Emma's hand. "You've got to go, daughter. I don't see how we can say no to family."

Emma went pale, but she nodded.

An icy sensation seized Jared right in the heart. They'd agreed to marry five minutes ago. Was she now about to up and leave him?

Her nod turned to a shake of her head, and her eyes narrowed like when she didn't like something. A glimmer of hope lit up inside of Jared.

"Why would Aunt Maggie ask such a thing of me?" Her troubled expression turned angry. "I don't know anything about taking care of children."

No word coming out of her mouth could have shocked Jared more. Shocked him even more than the idea of her leaving to help her aunt.

She didn't know anything about taking care of children? And here he'd dreamed of having a passel of them with her. He'd made a terrible mistake to propose to her before talking about these things. How could he back out on her...again?

* * *

Emma had nothing against children. She liked the ones she knew. She just didn't know what to do with them. Working alongside Pa, she hadn't gone with Ma to visit friends with young ones as Julia had.

In response to her outburst, Ma shed a few more tears. "That's my fault, Emma. You've always been so busy helping your pa, and I neglected to teach you. I'm sorry for that."

Pa appeared stunned by Aunt Maggie's request. Ma didn't know Jared had proposed, but Pa did. Did he understand she couldn't leave now? Not when her dream of a happy life was about to come true. Jared's face closed up tight, but she could see anger under his blank expression. He turned away and walked outside, putting his hat on his head as he went. From the way his shoulders slumped, she guessed he was thinking he was about to be abandoned again.

Deep inside she knew she had to go to Aunt Maggie. What choice did she have? Decent folks helped those having difficulties, especially family. If it hadn't been for their neighbors helping them, they'd never have gotten the barn built. While it was a grand thing to have it done for Las Posadas, in truth, the family desperately needed it for the winter.

Now a family member required help, and Emma was the only one who could go. Julia and Cal had planned their marriage first, and they deserved their happiness. With Cal staying on the ranch, Pa wouldn't need Emma's help as much. Two couples could manage to run the place.

As much as she didn't want to go, how could she pray to the Lord about anything if she didn't surrender herself to do His will? She took Ma's boney, weathered hand and gently squeezed it.

"You can wire Aunt Maggie and tell her I'll come right after Julia's wedding." She'd allow herself that one pleasure before abandoning Jared. Before abandoning all she'd ever known.

Ma gave her a weary smile. "I knew you'd do what's right, dear. And don't fret about tending the children. You'll figure it out just fine."

"Emma, are you sure about this?" Pa reached over and placed his large, callused hand on top of hers. His frown said more than his words. "Once a man's proposed, he don't like to wait on his woman, 'specially when he has no idea how long she'll be gone."

"Jared proposed?" Ma and Julia asked in unison. Julia squealed, but Ma sighed deeply and wearily.

"Oh, my dear." She gave Emma's hand a sympathetic squeeze and then gave Pa one of their special looks. "When you think about it, it's no different from a man going off to war and his woman not knowing when—or if—he'll come home."

"That's true, Annie." Pa echoed her sigh. "I'm grateful to the Lord for bringing me home to you and Emma, and for sending us Julia nine months later."

"Pa!" Julia's cheeks flamed. Any other time, Emma would have snickered at her sister's prudishness. Julia was the one who'd been disappointed about not seeing the kittens born.

Pa and Ma shared a laugh, a soft, cozy sound that had always made Emma glad. Today, though, it reminded her that she might never share such sweet closeness with Jared. Not if he wouldn't wait for however many years it took to help Aunt Maggie care for her young'uns. She'd best face it head-on and find out what he was thinking.

"Well, I have some stalls to finish." She shoved away from the table and stood. "Mostly, I need to talk to Jared."

Ma and Pa looked at her with identical worried expressions, so she forced a smile.

"Don't worry. The Lord will work it out." She gave voice to a conviction she wasn't exactly feeling at the moment.

They both returned a smile, so she knew she'd done right by them. As the oldest daughter that was her job in life: sacrificing her own happiness for a stretch of time to take care of family. Now to take care of the man she loved. The man with whom she hoped to build her own family. Someday.

Holding up a hand to shield her eyes from the glare of the sun, she could see him back up on the roof nailing shingles into place. The determined look on his face and the power of his hammering indicated he was intent on completing a large part of the roof this afternoon. With a heap of building to do inside the barn, she pondered whether to climb the ladder and talk now or wait until he came down. It was best not to alarm a man on a roof, so she decided to get on with her own work. Besides, he probably needed some time to himself. She'd grant him that. She could use a little thinking time herself right about now.

Inside the barn Paco was putting boards in place between two stalls. She arrived just in time to help him secure them with nails.

The work stretched on until suppertime. To her disappointment, Jared didn't check on her all afternoon. When the hour arrived for them to quit, he didn't even come inside the barn to walk her to the wash tables on the back porch. In fact, he and Cal were already washing up when Emma and Paco arrived.

From the obvious way Jared ignored her—turning the back of his shoulder her direction, Emma could see big change coming from their days of teasing, and she didn't like it one bit. When he broke off courting her two years ago, he'd never explained himself. Even though she'd figured it out after he'd told her about the kitty that had comforted him after his ma left, he'd never come out and said he didn't trust Emma to stay. Was that how he felt now? If he wouldn't talk things out with her, like Ma and Pa did when they had a hard situation to deal with, maybe it would be a mistake to marry him.

Surely he understood about family. She knew he and his brothers worked together, stuck together, no matter what. No doubt each one of them had sacrificed something along the way for the good of the others. Sure, he had to sort things out about this situation, but what if he didn't sort them out the way she hoped? His quiet, distant manner continued through supper and into the evening, and she had a terrible feeling he didn't trust her enough to discuss it for fear of what she'd say. Well, if he wouldn't talk to her, she wouldn't talk to him. After all, she had her pride.

No longer feeling a part of the Sharp family, Jared couldn't bring himself to look at Emma as they all sat in the parlor that evening. However, he couldn't escape the clicking sound of her knitting needles and knew she was still making Christmas presents, just as he was. Last night he'd finished her comb and now almost had

Mrs. Sharp's apple wood spoons done. Mr. Sharp's bolo tie was finished, and the wooden slide only needed a bit more sanding.

"Say there, Emma." As always in the evenings, Mr. Sharp held his large Bible on his lap. "Those socks you're knitting are a mite small. Who're they for? You taking them to Cleveland with you?"

She blinked in that pretty, surprised way of hers that Jared found so appealing. It was hard to shut down his feelings after growing fonder of her every day, after thinking of all the ways he might take care of her and please her.

"No, sir." She held up the half-done sock. "I'm making them for Robby." Her expression turned sheepish. "Last week I asked Rob if I could give Robby some candy for Christmas, and he said that was fine. I hope he doesn't mind me adding something more practical." She gave Jared a shy smile. "Jared said his family doesn't celebrate Christmas, but I figured a boy ought to have Christmas presents, even if one of them is a pair of socks."

While everyone else chuckled, Jared could only stare at Emma. Was this the same gal who, not four hours ago, had said she didn't know much about children? Yet here she was making a present for Robby and planning to buy him some candy. Maybe she knew more than she thought. At least a day before her aunt's letter arrived, she'd begun to knit those socks for his nephew, who'd received far too few gifts in his young life. That was way more than generous. It was downright *magnanimous*, the word he'd spelled correctly in the eighth-grade spelling bee back in Charleston, beating out his entire school. He'd earned the top prize for it, the five-dollar gold piece he'd be giving Cal and Julia on Christmas Day. Right now, though, he had the feeling a much finer prize was about to slip through his fingers.

"That's a mighty good thing to do, Emma." Mr. Sharp opened the Bible and thumbed through the pages. "I'm sure the boy will be delighted."

Although Jared agreed, he still had much to think about before he could figure out his future with Emma. That was, if he still had a future with her.

Mr. Sharp found his place and smoothed a hand across the page. "As Emma just showed us, Christmas is all about giving. So let's take a look at the greatest gift the Almighty gave us on that first Christmas, starting at Matthew, chapter one, verse eighteen. 'Now the birth of Jesus Christ was on this wise: When as his mother Mary was espoused to Joseph, before they came together, she was found with child of the Holy Ghost.'"

As the older man continued to read, Jared couldn't keep his mind from scampering down a rabbit trail. He'd always felt a little sorry for Joseph when he found out his bride-to-be was expecting, knowing full well he wasn't the father of her child. But the Lord had chosen him to be Mary's husband because he was a "just" man, one who would stand by Mary in spite of rumors. Of course, according the scripture, the Lord had it all worked out since the beginning of time: Mary's baby was the long-promised Messiah. Because of Joseph's character and faithfulness, he would be granted the great privilege and responsibility of serving as the earthly protector of God's own Son.

Jared wouldn't be so bold as to compare himself with Joseph. But he'd learned from Pastor Daniel that every story in scripture held a lesson a man could apply to his own life. While no rumors were attached to Emma, maybe the Lord wanted him to be as supportive of her as Joseph had been to Mary in the job she had to do. In Emma's situation, that meant he would have to support her decision to help her family rather than marry him, even though the idea cut into him painfully.

Mr. Sharp read the passage in Matthew clear through to chapter three, where the Lord told Joseph to take the Christ Child home from Egypt to settle in Nazareth. From then on, only one further story referred to Joseph, although Mary was mentioned in several passages about Jesus's ministry. Joseph seemed to have simply and quietly passed from history.

Jared released an inaudible sigh. Was his lot in life to quietly disappear? To have no further significance after the barn was built to protect the Sharps' livestock and serve as a place for the community to celebrate the last night of Las Posadas?

As one of five sons, he'd always had a hard time getting attention. Not that he wanted to be famous or anything. All he wanted was his own piece of land and a wife to share it with. Was it God's will for him to lose Emma's wifely companionship because her responsibility to her family was more important than marrying him? He'd do what the Lord instructed, but that didn't soften the sting of being abandoned by the woman who was supposed to become the center of his life. Abandoned *again*, he reminded himself. How many times could he be expected to endure such treatment?

Yes, he'd obey the Lord. However, he would not let Emma leave for Cleveland without telling her he'd wait for her and give her a chance to make a similar commitment to him. He'd tell her about his hopes of buying that ranch in Colorado and building a house for her there. Would she like that? As soon as Mr. Sharp finished reading, he'd ask permission to speak to her privately while the others went to bed.

Mr. Sharp closed his Bible and offered a prayer. Then he stood and reached out to Mrs. Sharp. "Annie, let's get those *farolitos* made."

Jared had forgotten they'd planned to do that this evening. He couldn't very well talk about private matters in front of Emma's whole family. For now all he could do was encourage her.

While the ladies gathered the sacks and candles, Jared and Cal went outside to retrieve the buckets of sand they'd fetched from the riverbank earlier. They all stood around the kitchen table to work on the project. Jared took his place beside Emma and offered a smile. She looked mighty tired, so he'd make sure they had a chance to talk in the morning.

Then, as he thought more about it, he decided he should first tell Pop about proposing to Emma and about her having to leave for a long spell. He also needed to discuss his dream of buying a ranch in Colorado, since Pop would have to give him his inheritance to make that happen. With only a few days before Cal and Julia's wedding, and then Emma leaving the next day, he must not wait any longer. If Pop didn't agree to Jared's plans, Jared would have to find another solution. If Pop approved, Jared could take the next step of talking to Emma.

In the meantime, he needed to show Emma he hadn't given up on her without saying too much. "Say, you sure do a good job of making those candles stand up."

She responded with a sad, rueful smile and slumped shoulders. He longed to encourage her, but with his hands deep in damp sand and her family all around, Jared couldn't exactly give her a big hug. But, Lord willing, he'd make it up to her real soon.

Chapter Six

The next evening, as twilight faded and stars appeared in the black sky over Riverton, Emma, Julia and Cal joined the procession walking behind Jose and Maria Mendez. Maria made a beautiful "Mary." Her baby was due soon, and Emma sensed she understood very well how Mary had felt on her long journey from Nazareth to Bethlehem, where Baby Jesus was born. Jose also played his part as Joseph well, making sure Maria sat comfortably and securely on her burro as he led the animal with care over the uneven ground. The couple's heartfelt portrayal helped everyone in the community get into the mood of the occasion.

Observing Maria's serene countenance, Emma wanted more than anything to be a mother one day, too. Wanted it so bad she'd be willing to sacrifice her pride and talk to Jared if he didn't approach her first. Tonight would have been the perfect time, but he'd gone home this afternoon without explanation, so she'd have to wait. The Lord surely was teaching her patience, a quality she'd never been able or even wanted to claim.

The procession began at the church and continued

to the Martinez home a quarter of a mile away. Ahead of Maria's burro, a small boy carried a candle to light the way through the darkness. For the safety of all, several other people also carried candles or lanterns.

"See the *farolitos*," someone cried with an enthusiasm that belied the fact that they'd already done this for seven nights in a row.

"Luminarias!" someone else corrected, and everyone laughed.

According to Brother Miguel, both Spanish terms applied to the candlelit paper bags. The folks who hailed from south of La Bajada, New Mexico, insisted that *luminarias* was the proper term, but those from Santa Fe proclaimed the lights must be called *farolitos*. For the good of the community, everyone agreed to disagree.

This being Emma's first night to participate, she decided to set aside the depression that had held on to her since yesterday when Ma received Aunt Maggie's letter. For just this one night, she gave herself permission to enjoy the excitement, especially as she observed the expressions of happiness and camaraderie on the faces of her companions, Mexicans and Americanos alike. If this mood continued beyond the Christmas season, or *Navidad¸* as the Mexicans called it, the pastors could count their efforts to unite the communities a success. Her heart uplifted by it all, Emma prayed she and Jared could have similar success at uniting their lives.

As the procession made its way up the lighted pathway to the house, Mr. Martinez, the "innkeeper," opened the door. Jose asked if he had any room in the "inn." In a deep baritone voice, Mr. Martinez sang a Spanish song of welcome, while Mrs. Martinez emerged from the house with a tray full of refreshments. On a tree in the front yard hung a star-shaped clay piñata, which the children broke with sticks. Wrapped homemade candy flew everywhere to the delight of the little ones, who scrambled after it.

Caught up in the celebration, Emma could hardly wait for her family's turn to welcome Mary and Joseph, especially for the children. Pa had bought a clay piñata, and Ma had been making candy for days in anticipation. Emma turned to Julia to share one of their sister smiles, but Julia had eyes only for Cal. They'd already entered that secret world where happy couples lived. Emma sighed. Would she and Jared ever live there?

The next day the sun shone bright and warm enough so everyone could work on the barn in their shirtsleeves. By noontime, Emma and Paco had finished the inside of the barn less than an hour before Jared and Cal hammered nails into the last shingles on the roof.

Buoyed by her sense of accomplishment, Emma decided the time had arrived to deal with Jared. As he came down from the roof, she leaned against a sawhorse with her arms crossed and pasted on a smirk she didn't feel. What if he couldn't forgive her for abandoning him? What if he'd decided to avoid the pain and just not care for her anymore? Still, she had to try.

"I suppose it's safe to say Paco and I won the competition."

He took off his hat and swiped a sleeve over his forehead. "I suppose." The glimmer of good humor in his gray eyes gave her hope.

"You want to talk?"

"Do you?"

She nodded. "Let's clean up and get changed. I'll meet you in the parlor in a half hour."

"Fine by me."

This time, instead of walking away from her, he walked beside her to the wash table, which encouraged her about their courtship for the first time since Aunt Maggie's letter arrived.

As she washed her face and hands, she had a mind to dump her porcelain bowl on Jared, but he beat her to it. Being considerably taller, he managed to pour the soapy, lukewarm water down her back. She squealed with false indignation, grabbed her own basin and flung it in his direction. He couldn't quite dodge the spray of water, and it splattered down his front. Not to be left out, Cal and Paco emptied their bowls, partly on each other and partly on Emma and Jared. Laughter rang across the barnyard in celebration of the barn's completion. It didn't take long for the wind to cut through their wet shirts, so everyone scurried into the warm kitchen.

"Oh, my, just look at all of you." Ma stood over the stove stirring a pot of her special taffy. "You'd better get changed before you catch your death. Paco, you stay here, and Job will fetch you a change of clothes from the bunkhouse. By the time everybody's dressed, I'll have dinner ready."

Changing clothes and stoking fires to ward off their self-inflicted chills took a while, but at last Emma and Jared made it to the parlor. As if understanding their need for privacy, everyone busied themselves elsewhere. Emma's pulse raced as she sat on the settee, hoping Jared would sit beside her rather than in a chair.

* * *

Jared would have preferred to face Emma for this conversation, yet her vulnerable expression gave him no choice but to sit beside her. He'd come to recognize the subtle dip in her eyebrows and downward turn at the corner of her lips that said she feared being hurt. As he'd promised himself since coming to the Sharp ranch, he would never willingly hurt her again.

Just for fun and to lighten the moment, he sat as far away from her on the settee as he could and leaned in the opposite direction. "Ahem. I understand, Miss Sharp, that you wish to speak to me."

She gave him the smirk he'd hoped for. "I did, indeed, Mr. Mattson." She cupped a hand beside her mouth as if calling across a far piece. "But not if I have to holler at you way down there at that end of the settee."

He wasted no time in closing the gap between them, coming near enough to brush against her shoulder. "That better?"

She lifted her chin and gave a fake sniff. "If that's the best you can do."

Nothing she could have said would have made him feel better. "Is that an invitation?"

"If you want to take it that way."

Now she looked downright cute with those blue eyes looking up at him and her full, black hair framing her pretty, tanned face. For the first time since knowing her, he noticed three or four tiny freckles on the bridge of her straight, slender nose. Oh, my, how he wanted to kiss those freckles. But they had important things to square away before he had that right. Instead, he accepted her invitation and put one arm around her slender shoulders.

"That better?" he asked.

The way she snuggled up close to him gave him the answer he'd hoped for. He pulled in a long breath. Although he'd been planning what to say since talking to Pop the other night, he was afraid to begin, afraid he'd say it wrong.

"Jared, I—"

"Emma, would you—"

They started and stopped together and then laughed.

"You first." He gave her shoulders a gentle squeeze.

"All right." Tears came to her eyes, but he'd been prepared for that, so it didn't throw him off. "I *have* to go help Aunt Maggie."

He nodded but kept quiet. The other night, Pop had told him how much he regretted not listening to Mama. *Women need to talk things out, son, so we need to listen to them.*

"I felt awful telling you I'd marry you and then five minutes later saying I'd go help her." Emma sniffed, this time for real. "But I do have to go," she repeated, and her voice broke at the end.

She looked up at him with those blue eyes all rimmed with tears, and he had a hard time breathing. If she expected him to speak, he wouldn't be able to. He gave her a rueful grimace and nodded again.

"What are we going to do?"

Her question surprised him. This was his smart, feisty Emma who always had an answer for everything and everybody. Yet she was asking him what they should do. All the ideas he and Pop had talked about the other night came clear in his mind, with one addition.

"First, we're gonna pray."

Seeing her trust-filled eyes and eager nod, he removed his arm from around her and gripped her hand. "Lord, give us Your direction about what You want us to do. We know Aunt Maggie's in need, and we want to help." Something vague itched in the back of his mind, but he couldn't pull it into focus to scratch it, so he continued. "You know I've got a plan, but please show us what Your will is real clearly, 'cause sometimes we're as dumb as old Homer the mule. Well, I am, at least. Emma's not. She's…"

She nudged him with her elbow and giggled in her cute way.

"Anyway, Lord, please guide us. Amen." He finished and looked down at her. Those blue eyes sparkled with admiration, and his heart warmed as never before. *Tumbleweed!* He felt proud having this sweet little gal love him. "Sweetheart, I've worked out a plan with my pop, and if you like it, it's what we'll do." He needed another deep breath before continuing. "You can probably guess how crowded things are over at our place with Pop, five grown sons and a grandson. Even with Cal's moving over here, it'll still be crowded."

"I've wondered about that." Curiosity and a hint of hope now filled her eyes. Maybe they'd gotten past the emotional part of their talk. "What's your plan?"

"Being one of the younger sons, I've always dreamed of having my own place where I can spread out and be my own person instead of taking orders from Pop and Rob and Will and Andrew and—well, you get the idea."

"I do." She grinned, so he kept on going.

"Pop's going to stake me in buying a ranch in Colorado."

She sat up straight and pulled away from him. "Colorado? Why Colorado?" Tears started again, so he hurried to explain.

"If I can get a ranch built up while you're in Cleveland, then you'll have a place to come home to. One that I've built for you so you don't have to do a man's work anymore."

She looked away and pondered his idea for a moment. "That doesn't sound half-bad." Even so, she slumped against his shoulder. "I don't know how long I'll be with Aunt Maggie. It may be years. I don't know whether I can wait that long to marry you."

Jared gave her another encouraging squeeze. "Remember the Bible story where Jacob worked seven years to earn the right to marry Rachel? Then when Laban gave him Leah instead, he worked seven more years to earn the wife he wanted?"

"*Humph.* I don't much like that story. Doesn't seem fair to Leah *or* Rachel." She eyed him. "Don't you be thinking of marrying somebody else while you're working on *our* ranch."

"No, ma'am, I won't. But you missed my point. The Bible says those years passed quickly because of the great love Jacob had for Rachel."

She gave him her saucy grin, even though her eyes still held sadness. "Are you saying you love me? 'Cause if you stop and think a minute, you may recall you've never said that to me."

"Did, too."

"Did not."

He thought real hard for about half of that minute.

"*Tumbleweed!* I do think you're right." He slid off the settee down onto one knee and grasped her hands. "Miss Emma Sharp, I love you more than anything in this world, more than anything in the universe except the Lord. There, now. What do you think of that?"

All serious now, she gazed at him with a tender look that near to melted his heart. "Mr. Mattson, I do love you the same, only more so." Even with that joyful confession, tears rolled down her cheeks, and she closed her eyes. "Oh, Lord, make those years pass quickly. Help us both endure through them, and may we both live long enough to see our dreams come true."

A cold chill swept through Jared. He'd never considered one of them might…but he wouldn't think about that now. Pop's frequent admonition of "No time like the present" came to mind, but this was one time it wasn't the best advice.

"Emma, may I kiss you?"

"You may."

He stood and pulled her up into a gentle embrace. For all her hardiness, she was still a fragile soul. In fact, at the moment, he wouldn't make claims to being all that strong himself, 'cause his knees felt like jelly. He brushed back her wonderful, unruly hair and kissed those sweet full lips. This was the first time he'd ever kissed a girl. From the way she stood on tiptoes and kissed him back, he must have been doing it right.

Emma had never been kissed. When she'd seen Cal kiss Julia after they got engaged, she'd wondered what all the fuss was about. Now she knew. As she melted into Jared's embrace and he touched her lips with his, a brand-new kind of happiness filled her being. Did he feel it, too? From his soft sigh, she reckoned he did. But all that happiness was tempered by thoughts of their coming separation. Now that they'd kissed, it was just about unbearable to think of leaving him.

They sat back down on the settee, and he took her hand again. "Tomorrow, Cal and I can haul hay into the barn and make sure the bull and the milk cows are settled. Then it'll be ready for tomorrow night's guests." He thought for a moment. "Your pa plans to go down to Riverton this afternoon and pick up some replacement supplies, so maybe you and I could go with him."

Ordinarily, Pa told Emma about such plans. Even so, it didn't bother her that he'd told Jared instead. It showed how much Pa respected the man she loved. "I'd like to go. I still haven't bought that candy for Robby. Ma's taffy can't be beat, but store-bought penny candy is something special."

Jared got a speculating look in his eyes. "You like young'uns, don't you?" His words held a pinch of doubt.

She knew why. Her outburst over Aunt Maggie's letter when she said she didn't know anything about taking care of children. "I do like them." Should she tell him more? Did a lady say such things? Maybe not. Yet they'd watched together as the kittens were born. They planned to marry one day. So it wasn't as if she was speaking the unspeakable. Still, she felt her cheeks warming up something fierce. "I'd like a half dozen or so of my own. How about you?"

His grin was a mile wide, and his eyes beamed with relief. "I'd say a half dozen would be just about right."

Even with their shared joy, the next day Emma couldn't help feeling sad. With some difficulty, she managed not to show her growing depression as they made their way to Riverton Mercantile with Pa. Thanks to their good neighbors providing supplies to rebuild the barn and being willing to wait for payment until after spring sheep shearing, Pa had enough money to buy tack, chicken feed and a host of other items to replace those lost in the fire. Jared bought a new whetstone, and Emma bought a pound of candy. In addition to Robby's gift, she'd need to have something for her little cousins.

December 24 arrived, and with it an overcast sky that threatened snow. Messages were sent back and forth among the townsfolk about whether to celebrate this last night of Las Posadas. When the sun made a midafternoon appearance, everyone agreed to proceed as usual.

Emma had long looked forward to entertaining the community for this event, but now she wished she could pull back on the reins of time to slow down the day of her departure. Each look she traded with Jared conveyed an increasingly sadder mood in each of them. As much as she tried to shake it off and enjoy the beauty and wonder of Christ's birth, her own longings intruded all too often.

Because Pa was to play the part of the innkeeper, the family didn't join the procession from town but instead stayed home to finish decorating. A tree graced the parlor, covered with ribbons, bits of lace, strings of popcorn and two hand-painted glass ornaments, and grandly topped with a silvery glass star Pa had bought for Ma some years ago. The house and barn doorways were festooned with evergreen branches tied with red ribbons. In anticipation of a grand feast, plank tables in the center of the barn awaited food now being kept warm in the house, with more expected to arrive with their guests. And, of course, the clay piñata hung from the cottonwood tree in the side yard. Finally, as darkness descended, Jared and Emma prepared the *farolitos* that lined the path from the road to the barn. When the last candle was lit, Jared put his arm around Emma's shoulder.

"My, what a beautiful sight."

Emma nodded. "They are, aren't they?"

He chuckled. "I wasn't talking about the *farolitos*."

She looked up into his adoring gaze. "You don't look so bad yourself, cowboy."

He placed a quick kiss on her nose. "Better get that done before everybody arrives."

"Yes, you'd better, 'cause here they come."

The procession appeared in the distance, this time led by a little girl dressed all in white and carrying a candle. Behind Maria and Jose, lanterns and candles held back the darkness. As they drew nearer, Emma's heart lifted. She would choose to enjoy this celebration. She *would*. God had been merciful to her family when the old barn burned down and in the building of this new one. Surely He could be trusted to take care of her future with Jared.

Taking her sweetheart's hand, she hurried to the barn to join her family in greeting their guests. Just as the procession reached the drive from the road to the barn, snow began to fall lightly across the landscape.

Jose led Maria's burro to the barn and asked, as he had for the eight previous nights, "*Señor*, my wife is about to give birth. Do you have any room in your inn where we might rest?"

Due to Pa's heightened emotions, his eyes were rimmed with red, a rare thing. "I sure do. Come on in." It wasn't exactly the script, and everyone laughed with good nature and high spirits.

Perhaps forty people crowded into the barn to hear Emma and Julia sing "Silent Night" as their song of welcome, accompanied by Ma on her concertina. Then food was laid out on the planks, coffee served, and everyone filled their plates high. Jared sat on a blanket beside Emma eating a bowl of chili, while she chose a tamer dish of fried chicken.

"Uh-oh. Look at that snow." Jared jutted his chin toward the open barn door.

Indeed, the white sprinkle had turned heavy, with a howling wind stirring it up into frantic flurries.

"Oh, my." Emma liked snow, but not blizzards.

"Folks," Pastor Daniel said, "I think we should return home before it's too late."

"Sí," Brother Miguel said. "If all these *amigos* get snowed in, the Sharps will not appreciate it much."

Laughter filled the barn as the guests scrambled to gather their belongings and leave in groups so no one would be lost in the snow on their way home. Emma and Jared did what they could to help everyone get away.

"Just rest, my dear." Ma knelt beside Maria, who sat on a bale of hay. "You'll be fine."

Beside them, Jose chewed his lip. "Señora Sharp, it is not her time."

Her hand on Maria's belly, Ma gave him a kindly smile. "Babies make their own time, son. And blizzards can provoke an untimely birthing. I think we'd better make a bed over there in that stall." She nodded toward an empty one. "This little tyke's bound and determined to make his appearance real soon. Emma, get some blankets. Job, you go to the house and fetch some towels and boiling water from the stove tank. Cal, you help him."

Wide-eyed, Cal helped Pa tie a rope around his waist and then did the same for himself, finally tethering them both to rails in the barn. They ventured out across the barnyard toward the dimly lit house, holding on to the ropes for dear life so they wouldn't lose their direction.

Emma and Julia scurried to gather the blankets they'd brought out for people to sit on, while Jared helped Jose make a thick bed of hay for the little mother. As she worked, Emma noticed Ma's steady nerves, and it helped her remain calm, too. Even when Maria cried out, Ma cooed soft words of encouragement to her. Even when Jose wrung his hands, she reminded him that they'd all survived being born, and his son would, too. Hearing that promise, Emma's heart ached. Ma had lost several sons, yet not her faith.

By the time Pa and Cal had returned with the water, it had gone lukewarm. Cal went out again, this time with Paco to the bunkhouse to fetch the brazier. That done, they started a fire in the small cast-iron stove, taking great care to avoid another barn fire. Now they had only to wait for the baby's birth. Here in a barn. Among the animals. With old towels folded and waiting to become swaddling clothes.

Emma looked around at her family, soon-to-be family members and friends. As unusual as the circumstances were, they all seemed aware of how special this birth was and how it mirrored the birth of Jesus.

It helped Emma set aside for good her grief over having to leave Jared. God was in charge, and He would take care of her marriage to Jared, too.

Jared couldn't take his eyes off of Jose. The young husband hadn't left Maria's side the entire evening. Now that she was about to give birth, Jose sat beside her on the straw holding her hand. Mrs. Sharp's wise words had brought a change in him, for he no longer wrung his hands or bit his lip. Instead, he gazed lovingly at his wife. At one point, Maria thrashed about and yanked her hand from him, speaking angrily to him in Spanish. Confusion filled Jose's eyes, but Mrs. Sharp assured him that all was well. Jared would have to remember when—and if—he and Emma were married and blessed with that passel of children they agreed on having.

A few feet away, Julia slept against Cal's shoulder, just as Emma rested against Jared's, all three getting some much-needed sleep. Jared's mind churned with too many thoughts to let him give in to slumber. This situation was a whole lot like the night Jesus was born to Mary. Had the innkeeper's wife helped with the birth like Mrs. Sharp was doing? Or had Joseph been left on his own to deliver the holy infant? If Jared and Emma lived on a remote ranch in Colorado, he'd have to be prepared for whatever happened. Just the thought of Emma having to go through childbirth without her mama worried him.

When he considered Joseph's obedience to God, a new thought took root in his mind. Long before Paul wrote the verses in Ephesians about a husband loving his wife and giving himself for her, Joseph had sacrificed all he had so he could take care of Mary. Could Jared do the same for Emma? The answer came quick and clear: yes! He could sacrifice his dream of owning a ranch in Colorado. Instead, he could marry her the same day as Cal and Julia and go with her to Cleveland. There he would take whatever job he could find to support them, maybe in the steel mills. After enjoying all the fresh air out here in New Mexico, he wouldn't like to work inside an oven-like building, but for Emma's sake he could do it. And together they would help Emma's aunt Maggie to raise her children.

Lord, if that's what You want me to do, please give me a sign.

In spite of the icy cold of the dimly lit barn, a deep certainty warmed Jared from the inside out, and it felt mighty good. With the snap of a finger, he could forget Colorado, forget his dream of buying his own place, thus surrendering the pride that accompanied such ownership. The idea didn't give him the slightest grief or regret. Surely that was the sign from the Lord he'd just asked for.

He tugged Emma's blanket up around her neck and then leaned back against the hay. It seemed his eyes hadn't been closed more than a minute when a baby's cry startled him awake. Emma and the others, too.

"A boy!" Jose's voice rang throughout the barn. "A son."

Emma and Julia jumped to their feet and scurried to help their mother clean and wrap the newborn. Cal stayed by the brazier to guard against a spark flying out to start a fire. Jared looked to Mr. Sharp for instructions.

"Time to do chores," the older man said. "Weather permitting."

Jared opened the barn door and peered out. Dawn was slow in coming due to cloud cover, but at least the snow had stopped. A brand-new day had arrived. Christmas Day. And he had a gift for Emma that was far finer than a hand-carved comb.

While Jared and Cal hitched up the wagon and took the Mendez family back to town, Emma helped Julia prepare breakfast in the kitchen. Ma was busy stuffing the turkey Paco had shot yesterday afternoon, and later today, Xavier and Angelique Elizondo would leave their house by the sheepfold and come for Christmas dinner. Tomorrow was Sunday. Then on Monday, Jared's father and other brothers would again meet the family at the church. Emma would give Robby his candy and socks then. She'd managed to wrap her handmade gifts in brown paper and tied them with ribbons.

In spite of her constant awareness that she would soon be leaving all that she loved, Emma found herself at peace. In fact, a peaceful feeling had come over the whole ranch since the arrival of Maria and Jose's baby. A new life brought hope for the future, and Emma latched on to hope with all her heart.

Beside the stove Mrs. Cat finished feeding her babies and wandered over to the saucer of milk Ma had set down. All of the kittens' eyes were halfway open, and the firstborn black one seemed determined to climb out of her wooden box to go exploring. Oddly, Ma had taken to the kittens from the first and sometimes acted as if it was her idea to bring the mama in for their births.

After Jared and Cal returned and everyone had eaten breakfast, the family gathered in the parlor. As always, Pa read the Christmas story from the second chapters of Luke and Matthew so they all would remember the true meaning of this day.

"Just as the magi gave gifts to the Christ Child, we give gifts to each other." Pa proceeded to pass out his presents, as did everyone in turn.

When Jared handed Emma a hand-carved comb, she felt a rush of emotion that almost made it impossible to speak. Almost. "Oh, Jared, it's beautiful. You sure do have a gift for carving." She ran a finger over the smooth wood.

"Here." Julia took it from her. "Let me." She undid the ribbon from Emma's hair and pulled the locks up, securing them with the comb. "Finally. Something to keep your hair in place."

Emma laughed. She and her sister had often teased each other about such things.

After everyone exclaimed over the rest of Jared's gifts, Jared and Cal heaped praise on Emma for hers.

"Here's a gal who can beat us in building a barn and knit fine stitches, too." Cal held up his gloves and grinned in his teasing way. "Jared, I don't think you should let this little lady get away." He waggled his eyebrows at his brother in a knowing way.

Jared gave him a sidelong look that hinted at mischief to come. "Why, Calvin, I'm glad you brought that up. I've been thinking on it, and I believe I'll hang on to her...all the way to Cleveland."

"What?" Emma's heart jumped into her throat. "You mean to go with me?"

"Ahem." Pa was clearly in on Jared's plan, if his wily grin was any indication. "If you intend to travel clear across the country with my daughter, young man, you'd better get hitched first."

"Why, Mr. Sharp, that's my intention." Jared turned to Emma, and his joking expression turned tender. "That is, if she'll have me."

Emma couldn't get out of her chair fast enough. She scampered across the room and plunked herself down on his lap, throwing her arms around his neck. "Oh, honey, I never would have asked you to go, but if you do, I'll be the happiest woman in the world." Not caring a minute what her parents thought, Emma planted a kiss right on Jared's lips. And from the laughter echoing throughout the parlor, she had a feeling they didn't mind at all.

The day after Christmas was Sunday, so Emma got to share her good news with her friends in town. She thought Suzette Pursers might be jealous, since just a week ago, she'd come close to asking Emma's permission to flirt with Jared. But Suzette had already turned her attention to another Mattson brother. Will didn't seem quite as scornful of marriage as the older two brothers were…as Jared had been. Emma wished Suzette well in her pursuit.

Since most folks had just made the trip into town on Sunday, the double wedding on Monday was meant to be a simple affair with only family and a couple of friends in attendance. Of course with all the Mattsons in the church pews, that would still make for a sizeable group. Emma, Ma and Julia had gotten up early to fix a chicken dinner for everyone, to be served after the ceremony. Emma and Julia wore their yellow dresses made from the same bolt but in different patterns. As always, Emma preferred a simpler design. She just hoped Jared approved. If his whistle and raised eyebrows were any indication, he did.

They all drove into town and found the church full, with many people wanting to share their joy and willing to make another trip to do so. It didn't take long for Pastor Daniel to join the two couples in holy matrimony. Then everyone headed back to the ranch for dinner. As if trying to make up for the way the Christmas Eve Las Posadas celebration had been cut short, folks brought piles of food and spent the entire afternoon.

Mr. Branson, the postmaster, brought along some mail that had been piling up for the folks who didn't get to town often. He handed Pa several letters and a brand-new Montgomery Ward catalogue. Julia seized the large book and started to pore over its pages with some of the other girls. Pa set the other mail on the dining room buffet and mingled with his guests.

Most of the time Emma respected Pa's right to hand out the mail as he saw fit. But when she saw a yellow corner sticking out from among the other correspondence, she snatched it up. A telegram! *Mrs. Sharp* was written on the outside.

With a deep sigh, she pondered what to do. Ma was busy in the kitchen, where Emma ought to be helping. She ought to be enjoying her friends, whom she wouldn't see for who knew how long. But curiosity got the best of her. Ma had already wired her sister to say

Emma would arrive a few days after Christmas. What more did she need?

"What's that?" Jared came up behind her and put an arm around her waist.

She leaned into his shoulder and gazed up into his beloved face. "A telegram. I think it's from Aunt Maggie." She couldn't keep the sadness from her voice.

He nodded and then seemed to force a grin. "Maybe she's changed her mind. Maybe she doesn't need you after all."

"Hmm." This time, Emma couldn't match his humor.

"Only one way to find out." Jared snatched the letter out of her hand. "Let's go talk to Ma." He marched toward the kitchen like a man on a mission.

Hearing him say "Ma" made Emma's heart bounce like a rubber ball. He didn't know it now, but Emma had a feeling Ma would heap a prodigious amount of love on him and Cal that would help make up for their mama leaving all those years ago. As for Ma, she had a couple of sons at last.

Just ten days ago, Emma wouldn't have let Jared grab her mail. Wouldn't have let him tell her what to do. My, how things had changed. Both of them had changed, and all for the better. She hurried after him.

"Now, son." Ma eyed Jared briefly while mashing some cooked potatoes. "You'd do well to stay out of the kitchen for a bit longer so we ladies can get the meal on."

"Now, Ma." Jared echoed her tone. "Sometimes we men have important business that makes the interruption worthwhile." He held out the telegram.

Ma's face grew pale. "Oh, my. I hope it's not more

bad news." She dried her hands on her apron and snatched the paper, unfolding it with care. Her wary, worried expression turned surprised and then happy. "Thank You, Lord." She gave the telegram back to Jared and returned to her mashed potatoes.

"Hey." Emma reached for it, but Jared held it over his head.

"Let's go to our room and read it together."

"Jared!" Emma's face burned at his suggestion.

Several ladies helping in the kitchen laughed and whispered.

Then Emma remembered. She was married, and being alone in a bedroom with Jared wasn't the slightest bit scandalous. "*Our* room." She giggled. "All right."

Once there, they read the wire together. "Bessie came. Don't send Emma."

"I don't know who Bessie is." Jared's dark gray eyes twinkled. "But I already love her."

"She's Aunt Maggie's late husband's sister and also a widow." Emma couldn't hold back her tears. "We don't have to go. We can go to Colorado and buy that ranch you dreamed about."

"Darlin', I've been talking to your pa." Jared held her tight. "He says there's room enough for all of us here." He set her at arms' length. "Which do you prefer? Colorado or New Mexico?"

"Jared, I want you to be happy."

"And I want you to be happy."

"I'll be happy as long as I'm with you."

"And I'll be happy as long as I'm with you."

Jared laughed, and Emma couldn't hold back a giggle. Here she'd thought Julia and Cal were too agreeable with each other to ever make up their minds about anything. Somebody in this marriage had to make a decision. It might as well be her.

"Very well, Mr. Jared Mattson. I do believe you're stuck right here on the Sharp ranch. What do you think of that?"

He pulled her back into his arms. "Mrs. Mattson, I can't think of anyplace I'd rather be." And he sealed that thought with a kiss.

* * * * *

Dear Reader,

Thank you for choosing to read *Yuletide Reunion* during this Christmas season. I hope your Christmas will be filled with joy as you celebrate the birth of our Lord and Savior Jesus Christ.

Yuletide Reunion is set on a fictional ranch beside the Rio Grande near the fictional town of Riverton, New Mexico. My sister lives in a beautiful, real-life adobe house beside the river, and during my many visits to see her, I have been inspired by the history of the area. I've long wanted to write a story set on her land, although I've tweaked the descriptions for this story's sake. After all, it takes place in 1886, and of course life was harder back then. No phones, no television, no running water. Meals were cooked on woodstoves. Many natural and human dangers faced the settlers every day. Still, our hardy ancestors managed to survive and build strong communities. They also loved to celebrate Christmas, just as we do today.

Our family has many traditions that we enjoy at this time of the year. Perhaps your family does, too. One of the traditions that takes place in New Mexico each year is Las Posadas, a nine-day celebration of *Navidad*, Spanish for "Christmas." When learning about the difficulties of past generations, I'm also struck by the attempts of some people to get along with their neighbors. I was inspired to write about two such groups within my fictional community.

For hundreds of years, Mexicans had settled in the land we now call New Mexico, then known as New Mexico Territory. After the 1848 "Treaty of Guadalupe Hidalgo," new boundaries were drawn, giving the territory to the United States. The Mexicans living there were given the opportunity to move to Mexico or remain on their land. Numerous families remained. At this time, many Americanos moved into the area, and animosities sprang up between the two groups. In my idealistic community, the pastors of two different local denominations decide to set the example and bring their congregations together, concentrating on their common belief in Jesus Christ instead of their differences.

I love to hear from my readers, so if you enjoyed *Yuletide Reunion*, please write and let me know. Please also visit my website: *http://blog.Louisemgouge.com*.

God bless you.
Louise M. Gouge

Turn your love of reading into rewards you'll love with
Harlequin My Rewards

**Join for FREE today at
www.HarlequinMyRewards.com**

Earn **FREE BOOKS** of your choice.

Experience **EXCLUSIVE OFFERS** and contests.

Enjoy **BOOK RECOMMENDATIONS**
selected just for you.

PLUS! Sign up now
and get **500** points
right away!

Earn
FREE
REWARDS
HarlequinMyRewards.com
Join
Today!

MYR16R